Library of
Davidson College

URBAN AND REGIONAL ECONOMICS:
PERSPECTIVES FOR PUBLIC ACTION

Edited by Joseph E. Haring *Occidental College*

HOUGHTON MIFFLIN COMPANY · BOSTON
New York · Atlanta · Geneva, Illinois · Dallas · Palo Alto

301.36
H281u

Copyright © 1972 by Houghton Mifflin Company.

The selections reprinted in this book are used by permission of and special arrangement with the proprietors of their respective copyrights. All rights reserved. No part of this work may be reproduced or transmitted in any form or by any means, electronic or mechanical, including photocopying and recording, or by any information storage or retrieval system, without permission in writing from the publisher.

Printed in the U.S.A.

Library of Congress Catalog Card Number: 70-160034

ISBN: 0-395-12337-2   77-2296

For Loreen, Crystal, Arianne, Elisa, and P. J.

PREFACE

OUR CITIES AND REGIONS are beset by a number of severe problems that may be solved, at least in part, by the application of urban and regional economics. The attack on ghetto labyrinths, transportation jams, police patrolled schools, rising crime rates, and unstable economies involves the contributions of a number of disciplines; and this interdisciplinary approach calls for the joint efforts of economists, city and regional planners, sociologists, educators, and experts in the fields of public health and finance.

In this book we present the work of experts in all of these areas within the context of economics. The thirty-two articles the book contains have been selected with care to emphasize economic and public policy. Following the lead of economists George Stigler, J. J. Spengler, Albert Hirschman, James Dusenberry, and John Kenneth Galbraith, I have sought solutions wherever they can be found. My use of economics is broad. It includes both microeconomic and macroeconomic theory and also techniques which lie at the very "cutting edge" of urban and regional economics, such as process analysis planning, simulation models, and benefit-cost analysis.

This volume has been designed for the undergraduate student. It can serve either as a basic text or as a supplement in the many courses now available in urban and/or regional economics and in urban problems. It will, I trust, be comprehensible to undergraduates with only a minimal knowledge of economics, raise their level of knowledge, and prompt them to read further in both "positive" and "normative" economics.

The book comprises four parts: Part One — "An Urban Overview"; Part Two — "Urban Issues" (covering "Poverty, Unemployment, and the Welfare System," "Housing," "Transportation," "Public Health and Education," and "The Economics of Crime"); Part Three — "Urban Financing"; and Part Four — "The Regional Context." A headnote precedes and places each of the articles. Introductions to the book's four parts form in themselves a general and brief textual analysis of urban and regional economics.

My approach then is problem-oriented and action-directed. It is, I believe, timely and relevant to conditions in the United States in the 1970s. Indeed, I believe that it will give students sound perspectives for the public action in which they engage.

Colleagues and friends at Occidental College and Harvard, Princeton, Yale, and Columbia Universities provided background for the selection of many of the articles. The urban studies staff of the Jet Propulsion Laboratory, California Institute of Technology, as well as members of the Urban Planning Department and the Graduate School of Business Administration at the University of Washington, participated vigorously in discussions of some of the issues presented. I also acknowledge with gratitude the support and encouragement of Occidental College.

JOSEPH E. HARING
Occidental College

CONTENTS

Preface v

PART ONE · AN URBAN OVERVIEW 1

1 The Changing Economic Function of the Central City: the Central City in Transition · *Raymond Vernon* *3*
2 The Economic Future of City and Suburb · *David L. Birch* *21*
3 Strategies for Helping Cities · *Jane Jacobs* *30*

PART TWO · URBAN ISSUES 37

A Poverty, Unemployment, and the Welfare System 40

4 Poverty Amid Plenty · *President's Commission on Income Maintenance Programs* *41*
5 Negative Taxes and the Poverty Problem · *Christopher Green* *49*
6 The Case for the Negative Income Tax · *Milton Friedman* *58*
7 Guaranteed Income · *Congressional Quarterly Almanac* *60*
8 Work Orientations of the Underemployed Poor · *Leonard Goodwin* *66*
9 Differences Between Economically Disadvantaged Students *Edsel L. Erickson, Albert Ritsema, Wilbur B. Brookover, and Lee M. Joiner* *76*

B Housing 82

10 Population Pressure, Housing and Habitat · *Joseph J. Spengler* *84*
11 The Tenement Landlord: Lessons from Newark · *George Sternlieb* *100*
12 Urban Renewal: Weapon Against Slums · *Maxwell Stewart* *108*
13 Housing Segregation, Negro Employment and Metropolitan Decentralization · *Joseph D. Mooney* *113*
14 The Housing Market in Racially Mixed Areas · *David McEntire* *123*

C Transportation 134

15 Urban Transportation in Summary and Perspective · *John R. Meyer, J. F. Kain, and M. Wohl* *135*
16 Planning Adequate Transportation for Southern California: a Case Study · *Joseph E. Haring* *142*

D Public Health and Education   153

17 Physical and Mental Health in the City · *E. James Lieberman and Leonard J. Duhl*   154
18 Neighborhood Health Centers · *Seymour S. Bellin and Peter Kong-ming New*   165
19 Academic Motivation and Equal Educational Opportunity *Irwin Katz*   167
20 Educational Vouchers: An Overview · *Center for the Study of Public Policy*   174

E The Economics of Crime   184

21 The Economics of Defense Against Crime in the Streets *Martin T. Katzman*   185
22 The Clandestine Distribution of Heroin, Its Discovery and Suppression · *Simon Rottenberg*   197

PART THREE · URBAN FINANCING   209

23 Reforming the Real Estate Tax · *James Heilbrun*   212
24 Alternatives to the Property Tax · *Dick Netzer*   225
25 Beyond Grants-in-Aid · *Walter W. Heller*   229
26 Tax Credits · *Harold Somers*   232
27 General and Specific Financing of Urban Services *William W. Vickrey*   234

PART FOUR · THE REGIONAL CONTEXT   259

28 Reshaping Government in Metropolitan Areas · *Committee for Economic Development*   261
29 Metropolitan Growth and Regional Policy · *James L. Green*   271
30 Exports and Regional Economic Growth · *Charles M. Tiebout*   280
31 A Reply — to Professor Tiebout · *Douglass C. North*   286
32 The Economic Impact — Industrial and Regional — of an Arms Cut *W. Leontief, Alison Morgan, Karen Polenske, David Simpson, and Edward Tower*   291

Bibliography   303

PART ONE

AN URBAN OVERVIEW

CITIES ARE THE NERVE CENTERS of civilization. Historically, cities have been the places where trade occurred, where new ideas were exchanged, where men recorded their deeds and interactions. Located at the intersections of transportation arteries, cities everywhere have created the social and economic interconnections among groups of people.

In political terms, cities are an old-fashioned unit of government that developed when urban communities were small and the agricultural hinterlands large and important. Today, metropolitan areas are "home" for many millions of people: in the United States, almost eighty-five per cent of the population live in or near them.

Unfortunately, metropolitan areas have not developed a form of government suitable for managing the conglomerations of cities (the concentric rings of suburbs incorporated as separate cities) formed around the old central cities — albeit New York and Chicago, for instance, have given their names to what we now call *standard metropolitan areas*.

In economic terms, cities are the locations of market activities — locations which make possible specialization of labor and of machine. The increases in output and productivity which result from such specialization are great. The increases in congestion, pollution, slums, to name a few problems, are also great. And, with mounting urgency, they are claiming the attention of economists and policy makers who, through the field of urban and regional economics, are extending traditional economic analysis in a search for solutions.

Traditionally, economics has been defined as the study of scarcity, or stated more completely, as the study of the allocation of scarce resources to achieve stated goals. Economic theory has been divided into *microeconomics,* the study of how supply and demand interact to determine prices and output; and *macroeconomics,* the study of the size and flow of income from the processes of production. Microeconomics, sometimes called price theory, was developed by the great classical economists following Adam Smith — particularly Ricardo, John Stuart Mill, Alfred

Marshall, and A. C. Pigou. Macroeconomics is associated with the name of John Maynard Keynes, who published his *General Theory* in 1936. By now, of course, the thinking of many economists, prior to (and since) the 1930's, has been incorporated into the Keynesian school of thought.

Recently, economists have used the tools of mathematics and statistics in constructing models of economic behavior which simulate actual conditions, describe how a system works, and yield implications capable of being tested to verify or contradict theory. Although the simulative models which describe the process of economic interaction are fashioned on the foundations of microeconomics-macroeconomics, they are not restricted to either side of the "fence." They can describe the economic process much more adequately because they permit special limiting or expanding assumptions to be built into the analysis — assumptions which approach much more closely to the reality: there are two sides to every fence. This is where urban and regional economics is "at" — the process or simulative model stage.

Sometimes economic and social processes operate in ways considered undesirable, as in the creation of slum conditions. At other times supply and demand do not meet at price and output levels judged fair or adequate. Often this means that government regulation, expenditures, and taxation must be increased or decreased to correct the situation. The "need" for more low-income housing is a problem widely discussed by economists; some planners and politicians have devised housing programs to alter the forces which operate in this field. Planning activities begin with the value judgement that housing, or whatever, is inadequate, and then proceed with analyzing the processes which have created the inadequacy. Imperfections of supply and demand and other factors are identified; corrective and compensatory policies are developed.

Since these planning activities include goal and value statements, they involve more than objective analysis of economic problems (sometimes called "positive" economics). Planning is a part of what is called "normative" economics.

Normative economics in the fields of public policy — especially in urban and regional public policy — often is associated with "benefit-cost analysis" which provides a systematic method of evaluating a proposed (or planned) program of public service. For instance, the private and public benefits of a city sewer system can be compared with the costs of that system to aid in determining whether the system is worth implementing.

In this book we use a broad definition of economics — including not only microeconomic theory and macroeconomic theory, but also process or simulation models, planning, and benefit-cost analysis. For these last three are at the "cutting edge" of the field of urban and regional economics.

1 The Changing Economic Function of the Central City: the Central City in Transition

RAYMOND VERNON
Harvard University

Technological revolutions in transportation and communication have fostered changes in the central cities — generating powerful economic and social pressures. To these, the historical institutions and current practices of cities adapt with a painful slowness, one which accelerates the flight of commerce, industry, and population to the periphery — toward more flexible patterns of land use. The hand-me-down dwellings from which commerce, industry, and population flee go through a process called "filtering," the end result of which is called a "slum."

By almost any objective standard, the major central cities of our nation over the past fifty years or more, have been developing more slowly than the suburban areas that surround them. By many such standards, this *relative* decline has lately begun to appear as an *absolute* decline as well.

Neither the relative nor the absolute decline, considered by itself, is conclusively a sign of deterioration in the central city's economic or social life. But the signs of an absolute decline do raise questions which the relative decline did not. They suggest the possibility of a flight from an environment whose deterioration might conceivably be arrested. They suggest the abandonment of public and private capital which might conceivably still have economic use. They suggest also the possibility that precious space may be available in the central city for conversion to new uses, if only the processes of abandonment were understood and the new uses defined. Our job here is to try to understand the forces which lie behind these trends.

POPULATION MOVEMENT

The placement of American cities has typically been dominated by problems of transportation — problems of servicing the movement of goods and people across oceans, down rivers, and through mountain passes. Sheer chance also played a

From *The Changing Economic Function of the Central City*, by Raymond Vernon, New York: Committee for Economic Development, 1959, pp. 40–67. Reprinted with permission.

part, no doubt, in their original placement: sheer chance reflected in the sequence by which various land areas were explored and settled or by the special enterprise of some individual or group.

At any event, almost from the moment the first house was erected, the first street laid, and the first drainage ditch dug in any of these embryo cities, a process of obsolescence took hold which dominated the pattern of subsequent development. This obsolescence, one should note, developed not only in the private structures but also in the public domain. It was not only that the first dwellings soon became inadequate by the standards of the people who lived in the city, but also that the street layouts, the sewage systems, and the water supply systems also became obsolescent. Almost from the first, then, there was rebuilding as well as building: a tearing down and reordering of structures and public facilities. "New York will be a great city," a visiting Englishman remarked a century ago, "when it gets built."

In the course of this building and rebuilding, however, the general tendency was to add to the ossification of the structure: to surface the public streets more permanently and to cram their sub-surface with more and more cables, mains, and transit conveyances; to replace wood dwellings with stone, and one-story structures with three- and four-story dwellings and factories. Each rebuilding, therefore, tended to make the next one a little more difficult than the last.

But the obsolescence process went on. In middle income homes, sanitary facilities and water supplies were brought into the home; gas mantles were replaced by electricity; the servant's bedroom gave way to the utility closet and the dishwasher; the private automobile supplemented shank's mare, the bicycle, the horse trolley and the subway.

The response of families who could afford it, at one stage or another in most central cities, was to abandon the original residential neighborhoods and to build new neighborhoods elsewhere at points further removed from the city center. Step by step, Bostonians retreated from the Commons, Philadelphians from Independence Hall, New Yorkers from Astor Place. By 1881, Henry James — speaking through one of his fictional characters — was saying:

> "... At the end of three or four years we'll move. That's the way to live in New York — to move every three or four years. Then you always get the last thing. ... So you see we'll always have a new house; you get all the latest improvements...."[1]

By the beginning of the twentieth century, the electric trolley and the suburban railway were quickening the moving process. By the 1930's, the automobile and the bus had speeded the movement even more.

This tendency produced a typical growth pattern around our central cities. At any stage, one could discern points outside the older areas — points where the rail lines and public conveyances ran — where new residential construction was at a peak and populations were increasing at a rapid rate. As time went on, these points where maximum growth rates were being registered were further and further removed from the center of the city, and when the automobile came they were no longer isolated points but a continuous band of maximum growth ringing the central city.

Thus, during the decade of 1900 to 1910, the most rapidly growing parts of metropolitan areas were the central cities themselves. In 1910 to 1920, the maximum growth rates occurred in a five-mile wide ring surrounding the edges of the central cities. In the next three decades, the high growth rates had moved outward still further to a ring 5 to 10 miles from the central city.[2] By 1956, the outward tendency was so marked that over three-quarters of the major metropolitan areas' new dwelling units, measured by number or value, were scheduled for construction outside the central cities.[3]

The result of this pattern of development is suggested by Chart 1. In every case, it will be noted, populations in the central city depicted in the chart tended to decline in relation to the metropolitan area of which it was a part. This, of course, reflects relative rather than absolute decline. After 1950, however, New York City's populations declined in absolute terms. The odds are high that a few others may also have done so.

To account for the absolute decline in New York City's populations and to appreciate why other cities are likely to experience a similar pattern, one must return to a consideration of the process of growth and structural obsolescence which dominates the central cities. Earlier, we carried the story to the point at which the middle-income groups moved to new neighborhoods further removed from the city's center. But this was not typically the end of the economic life of the structures vacated by them.

The next stage was the familiar one, almost universally observed in the nation's central cities. Most of the structures abandoned by one income group were filled by another group several rungs lower on the income ladder. The new tenants crowded the old structures much more than their predecessors had done. Maintenance and repair standards deteriorated. Ultimately, the middle class areas became slums.

But a careful observation of the neighborhood patterns within central cities indicates that the slums, in turn, are having a population cycle of their own. An initial heavy crowding is eventually followed by a tapering off of populations in the slum areas. The ring of slum population growth crawls outward from the center of the city in a belated imitation of the middle-income group that preceded.

The pattern is illustrated by developments in Philadelphia in recent years. The greatest concentration of old dilapidated structures in that city is found in its southeast section, bounded by the Schuylkill and Delaware Rivers. Seven out of eight of the one-family dwelling units in this area had been built before 1919 and 26 per cent of the dwelling units in the area were sub-standard by 1950. In the rest of the city, such dwelling units were much less aged and less dilapidated on the average. The differences were reflected in population changes during the 1940–1950 decade. While the southeast area's population declined by 3 per cent, that of the rest of the city rose by 10 per cent.

The same pattern appeared in Manhattan's lower East Side, at an even earlier date. Here, about two-thirds of the dwelling units had been erected before 1919 and about half of the dwelling units were classified as substandard in the 1940 census. From 1930 to 1940, population on the lower East Side declined 19 per cent while that in the rest of the borough rose 3 per cent. To be sure, some razing of slum structures has occurred in these old areas and elsewhere, a fact which has either hastened the population decline of deteriorated areas or tended to reclaim depopulated areas for other uses. On the whole however, such razing has commonly failed to match the population decline in the slum districts where it occurred. The picture is one of the reduced use of old slum dwellings and the development of new slums to replace them.

Chart 1

Population of Thirteen Central Cities (as Proportion of Their Corresponding Metropolitan Areas, 1900-1950)

Source: Donald J. Bogue, *Population Growth in Standard Metropolitan Areas 1900-1950* (U.S. Housing and Home Finance Agency, Washington, D. C. 1953), Appendix.

RETAIL JOB MOVEMENT

Inevitably, the number of retail jobs in central cities has changed with the changing pattern of their populations. As households have shifted outward toward the suburbs, the neighborhood retail trade has gone along. This is illustrated by Chart 2, which shows how the central city's proportion of retail trade in their respective metropolitan areas has changed in the past quarter century.

But something more than a simple proportionate shift in retail trade has occurred, as evidenced by trends in retail trade in the central business districts of these cities. These districts, as delineated by the United States Bureau of the Census, typically embrace the main city shopping centers and typically draw their trade from all corners of their respective metropolitan areas. From 1948 to 1954 — while the central cities as a whole were slipping in relative positions as retail trade centers — the central business districts of these cities were slipping even faster. Whereas 13 central cities registered a decline of one-tenth in their share of the 13 metropolitan area's retail trade employment in which they were located, the 13 central business districts' share fell by one-quarter. Indeed in seven of these central business districts, there was not only a relative decline in retail sales but an absolute decline as well, a decline all the more remarkable because it occurred during a period when retail sales in the nation were growing prodigiously.

Behind this decline in the central business district's role as a retail shopping center, there lie three main forces. One of these already has been mentioned — the fact that populations in the oldest portions of the central city have tended to grow more slowly than for the city in total or have actually declined in absolute number in some neighborhoods. Another force has been the relatively slower rate of growth of the number of jobs of all kinds in the central cities, a tendency which has reduced the number of prospective "downtown" shoppers; we shall have more to say about this tendency at a later point. Finally — perhaps most importantly — there has been the almost universal preference of the shopper to use the automobile instead of mass transit facilities in the journey from home to bargain counter.

There is not much need to labor the point that a revolutionary shift in transportation preferences has been occurring. The shift has been documented copiously in other sources.[4] The implications of the shift are pointed up by the experience recorded in New York City's central business district. Between 1940 and 1956, the number of persons entering the district on a typical business day had barely changed; it was 3,271,000 on the earlier date and 3,316,000 on the later. Yet during this same period, the number of motor vehicles entering the district had risen from 351,200 to 519,300 daily, a rise of 48 per cent. One can also be reasonably certain that the number of cars circulating entirely within the central business district rose by something like the same magnitude during the 16-year period.

This rise, one need hardly point out, has taxed the obsolescent street system of the area almost beyond endurance. Congestion has always been characteristic of some obsolescent sections in most central cities; Boston's narrow crooked street system in the neighborhoods of Scollay Square and the Washington Street area, New York's street system in the Greenwich Village district, and the narrow north-south streets of Philadelphia's and Baltimore's downtown grids were never designed for the automobile and could scarcely accommodate the horse-drawn dray. But the revolutionary shift away from mass transit has made congestion throughout these

Chart 2

Retail Trade Employment (of Thirteen Central Cities as Proportion of Their Corresponding Metropolitan Areas, 1929-1954)

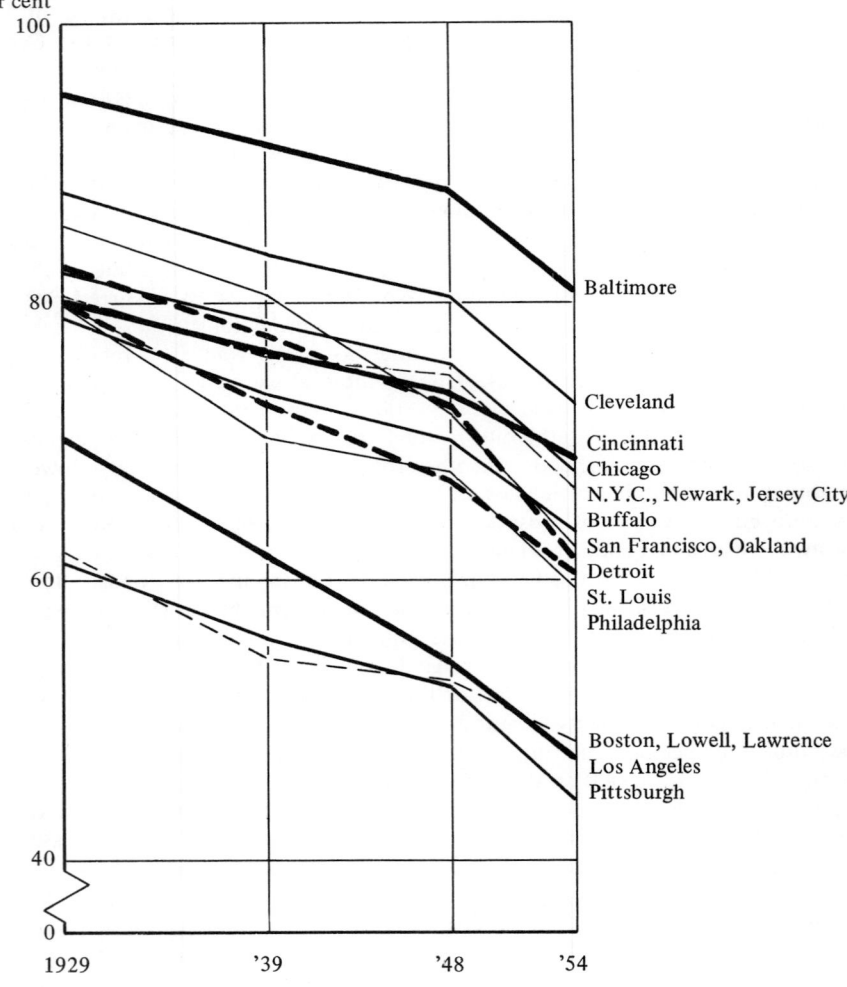

Source: U. S. Census of Business, 1929, 1939, 1948, 1954.

and other central city areas widespread and endemic; and some of the results are seen in the decline of shopping in the central city.

WHOLESALE JOB MOVEMENT

From the ancient days when central cities were principally market towns, wholesaling has been a significant feature of city activity. Goods carried overseas by ships to Atlantic or Pacific ports; articles floated on rivers and lakes or dragged overland to St. Louis, Chicago, Pittsburgh and Denver; these formed the nucleus for the wholesaling function in the towns which were to become our great central cities. Here, the goods were weighed, inspected and bought on the spot.

The ties between wholesaling and the institutions of the city grew more and more firm with the passage of time. In the 19th century, the city was the mecca where the wholesaler from distant markets arranged his financing, indulged his more exotic appetites, and acquired his trade intelligence. Reminiscing about that period in New York, Jacob Knickerbocker says:

> "In the 50's (the 1850's), the wholesale business was located in the lower sections of the city. . . . The position and activities of the salesmen were rather unique. Each had his list of customers from the various sections of the country. When they came to New York to purchase most of them also expected to have a 'good time' and looked to the salesmen to provide it for them. Sometimes the entertainment graded the extent of the purchases. . . ."[5]

So dominant was the central city in this type of activity that even as late as 1929, the central cities in 13 metropolitan areas accounted for over 93 per cent of the wholesaling jobs in those areas. From that date on, however, there was a rapid decline in the relative importance of wholesaling jobs in all these cities, as Chart 3 shows.

Once again, the forces which lie behind this shift can be traced in part to transportation changes and to the advanced state of obsolescence of the central city. On the transport side, the shift in goods movement from rail to truck has freed wholesalers from the compelling need to be on a rail line and has weakened the advantage of being close to a rail junction. As long as wholesalers relied principally on the rail lines in our principal central cities, the fact that the point of convergence of different lines was typically within the central city acted as an attractive force. Once the truck began to be used, however, the attraction of the central city as the preferred distribution point for wholesalers was weakened.

Yet it should not be assumed that the shift from rail to truck is the only transportation force which is pushing wholesalers with stocks from locations in the central city. As we indicated earlier, the best location for distribution to local markets is not necessarily at the center of the market. As the proportion of the total market outside the congested center grows, and as the relative level of congestion in the center area increases, the case for locating outside the center progressively improves. This is one of the elements which has produced the trend shown in Chart 3.

Some of the forces which have pushed wholesaling and distribution from the city centers, however, stem from changes within the warehouse. Goods-handling has been undergoing a technological revolution in recent decades. In some instances, the city-style multi-story warehouse has been readily adaptable to these changes.

Chart 3

Wholesale Trade Employment (of Thirteen Central Cities as Proportion of Their Corresponding Metropolitan Areas, 1929-1954)

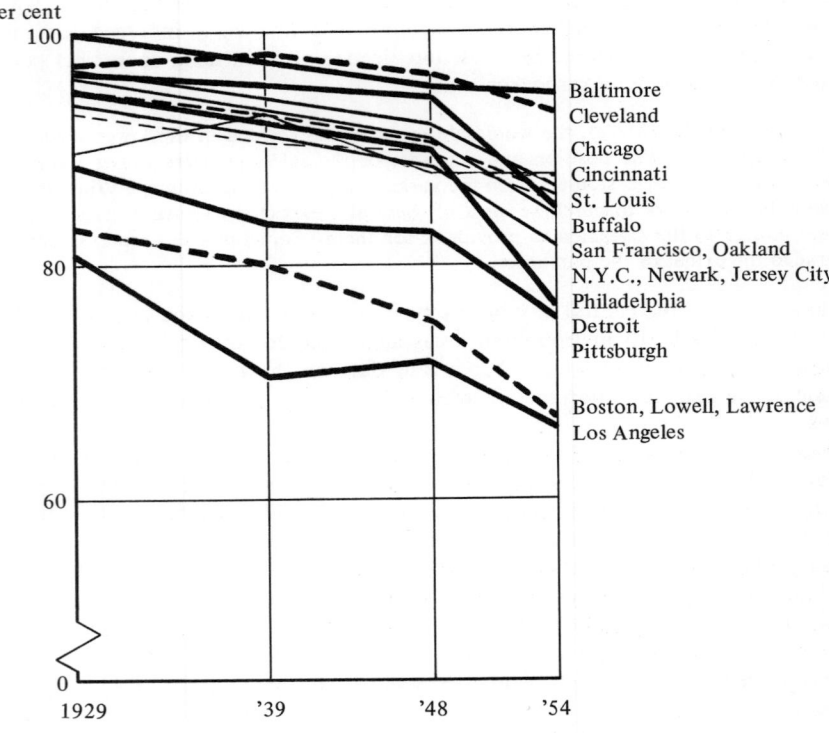

Source: U. S. Census of Business, 1929, 1939, 1948, 1954.

But for the most part, the palletizing of goods and the use of fork-lift trucks and drag lines have created a substantial demand for horizontal warehousing space, with wide bays and high ceilings. These are developments which have not yet spent their full force.

MANUFACTURING JOB MOVEMENT

For as long as the record can be constructed, the major central cities of the nation have been declining in importance as manufacturing centers relative to their suburban hinterlands. As Chart 4 shows, virtually every one of the 13 metropolitan areas depicted there experienced this relative decline of the central city.

Once again, it is well to make a distinction between a *relative* decline and an *absolute* decline in the jobs contained in the central city limits. In recent years — from 1947 to 1954, for example — the cities of Boston, Chicago, Detroit, Pittsburgh, St. Louis, and San Francisco recorded not only a *relative* decline but also an *absolute* decline in the number of these jobs.

Manufacturing enterprises can differ so much from one another in their locational needs that one hesitates to generalize about the movement of these jobs out of the central cities. Some industries have been quite invulnerable to the creeping obsolescence of the central city's environment; others have been highly sensitive to it. Some have departed from their central city location at a precipitate rate; a few are still as highly concentrated in central city locations as they were a quarter century ago. Nevertheless, there are a few generalizations which apply in some degree to most of the manufacturing economy found in large metropolitan areas.

To understand the forces which determined industrial location in our major central cities a century or two ago, one has to turn once again to the overwhelming restraints imposed by problems of transportation. When these cities were in their embryo state, such industry as existed — the mills and metal-working shops, and even the tanneries and abattoirs — necessarily lay inside or close by the city. For the city itself typically sat athwart the natural transportation routes of the area, such as the rivers, lakes and mountain passes. And the city typically provided much of the market and all the labor which the factory employed.

By the middle of the 19th century, however, the problem of industrial location had grown rather more complex. By this time, large manufacturing plants were no longer a rarity and the development of the railroad and the horse trolley were offering them a little more latitude in the choice of a site suitable for the construction of substantial factory structures. Still, these plants were as reliant as ever on rail or water for their transport needs. And since the major rail junctures had commonly developed within the limits of the larger cities, special advantages still existed in remaining in the vicinity of the cities. What is more, homes and factories still could not be too far apart — no further than an hour's journey by foot, ferry or trolley. This, too, contributed to the cohesive development of the city.

In the course of time, however, some of the more noisome industries began to feel the pressures to locate in less constricted spaces. Abattoirs, smelters, and other unsocial industries began to look for sites where no inhibitions would exist to polluting the air or water. Industries of this sort accordingly began to locate in what was then regarded as the far outskirts of the growing cities.

Nevertheless, though the sites which they selected in the late 19th century often seemed remote from the city limits at the time, the cities' growth over the next

Chart 4

Manufacturing Production Workers (of Thirteen Central Cities as Proportion of Their Corresponding Metropolitan Areas, 1899-1954)

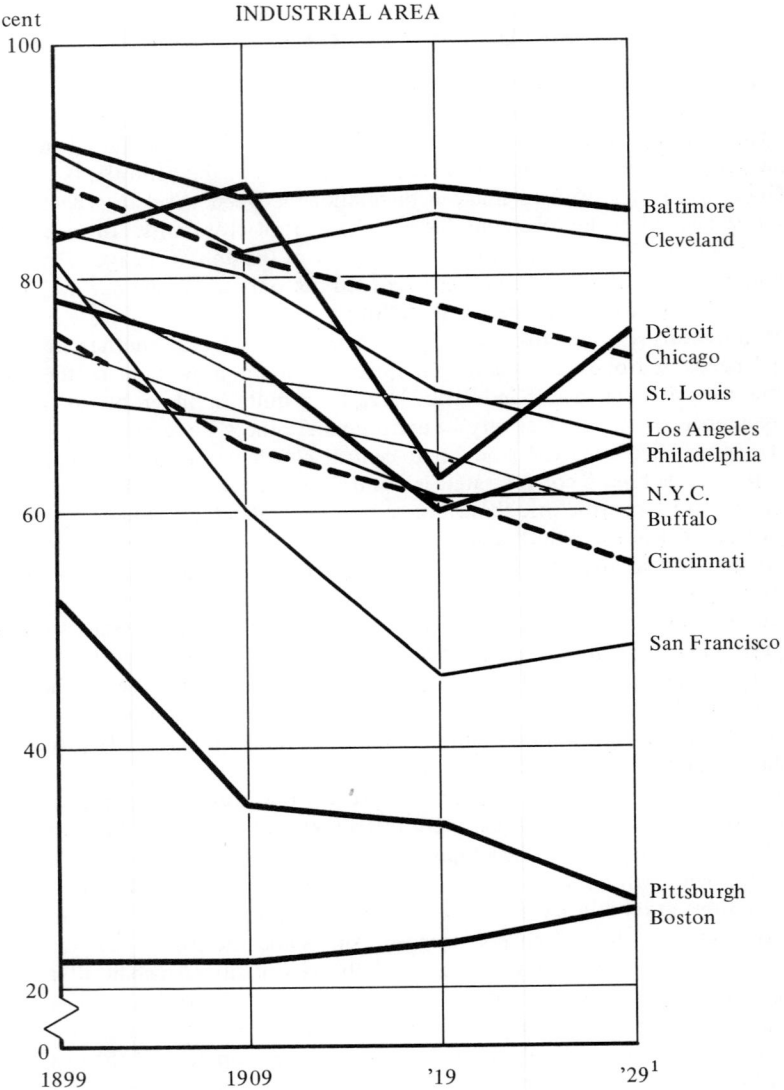

[1] Discrepancies between the two sets of 1929 percentages may result from either changes from Industrial Area to Standard Metropolitan Area or changes in the definition of central city, or both.

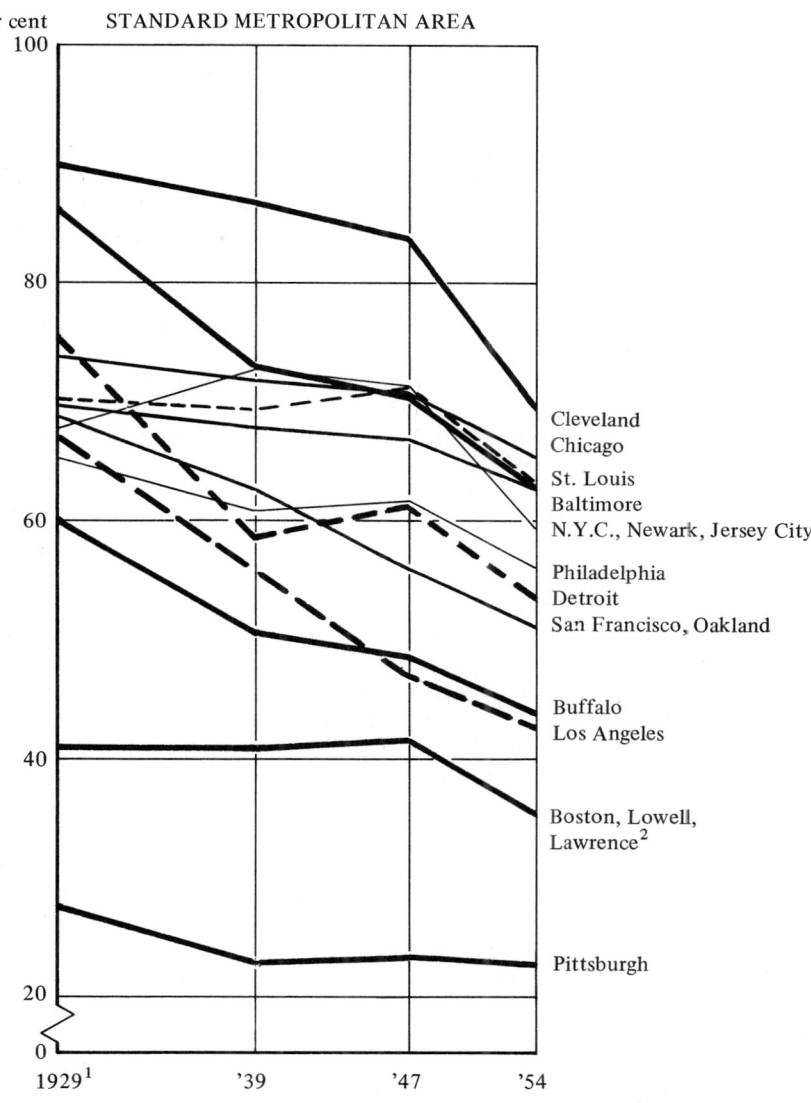

[2] As per cent of Industrial Area

Source: Glenn E. McLaughlin, *Growth of American Manufacturing Areas (Pittsburgh, 1939)*, p. 29. Evelyn M. Kitagawa and Donald J. Bogue, *Suburbanization of Manufacturing Activity within Standard Metropolitan Areas (Oxford, Ohio, 1955)*, pp. 132-139. U.S. Census of Manufactures, 1954 . . .

several decades soon engulfed them. Today, these industries often sit in little enclaves surrounded by urban development; within these enclaves they share a blight perpetuated by the sometimes unavoidable by-products of their operations. Yet in many cases, these industries have little apparent choice but to remain where they are. For their next move — overleaping and locating beyond the urban development which surrounds them — would frequently carry them into territory well removed from their markets or their labor force.

Most of the movement from the central city, however, came later and was spurred by other factors. As time went on, manufacturing structures, like residential structures, became obsolescent. The process of obsolescence was greatly accelerated by the introduction of assembly line techniques in manufacture and by revolutionary developments in materials handling to which we earlier referred. As a result of these changes, as we now all know, the old multi-story mill-style building became increasingly inappropriate for many operations which it had previously housed. The preferred type of structure became the elongated one-story building, laid out on large sites with the easy possibility of expansion in any direction. The advent of trucking was of course of considerable importance in this development. No longer confined to railside or waterside locations, manufacturers were free to look for sites over much more extensive areas.

There were times, to be sure, when the manufacturer replaced his obsolescent old structure on the very site where his original plant had stood or on a site nearby. There were numerous advantages in such a course: Some of the sunk capital in the old site could be salvaged by such a process; some of the old labor force could be retained; some of the neighborhood contacts in the central city, such as repair services and supply sources, could still be utilized.

By and large, the possibility of carving out a new site or greatly enlarging an old site in the central city became increasingly difficult with the passage of time. Zoning regulations were a part of the problem; these regulations, which first appeared in American cities to any extent in the 1920's, often inhibited the expansion of manufacturing in neighborhoods where some manufacturing already existed. To be sure, such restraints ordinarily did not apply to plants in existence prior to the adoption of the zoning requirements. But they did operate to discourage the radical expansion or total replacement of plants in many city areas.

Even where zoning ordinances played no role, however, the assembly of a city site was a formidable operation. As the city developed, most of its land was cut up in small parcels and covered with durable structure of one kind or another. The problem of assembling these sites, in the absence of some type of condemnation power, required a planning horizon of many years and a willingness to risk the possibility of price gouging by the last holdout. Moreover, once a site was acquired, razing costs alone could easily run on the order of $50,000 an acre in current dollar terms. All told, the value of the site could amount to 20 or 30 times more than that of an equivalent area in a developed suburban location. In these circumstances, it was small wonder that many manufacturing establishments chose a suburban location in replacing their obsolescent structures.

Other factors were also operating to push manufacturing into the suburbs. Some of the main forces which previously had drawn manufacturing plants to the centers of the old cities were being weakened by technological change. We have already observed how the truck and the automobile were providing a new mobility to goods and to the labor force, allowing manufacturers to locate at greater distances from existing clusters of homes and factories. In addition, some of the other features unique to the old cities — some of the "external economies" of such cities — were being found over increasingly wider areas. Special power facilities, special transportation services, a variety of repair services, all of these were being extended in the course of time to an increasing number of points outside the older industrial districts.

In tracing the outward movement of manufacturing plants for the central city, one must not overlook the special problems of the plant which operates from industrial lofts and other multi-tenanted quarters. Plants of this sort, anxious to avoid any investment in bricks and mortar, typically have had to take their space where they found it. Accordingly, they have been limited in their locational choices either to industrial buildings constructed for multiple tenancy or to obsolete factory buildings abandoned by their original users.

Establishments of this sort also have tended to move outward from the central city. For with the passage of time, factory buildings have become available to an increasing extent for subdivision and rental in suburban industrial areas. And the scale of existing rentals for such space has been sufficiently low to prevent the construction of new industrial loft structures either in the central cities' confines or elsewhere.[6] Besides, the fact that some of the "external economies" unique to the old cities were appearing on the outskirts as well, removed a major obstacle to suburban locations for many small firms.

The net effect of these outward tendencies has been to delineate more sharply the special characteristics of the central city as a site for manufacturing operations. More and more, the central city has come to specialize in the "communications-oriented" segment of manufacturing. More and more, too, the emphasis has been on the "unstandardized," the uncertain, and the exotic type of manufacturing specialization. And there is every reason to expect that, to the extent that manufacturing remains in the central city, these forms of specialization will grow more pronounced still.

OFFICE JOB MOVEMENT

Those who are concerned with analyzing the economic future of central cities are dogged at the outset with special problems of data gathering. For enough has been written here to underline the point that the business of cities is of a kind which tends to evade the census-taker and which, once detected, resists statistical classification — namely, the new, shifting, different, "unstandardized" operation.

The problem reaches new intensity with respect to the activities which go on in the offices of the nation's great central cities. Whereas manufacturing, transportation, retail trade, and wholesale trade are economic activities whose existence is easily recognized and catalogued, many aspects of office activity are more difficult to classify. Where the work of a firm or an institution is such that all of it is performed in an office setting — as is the case with banks, insurance companies, securities dealers, and related institutions — the problem is not so difficult. But most office activities — most recordkeeping, data-processing, purchasing, routing, billing, controlling, expediting, designing, scheduling, and researching — have developed as adjuncts of producing, transporting, and selling and are not ordinarily identified and enumerated as an independent operation. Yet because the central cities are coming more and more to be reliant for their economic existence upon office activity, it is indispensable to probe into this amorphous group of operations and to draw what generalizations can be pulled out of the unstructured and unsatisfying data.

The financial institutions, we have observed, were among the more easily recognized office activities. From their earliest beginnings, these activities sought out central city locations. We have dwelt upon the forces conducive to central city growth enough by this time to have indicated why banks and security markets should have gravitated toward the very heart of the old cities. "Information" was the greatest stock-in-trade of the security dealer and the banker — information about the credit of an individual, the affairs of an enterprise, the condition of a trade, the politics of a nation; in the ordinary course, such information could best be acquired at the points where ships arrived and departed, where travelers congregated, where news was gathered, and where the posts were swiftest and most frequent.

Besides, the most critical business of these financial entities ordinarily was that of negotiation — the subtle jockeying between buyer and seller, borrower and lender. This is a type of activity which one could scarcely leave to the mails, to the telegraph, or even to the telephone, except where the negotiations were perfunctory, routinized and repetitive.

The pull of the big cities was not due solely to these factors, however. Some aspects of the financial community's activities were indeed sufficiently routinized and standardized that a central city location would not have been absolutely compelling. Insurance company activities, for instance, are largely of a routine and repetitive character. Where such companies chose to centralize their record keeping activities in a single office, the problem was to find a large enough pool of literate clerks to handle the volume of work generated by such an office. In general, women did better than men at this sort of work. Accordingly, the problem became one of locating at a point where a large number of literate women would be assembled daily. The obvious location indicated was a large city, where literacy rates were high, at a point in the city close by mass transit facilities.

The affinity of the financial institutions for the central city was so marked in 1947 that in eight metropolitan areas every major branch of the financial community — banking, insurance, and securities dealers — had more than four-fifths of its employment in the central cities.

As the nation's larger manufacturing, transport, and utility companies developed central offices sufficiently large to make a separate establishment feasible, they too were pulled to the downtown areas of the cities, reacting to much the same forces as had drawn the financial institutions to such locations. One of the functions of these central offices as they developed was to be close to the trade currents — to know what was going on in markets, in technology, in finance. Another was the subtle business of negotiation. Besides, like the insurance companies, their labor requirements were large quantities of literate clerks and stenographers. Their indicated locations, therefore, were the downtown sections of the nation's great cities.

In the end, this use of the central business district tended to elbow out competing uses. The capacity of the office to preempt the downtown area stemmed in part from the relative intensity of its need for central locations. It arose in part also from the special insensitivity of many office activities to the cost of space. Office space costs constitute an incidental fraction of the total costs of manufacturing companies; they involve the prestige center of the enterprise; they affect the daily surroundings and contacts of the firm's elite; accordingly, their location is less prone to determination on a dry-as-dust least-cost calculation than a manufacturing facility or than a warehousing location would be.

As a major fount of employment for a variety of related services, the central offices and the financial institutions managed to draw to the downtown portions of central cities a considerable variety of appended activities. Advertising agencies, employment agencies, management advisory services, addressing and mailing services, all were drawn to the area, where they might provide the type of service which their customers demanded. In 1948, the 13 central cities covered earlier accounted for 94 per cent of the employment in their metropolitan areas' business services.

Nevertheless, although all of these activities have grown in the central city, they have also shared to some degree in the general outward redistribution of population and jobs. In the first place, a considerable proportion of the financial community's activities has come to be oriented to residential neighborhoods. With the much more widespread ownership of personal savings and checking accounts and with the growing use of consumer credit, a considerable segment of banking activity has taken on the locational attributes of any consumer-oriented service. The outward shift of residences, coupled with that of manufacturing, wholesaling and retail trade, has accordingly led to a redistribution of the financial facilities which service them. The impact of this shift can be seen in Chart 5. In the brief period from 1947 to 1956, for eight selected metropolitan areas, there was a modest outward shift in each category of financial facilities except insurance carriers.

This still leaves a significant nub of office employment, located in the central city, which has no obvious reason for dispersal to the suburbs. Just how large this cluster may be is quite unclear, since the statistics seem hopelessly incomplete on this score. But many central offices, business service offices, insurance companies, and "downtown" financial institutions must probably be counted in this category.

By all the signs, the activities of this sector of the nation's economy should continue to grow, perhaps at a rate much faster than of the economy as a whole. Yet even here — even in this stronghold of big city employment — there are certain factors to be taken into account in appraising the future ties to the central city.

One of these is the fact that as central cities decline in population, and as Negroes and other groups with more restricted job opportunities constitute a larger proportion of the population that remains, the young women who have constituted so large a proportion of the labor force of these office installations will become more and more remote from the downtown portions of the central cities. With commuting distances lengthening and mass transit facilities deteriorating in most cities, the question is raised whether the downtown area will continue to be the optimum point at which to collect the preferred office labor force.

A second factor which could affect the growth of central city office employment is the impact of new data-processing and communication techniques on employment. One must be careful not to exaggerate the speed or extent of the shifts which these developments will produce. The introduction of new data-processing systems is a slow and costly business. Besides, its introduction often stimulates the demand for new and timelier data in the firm, thus blunting its labor-displacing effects. Yet there is no denying that such innovations can suppress the growth in office manpower, change the nature of required office skills, and shift the preferred

Chart 5

Finance, Insurance, and Real Estate Employment (of Eight Central Cities[1] Compared with Their Corresponding Metropolitan Areas, 1947 and 1956)

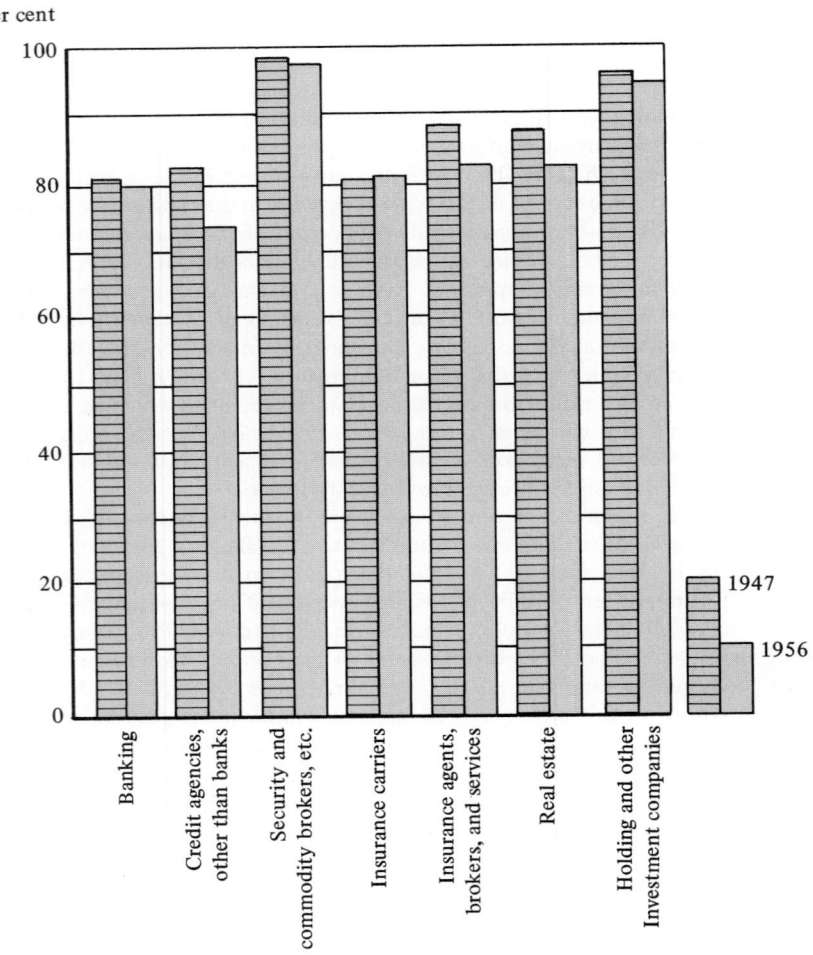

[1] Baltimore, Denver, New Orleans, New York City, Philadelphia, St. Louis, San Francisco, Washington, D. C.

Source: U.S. Bureau of the Census, and U.S. Bureau of Old-Age and Survivors Insurance, County Business Patterns, 1947, 1956.

location of some office functions out of the central city. The repetitive, standardized processes of the office are likely to be most amenable to an out-of-city location, while the elite functions are unlikely to be much affected.

The introduction of mass-data processing equipment has another implication for location. It opens up the possibility of central data-handling for the multi-plant or multi-warehouse firm which previously had been performing many of its office functions on a regional or local basis. This in turn creates the possibility of a redelegation of decisions to the central office — decisions on inventories, shipments, production schedules and the like. To the extent that the office function grows, therefore, the growth may well occur to a disproportionate extent in the office districts of the larger central cities, at the expense of the regional centers.

The possibility that only the largest cities may be the principal beneficiaries of continued office growth — indeed, the possibility that they may be the only beneficiaries — is raised also by the increased use of air travel by business executives. All of the locational implications of such travel are not yet clear. But one of the consequences of the use of such travel is that far-flung plants, warehouses and sales offices are no longer so remote from headquarters as they used to be. Accordingly, the risks of operating through absentee management and the need to delegate decision-making to the field may seem somewhat reduced.

Of course the development of air travel may be read two ways. For the availability of such air travel opens up the possibility of stationing key corporate offices in the field, yet being able to summon them to headquarters on a few hours' notice. But the odds seem heavy that the increased mobility among executives will not be exploited by dispersing them to the field but rather by gathering them in to central points; that in the rival pulls for more face-to-face contact among top executives and more face-to-face contact with plant managers, the former pull will be the stronger. This, too, suggests that "central office cities" may grow more so, at the expense of the lesser regional office centers. But it would be comforting if hard data could be brought to bear to test these conjectures.

SUMMARY

As one fits these various trends into a coherent whole, they suggest the possibility that we may have entered upon a new phase in the development of the large central cities of the nation. At the very center of such cities — more so in the larger than in the smaller ones — there is every reason to expect continued vitality. Office activities in the nation are expanding and will continue to expand. The central cities may not capture quite as high a proportion of such activity as they have in the past, but there is not much doubt that absolute increases in such employment will occur. Nor is there much doubt that, to the extent that they occur, they will offer a continued stimulus to some central business districts.

This activity aside, one sees only a growing obsolescence in the rest of the central city beyond its central business district. There is nothing in view calculated to interrupt the cycle so far evident in the old cities. When middle income structures reach an advanced stage of obsolescence, they will be converted to intensive low-income use. The ancient slums will be partially abandoned, as they have been in the past, for the newer ones; populations will thin out in the former and rise in the latter, in a wave which moves gradually outward to the edges of the city and into the older portions of the suburban towns.

The outward movement of people will be matched by an outward movement of jobs. Retail trade will follow the populations. Manufacturing and wholesaling establishments will continue to respond to obsolescence by looking for new quarters and by renting in structures in the suburban industrial areas where obsolescence is less advanced. The movement of jobs will reinforce the movement of residences.

Beyond the central business district, therefore, but within the confines of the central city, there is likely to be a long-run decline in the intensive use of space as sites for jobs and homes. Will such space be converted to other uses? It is difficult to detect any actual or incipient private demand for city space which is of a magnitude calculated to replace such prior uses. Modern factory space is ruled out by the high costs of recapturing the site; new multi-story lofts face a poor market, since they will be competing with obsolescent factories vacated by their prior owners; office space, however greatly it expands, can scarcely be expected to fill more than a minuscule area, largely concentrated toward the city center; high-income renters may fill a little more space, but not much.

This leaves two possibilities: that middle-income families may decide to return to the cities in great numbers; or that subsidized governmental intervention, such as low-income housing or open-space projects, may be expanded to such levels as to constitute a significant space-using force. The first possibility would fly in the face of deep-seated historical trends, based on powerful sociological forces. The latter demands a scale of intervention much larger than any which heretofore has been contemplated.

REFERENCES

1. Morris Townsend speaking in Henry James' *Washington Square*, reprinted in Modern Library Series (1950), p. 38.
2. Amos H. Hawley, *The Changing Shape of Metropolitan America*, (Glencoe, Ill., 1956), pp. 14–16.
3. Based on Balitmore, Boston, Buffalo, Chicago, Cleveland, Detroit, Los Angeles, New York-Northeastern New Jersey, San Francisco-Oakland metropolitan areas. U.S. Bureau of Labor Statistics, *Monthly Labor Review,* June 1957, p. 690. U.S. Dept. of Commerce and U.S. Dept. of Labor *Construction Review,* May 1956 to April 1957.
4. See particularly Wilfred Owen, *The Metropolitan Transportation Problem* (Washington, 1956).
5. Jacob Knickerbocker, *Then and Now* (Boston, 1939), p. 39.
6. Calculations based on the cost structure in the New York Metropolitan Region suggest that new multi-tenanted industrial structures — even if built on sites acquired at no cost — would have to command an annual rental of more than $3 per square foot whereas the prevailing rental rate in existing structures tends to be less than $1.00.

2 The Economic Future of City and Suburb

DAVID L. BIRCH
Harvard University

Our future may be quite different from our past — with the central city no longer able to function as a general-purpose economic system.

1. INTRODUCTION

At the turn of the century, the central city was the city. It was the place where business was concentrated. It was the place where the people who worked in the businesses lived. It was, in short, metropolitan America. The outlying towns were largely self-sufficient communities. Only a wealthy few could afford the train fare and the time required to commute from country to city.

All this, of course, has changed. The businesses and the people have spread out across the cities' boundaries, and long-distance commuting has become a way of life. When we speak of metropolitan America, we now refer to 233 standard metropolitan statistical areas, not to 233 cities.

The expansion has not been uniform. Businessmen who relied heavily on meetings with many different people to get things done kept their offices in the city. Small businesses needing low-cost floor space and a diverse source of suppliers stayed. Large office complexes that required large pools of clerical help could not move easily. Many wealthy families, especially those without children, preferred the concentration of opera houses, restaurants, museums, theaters, and nearby offices, and could afford the high cost of living near them. Many poor families had no alternative but to stay.

On the other hand, manufacturers who could take advantage of cheap land and large, single-level floor space moved out eagerly. Families that wanted more space for their children and privacy for themselves also left the city. At the same time, many new enterprises and families were formed outside the city rather than within it. Retailers, and eventually wholesalers, sprang up to service them. As a result of this selective relocation, the central city, which was once a concentrated, self-contained economic and residential whole, now finds itself becoming a relatively specialized segment of a rapidly growing area.

The pains and discomforts of conversion have been many. The plight of the poor, trapped, central-city resident has been publicized and has received a great deal of national attention. The congestion of the central cities' streets and the pollution

From *The Economic Future of City and Suburb*, by David L. Birch, New York: Committee for Economic Development, 1970, pp. 1–15. Reprinted with permission.

of their water and air have become extreme. The frustrations of central-city mayors, faced with a list of urgent needs and relatively static financial bases, are well known.

A critical question now facing the nation is how, and to what extent, we are going to meet the cities' needs. As a prerequisite to making that decision, we must understand in some detail how the central city is changing and what its probable future course will be. It is difficult to know where to begin. Shifts in employment cannot be considered apart from shifts in population; they are hopelessly intertwined. Jobs seem as logical a starting place as any, however, and this paper will begin with a description of how central-city employment has changed since World War II. As will be seen, the movement of people has been closely related to shifts in employment, and population shifts will be considered in the second main section. Finally, some attempt will be made to assess the strength of the trends affecting central-city development and the probable effect that several changes in policy and technology might have upon these trends.

2. THE CHANGING ECONOMIC FUNCTION

As Raymond Vernon pointed out ten years ago . . . (in *The Changing Economic Function of the Central City,* New York, 1959), on the surface there is little or no reason why economic activity should be located in the central city. Vernon found that, with a few exceptions, wage rates are practically indistinguishable between central city and suburb. He also found few, if any, advantages for businesses in the city in terms of space costs, transportation costs, and taxes. Manufacturing floor space in the central city is slightly more expensive in small quantities and a great deal more expensive in large quantities. Even taking into account the extra conveniences that must be built into new suburban locations, such as parking, shopping facilities, and cafeterias, space costs are more or less equal between city and suburb.

With rising congestion in the cities, rapid construction of circumferential highways, and the granting of advantageous city rates to suburban shippers, the cost advantage to a manufacturer or wholesaler of a central-city distribution point may no longer be substantial. For a retailer, the bulk of whose customers will not drive more than twenty minutes to get to his store, a central-city location can be a distinct disadvantage. Taxes in the central city are somewhat higher, and the differential can be expected to continue as the cities' needs continue to outstrip their resources.

With all these disadvantages in space costs, transportation costs, and taxes, how do we explain the tremendous concentration of economic activity found in today's central cities?

The first, and most obvious, explanation is that the central cities are where it all started. In the days when transportation was difficult and slow and the advantages of a harbor or a railroad intersection were great, the geographically concentrated city was the best solution for men of affairs and their families. *The* place to close a financial deal was the Cosmopolitan Club or Frank's Delicatessen. Out-of-town guests expected to be entertained at the 21 Club. Investments depreciate slowly and customs change slowly. If the central cities claimed no measurable economic advantages today, we would still not expect the concentrations that developed during the late nineteenth and early twentieth centuries to disperse rapidly.

But we must look beyond historical geography if we are to explain why so many central cities are still growing at a rapid pace. The search for a positive explanation led Vernon to identify three factors: (1) the communication factor, (2) the costs of uncertainty, and (3) the external economies of scale.

As Vernon saw it, face-to-face communication is very important to the small manufacturer who is dealing in a nonstandard product on a tight schedule. The producer of legal briefs or women's clothes or the seller of fresh produce must engage in all the subtleties of showing his product to the customer, reaching an agreement on the spot, and delivering the product — all in a very short period of time. The headquarters of business firms need to be in close personal contact with the bankers, the underwriters, and the stock brokers who provide them with funds, with the lawyers who protect and advise them, with the officers of other firms with whom they do business, and with a host of specialized suppliers. Taken together, the people in these firms constitute a number of closely knit communities that depend upon day-to-day personal communication to get things done. An entire community can be moved physically, as was the produce market in Paris and the garment industry in Amsterdam, but it must remain as a community in order to sustain the human relationships on which it depends.

Minimizing the costs of uncertainty by locating in a congested urban complex is once again primarily the concern of the small producer of nonstandard products. The small machine shop owner or the producer of advertising brochures is constantly seeking new business that may require the use of new materials and processing techniques. The risk of investing in equipment to produce his own materials for any particular order is very great as compared with the short-term savings he might obtain. He would much prefer to be in a position to call on a diversity of competing suppliers, despite the extra cost. Likewise, the man who runs a specialized lathe or printing process needs a great diversity of customers to assure him of steady production. He cannot afford to be dependent upon one or two customers whose individual needs for his special product might vary a great deal. This interacting group of suppliers and producers forms a community in which one relies on the other to minimize risk.

External economies of scale have long been put forth as a rationale for concentration. The city can provide for the smaller firm what the larger, suburban company might have to provide for itself, or do without. The smaller firm contracts, either directly or through taxation, for the partial use of a subway or an airport, a freight distribution service or a sewage disposal plant. Collectively, these smaller firms bargain together for lower shipping rates. They hire a part-time electrician by purchasing his services by the hour. Because the central cities are able to offer this opportunity to share large fixed costs, they serve as breeding grounds for small firms. Vernon was not surprised to find that 69 per cent of small plants were located in central cities, whereas only 45 per cent of their larger, more self-sufficient counterparts were situated in such centers. It is no accident that new firms spring up and die in the central cities at about twice the rate that they do in the suburbs. The ease of getting started is much greater when the burdens of getting started can be shared.

The advantages of close personal communication, lower costs of uncertainty, and external economies of scale are obviously greater for some firms than for others. Wholesalers and service firms, which tend to deal in specialized, nonstandard products, cannot completely ignore the advantages of a central location and thus tend to be more content in the central city. However, retailers, taking advantage of a short shopping radius, and manufacturers, attracted by the efficiencies of single-story plants, have increasingly located in the suburbs.

The City's Increasing Specialization

Attempts to document these observed trends have been frustrated for years because of the inadequate level of detail contained in census and other data. Detailed employment data for most central cities and suburban areas are available only for retail trade, wholesale trade, manufacturing, and selected services, which, in combination, account for only 55 per cent of total metropolitan employment and 58 per cent of central-city employment.

Accepting for the moment these shortcomings, an analysis of the four employment categories for which data are available supports our Darwinian assumption that some forms of activity survive better than others in a central-city environment, and that services survive the best. Looking at Figure 1, we note that, for a sample of seventy-three Standard Metropolitan Statistical Areas (SMSA's), representing 75 per cent of the total metropolitan population . . . there have been recent absolute declines in retail trade, relatively slow growth in wholesaling and manufacturing, and rather greater growth in service jobs.

As a further check on this pattern, we must look to "other services," a category which includes most nonbusiness organizations, such as hospitals, law offices, schools, and nonprofit membership organizations (ranging from the Knights of Columbus to the Elks to CORE). We must also examine jobs in such fields as finance, insurance, real estate, and government. Together, these additional sectors account for approximately 32 per cent of central-city employment, raising our over-all coverage to about 90 per cent.

Figure 1

Growth of Central City Employment by Major Industry Groups: 1948–1963

Distribution and Mean Annual Percentage Change for Seventy-Three SMSA's

EMPLOYMENT CATEGORY	PER CENT OF TOTAL CENTRAL CITY EMPLOYMENT IN 1963	MEAN ANNUAL PERCENTAGE CHANGE		
		1948–54	1954–58	1958–63
Retail trade	20.0	0.8	1.8	−0.9
Wholesale trade	5.7	1.6	2.3	1.4
Manufacturing	7.5	3.6[a]	1.1	1.6
Selected services	5.0	2.3	4.7	2.4

[a] Data pertain to 1947–1954.

Sources: National Planning Association, *Economic and Demographic Projections for Two Hundred and Twenty-Four Metropolitan Areas*, Regional Economic Projections Series, Report No. 67-R-1, Vol. I, II, and III; U.S. Department of Commerce, Bureau of the Census, *County Business Patterns*, 1948, 1956, and 1958; and U.S. Department of Commerce, Bureau of the Census, *Census of Manufacturers and the Census of Business*, selected reports for various years, 1954–1963. See Appendix II, p. 41.

Unfortunately, the data for these additional sectors are quite sketchy. There are only eight SMSA's for which central-city statistics are available, and then only because county and city boundaries happen to coincide in these eight instances, thus opening up the detailed data ordinarily available for counties. The figures for the eight cities reveal some support for the concept of growing central-city specialization in service-type jobs. In Figure 2, we note that hospitals, schools, and law offices are growing much more rapidly as a group than is any sector yet examined. The financial sector is also expanding quite rapidly. Government employment is growing more slowly, and there appears to be a trend for insurance and real estate organizations to abandon the city for greener pastures.

If these differential growth rates are as persistent over the next fifteen to twenty years as they have been since 1948 — and in the absence of dramatic changes in transportation or communication, we have every reason to believe that they will be — then it is reasonable to expect that the central cities will continue to become economic specialists. They will increasingly serve as the home for the hospital, the corporate headquarters, and the state office building.

The degree to which these trends persist will depend, of course, to a certain extent upon the relative growth of the sectors within the economy as a whole. If our greatest expansion as a nation over the next twenty to thirty years were to be in manufacturing or retail trade, rather than services, then the prospects for continued central-city growth would be diminished. However, one comprehensive projection, made by the National Planning Association, suggests otherwise. The NPA estimates summarized in Figure 3 indicate that it is the services (aggregated in this case), the financial community, and the government that can expect the greatest growth through at least 1975.

Thus, it can be assumed from the available evidence that, in aggregate, central cities will experience substantial growth in the white-collar, service-type job cate-

Figure 2

Change in Central City Employment by Selected Categories: 1948–1967

Distribution and Mean Annual Percentage Change for Eight Central Cities[a]

EMPLOYMENT CATEGORY	PER CENT OF TOTAL CENTRAL CITY EMPLOYMENT IN 1963	MEAN ANNUAL PERCENTAGE CHANGE	
		1948–56	1956–67
Finance	3.1	4.0	4.1
Insurance and real estate	3.9	1.8	−0.2
Government[b]	11.4	n.a.	2.0
Other services[c]	13.4	4.0	15.7

[a] Baltimore, Denver, New Orleans, New York, Philadelphia, St. Louis, San Francisco, and Washington, D.C.

[b] Data pertain to 1957–1962.

[c] Includes medical, legal, educational, and miscellaneous business services, as well as non-profit membership organizations.

Sources: See Figure 1.

Figure 3

*Growth of U.S. Employment by Major Categories
Since 1950, Projected to 1975*

Average Annual Rate of Change

EMPLOYMENT CATEGORY	ACTUAL 1950–57	1957–62	PROJECTED 1962–75
Retail trade	0.3%	0.8%	1.9%
Wholesale trade	0.9	0.6	1.9
Manufacturing	1.6	−0.3	1.2
Services	2.7	3.5	2.9
Finance insurance and real estate	3.6	2.7	3.2
Federal government	2.2	1.9	0.1
State and local government	3.4	4.5	4.2

Sources: See Figure 1.

gories. As manufacturers, wholesalers, and retailers settle elsewhere, the effect of the growth in services will be to alter the mix of activities going on in central cities, which, in turn, will quite probably have an influence on the kinds of people living there.

The Suburb Versus the City

Before we examine the residential function of cities, there remain two important economic questions. First, how are cities faring relative to suburbs in terms of economic growth rates? A basic consideration here is whether cities are capturing the bulk of the region's service jobs, and hence becoming service centers, or whether their specialization merely reflects an internal shift. Second, are all cities — large and small, young and old, north, south, and west — behaving in roughly the same fashion, or can we expect differences?

It is clear that the suburbs are growing much faster than the cities, despite the absolute gains of the central cities. As can be seen by a comparison of Figure 4

Figure 4

*Growth of Suburban Employment
by Major Industry Groups: 1948–1963*

*Mean Annual Percentage Change for
Seventy-Three SMSA's*

EMPLOYMENT CATEGORY	1948–1954	1954–1958	1958–1963
Retail trade	1.8%	15.5%	11.3%
Wholesale trade	4.5	17.6	9.4
Manufacturing	10.5[a]	6.3	9.9
Selected services	8.9	18.1	13.8

[a] Data pertain to 1947.

Sources: See Figure 1.

Figure 5

The Central City's Changing Share of Urban Employment: 1948–1967

Percentage

EMPLOYMENT CATEGORY	1948	1954	1956	1958	1963	1967
Sample of Seventy-Three SMSA's[a]						
Retail trade	78.9%	77.6%		72.4%	64.0%	
Wholesale trade	87.3	86.4		82.4	78.5	
Manufacturing[b]	65.9	64.4		60.8	57.6	
Selected services	88.6	83.1		79.5	75.0	
Sample of Eight SMSA's[c]						
Other services	81.4		83.6%			72.1%
Finance	90.4		86.8			82.9
Insurance and real estate	92.7		89.2			80.2
Government	n.a.		66.0			59.7

[a] Statistics for sample of seventy-three SMSA's described in Appendix I.
[b] Data pertain to 1947.
[c] Statistics for sample of eight SMSA's described in Figure 2.
Sources: See Figure 1.

with Figure 2, suburban growth rates are much higher (sometimes by a factor of ten or more) than those of the central city.

This rapid suburban expansion has had a predictable effect on the central-city share of total metropolitan employment: without exception, the central-city percentage is declining. (See Figure 5.) The difference in the central-city share as between one type of employment and another is less predictable, and perhaps more informative. In particular, the central city's relatively high share of service and financial jobs suggests that the city, by specializing in service work, has been able to attract and hold a great percentage of all high-priced service jobs in the region. It thus appears to be functioning as an elite service center.

The Life Cycle of the City

It must be emphasized, however, that not all central cities are undergoing the same kind of transformation at the same rate. If we compare large SMSA's (over 500,000 people) with smaller ones (less than 500,000 people), it is clear that cities in smaller SMSA's are growing much more rapidly than cities in larger SMSA's for each employment category. (See Figure 6.) In particular, manufacturers still appear to find the central cities of smaller metropolitan areas attractive, which would suggest that the problems of locating suitable building sites for efficient, one-story plants are not so acute.

Size, of course, is only one basis for comparing cities, and it is not a particularly useful one for prediction purposes. Intuitively, we would expect Phoenix and Albany, which are almost identical in size, to have quite different futures. Likewise, we might well anticipate different patterns for such matched pairs as Buffalo

Figure 6

Growth of Central City Employment by Size and Age of SMSA: 1948–1963[a]

Percentage Change for Seventy-Three SMSA's by Major Industry Groups

	OLD SMSA'S	MIDDLE-AGED SMSA'S	YOUNG SMSA'S	AVERAGE
Retail Trade				
Large SMSA's	−11.1%	19.8%	73.5%	4.2%
Smaller SMSA's	−13.0	11.7	26.5	18.6
Average	−11.2	15.7	37.7	9.5
Wholesale Trade				
Large SMSA's	4.1	43.9	111.6	23.6
Smaller SMSA's	17.0	26.5	54.2	42.2
Average	4.9	35.2	67.9	30.5
Manufacturing				
Large SMSA's	− 0.8	59.6	284.1	42.0
Smaller SMSA's	−10.9	52.6	89.8	69.9
Average	− 1.4	56.1	136.0	52.3
Selected Services				
Large SMSA's	31.5	56.6	162.1	50.6
Smaller SMSA's	21.2	37.8	67.8	54.3
Average	30.9	47.2	90.2	52.0

[a] "Old" SMSA's qualified as SMSA's before 1900; "middle-aged," between 1900 and 1930; and "young," after 1930. "Smaller" SMSA's have a population of less than 500,000; "large" SMSA's contain over 500,000 people.

Sources: See Figure 1.

and Houston, or San Diego and Cincinnati. For one thing, we would expect the younger city in each case to have lower densities and more room for expansion. In point of fact, the densities of these cities are roughly one-half the densities of the older cities. Furthermore, we would expect the younger cities to be built around road networks, rather than around the railroads and harbors of the earlier cities. The combination of open room for new housing and new plants and the greater efficiency of moving from the one to the other should give these younger cities a distinct advantage in attracting jobs and the people to fill them.

There is nothing to suggest, however, that young cities can avoid the life cycle that older cities have experienced. As today's young cities "fill up," new technology will favor the still newer SMSA's, which will be able to incorporate recent advances from the start. The young cities of 1970 will become the older cities of 2050 and, in the process, more than likely will pass through the typical phases of growth, saturation, and eventually stabilization and decline.

To test this conjecture, SMSA's were further grouped according to the year in which each qualified as an SMSA. The resulting categories were: old (before 1900), middle-aged (1900–1930), and young (after 1930). The results strongly support the life-cycle notion. As can be seen in Figure 6, invariably the older the SMSA, the less rapidly it is growing in economic terms. Of particular interest is the absolute decline of retail trade and manufacturing in the older cities. In sharp contrast is the rapid growth of central-city manufacturing in the younger cities regardless of size. If anything, these young cities are capitalizing on their roads and open spaces to become manufacturing rather than service specialists. And, as might be predicted from a life cycle model, the older a city gets, the less its tendency to rely on manufacturing for growth.

This suggests a sequence whereby younger cities chew up low-density land at a good clip with manufacturing floor space, parking lots, and road networks. The other economic functions develop more slowly. As the city ages and becomes more densely populated, central-city land becomes more expensive, and manufacturing declines in significance, as does retail and wholesale trade. Services, in contrast, appear to thrive on concentration, for all the reasons indicated earlier, and, through a process of self-selection and survival, emerge as the dominant economic force in the older, larger cities. The tendency of central cities to become elite service centers appears, like rheumatism and decaying teeth, to be a strong function of age.

One effect of this life cycle phenomenon will be to redistribute the location of economic activity over time. Most of the younger, growing metropolitan areas are found in the South and the West. Whereas at present these younger areas account for only about 25 per cent of total employment, over time their much greater growth rates will give them an increasing share of the nation's gross national product. Conversely the significance of the large northern metropolitan centers, which served as the nuclei of urban growth during the first half of this century, will decline in a relative sense. Companies will not automatically locate their headquarters in New York or Philadelphia or Chicago. A young man will no longer have to "make it" in *the* big city. There will be a larger number of significant and growing economic concentrations to choose from.

Summarizing, we can envision a future that is quite different from the past. The central city is no longer able to function as a general-purpose economic system. Specialization is taking place within the city and within the SMSA, particularly in the older areas. Those organizations which can thrive on the advantages that concentration and a large city government can offer are thriving. Others are leaving or, more importantly, not locating there in the first place.

The extent to which specialization takes place appears closely related to the age of the area in which the city is located. While central cities in older areas are declining absolutely in most non-service jobs, cities in younger areas are growing quite rapidly across the board. Since the younger areas are located primarily in the South and the West, one result of this life-cycle effect will be to alter substantially the location of economic growth during the next fifty years. The pillars of American urban society during the first half of the century will have to accept a relatively lesser role in the future.

Accompanying this shift in economic activity will be a marked shift in population . . .

3 Strategies for Helping Cities

JANE JACOBS
Author and Consultant

Jane Jacobs locates "the heart of the matter" — of helping cities — in city economic activity.

Americans, at present, use two national strategies that are presumed to help cities. One, which is impartial, is to dispense Federal grants to them, either directly or through the states, for specified physical and social programs. The other is to award war and space contracts to enterprises in this or that locality, frequently a city; while this is a by-product of other purposes, the contracts are regarded in recipient cities as aids to their economies and are highly valued for just this reason. I propose to question, from the point of view of cities' growth mechanisms, both these approaches and to suggest another strategy.

    The overwhelming fact about cities is that if they do not maintain self-generating economies, they will ultimately stagnate and decline. This is not true of rural areas or towns. New export work is often bestowed upon towns by enterprises that have transplanted their work out of cities. Rural areas prosper when their products are directly drawn upon by growing city markets and their productivity increased by city-created products and technologies. But, as for cities — even when a city receives a transplanted factory or office, the spin-off is from another city and has been "earned" by the growth of the receiving city's market or its array of input items, usually both. Rural technologies do not provide answers to unsolved practical problems in cities, nor does any city prosper and grow because of the markets provided by rural hinterlands. Cities, individually, must generate their own economic bases; and cities, taken collectively, must generate the innovations that make developing economies possible.

    A city employs two major growth and development mechanisms, each of which builds upon the other: it generates exports and replaces imports. Simply to maintain an export base, a city must continually find new exports because among other things the city must compensate for production transplanted out to towns and countryside, and for exports lost because they are produced eventually in former customer cities. Of course, many of a city's older exports become obsolete in the course of time. A city's stream of new exporting organizations emerges directly from, and upon, production of goods and services first undertaken for the city's own market. The other major mechanism, import replacing, operates — for obvious reasons — mainly through replacements of imports from other cities, but also on occasion (e.g., artificial refrigeration in place of natural ice) from rural areas. When a city replaces imports, it shifts its purchases to other, often newer, imports

---

From "Strategies for Helping Cities," by Jane Jacobs, the *American Economic Review*, September 1969. Reprinted with permission.

from other cities as well as to larger quantities of rural goods. Replacing imports creates a large multiplier and thus, from the vantage point of that city, also creates a greatly enlarged and diversified reservoir of potential export goods and services. Quite apart from the great problem solving innovations that arise in cities in the course of these events, the processes themselves, considered as sheer mechanisms, are vital to city economic expansion and to dynamic inter-city trade.

The defect of the national grant strategy, as far as these vital mechanisms are concerned, is precisely that it is national. The grant programs insure that many different cities concentrate on exactly the same collections of problems and approach them in similar ways. Once a grant program has been devised, much standardization of goods and services in its cause automatically follows. One does not build a city highway on Federal funds without meeting standard specifications, some of which are gratuitous but most of which are inherent in the prescription itself. Furthermore, since grants must be policed against corruption and egregious mistakes (e.g. housing with inadequate heating plants, hospital nursing units too small) or else their purpose is vitiated, it follows that most "correct" responses must be routinized; the policing, in any case a mammoth job, is impractical otherwise. What all this means, in sum, is that each city participating in a given grant program must respond with goods and services, whether imported or locally produced, very similar to those of all other cities participating. The very stuff of differential creation and dynamic city export generating and import replacing is being discouraged. This defect is more serious than the size of the grants alone would suggest. Since the grants are directed to glaring practical problems, they are automatically directed to activities, e.g. housing, transportation, health care, that have already become backward; these are precisely the problems, along with their associated economic activities, that most require development work, not premature prescriptions with their accompanying standardizations.

Not all countries, of course, have numerous cities as the United States does. Some have only one important metropolis. Denmark, Cuba, and Austria are typical instances of one-metropolis countries. Hong Kong is another, although an unusual case. In a one-metropolis country, national grant programs do not carry the defect of standardization to an extreme, simply because, in a one-metropolis country, the central government's writ does not run to the other metropolitan areas with which its own city trades most heavily. This suggests that a strategy which can work constructively in Denmark is inherently destructive in Britain. The same kind of distinction can be drawn between Hong Kong or Malaya and multi-city India or China; and between Cuba and multi-city Brazil or the Soviet Union. The point is that in a multi-city country, a national grant strategy per se must be at cross-purposes to the mechanisms of city economic growth and development, no matter what the specific content and quality of the programs may be.

In the United States, the high point of faith in the grant strategy may well have been reached at the time the War on Poverty was launching its Great Leap Forward in 1965, and now may be on the wane. I base this supposition on the observation that, until the past few years, constructive criticisms of the national grants were almost wholly concerned with tactics — that is, were directed to details of administration, sizes of appropriations, emphases or omissions of the programs, and the like. But interest is growing in Federal tax-sharing with cities, either as an alternative or a supplement to grant programs. This speaks, if only by implication, of growing skepticism concerning the grant strategy itself.

The other American national strategy for helping cities, the war contracts for which there is so much jockeying, also works at cross-purposes of city growth and development although probably more gradually and cumulatively. From the point of view of a modern city, the war goods produced are export items. Thus they increase, often enormously and abruptly, the city's export economy. The trouble arises because war goods and services are not imported by cities. All sections of the country are paying for them but are not receiving imports in return and this import deprivation inexorably affects their economic mechanisms.

A city develops and builds its economy upon its imports as surely as upon its exports; it does so most importantly during its periodic episodes of explosive economic growth when it is replacing many former imports rapidly, in a chain reaction, and shifting its imports rapidly to other kinds of goods and services. If import deprivation is temporary only, postponement of import replacing seems to be of no great moment. A dramatic example is afforded by Los Angeles at the end of World War II. This probably means that a country which only intermittently engages in heavy war production, as was the case in the United States until the time of the Korean War, reaps the stimulating effect without incurring any long range depressing effects on its cities' economies . . . (See Jane Jacobs, *The Economy of Cities,* New York, 1969, pp. 151–154.)

However, prolonged, heavy production for war is a different matter; it means that one after another, city after city is either being obstructed from replacing imports or the process is critically weakened, simply because, over a prolonged period, such large quantities of goods and services for which their people and enterprises have been paying have not reached the cities as imports. The effect must be a cumulative inhibition on new city exports too, because cities that are not replacing and shifting imports vigorously are not serving as rapidly growing markets for new kinds of exports from other cities; nor are they, themselves, building up in their own local economies their own great potential reservoirs of new kinds of exports. The cities' dwindling capacities for creating exports (and hence dwindling capacities for earning imports from other cities) reinforce the import deprivation caused directly by war production. This further undermines capacities to replace imports. In short, city economic mechanisms that ought to be building constructively upon one another are, at such a stage, converting to mechanisms of decline. A country does not have unlimited time to play games with its cities' economies.

If my reasoning is correct, it would follow that any other heavy and prolonged subsidy falling upon a nation's cities (e.g., very heavy and prolonged foreign aid consisting of goods from the donor country; heavy and prolonged exports of capital at the expense of city imports of goods and services) would also have the same effect. But so would diversion of the subsidies back into the cities themselves if they could not be used there to fuel revived and dynamic intercity trade in many new kinds of goods and services. We are back at the standardization defect of the grant strategy again, and this time I am pointing out the fallacy of supposing that cities will necessarily prosper if subsidies for war are simply replaced by equivalent subsidies for city grant programs.

Perhaps the society of the United States is already too distraught to be capable of instituting in an orderly and constructive way a different strategy for helping cities. The common values, the sense of joint purpose, and the trust necessary to great, orderly reforms and their adjustments may already have been irretrievably lost. But if reform is still available to the United States, this is the course I would suggest:

First, the grant strategy should be abandoned in favor of Federal tax sharing with localities. The cities' returned taxes (or as an alternative tactic, the reallocated taxing powers) would have to be given the cities themselves, not the states, because so many states contain two or more metropolitan areas, as well as smaller, and in many cases long stagnant, cities. Thus state administered standards or contingencies attached to the funds or powers would duplicate, on a smaller scale to be sure, the inherent defect of grant programs; and if no standards or contingencies were attached to the sharing, there would be no point in using states as conduits. The usual objection, that the cities cannot be trusted with these funds or powers because their governments are too corrupt, or because racial discrimination runs too deep in them, may be true; and if so, this is merely another way of saying that reform is no longer available to the United States, but only further city stagnation and decay, or revolution and counter-revolution. Supposing things not to be so hopeless yet, the funds swiftly released to cities in lieu of specific grants should be augmented by tax money withdrawn from military spending. We might expect, considering the ingenuity of American corporations when their well being is at stake, and the experience after earlier wars, that organizations losing military contracts would hustle to add new kinds of goods and services to their repertoires; the economy might thus get the famous "fall-out" of civilian technology which has so long been promised as a byproduct of the work of the military-industrial complex but has so little materialized. The objection that the government is, by definition, responsive to Congressional representatives of communities that have come to depend upon war work, and so cannot, or will not, take the step may, of course, also be true.

In effect, these suggested moves at the expense of the existing strategies would merely lift burdens that are now obstructing the normal growth and development processes of cities. In that sense, the reform would be negative. But I think a positive strategy is also desirable and probably necessary. To develop it would take somewhat longer.

The strategy would require a continuous program of data collecting, diagnosis and action, with the data collecting ideally coming first. But realistically, considering the need, diagnosis and action would be desirable at the same time data collecting was getting under way. The whole strategy would be directed at the heart of the matter: city economic creativity.

The relevant data would be economic development rates for cities. These could be determined by first compiling kinds and values of all goods and services, public and private, produced in each given city in a given year. The next compilations would sequester kinds of goods and services, and their values, produced in the city only since the preceding compilation; this would be expressed as a percentage of the value of all work shown in the preceding compilation, yielding a development rate of new kinds of goods and services. The second quinquennial compilation, which of course would yield up the first development rate figure, would afford a comparison of a given city's development rate with those of other cities, and so would subsequent compilations. The third quinquennial compilation (and all succeeding ones) would also indicate whether a given city's rate were rising or falling. I am of two minds about a compilation interval as short as five years. The urgency of our situation argues powerfully for it. But a ten year interval would shake out much ephemera and would give real weight, as the shorter span cannot, to the rapid growth of some innovations after their very early years. Perhaps the wisest course, at first, would be to make both five and ten year compilations. Indeed, to compare two successive five year spans, placing greater weight on ephemera, with a ten year span that allows greater weight to be given solid achievement, might be exceedingly enlightening. We know too little about these relationships.

In a city with a low or falling development rate, the job would be to diagnose, concretely, what factors were hampering the economic creativity of the city's people. This work should certainly not be approached with rigid preconceptions, but rather with hypotheses and these only because it is necessary to start somewhere. Some possibilities suggest themselves immediately: lack of venture capital; racial and other ethnic discrimination, as far as access to capital is concerned; presence of monopolies (e.g., those imposed by organized crime, by otherwise obsolete franchises and licenses, by shopping center developers in conjunction with zoning laws); unwillingness of local government to purchase experimental and innovative goods and services (e.g., for parks, schools, health services, sanitation work); unwillingness of local government to permit competition to its services (e.g., in public transportation, waste disposal); prevention, by existing enterprises, of breakaways of employees capable of organizing new enterprises; lack of independently produced or supplied input items, available to any potential producers requiring them; lack of incentives to purchase problem-solving goods and services (e.g., noise-combatting materials, pollution-catching equipment) such as could be afforded by intelligent performance zoning, for instance.

This is investigative work from which we would begin to learn, in concrete detail, much we don't now know about the effects of our laws, about the uses and sources of risk capital and, indeed, much about our own natures as city building (and city destroying) animals. To learn, and even to publish what has been learned, is by no means also to correct. But it is a beginning, if undertaken in cities where the power structure and the population are honestly concerned about city stagnation. The work could be financed in such cities by using funds now devoted to many unproductive planning studies and other expensive irrelevancies subsumed under city planning. Of course, resistance might defeat any changes required which is a way, again, of saying it may be too late for reform.

Getting back to development rate data, such figures would continuously be informative and useful for prospering cities as well as for those in desperate trouble. They would indicate when prospering cities were just beginning to stagnate and would signal that preventive diagnosis and action were required. Where development rates were high and rising, they would signal a city's capability for unusual development work on innovative, problem-solving goods and services, vital to the entire economy; if this were not actually coming about, the reasons why should be investigated. Where development rates had been unusually high, but were falling, the movement might represent only the downside of the normal city growth cycle; but the fall, if long continued, would be a danger sign. Development rates within varying districts of cities or metropolitan areas could be calculated and these would be extremely useful for diagnosis and action.

To achieve a rather refined portrait of a city's economy and the processes at work there, one would need data on the following: (1) which new goods and services (appearing since the last compilation) represented replacements of imports and, among these, which were transplants of production from elsewhere and which were locally originated; (2) which new goods and services represented new input items; (3) what input items had been lost since the previous compilation; (4) kinds and values of export work lost; (5) kinds and values of work exported and which of these represented new kinds of exports; (6) the genesis of these new exports (that is, whether produced by organizations that had already been exporting, by organizations set up *de novo* for export work, or by organizations formerly producing only for the local market); (7) numbers and types of new organizations created by breakaways from older organizations; (8) kinds and sizes of new organizations being financed locally as distinguished from those financed from outside, and the terms of investment; (9) changes in quantities and kinds of imports since the previous compilation. I have been rather reluctant to enumerate these because the list might suggest that to collect that data is the salient task. But it would be useful only where diagnostic and remedial work were already rather highly developed too. As far as data are concerned, the first need is for the development rates; and I think they are badly needed.

The general strategy would represent, in itself, a problem solving addition to economic life; that is, work which more than pays for itself, and does so even during its own period of development. There would be no need to begin the service in all cities at once in a multi-city country, nor need it be under the aegis of a single organization; it could be begun independently in various cities. To obtain useful comparative development rates it would, of course, be necessary to employ the same methods of compiling and computing in different cities but even these must at first be somewhat experimental because many difficult questions of judgment must be resolved in ways that will not, in fact, distort the realistic indications of economic innovation and creativity that are needed. The diagnostic and remedial work would be thoroughly experimental at first. Where any experimental work is concerned, an excellent ground rule is to encourage duplication, not monopoly, of effort. This, I should think, applies as surely to development of an effective strategy for helping cities as it does to the other creative efforts that this strategy would be identifying, measuring and — let us hope — liberating and stimulating.

PART TWO

URBAN ISSUES

THE URBAN AND REGIONAL ECONOMICS which is brought to bear on urban issues is distinguished from more general economics by three characteristics: (1) the importance of the location of economic activity; (2) the height and complexity of population densities; and (3) the uniqueness of the institutional conditions within an urban region.

LOCATION

Location, or the spatial dimension of economic activity, generates substantial benefits and costs, called external economies and external diseconomies, respectively. Ideally, a metropolitan area provides substantial benefits to firms: it affords a wide variety of labor skills at competitive prices; quick and inexpensive transportation because of the high priority availability of many types of facilities and services; and housing which already exists and is used by most of the people who live and work in the area. Business firms wishing to expand can have all of these benefits if they choose to locate in or near a metropolitan region.

Many of the benefits of conducting economic activities in close proximity to one another arise out of the interdependence of the labor market, consumption, and exchange. Many jobs and goods are readily available in a city. Workers commonly buy a wide variety of consumer goods for their families. Water, sewers, streets, schools, and other elements of a region's infrastructure can be used for both production and consumption purposes.

There are also, of course, extra costs associated with locating economic activity in an urban area. Most of these costs grow out of the congestion and confusion of high population densities and the associated movements of people and goods — out of the crowding, delays, and pollution of air, water, and other environmental elements. Where such costs are deemed great, economic activity may become decentralized, spreading to the outskirts of urban regions. The widely noted flight to the suburbs reflects a desire to avoid the diseconomies of urban congestion while retaining the benefits of a large metropolitan area.

POPULATION DENSITIES

High population densities alone create congestion and pollution of air, water, noise, space, and other elements of the environment. Pollution and other diseconomies of urban "togetherness" are called neighborhood effects. They are serious because they occur as side effects to economic activity — side effects for which no single participant in the community can bear responsibility. Where neighborhood diseconomies are negligible, as in small, isolated towns, they can be (and are) safely ignored by everyone. Neighborhood effects in densely populated areas are enormous and highly undesirable, though until very recently they have been ignored as much as the minor diseconomies of small towns. In older, blighted areas of large cities the numerous diseconomies combine to generate psychological and social tensions which add to frustration, crime, and expense.

Normally, collective action by a group or even a majority of neighbors in a densely populated area is required to reduce neighborhood diseconomies. Usually, such action leads to government action. Government must regulate or tax members of crowded communities in order to reduce the diseconomies.

Rapidly rising population densities in city centers and urban clusters generate serious diseconomies by clogging the streets and polluting the atmosphere of nearby and even rather distant communities. Central city business districts, for example, create congestion problems for a wide ring of residential streets, from which the inhabitants flee to the suburbs, where separately incorporated communities can protect themselves at least temporarily from the rising density patterns of the central area.

INSTITUTIONAL CONDITIONS

The growth of separately incorporated suburban cities has helped to create badly divided urban regions around the central cities. Single-purpose special districts for flood control, water, sewers, schools, rapid transit, and other functions have multiplied the layers of government dealing with urban problems. Unfortunately, these local governments are not obliged to cooperate with one another, and in some cases are restricted by law from considering factors other than the special purpose for which each has been created.

Thus governmental institutions for taxation, public expenditure, and regulation of urban economic behavior are fragmented — acting in ways that are contradictory and mutually self-defeating. Well-to-do suburban cities have been loath to contribute tax revenues to the central cities, where many suburbanites earn their livings, or to contribute to any other suburban city, however poor or needy. Worse, each city in a metropolitan region adopts zoning laws and variances for its own benefit, without regard to how much damage or cost such adoptions may create for a neighboring city or government unit. Land use, provisions for open space, transportation between cities in a metropolitan area, and the control of pollution are major problems that, because of fragmented governmental structures, have remained unsolved.

Economists dealing with environmental problems beyond the control of any one city seek to help meet the (politically determined) "needs" for orderly land use, open space, inter-city transportation, and a cleaner atmosphere. They may begin with a stated goal (say, cleaner air), write a plan to meet this goal (regulation or taxation of air polluters), carry out a cost-benefit analysis of their plan, compare it with alternative plans, and then choose the one which has the highest ratio of benefits to costs. Very often these plans involve large or small changes in the institutional conditions of a metropolitan area, especially regarding taxation, government expenditure, and regulation.

THE APPLICATIONS — OF URBAN AND REGIONAL ECONOMICS

In the application of urban and regional economics, the three best known problem areas are: (1) poverty and unemployment; (2) housing; and (3) transportation. Recently economists also have given major attention to the economics of (4) public health and education; and (5) crime, a special problem with high population densities. Finally, the fragmented governmental conditions of urban regions gives rise to (6) tax revenue imbalances; and (7) organizational friction. We shall discuss these seven urban issues in turn.

A

Poverty, Unemployment, and the Welfare System

Poverty has become a terrifying thing in the United States — not only for the poor but also for the rich. A recent *New York Times* quotes the doorman at a posh Manhattan apartment house: "The tenants are terrified — terrified for themselves and their cash registers." As for the doorman himself: "I carry a knife."

The poor, of course, have long known the severe limitations on their lives caused by low income — limitations on what they can buy and where they can go, on the types of housing in which they can live, on the sorts of education open to their children. The rich and the affluent awakened fully to poverty as a result of the riots that occurred in the low-income areas of most of America's great cities between 1965 and 1968. Indeed, people in every walk of life began to realize that poverty in any section of the city — or the town — endangers the whole community.

Conventional microeconomic theory begins to analyze poverty, and the unemployment which leads, in large part, to poverty, by studying the labor market in urban areas. If there is unemployment, then obviously there is a surplus of workers or a shortage of jobs or both. A closer look at the labor situation in inner-city ghettos suggests that neither an excess supply of workers nor inadequate demand for workers exists: the trouble is that the skills and aptitudes of the workers do not fit the requirements of the employers and so workers from other communities are hired; the ghetto denizen remains unemployed and therefore poor. To change the demand situation by bringing in additional employers seems attractive in some ways, but seldom has worked since urban and poverty areas already are heavily populated and industry is nearby. To change the supply of labor skills and aptitudes through education and training seems the next obvious step — one which would require, however, a quite complete understanding of the educational process, a will to change the educational system if necessary, and a careful benefit-cost analysis of the impact of alternative educational or training programs.

In the area of poverty, unemployment, and welfare much of the economic analysis is focused on the market imperfections brought about by discrimination, class distinctions, inadequate knowledge of job opportunities, poor transportation, and numerous other institutional factors which inhibit or destroy the effective working of a labor market in the poverty-stricken ghettos of inner cities.

Conventional macroeconomic theory would suggest that low income and low employment are due in part to inadequate aggregate demand, the solution for which is to stimulate the economy sufficiently to generate employment and income earning opportunities for the unemployed. But neither local nor regional governments can do much about aggregate demand, at least in the short run, so the macroeconomic solution becomes necessarily a national solution.

Simulation studies of poverty-stricken urban ghettos require an examination of the social and economic institutions which maintain class distinctions and other barriers. Here the economist borrows from the political scientist, the sociologist, and the psychologist, since discrimination on the basis of race, sex, religion, or ethnic background clearly is uneconomic — in the usual sense of that term.

Economic planning and benefit-cost analysis have been applied directly to poverty problems without reference to employment. Here the goal was to provide income and other economic support for indigent people. Several plans have been put forward and actually used in a variety of places. Many welfare programs of local governments have been criticized by economists, who recommend a national plan to combat poverty based around the (national) income tax, sometimes called guaranteed annual income.

4 Poverty Amid Plenty

PRESIDENT'S COMMISSION ON
INCOME MAINTENANCE PROGRAMS

A moving vignette of what it means to be poor; an analysis of current poverty programs; and recommendations for a new income maintenance program.

PROLOGUE

For the past 22 months this Commission has been studying the poor in America and the programs designed to help them. In the course of our investigations we have traveled throughout the country and talked with many of the poor as well as with public officials. We have found severe poverty and its effects throughout the Nation and among all ethnic groups. This poverty is not only relative to rising

---

From *Poverty Amid Plenty: The American Paradox*, by the President's Commission on Income Maintenance Programs, Washington, D.C.: U.S. Government Printing Office, November 1969, pp. 2–9.

American living standards, but is often stark and absolute. There are too many American families with inadequate shelter, inadequate clothing, absolute hunger, and unhealthy living conditions. Millions of persons in our society do not have a sufficient share of America's affluence to live decently. They eke out a bare existence under deplorable conditions.

We have concluded that more often than not the reason for poverty is not some personal failing, but the accident of being born to the wrong parents, or the lack of opportunity to become nonpoor, or some other circumstance over which individuals have no control.

In addition to the current poor, we have been concerned with others who easily could become poor. Most persons who depend on earnings for their incomes face the risk of losing that access to prosperity through accident, disability, loss of a breadwinner, or obsolescence of skills. Few Americans are wholly free from the economic vicissitudes of life.

We have found that existing Governmental mechanisms and institutions are simply inadequate for alleviating existing poverty and protecting the nonpoor against risks that they are incapable of dealing with themselves. We have found that there is no overall system of economic security. But the Commission feels strongly that the problem of poverty must be dealt with by the Federal Government. It is possible to assure basic economic security for all Americans within the framework of existing political and economic institutions. It is time to construct a system which will provide that security.

THE POOR

At the end of 1968 there were 25 million poor Americans as measured by the Federal Government's poverty index. This index allows a nonfarm family of four $3,553 per year, or $2.43 per person per day, to meet all living expenses. In contrast to the poverty index, a recent Department of Labor study found that an urban American family of four needed at least $4.05 per person per day to meet its needs. Using the lower, official poverty definition, we find that: about one-half of all poor families live in the South; two-fifths of the poor are children under 18; two-thirds are white; one-fifth are over age 65; and perhaps most striking of all, over one-third of the poor live in families in which the family head works throughout the year. Among the "working poor" the average gap between family income and the poverty line exceeds $1,000.

These figures, by themselves, do not convey the barrenness of poverty, or the humanity and diversity of the poor. Such qualitative aspects are not easily captured by a statistical profile. It is difficult to discuss analytically the consequences which stark poverty imposes on people's lives. But a visitor feels these consequences in a two-room shack in the Kentucky Appalachians inhabited by an unemployed miner, his wife and his seven children; or in seeing the ugly decay of urban tenements; or in the dirty hands and faces of rural children, whose families depend for water on open wells which may go dry in summer and which may be located downhill from the neighbor's privy. And as one talks to families with small children who have "water gravy" for breakfast, one is reminded of recent studies showing a high correlation between malnutrition and mental retardation.

The barren life styles of the poor are not primarily the result of ignorance or indifference but rather the result of insufficient money with which to purchase proper food, housing, medical attention, and other basic amenities of contemporary life. The urgency of the problems of low-income persons and the lasting effects of their day-to-day deprivation are compelling.

In many cases the possibility for improvement is not realistically within the power of the poor. In talking and listening to the poor, one is struck by the vicious circles which characterize poverty. Rising from poverty seems inordinately difficult for the ordinary man. We recognize this unconsciously in our strong admiration for those who manage to escape poverty on their own, but we seldom note how few they are.

Very few people seem poor because they are shiftless. Fully 70 per cent of the nonaged heads of poor families worked for part of the year in 1966. And most of those who did not work at all were ill or disabled or were women with absent husbands and young children. Some of the poor are older people who *became* poor when they no longer could work; some were born in poor families and never gained sufficient education or skills to command decent jobs; some are now children in poor families who will make up the next generation of poverty. Many are physically disabled, or retarded, or trapped by discrimination. Many are poor by sheer chance.

The simple day-to-day effort to survive may require all of a poor person's will. The disabled man or the elderly couple can do little to escape poverty. The woman with several children cannot manage a household while simultaneously looking for work or being trained. The unskilled, middle-aged, unemployed laborer is helpless in the face of unemployment.

Finally, we must note that the problem will not solve itself in time. The poor will not be able to become unpoor without Government aid. The challenge we face is to develop the means of assuring economic security for all Americans. In order to develop an effective program, we must learn the lessons of earlier Federal efforts. Existing Government programs have a major role to play in achieving this objective, but new programs also are needed. For the existing programs do not constitute the broad system that is required.

CURRENT PROGRAMS

The Origins of Existing Programs

Existing income maintenance programs originated in the Depression of the 1930's when millions were unemployed. Underlying the design of these programs was the notion that in our society employable people should obtain their income through employment. If there were enough jobs, adequate education would assure young people a place in the labor force when they left school. Then families and individuals would need protection only against changes in the unemployment rate, and against the crippling losses of income if the breadwinner retired, died, or became disabled. Public Assistance would be needed as a "residual program" to aid those considered unable to enter the labor force.

This analysis gave birth to the Social Security system, which provided partial income replacement to workers and their families in the event of retirement or death. More recently it has provided income to disabled workers and health insurance for the aged. State Unemployment Insurance programs were created to keep those who were unemployed briefly from becoming pauperized. And the welfare system was constructed as an optional State program, jointly financed by all levels of government, to provide aid for particular categories of the needy: the blind, the aged, the disabled, and dependent children. Generally able-bodied male workers were ineligible for assistance under any of the welfare programs.

In the mid-1960's an effort was made to mount a war on poverty, but the strategies adopted were focused primarily on long-run creation of opportunities. This strategy did little to affect incomes directly. Existing income maintenance programs have been broadened, but their structure has not been changed. This structure — and the strategy underlying its development — has severe flaws that prevent it from reaching all of the poor effectively.

The Employed and Employable Poor Are Excluded From Cash Transfers

Largely because of the assumption that everyone who is employable could work at adequate wages, no Federal income transfer programs have been enacted to supplement the earnings of the employed poor. Yet one-third of all persons in poor families in 1966 lived in families headed by full-time employed male workers. If the head of a family of four worked forty hours a week, fifty-two weeks a year, at the minimum wage of $1.60 per hour, family income would still fall below the poverty line. Yet nearly one-half of the working poor families have six or more members, so that full year employment at more than $2.00 per hour would be required for them even to reach the poverty level. And jobs with low wages often are characterized by layoffs, short weeks, or seasonal employment which further reduce the family's potential income. There are at least 10 million jobs in this country — including some State and municipal government jobs — which pay less than the current Federal minimum wage.

The major program dealing with the temporarily unemployed, but employable, person is Unemployment Insurance. However, it did not provide benefits for nearly two-thirds of total unemployment in 1968 because of gaps in coverage and expiration of benefits. Unemployment Insurance programs, which pay benefits for only a specified number of weeks, have payment levels below the poverty line for families in most States.

The Aid to Families with Dependent Children program (AFDC), which is aimed primarily at families with absent or incapacitated fathers, can provide for the unemployed able-bodied male head of the household, but the eligibility requirements for this component of the program are very restrictive. Only 25 States have chosen to implement this component since its enactment in 1961, and less than 100,000 families are benefiting from it.

The structure of the Aid To Families with Dependent Children program thus makes it profitable in many cases for families to break up. AFDC benefits vary by family size and need for income. They provide a predictable income, while wage income is subject to vagaries of a labor market which has a diminishing need for low-skilled workers.

The lack of a program which aids working men and women not only creates economic disincentives and encourages family breakup; it also is socially divisive, because it is possible for incomes of some aid recipients to exceed the incomes of low earners. Viewed in this context, some of the resentment that has developed against welfare programs may have sprung from a sense of injustice about programs which reverse positions and ranks in the income distribution for no equitable reason.

Under the welfare system we have clung to the notion that employment and receipt of assistance must be mutually exclusive. This view is untenable in a world in which employable persons may have potential earnings below assistance standards. Thus, it is possible to reverse positions in the income scale. Exclusion of the employable and the working poor from categories aided by the Government would be justifiable only if all who worked achieved adequate incomes. But that is simply not true, and the prospects for it becoming true in the near future are dim.

Programs that place the hard-core unemployed in the labor force and upgrade the skills of those employed at very low wages can and do work. But they are expensive and slow.

Currently, such programs are reaching only a few hundred thousand of the poor annually, and not all of the programs are successful. It has been estimated that reaching all of the employable poor who could benefit from manpower services and training would require making such services available to 11 million persons. Current employment and training programs can and should be expanded. But even if funding levels were increased substantially, training and manpower programs can be viewed only as a long-term solution. The number of persons in need of services is too large to serve quickly. And even completion of a training program and placement on a job does not guarantee an adequate income to a family with several children.

Social Insurance Benefits Depend on Earnings

Social insurance programs protect workers and their families against the loss of earnings from some of the hazards of industrial life. Each social insurance plan is built around a particular risk that has been identified as a potential interruption to earnings. Old Age, Survivors, and Disability Insurance, Unemployment Insurance, and other forms of social insurance generally are financed through contributions based on wages, and they pay benefits based on earning levels before employment is interrupted.

Social insurance benefits also are provided to some persons who have contributed little or nothing, and the ratio of benefits to earnings declines as earning levels increase, thereby focusing benefits somewhat on the lowest income earners. Despite attempts to replace a higher proportion of earnings for lower-income workers, however, social insurance programs still do not provide adequate benefits to the poorest. They pay adequate benefits only to those with strong labor force attachments and relatively high earnings records. Because social insurance is related closely to employment, it cannot reach effectively those with fleeting or irregular labor force ties. Low-wage earners will receive low social insurance benefits; thus the poor worker becomes the poor beneficiary. And many jobs are not covered by insurance.

Social insurance programs do a great deal to insure that the average worker does not become poor upon retirement, disability, or short-term unemployment. They prevent many persons and families from falling into poverty upon the death of a worker. But adequate insurance benefits simply cannot be provided to the worker with inadequate earnings in an earnings-related benefit system.

Public Assistance Benefits Are Low and Program Coverage Is Restricted

The target population of Federally-aided welfare programs has never included all of "the needy." The working poor and the employable but unemployed poor, for example, are excluded from potential eligibility.

Many of those who might be eligible for existing assistance programs — the aged, blind, disabled, dependent children and spouses — do not qualify for benefits because of the variety of Federal, State, and local nonfinancial eligibility requirements. Program features and regulations often seem designed to restrict benefits through the imposition of residence requirements, tests of "moral worthiness," mandatory acceptance of social services, overly stringent asset tests, income limits set below the poverty line, and the like.

These requirements vary considerably from program to program and from region to region. Persons eligible for benefits in some States may be ineligible in others, although their financial need may be identical. Some persons do not receive benefits because they are not aware of their eligibility. Some persons decline to participate in welfare and food programs because of demeaning administrative techniques. Many people never are eligible for some programs because the States, counties, or cities in which they live have not elected to participate in the programs. And, of course, those who are not aged, blind, or sufficiently disabled, and who do not have dependent children, are ineligible for any Federally-aided Public Assistance program although they may be in need.

Those who do meet all of the requirements for eligibility receive income support that is generally inadequate. Nationally, the average payment per recipient in January 1969 was $43 per month for AFDC, and $70 per month for Old Age Assistance. Moreover, there are wide differences in the treatment of needy individuals who fall into the same categories because of State variations in payment levels. Within AFDC, for example, average grants per recipient ranged from $10 per month in Mississippi to $65 in Massachusetts in January 1969. For Old Age Assistance the range was from $36 in Mississippi to $115 in New Hampshire.

THE ROLE FOR NEW PROGRAMS

Clearly, the three-pronged strategy of the 1930's — relying on employment to provide adequate income to workers and their families, social insurance to maintain incomes of workers forced out of their jobs, and residual aid to those who are unemployable for non-insured reasons — has not eliminated poverty, and it cannot.

Such a conclusion does not preclude improvement in existing programs. Improvement in training programs, social insurance programs, and similar reforms are important. But a new program is required to achieve objectives that existing programs cannot reach.

This Commission has concluded that there must be a larger role for cash grants in fighting poverty than we have acknowledged in the past.

We have reviewed many proposals for new programs and for reforms of existing programs. We have concluded that a new income maintenance program is needed, a program which directly increases the incomes of the poor. The new program should be adopted along with specific changes in existing programs.

RECOMMENDATIONS

Our main recommendation is for the creation of a universal income supplement program financed and administered by the Federal Government, making cash payments to all members of the population with income needs. The payments would vary by family size and would provide a base income for any needy family or individual. The basic payment would be reduced by 50 cents for each dollar of income from other sources. This formula would encourage recipients to continue working or to seek employment and would not discourage continued development of private savings and insurance, and social insurance systems. We propose that the program be initiated at a level providing a base income of $2,400 to a family of four. Families of four with other income up to $4,800 thus would receive some supplementation. This program would provide an estimated $6 billion of net added income to 10 million households in 1971.

Since $2,400 is below the poverty line for a family of four, the basic benefit would not meet the full income needs of families with no other income. *This level was not chosen because we feel that it is an adequate income, but because it is a practical program that can be implemented in the near future.* The level can be raised to an adequate level within a short period of time. Of the $6 billion added to disposable household income, $5 billion would go directly to the poor, and the remainder to those somewhat above the poverty line. Half of the income needs of the poor would be met by this program alone.

The Commission strongly recommends that the benefit levels be raised as rapidly as is practical and possible in the future. To set payment levels at the poverty line immediately would cost an estimated $27 billion, and provide income transfers to a total of 24 million households. We believe that a program of that potential magnitude must be adopted in steps. We have recommended a feasible first step.

This basic program can be adopted with no statutory changes in other programs since benefits of other income-tested programs would decline automatically under current law or practice. The program would have the immediate effect of improving the income position of most of the poor — the working poor as well as the unemployed, couples without children, single individuals, the aged, and female-headed households in locations where AFDC payments are very low. It would also improve the income position of many poor persons who are reluctant to apply for Public Assistance. The long-run impact of the program could be a reduction in variations of living standards throughout the country.

Any program which provides income without work may have some effect on labor force participation. Some secondary and part-time workers as well as primary workers may withdraw from the labor force or reduce their hours worked. However, we do not believe that work disincentive effects of the proposed program would be serious. The level of income provided is low, and we do not believe that the poor are anxious to receive less income rather than more. The proposed program would always result in significantly higher income for those who work than for those who do not. We feel that reduced work effort is likely to be concentrated among secondary family workers, female family heads, and the elderly, rather than among nonaged male family heads. Thus, reduced work effort may be desirable for some of those affected.

The focus on the possible work disincentive effects of transfer programs has in the past been used to avoid serious consideration of such programs. It has led policymakers to overlook the crippling effects of absolute poverty. Men and women without income cannot afford to take risks even for a day; they cannot take advantage of opportunities for future improvement which require a current investment of time and money. We believe that only when the poor are assured a minimum stable income can the other mechanisms in our fight against poverty — education, training, health, and employment — begin to function adequately.

The Commission recommends that Federal participation in existing Public Assistance programs be terminated. One objective is to replace the existing categorical Public Assistance system with a universal Federal program. Thus, Federal funds should be used to raise the proposed new program to adequacy as rapidly as possible rather than to extend the Public Assistance program. In some States current Public Assistance benefit levels exceed the proposed initial level of the Federal income supplement program. The Commission strongly urges that those States pay supplemental benefits to those currently eligible for aid with the savings generated by the new Federal program. If States supplemented incomes of current assistance recipients after adoption of a Federal income supplement at the recommended level, they would still have savings of an estimated one billion dollars in 1971. Thus, the program has an implicit revenue-sharing feature.

The Commission recommends Federal matching funds be made available for a new, locally-administered, noncategorical, Temporary Assistance program. This program would provide for short-term emergency income needs which could not be met under the basic Federal program because of time lags. The Federal Government would pay 50 per cent of the costs of such assistance up to the level of the full Federal program, but only during periods when the individual's income was below his maximum payment under the direct Federal income supplement program. Estimated total cost would be $600 million. The Federal share would be $300 million.

The Commission recommends that coverage under Unemployment Insurance programs be broadened, and benefits raised to provide more adequate protection to workers against unemployment. Benefit schedules under Society Security programs should be reconsidered in the light of adoption of a universal income supplement plan. The need for welfare considerations in setting benefit levels would be considerably weakened.

The Commission regards the provision of income-in-kind as a poor substitute for providing adequate cash incomes to the poor. *Special programs providing food to poor families should be phased out and equivalent assistance given in cash.* Income supplements, when they approach adequate levels, also would allow housing programs to be phased out as soon as the market could meet the demand for low-cost housing.

Manpower and training programs require continued development, modification, and careful evaluation. These programs have great potential for helping many individuals find jobs and for improving the functioning of the economy. In the long run they may reduce the need for transfer programs. In the few years that they have operated, they have shown considerable promise. *We recommend consolidation and improvement of existing programs, and expansion of the range and scope of manpower and related services offered.*

One major cause of poverty is that many families have more children than they can afford. While we believe an effective income maintenance program must assure that no child is deprived of the necessities of life, we feel equally strongly that family planning aid should be made available and accessible to those who want it. *Therefore, we recommend an expanded program of birth control information and services.*

The overall annual added Federal cost of our recommendations, including the basic plan, is estimated to be under $10 billion. While this is a large amount of money, it does not meet fully the obvious need. Rather than propose a panacea, the Commission has chosen a course that can be followed quickly and, we believe, can achieve a great deal with few adverse side effects.

The relatively low dollar cost of the program recommended should underscore the fact that these proposals are not designed to solve all the Nation's social problems. But the level of this universal program, which equitably and simply transfers cash income to the poor, can be raised in the future. With such a basis we shall have gone far towards solving the critical problem of poverty in this Nation. By approaching this goal in a manner that reaffirms our society's respect for the worth and dignity of all its citizens, we shall have recognized the responsibilities of affluence and, in doing that, we shall have improved the quality of our National life.

5 Negative Taxes and the Poverty Problem

CHRISTOPHER GREEN
The Brookings Institution

Negative taxes or "transfer-by-taxation" plans usually differ from current public transfer programs in their focus on closing the poverty gap; in their emphasis, for the purpose of determining eligibility, on income (as related to family size) rather than on such characteristics as age, physical disability, work history, or dependent children; in the degree of their use as a vehicle for transferring income.

Since the Depression of the 1930's, public programs to improve standards of living have received increasing support in the United States. The most well-established and far-reaching of the federal programs are public assistance to the traditional categories of the poor — the aged, the disabled, and dependent children — and the wage-related social security and unemployment insurance programs. More recently, with the start of the war on poverty, programs were introduced to provide opportunities for better training and education of the poor.

While these programs have helped to reduce poverty and its accompanying social and economic problems, about one-fifth of the U.S. population still ekes out a living on an income below the so-called poverty line — the amount of income recognized in the United States as that required to maintain a decent standard of living. And of this fifth of a nation, a surprisingly large proportion of the very poor families receive no direct assistance other than the public services available to everyone, whether rich or poor.

From *Negative Taxes and the Poverty Problem*, by Christopher Green, Washington, D.C.: The Brookings Institution, 1967, pp. 1–12. © 1967 The Brookings Institution. Reprinted with permission.

In recent years, there have been a series of proposals to supplement or complement the present programs by using the federal tax system to close all or part of the poverty gap — that is, the gap between the income of poor families and the income they need to move above the poverty line. The proponents of these proposals are in favor of extending the income tax system into the lowest income brackets through the adoption of negative, rather than positive, tax rates. By making payments based on negative tax rates to persons who have incomes below some specified line and by collecting positive taxes from persons with incomes above that line, the government could operate a single system for the giving and taking of income. Some advocates of these proposals also believe that such a system might increase work incentives by removing many poor persons now receiving public assistance from what amounts to a 100 per cent tax bracket, since many payments under these programs are reduced by a dollar for each dollar earned.

These tax-transfer proposals are called "transfer-by-taxation." Although the transfer-by-taxation plans differ in detail, most are distinguished from present public transfer programs by: (1) the focus on closing the poverty gap; (2) the emphasis upon income — usually related to the size of the family — in determining whether a given unit is eligible for allowances, rather than upon basing eligibility on such characteristics as age, physical disability, work history, or dependent children; and (3) the degree to which the tax system is used as a vehicle for transferring income.

In general, the plans are of two basic types. One, social dividend taxation, would fill the whole poverty gap and substantially alter the entire income distribution. The second, negative rates taxation (more commonly, but less precisely, known as negative income taxation), would close a portion of the poverty gap. Other proposals do not fit neatly into either of these types, but have some features of one or the other or of both types.

POVERTY IN THE UNITED STATES

Two general, but fundamental, assumptions underlie this study of negative taxes: There is still a serious poverty problem in the United States in spite of continuing efforts during the past several decades to do away with it. More and more, society as a whole seems willing to try new ways aimed at reducing and eventually eliminating the remaining hard core of poverty. Although the extent and nature of poverty are not extensively analyzed here, a brief review of statistics on the subject serves as useful background for subsequent discussion.[1]

There were about 35.3 million "poor" persons in 1963 and 34.1 million in 1964.[2] Thus about one-fifth of the people in the United States are poor. How poor are they? The poverty index of the Social Security Administration (SSA) defines a nonfarm family of four persons as "poor" if its 1963 income was less than $3,130. For smaller and larger families, the poverty index differential is about $500 a person. What would it take to raise the income of these persons so that they would no longer be poor? As estimated by Mollie Orshansky, the poor needed $28.8 billion to cover their basic requirements in 1963. Since the poor in that year had an income of $17.3 billion, the deficit, or poverty income gap, was $11.5 billion.[3]

The continued rapid growth of personal income since 1963 has undoubtedly narrowed the poverty income gap. But other changes also could have affected the gap. Disposable income has increased as a result of changes in the income tax but decreased because of extra social security taxes; prices have increased as a result of inflation but decreased because of excise tax cuts; and the need for dollars by the aged has been reduced by the new Medicare program.

Table 1 shows that poverty was not confined to a few demographic groups. The poor are found in big and small families, in rural and urban areas, among the young and the aged, among the employed as well as the unemployed. As Table 1 shows, the chances of being poor are substantially higher than average if the family is not white or is large; or if the head of the family is old or a female, or is not in the labor force. But, in 1963, the heads of two million poor families worked from 50 to 52 weeks; 70 per cent of the poor families were husband and wife families; 72 per cent of the poor families were white; and the heads of 54 per cent of the poor families were between 25 and 54 years of age.[4]

Since these figures overstated the number of poor by not accounting for assets and understated the number by omitting the "hidden poor,"[5] Miss Orshansky later attempted to make a rough adjustment for these factors. When allowance is made for the increased consumption power that would arise if all the assets were used over the aged family's remaining expected years of life, the number of aged families and unrelated individuals in poverty is reduced by only 500,000 — from 5.2 million to 4.7 million.[6] However, there were 2.9 million hidden poor to offset this figure.[7]

The data indicate that disadvantages are associated with certain demographic characteristics. But the pervasive character of poverty amid affluence — although the poor are often hidden from sight, as Harrington has observed[8] — undoubtedly explains why a broad-ranging war has been declared on poverty. If poverty were confined to a homogeneous group, a multifaceted antipoverty program would be less necessary.

UNIQUE FEATURES OF AN INCOME-CONDITIONED PLAN

Present public transfer programs vary in coverage, eligibility for benefits, and type of benefit. These differences in such programs as social insurance, public assistance, veterans' benefits, and special subsidies largely reflect differences in philosophy. For example, the social insurance programs are based on what amounts to a contract between the employee and the government, with coverage extended to almost all wage earners. Eligibility for benefits is not based on whether a person is or is not poor. Instead, eligibility is confined to persons who are retired or unemployed through no fault of their own or who in some way are handicapped, either because of old age or because a family's main wage earner has been disabled or has died. With the exception of health benefits, the payments for these present social insurance programs are in cash.

In contrast to the social insurance programs, public assistance is designed to meet the "needs" of some of the poor where need is measured in terms of a means test. For public assistance, a line is drawn between those persons who are able and expected to work, and those persons who are not. Most public assistance has not been aimed at helping poor families headed by an able-bodied earner. Work relief, retraining, and minimum wage legislation have been the order of the day for the able-bodied. Public assistance categories pinpoint families that are unlikely to have an able-bodied person who is expected to work. Thus, the two most important public assistance programs are old-age assistance and aid to dependent children. The general assistance (or "relief") program is an exception to the rule regarding

Table 1

Characteristics of Poor Families, 1963[a]

CHARACTERISTIC	NUMBER OF POOR FAMILIES (MILLIONS)	POOR FAMILIES AS PERCENT OF ALL U.S. FAMILIES	PERCENTAGE DISTRIBUTION OF ALL POOR FAMILIES
All poor families	7.2	15	100
Residence:			
Farm	.7	23	10
Nonfarm	6.5	15	90
Race of head			
White	5.2	12	72
Nonwhite	2.0	42	28
Age of head:			
14–24 years	.7	26	10
25–54 years	4.0	13	54
55–64 years	1.0	13	14
65 years and over	1.5	24	22
Type of family:			
Husband and wife	5.0	12	70
Wife in paid labor force	.9	7	13
Wife not in paid labor force	4.1	15	57
Other male head	.2	17	3
Female head	2.0	40	27
Size of family:			
Two persons	2.5	16	34
Three persons	1.0	11	14
Four persons	1.0	10	14
Five persons	.9	14	13
Six persons	.6	19	9
Seven persons or more	1.2	35	16
Related children under age 18:			
None	2.4	13	34
One	1.1	12	15
Two	1.0	11	13
Three	1.0	17	14
Four	.6	23	9
Five	.5	36	7
Six	.6	49	8
Earners in family:			
None	2.0	53	27
One	3.3	16	46
Two	1.5	9	21
Three or more	.4	7	6
Employment status and occupation of head:			
Not in labor force[b]	3.0	34	42
Unemployed	.4	28	6

Characteristics of Poor Families, 1963[a] (cont.)

Employed	3.7	10	52
Professional, technical, and kindred	.1	3	2
Farmers and farm managers	.5	29	8
Managers, officials, proprietors (nonfarm)	.3	5	4
Clerical, sales, and kindred	.2	4	3
Craftsmen, operatives, and kindred	1.2	8	17
Service, including private household	.6	20	8
Laborers (except mining)	.7	30	10
Work experience of head in 1963 (civilians):			
Worked	4.6	11	64
Worked at full-time jobs —	3.6	10	50
Worked 50 or more weeks	2.0	7	28
Worked at part-time jobs	1.0	36	14
Did not work	2.6	38	36

Source: Based on Mollie Orshansky, "Counting the Poor: Another Look at the Poverty Profile," *Social Security Bulletin,* Vol. 28 (January 1965), Table 2, p. 12. Miss Orshansky's data were derived from special tabulations by the Bureau of the Census for the Social Security Administration.

[a] Poor families, defined in the text, are those with incomes below the SSA "economy level" or poverty index.

[b] Includes approximately 900,000 family heads in the Armed Forces, of whom about 100,000 have incomes under $3,000.

the able-bodied poor, but the number of persons currently receiving general assistance . . . is small, indicating that they are exceptions that tend to prove the rule . . . Public assistance benefits may be in cash or in kind — that is, they may include housing, food, counseling, etc., as well as cash.

Coverage under the program for veterans is based on the status as a veteran. Eligibility for benefits is sometimes, but not always, based on need. Some of the benefits are in cash, others are payments-in-kind in the form of medical and educational services. In the United States, the veterans' program is the only public transfer program of the federal government which is so clearly based on status. In other countries, an aged person or a dependent child automatically qualifies for a "demogrant" — that is, a payment based on demographic status.

Beyond the public transfer programs, numerous public expenditures are designed to provide for such "social wants" as public health and for "merit wants" such as education, medical care, and housing.[9] Public programs also pay subsidies to producers on the basis of social needs (for example, airline subsidies) or preferred occupations (for example, farm subsidies). These programs are outside the scope of this book, but warrant mention to help illustrate that public programs making cash payments and payments-in-kind to individual households and firms embody many different philosophies.

The rationale of transfer-by-taxation differs from present public transfer, service, and subsidy programs in that coverage is universal and all payments are in cash. Benefits are determined under a transfer-by-taxation plan with no attention paid to why a person or family is poor. As a matter of "right," everyone has access to the benefits, which are conditioned only upon the level of the person's or family's income. This contrasts especially with the view implicit in the public assistance and unemployment compensation programs that, in providing assistance, society must be protected against the loafer — the person who can work but is unwilling to do so. The refusal to draw a line between the able-bodied poor and those persons with some form of disability seems to be at the heart of the difference between transfer-by-taxation and present income maintenance programs, especially public assistance. And unlike some of the public transfer programs, transfer-by-taxation is designed to supplement the earnings of the working poor. Of course, a transfer-by-taxation plan could include a provision that individuals, or families with heads who are able but unwilling to work, are not eligible to receive transfer-by-taxation allowances. However, such a provision is rarely contemplated in negative tax proposals.

Transfer-by-taxation seems to differ from the public assistance programs in another way by taking an aggregate approach to poverty. It concentrates on closing the poverty gap by transferring income from those with higher incomes to those who are poor. While public assistance contributes to the alleviation of poverty . . . its emphasis — as indicated by the role of the social worker — is upon the individual and the reasons why he or she is poor.[10]

Transfer-by-taxation has a superficial similarity to a minimum wage law, but there are important differences. Explicit in a minimum wage law is the philosophical view that no one should work for less than a specified amount. Implied, then, is some notion of a minimum income. However, a minimum wage law not only fails to touch families without an earning member, it may also backfire if unemployment is produced because the minimum wage guarantees hourly earnings in excess of the value of the product of some workers.[11] In contrast, the proposed tax-transfer plans can guarantee a minimum income without creating the involuntary unemployment often associated with minimum wages.

The transfer-by-taxation proposals contrast with — but are certainly not incompatible with — the antipoverty programs originating under the Economic Opportunity Act. The programs under the Economic Opportunity Act are aimed at making the poor more productive future earners; the transfer-by-taxation proposals would give dollars directly to the poor. Thus transfer-by-taxation can be considered as a complement of the antipoverty programs; and, as a complement, it could open up a new front in the war on poverty. It is not inconsistent to provide money income for the poor and at the same time to make government expenditures for raising the productivity of the poor. An important purpose of transfer-by-taxation and other income maintenance schemes is to break the vicious circle of poor education, low productivity, and low income. Transfer-by-taxation also embodies the principle that the poor can be trusted to allocate their own funds without government supervision. Those who support transfer-by-taxation believe that public programs should increase individual freedom of choice and reduce impediments to the operation of the market system.

TRANSFER-BY-TAXATION AND PROGRESSIVE TAXATION

Use of the federal income tax system to close the poverty gap would imply that society will go beyond the ability-to-pay justification for progressive income taxation. Under transfer-by-taxation, the income tax system would be used directly to reduce income inequality, although such reduction may not be the main objective of a given transfer-by-taxation plan. This raises serious philosophical issues that have been debated at length.[12] ... Two comments are warranted (here).

The ability-to-pay principle is not necessarily incompatible with a plan for reducing economic inequality directly. True, some early proponents of the ability-to-pay principle held that it is not the function of the income tax system to reduce economic inequality; that social reform should be effected through government expenditures and not by taxation.[13] By extending tax rates below zero to negative levels, the income tax system can reduce income inequality through transfers. Early proponents of the ability-to-pay principle excluded from the list of services to be paid for out of income taxes the service of providing a guaranteed minimum income. But once this service is included, it is hard to avoid the conclusion that the ability-to-pay principle is inseparable from at least one form of reduction in economic inequality — that is, cutting off the lower end of the income distribution.

The relationship between transfer-by-taxation and the progression issue can be considered in another way. This approach begins by noting that the personal exemptions in the present income tax system add an element of progressivity that would remain even if the graduated marginal rates were abandoned in favor of a single income tax rate. The main justification for personal exemptions stems from the view that only "clear income" is taxable, that providing the basic necessities of life is a cost to be deducted from gross income in arriving at net (taxable) income. Transfer-by-taxation adds the view that the tax system should, in the absence of taxable income, make refunds in some proportion to the failure of a family to achieve a clear income. A similar proposal is to give each taxpayer and dependent a tax credit which is equal to, or some fraction of, the costs of subsistence. Possibly transfer-by-taxation may add a dimension to the concept of personal exemptions which has not been contemplated by the proponents of a clear-income basis for income taxation. But this new dimension is a logical extension of the clear-income concept. Proponents claim that transfer-by-taxation avoids the "stigma" attached to allowances viewed simply as a subsidy to social outcasts, and rest their case on the added protection or economic security afforded every family by an income tax system with rates which do not stop at zero.[14]

THE MAIN ISSUES

The main issues, in brief, follow:

1. The existing system of monetary transfer payments closes about three-fifths of the before-transfer poverty gap. In doing so, about one-third of the families who had been poor before the transfers are pulled out of poverty. Some of the remaining two-thirds receive transfer income that closes less than 50 per cent of that group's before-transfer poverty gap.

2. There are several alternative ways further to reduce the poverty gap. The present social insurance and public assistance programs could be broadened to contribute more in filling the poverty gap. However, since public assistance is directed only to the disadvantaged poor in specific categories and social insurance is related to wages in the United States, the nature of these programs seriously limits their effectiveness as antipoverty tools. Family allowances have a good deal in common with transfer-by-taxation — especially the social dividend type of transfer, which would fill the whole poverty gap. The main difference is that payment of such allowances is limited to families with children.

3. All transfer-by-taxation plans have in common at least three basic variables. Each has a guaranteed minimum level of income; a "tax" rate at which allowances are reduced for each dollar of increase in before-allowance income; and a break-even level of income at which the allowance is reduced to zero. The magnitudes of two of these variables determine the magnitude of the third, and transfer-by-taxation plans differ to the extent that the three magnitudes differ. In fact, these comments extend to any type of proposal assuring a minimum income to everyone.

4. A negative rates taxation plan would not necessitate any major changes in the present positive individual income tax system. A social dividend plan, however, would be so expensive, and would pay net allowances to so many persons who now pay taxes, that the present individual income tax system would have to undergo major changes.

5. The income measure used for determining the level of negative rates taxation allowances should reflect a welfare concept of income. The family's money income more nearly approximates a welfare definition than does adjusted gross income — the definition which is now used for income tax purposes. Financing a social dividend plan would require a tax base considerably broader than the present definition of taxable income.

6. The tax unit used for determining eligibility for transfer-by-taxation allowances should reflect a welfare unit. The family would seem to be a better approximation of the basic welfare unit than the present tax unit which is composed of the individual and his or her dependents.

7. The problems involving determination of eligibility for allowances, the timing of allowance payments, and administration of allowance payments are difficult but it is by no means impossible to solve them.

8. Evidence on the probable effects of representative transfer-by-taxation plans on work incentives and on birth rates is inconclusive. Most of the studies of the effects of high tax rates on work incentives are based on upper income groups. It is not clear that the findings would carry over to groups with low incomes. The probable effect of such a tax plan upon the total birth rate is small, although there might be an initial stimulus to the birth rate among poor families.

9. Representative plans for negative rates taxation would cost from $5 billion to $9 billion a year. A typical social dividend plan would cost about $30 billion annually. There is no wholly satisfactory way to eliminate the income gap of poor families in the United States. Raising revenues only to match the $12 billion poverty gap would not prove to be an undue economic burden. But to close the gap completely would undoubtedly require far more than $12 billion in transfer-by-taxation allowances. Filling the gap would require an effective tax on before-allowance income at a 100 per cent rate and, therefore, would encourage many earners to reduce their work effort. This difficulty cannot be avoided by using any one of the alternative income maintenance programs such as public assistance or social insurance . . .

REFERENCES

1. I have relied for most of these statistics on detailed analyses reported by Mollie Orshansky of the Division of Research and Statistics, Social Security Administration.
2. Orshansky, "Who's Who Among the Poor: A Demographic View of Poverty," *Social Security Bulletin*, Vol. 28 (July 1965), p. 4. These figures are based on a poverty

index developed by the Social Security Administration of the Department of Health, Education, and Welfare.
3. Orshansky, "Counting the Poor: Another Look at the Poverty Profile," *Social Security Bulletin,* Vol. 28 (January 1965), pp. 9 and 13.
4. When Miss Orshansky followed up her "Counting the Poor" (*op. cit.*) article with that on "Who's Who Among the Poor" (*op. cit.*), which concentrated on the demographic aspect of poverty, her later findings reinforced her earlier conclusions as to the particularly disadvantaged position of the aged, children in broken families, children in large families, and the nonwhite family whatever its make-up.
5. "Who's Who Among the Poor," *op. cit.,* p. 5. The "hidden poor" are defined as individuals or subfamily members with own income below the poverty level but living in a family above the poverty line. A subfamily represents a married couple with or without children or a parent and 1 or more children under age 18 residing in a family as relatives of the head." These persons are of interest because programs aimed at reducing poverty might bring out of "hiding" a number of persons potentially poor, but presently not counted as poor.
6. *Ibid.,* p. 13. In taking account of assets, Miss Orshansky was limited by insufficient data to analysis of the assets of the aged.
7. *Ibid.,* Table 1, p. 5.
8. Michael Harrington, *The Other America* (New York: Macmillan, 1926), pp. 2–4.
9. Social wants have been defined as "those wants satisfied by services that must be consumed in equal amounts by all. People who do not pay for the services cannot be excluded from the benefits that result." Merit wants were defined as wants "that could be serviced through the market but are not, since consumers choose to spend their money on other things." Budgetary action is taken to correct individual choice. See Richard A. Musgrave, *The Theory of Public Finance* (New York: McGraw-Hill, 1959), pp. 8–9.
10. For a discussion of the role of the social worker — which may be defined broadly as the art of helping people to help themselves to cope more effectively with their problems — see Helen H. Perlman, *Social Casework: A Problem Solving Process* (Chicago: University of Chicago Press, 1957); Rex A. Skidmore and Milton G. Thackeray, *Introduction to Social Work* (New York: Meredith Publishing Co., 1964); Herbert H. Stroup, *Social Work: An Introduction to the Field* (New York: American Book Company, 1953).
11. The classic debate on the employment effects of higher wages is that between Lester, Machlup, and Stigler. Richard A. Lester, "Shortcomings of Marginal Analysis for Wage-Employment Problems," *American Economic Review,* Vol. 36 (March 1946), pp. 63–82. George Stigler, "The Economics of Minimum Wage Legislation," *American Economic Review,* Vol. 36 (June 1946), pp. 358–65. Fritz Machlup, "Marginal Analysis and Empirical Research," *American Economic Review,* Vol. 36 (September 1946), pp. 519–54. Lester's Reply and Rejoinders by Stigler and Machlup are in the *American Economic Review,* Vol. 37 (March 1947). Also see Fred Blum, "Marginalism and Economic Policy: A Comment," *American Economic Review,* Vol. 37 (September 1947), pp. 645–52. More recent work has been done by John Peterson in "Employment Effects of Minimum Wages, 1938–1950," *Journal of Political Economy,* Vol. 65 (October 1957), pp. 412–30; and "Research Needs in Minimum Wage Theory," *Southern Economic Journal,* Vol. 29 (July 1962), pp. 1–9.
12. See E. R. A. Seligman, *Progressive Taxation in Theory and Practice,* publication of the American Economic Association, Vol. 9, Nos. 1 and 2 (1894); Henry C. Simons, *Personal Income Taxation* (Chicago: University of Chicago Press. 1938); Elmer F. Fagan, "Recent and Contemporary Theories of Progressive Taxation," *Journal of Political Economy,* Vol. 46 (August 1938), pp. 457–98; Walter J. Blum and Harry Kalven, Jr., *The Uneasy Case for Progressive Taxation* (Chicago: University of

Chicago Press, 1953); Harold M. Groves, "Toward a Social Theory of Progressive Taxation," *National Tax Journal,* Vol. 9 (March 1956), pp. 27–34.
13. Seligman, *op. cit.,* p. 69. Simons, *op. cit.,* p. 16, is roundly critical of Seligman's argument that expenditure, but not taxation, is the tool for improving income distribution. However, Simons did not reach the conclusion that the tax system should redistribute income directly through the process of transferring income.
14. The case for transfer-by-taxation does not rest only on the modicum of economic security that it affords to every family. The discussion in Chapter III suggests that it may be the most efficient way to reduce the poverty income gap.

6 The Case for the Negative Income Tax

MILTON FRIEDMAN
University of Chicago

A "last word" in a National Review-Freeman *exchange: the author insists that the Right has misunderstood his "negative income tax" proposal — and he explains why he considers it better than current government welfare programs.*

[... *National Review* ran an editorial remarking on several proposals for a guaranteed minimum wage, some of which would achieve their aim by means of a "negative income tax." Our editorialist concluded:

> Now the July issue of the Freeman carries a brilliant essay by Mr. Henry Hazlitt on the whole topic, and the fat's in the fire. For Mr. Hazlitt, a pillar of free-market wisdom, rightly tags Prof. Milton Friedman, another pillar, with the responsibility for giving the greatest recent boost to the idea of a guaranteed annual income. . . . A lot of people think Friedman was tongue-in-cheek, hoping to smoke the liberals out into the open where they'd have to admit they don't think the poor folk have enough sense to spend real money properly, and therefore they have to be given services in lieu of cash. Friedman hasn't offered any reply, at least on the Machiavellian level. Now Hazlitt has demolished Friedman on every level but the Machiavellian. We have not heard the last from the guaranteed income, nor, we hope, from Mr. Goldwater's chief economic theorist of 1964, the illustrious Prof. Friedman to whom, herewith, an open invitation.

The good Professor replied with a will, and we are pleased to print . . . his response to our editorial . . .]

I am delighted to accept your open invitation to reply to your comments on proposals for a guaranteed annual income.

My support of a negative income tax has been and remains entirely serious,

---

From "The Case for the Negative Income Tax," by Milton Friedman, *National Review,* Volume 19, Number 9, March 7, 1967, pp. 239–240. Reprinted with permission.

neither tongue-in-cheek nor Machiavellian. The case I made for it in *Capitalism and Freedom* still seems to me entirely valid; indeed, further thought has only reinforced my belief in its desirability.

Your paragraph, like so much writing on this subject, confuses labels with substance. The elementary fact is that we now have a governmentally guaranteed annual income in substance though not in name. In effect, that is what our grab-bag of relief and welfare measures is. In some states, it is even written into the law that anyone whose income is "inadequate" is entitled as a matter of right to have it supplemented and brought up to an "adequate" level, as judged of course by the welfare agencies. And whether explicitly specified in law or not, the same thing is true almost everywhere in the U.S.

Our present de facto guaranteed annual income is a mess. It is expensive and most of the money goes to people who are not by any stretch of the imagination poor. It involves a tremendous bureaucracy, widespread intervention into the operation of the market system in areas that have nothing to do with poverty, and inexcusable interferences with the individual freedom and dignity of the truly poor who receive assistance, let alone of the rest of us. Equally serious, it has the worst possible effect on incentives, because a dollar earned and revealed is a dollar of relief lost. It tends to produce poor people, and a permanent class of poor people living on welfare, rather than to help the unavoidably indigent.

I favor the negative income tax because it would be vastly superior to our present guaranteed annual income. It would cost much less, give more help to the truly poor, avoid interference with personal freedom, preserve some incentives to work, and drastically reduce the present bureaucracy.

If we lived in a hypothetical world in which there were no governmental welfare programs at all and in which all assistance to the destitute was by private charity, the case for introducing a negative income tax would be far weaker than the case for substituting it for present programs. For such a world, I might very well not favor it. But, whether desirable or not, that is not our world and there is not the remotest chance that it will be in the foreseeable future.

Mr. Hazlitt does not in any way whatsover "demolish," as you put it, my arguments for the negative income tax. On the contrary, he grants them. He rejects the negative income tax on very different grounds: that it is not politically feasible to get it adopted, either as a substitute for present measures or otherwise, because it will be converted to a wholly different proposal that I oppose as fully as he does.

Mr. Hazlitt may be right. He almost surely will be if every libertarian and conservative attacks the negative income tax on his grounds, even though each would vastly prefer it to our present welfare measures. That is truly to let the best be the enemy of the good. Unless we propose an alternative and fight both to have it introduced as a substitute for present programs rather than an addition to them, and also to keep it to a modest and acceptable scale, just who is likely to do so? It is most uncharacteristic of both Mr. Hazlitt and NATIONAL REVIEW to give up a fight on grounds of political feasibility.

It will be a tragic wasted opportunity if libertarians and conservatives fail to support a program that is consistent with their own values and that seems to me the only practicable route so far proposed for dismantling gradually but thoroughly the jerry-built structure of government interferences with the market and with individual liberty that have been adopted in the name of welfare.

Finally, may I say how refreshing I find it to be attacked for a change from the Right and welcomed by the Left? The Left, if it accepts the programs, will find that it has bought a Trojan Horse. As to the Right, we need to recognize that our growing strength brings the responsibility to suggest reasoned alternatives to present programs that will permit a gradual withdrawal from them. We will only harm our own cause by an unreasoning retreat to a dream world.

7 Guaranteed Income

CONGRESSIONAL QUARTERLY ALMANAC

Economists of the Left, who include John Kenneth Galbraith of Harvard University and James Tobin of Yale University, find the solution to poverty in a "guaranteed annual income." Here, the findings and arguments of both Right and Left are shaken down to a comparative system.

The controversial concept of a Government-guaranteed minimum income for all Americans drew new interest in 1967 as President Johnson decided to appoint a commission to study the matter.

The President first proposed such a commission in his Jan. 26 Economic Report. At that time, acknowledging widespread interest both inside and outside the Government for various income maintenance programs, the President said: "Their advocates include some of the sturdiest defenders of free enterprise. These plans may or may not prove to be practicable at any time. But we must examine any plan, however unconventional, which could produce a major advance."

It took the President nearly a year to fulfill this pledge. However, in signing the Social Security Amendments of 1967, Mr. Johnson Jan. 2, 1968, announced that he was appointing a Commission on Income Maintenance to study all aspects of public welfare, including minimum-income proposals. Named to head the Commission was Ben W. Heineman, chairman of the board of the Chicago and Northwestern Railway.

Meanwhile, the concept received another boost when Arjay Miller, president of the Ford Motor Co., Nov. 30, 1967, became the first major business executive publicly to support the guaranteed annual income.

Following is a discussion of the guaranteed income controversy as it stood in 1967.

THE ISSUE

In simplest terms, the issue at stake is whether the Federal Government, by one means or another, should take it upon itself to guarantee that every individual and

From "Guaranteed Income," *Congressional Quarterly Almanac,* Volume 23, 1967, pp. 993–995. Reprinted with permission.

family in the United States receives a certain level of income each year. The guaranteed income would bridge whatever gap existed between some predetermined break-even point and the amount of money a family actually earned. Presumably the break-even point would be high enough up the income scale to enable a family to enjoy a decent standard of living.

Support Plans. If it were decided that the Federal Government should make such a commitment the question then would be how the guaranteed income would be provided. The suggested mechanisms for guaranteeing income or for providing income support or income supplements are as diverse and numerous as the myriad persons who have addressed themselves to the problem.

Among the most widely discussed mechanisms are the outright cash payment up to a specified total level of income; the negative income tax of payment related to the number of persons in a family and their combined income; a children's or family allowance; a many-faceted approach for bolstering income and finally, a program of guaranteed employment for all.

Background

Debate about a guaranteed income went back only to the early 1960's. Interest in and support for a program of guaranteeing certain minimum income standards could be found in many quarters, crossing and criss-crossing partisan political lines and ideological positions. There was no single liberal or conservative posture on income maintenance. The arguments for and against a guaranteed income took many forms.

Some experts argued that such a program of income support would be mandatory as more and more Americans are thrown out of work by automation. Others saw a single, direct cash payment to all as the simplest and best method of attacking poverty. After all, the argument went, people were poor because they lacked money. Give the poor money and most, if not all, poverty-related problems could be solved or at least eased, it was argued.

Others considered the guaranteed income as one potential solution to the alleged defects, inadequacies and inequities of the nation's public welfare system. A program of guaranteeing a decent standard of living for all would make the Federal Government the paramount force in aiding the poor. Currently, under existing public assistance programs, the states were the dominant agent in determining who received welfare payments — and how much. Liberals and conservatives alike were unhappy with the current $6-billion-a-year public assistance program.

Finally, some experts saw the adoption of a guaranteed income as the natural and proper evolution of a society not only rich but moral.

Arrayed against the guaranteed income were those who saw it as patently immoral, and totally alien to the work-oriented American way of life. Critics of a guaranteed income contended that all incentives and motivation to work would be wiped out if every American were given an iron-clad guarantee that he would receive a certain amount of money each year as a matter of right whether he worked or not. They argued that bolstering a person's self-respect, not eroding it, was what was needed if the poor were to be lifted out of poverty.

Furthermore, some persons who opposed the idea of income guarantees did so on the grounds of economy, pointing out that preliminary estimates of the cost of various proposals ranged from $5 billion to $30 billion a year.

Reports

There is no question that the concept of a guaranteed annual income is a break with tradition. The President's decision to set up a commission to study the matter is the most significant recognition to date in official policy-making circles of the widespread interest in income guarantees that has been churned up by debate among economists, sociologists, civil rights leaders and businessmen.

Crime Commission. A new voice was added to the debate on Feb. 18 when the President's Commission on Law Enforcement and the Administration of Justice, among its more than 200 recommendations, said that "efforts, both public and private, should be intensified . . . to devise methods of providing minimum family income." The Crime Commission did not elaborate on its recommendation.

The President's interest in exploring income guarantees came closely on the heels of two other reports that touched tangentially but importantly on the question of a guaranteed income.

Technology Commission. One report was issued February 1966 by the National Commission on Technology, Automation and Economic Progress; the other was released June 29, 1966, by the Advisory Council on Public Welfare.

The Technology Commission report, as it came to be known, suggested that Congress go beyond merely improving such existing systems of income support as Social Security and "examine wholly new approaches to the problem of income maintenance." The Commission urged that Congress give "serious study to a minimum income allowance or negative income tax program . . . to approach by stages the goal of eliminating the need for means test public assistance programs by providing a floor of adequate incomes." That recommendation could not have been more forthright. The report, however, did not gain widespread attention.

Advisory Council. The Advisory Council on Public Welfare, in a severe indictment of existing welfare efforts, called for sweeping changes in both welfare concepts and programs. Among its recommendations, the Advisory Council proposed establishing a single criterion for eligibility for cash aid — need. Everyone who was poor would be eligible for aid. Currently, there were a number of categories of assistance based on physical as well as economic criteria — e.g., old age assistance, aid to the blind, to the disabled, to the medically indigent, and to families with dependent children.

More importantly, the Advisory Council called for setting a national floor for public assistance payments. Each state now sets the level of welfare payments, which vary strikingly from state to state.

Although it did not say so, the Advisory Council was in effect proposing a guaranteed minimum income. That is, if there were to be only one criterion for eligibility — need — then all poor people would be covered by welfare. Then, too, everyone who was in need would receive assurance of minimum payments. The clear thrust of the Advisory Council report was in the direction of a minimum income guarantee for all Americans. Predictably, the Council's report became the source of a great deal of controversy.

Mechanisms for Support

Among the earliest proponents of some form of new income maintenance program were the British economist and sociologist, Robert Theobald, Professor Milton

Friedman of the University of Chicago and Professor Robert Lampman of the University of Wisconsin.

Before discussing details of their proposals, it should be pointed out that those in favor of a guaranteed income are not necessarily wedded irrevocably to a specfic income guarantee. Rather, the proposals or examples they employ in explaining their programs are offered more for the purpose of illustration than as a precise income support program.

Full Cash Payment

The way to eliminate poverty "is to supply money rather than moral uplift, cultural refinements, extended education, retraining programs or makework jobs," says Theobald, considered by most observers as the most radical of the income guarantee champions.

Theobald argues that a program of income guarantees is necessary because automation ultimately will erode the availability of conventional jobs and make necessary a substitute system of providing income unrelated to work. Such a program, which he calls Basic Economic Security (BES) would establish an economic floor for each individual. BES "should be given as an absolute constitutional right," Theobald argues, to provide each American with an income "sufficient to live with dignity." Eventually, this guaranteed income would take the place of all existing income maintenance plans such as welfare, minimum wage, Social Security and unemployment compensation.

As a starter, Theobald has proposed a $1,050-guarantee for every adult and $650 for each child or a total of $3,400 for a family of four. There would be annual recalculations of these amounts and no requirement that the recipient work.

Under the Theobald plan, if a family of four received no private income, it would get a full Government allowance of $3,400. If it had an income of $2,000 it would be entitled to $1,400 in Government payments and on top of that would get another $200 as a 10-per cent premium for having earned $2,000 on its own. This latter feature, the premium, was added recently by Theobald to his BES program to meet the charge that his original plan contained "disincentives" to work and earn. If a family had income in excess of $3,400, it would not be entitled to any Government payments. Theobald estimated that at the outset about 20 million Americans would receive BES payments.

Theobald's plan has been severely criticized by some who say that by offering full income guarantees, Theobald not only discourages those without jobs from seeking employment but actually would encourage those with jobs to quit them and go on the "dole." Theobald counters by saying that his underlying premise is that BES is designed to deal with the eventual economic situation of a shrinking job market and that BES is a replacement for the traditional job-wage concept.

Negative Income Tax

Friedman. Another pioneer in the guaranteed income debate is Friedman, who developed the concept of the negative income tax in his 1962 book, *Capitalism and Freedom.* He proposed the negative income tax idea "as a substitute for present welfare programs; as a device for accomplishing the objectives of those programs more efficiently, at lower cost to the taxpayer and with a sharp reduction in bureaucracy." Also, he says, his plan, unlike the Theobald plan or other versions of the guaranteed income, contains important and crucial incentives for those with low incomes to earn more.

As explained by Friedman, under current tax law, a family of four has exemptions plus standard deductions equal to $3,000. Hence if the family had income of $3,000 it would pay no tax — $3,000 would be the break-even point in other words. Above that point, the family would have to pay the Government a tax.

Under the Friedman plan, if the family of four had no income, it would receive a payment from the Government of $1,500 or 50 per cent of the $3,000 break-even figure. If the family had a pre-tax income of $2,000 it would have a negative taxable income of $1,000 and thus would be entitled to a $500 payment from the Government.

The critical difference between the Theobald and Friedman plans is that Theobald would pay a family the full amount between what the family earns and an acceptable break-even figure. Friedman would pay only a percentage of the difference and as he has said: "50 per cent is the highest rate that seems to me feasible." He argues that "the 100 per cent rate (favored by Theobald) removes all incentives to earn any income . . . such a scheme would create a quasi-permanent class of the professionally indigent for whom living on the dole was a way of life." Theobald, of course, would see no benefit in providing work incentives if all work were being done by machines anyway. Friedman would replace all other income maintenance programs with the negative income tax plan.

Tobin. A more generous version of the Friedman negative tax scheme has been advanced by Professor James Tobin, a Yale University economist and former member of the President's Council of Economic Advisers under President Kennedy. This plan could cost some $14 billion a year compared to Friedman's $7 to $9 billion program. Under the Tobin plan, the break-even point at which all Government supplements would stop could go as high as $7,500 with an absolute guaranteed floor of $2,500. Tobin has estimated that "an adequate program" of income maintenance, that would eliminate most public assistance expenditures, might cost as much as $25 billion a year.

Family Allowance

Another widely discussed mechanism for providing the poor with an adequate income is a children's or family allowance. Two of the leading exponents of this plan are Alvin Schorr, former deputy director of research for the Office of Economic Opportunity and now Deputy Assistant Secretary for Individual and Family Service at the Department of Health, Education and Welfare, and Daniel P. Moynihan, former Assistant Secretary of Labor in the Kennedy and Johnson Administrations, and now director of the Joint Center for Urban Studies of Massachusetts Institute of Technology and Harvard.

Criticizing a negative income tax system of income maintenance as totally inadequate and set "in a poor-law framework," Schorr has argued that a family allowance plan would be simpler to administer, more equitable and have the added benefit of being essentially an income-by-right program. He has said that civil rights leaders are opposed to the negative income tax idea because it still casts the poor in the role of supplicants. One Negro leader, Bayard Rustin, executive director of the A. Philip Randolph Institute, has been critical of the negative income tax on just that score. At the same time, it should be noted that two other Negro leaders, the Rev. Martin Luther King of the Southern Christian Leadership Conference, and Floyd B. McKissick, national director of the Congress of Racial Equality (CORE), in testimony before the Senate Government Operations Subcommittee on Executive Reorganization studying the federal role in urban affairs, proposed some form of guaranteed annual income, mentioning as one possibility adoption of a negative income tax program. (*For hearings highlights see 1966 Almanac p. 231.*)

Schorr Plan. Under Schorr's family allowance plan a benefit of $50 a month would be paid for each child under six years old and $10 a month for each older child, in rich and poor families alike. Present income tax exemptions for children would be eliminated and the allowance itself would be taxed. Thus, high income families would have to pay more taxes; low income families would have a net gain in income. The cost of the program, estimated by Schorr at about $12 billion a year, would be met out of general revenue.

Such a program, Schorr says, would take three out of four children out of poverty, does not interfere with work incentives for the family and would not affect the birth rate.

Moynihan Plan. Commenting that almost 60 nations have adopted such an allowance program, Moynihan has contended that while some well-off families might benefit from the program "this small inequity is paid for a universal system that does not separate the poor from the rest of the population and does not require an army of investigators to administer." Moynihan has advanced a family allowance program that would cost $9 billion annually.

Pluralistic Approach

Schorr points out that a family allowance is only one means of bolstering income in order to close the widening gap between the haves and the have-nots. Beyond the family allowance, Schorr is an advocate of what has come to be termed a pluralistic approach to the matter of a guaranteed income.

Leon H. Keyserling, economist and former chairman of the Council of Economic Advisers under President Truman, argues that a guaranteed annual income would be achieved if "an adequate, national full-employment-and-income policy" were adopted, which, he adds, was really the mandate of the Employment Act of 1946. Grafted on that, he says, should be guaranteed incomes to "those who cannot or should not" qualify for gainful employment because of age or other disability.

A pluralistic approach to a guaranteed income for all calls for better wages for those who have jobs, expanded job opportunities for those without jobs as well as expanded job training programs, improved unemployment benefits for those temporarily out of work, increased wage-related benefits such as Social Security for those too old to work and, finally, some form of limited income tax plan for those unable to work.

Labor Attitudes. Union leaders for the most part are extremely uneasy about proposals such as Friedman's which seek to replace in a single stroke all of the programs and benefits that labor has managed to secure through the years. There is an honest fear that programs such as Social Security, unemployment compensation and even the minimum wage would be jettisoned completely if a negative income tax plan were adopted. Labor is not sure it wants to make such a swap.

Moreover, those supporting the pluralistic approach to a guaranteed income view it as the most politically realistic way of bringing the poor into the mainstream of American life. It is an evolutionary rather than revolutionary program, they say, requiring no sharp break with tradition. As one labor spokesman told CQ: "We've got to keep pushing on all fronts, no one thing is the answer."

Guaranteed Jobs

A final proposal aimed at raising incomes to certain acceptable minimum standards is a program of guaranteeing jobs for all who want them.

Sen. Abraham A. Ribicoff (D. Conn.), whose Subcommittee on Executive Reorganization held extensive hearings on urban problems in 1966–67, has said: "I am convinced that the best majority of Americans — in every income category, of all races, in every part of the nation — want jobs: not relief. They want employment, not handouts."

This proposal became known as making the Federal Government the employer of last resort. Even President Johnson in a Dec. 18, 1967 statement cautiously endorsed the idea. However, he said first private industry should be given a chance to put the hard-core unemployed to work before the Government stepped in and provided jobs for any person who was unable to get a job in industry.

8 Work Orientations of the Underemployed Poor: Report on a Pilot Study

LEONARD GOODWIN
The Brookings Institution

Interviews with low-income black, and middle-class white, teenagers indicate, among other things, the probability that different kinds of job training opportunities should be provided for teenagers of different psychological and social positions.

A substantial portion of public and private effort aimed at helping the poor is based on the assumption that work is appealing to persons who are not regularly employed. Welfare efforts are oriented towards helping the poor obtain a pay check rather than a relief check. Training programs are meant to provide poor persons with the skills needed to obtain jobs. Thought is being given to the implementation of some form of guaranteed income that would provide poor people with an incentive to obtain jobs and add to the minimum income provided. The assumption that people want to work is not unreasonable.[1] Yet, the fact that relief rolls continue to grow and that substantial numbers of men are out of work during

---

From Leonard Goodwin, "Work Orientations of the Underemployed Poor: Report on a Pilot Study," *The Journal of Human Resources,* Volume 4 (© 1969 by the Regents of the University of Wisconsin), pp. 508–519.

times of high general employment raises the possibility that these persons may have a sharply different orientation towards work.[2]

An enormous literature exists on the attitudes of regularly employed workers towards job conditions. Relatively little emphasis has been given to the place of work in the total life picture of regularly employed persons.[3] The place of work in the life of the underemployed has been virtually ignored. Of the small amount of data that does bear on the underemployed, much is anecdotal. The latter material provides insight into, but not systematic examination of, work orientations.[4] Where quantitative data have been gathered, they are usually a small part of some broader effort so that an insufficient picture of work orientation has been gained.[5] The present paper reports some of the initial findings in a two-year study of how various elements of the poor population view work. In particular, the responses of teenage males in the pilot study are presented. It was possible to build upon certain procedures and results of a national study of occupational values which the Brookings Institution had completed earlier;[6] a comparison between the responses of a national sample of regularly employed workers and those obtained during the pilot effort are presented below.

THE QUESTIONS AND THE POPULATIONS

The major means of gathering data was the personal interview, using a questionnaire with both open-ended and structured items. Open-ended items permit respondents to express their feelings and ideas in their own ways. The format used for these items, called the self-anchoring scale, was used in the earlier Brookings study of occupational values.[7] During the present study, each respondent was asked to describe in his own words what the best kind of life would be like. He then was asked to describe the worst life. Through a content analysis of these responses, it was possible to determine not only the kinds of events that poor persons attribute to the best and worst life, but also the saliency of a job in their picture of life. Other open-ended questions asked about such matters as the best and worst ways of "getting enough money to live on," whether one would work if he inherited enough money, and what one needs to do in order to move up in life.

Structured items in the Brookings study consisted of statements about work with which the respondent was to agree or disagree by giving a rating on a ten-point scale. A number of these items were selected for inclusion in the present study. All items were pretested in a series of group interviews with low-income Negroes who had entered a job training program in Washington, D.C. The results led to a revised questionnaire which was then used in carrying out personal interviews with two populations of teen-age males.

The first population consisted of low-income males living in a poor Negro community outside Washington, D.C., which will be called Hickory Hill in this report. An indigenous teenager was hired to carry out the interviews. For purposes of comparison, a set of middle-class white teen agers from the Washington area was interviewed by the author.

RESULTS FROM THE LOW-INCOME COMMUNITY

A major advantage in interviewing in Hickory Hill was that Derek Roemer of the National Institute of Mental Health had studied the teenage peer groups of this low-income all-Negro community. The results of his research made it possible not only to recruit an able interviewer from the area but to choose respondents so as to constitute two sets. Set 1 included teenagers who were very poor and were regularly involved in legally marginal activities such as stealing, gambling, and drug use. This set consisted of 15 males representing essentially three peer groups. Set 2 included those males who were not habitually involved in illegal activities and were in somewhat better economic circumstances than the first set. This second set consisted of 28 males representing essentially four different peer groups. It was posited that the second group had a more positive orientation towards work than the first. The interviewer in Hickory Hill was a 17-year-old male who was completing high school in that poor community and who had previous experience in interviewing his peers. It was expected that the use of an indigenous interviewer would heighten the validity of interviewee answers.

In order to place responses of the Hickory Hill youth in broader perspective, responses also were sought from a group of middle-class male teenagers living in the suburbs of Washington. Seventeen white members of a social club, who lived in a middle-class neighborhood a few miles from Hickory Hill, volunteered to complete the questionnaire. The interview schedule was adapted slightly for self-administration and was distributed to the teenagers during a regular meeting of the club.

Responses to Open-Ended Questions

Tables 1 and 2 present responses of the two Hickory Hill teenage groups as well as the Suburban group to the questions about the ideal and worst life. "Medium H. Hill" refers to the Hickory Hill teenagers in better circumstances, while the group

Table 1

Attributes of the Ideal Life as Seen by Hickory Hill and Suburban Males

(*presented in percentages of persons responding*)

	SUBURB. MALES N = 17 AGE 16	MEDIUM H. HILL MALES N = 28 AGE 18	LOW H. HILL MALES N = 15 AGE 19
Economic: Have enough money, a nice house, car.	59%	79%	87%
Job: Have a job, be self-employed, interesting work.	53	39	13
Family: Get married, raise a family, have good family life.	29	54	33
Enjoyment: Have a happy life, live it up.	35	14	27
Social environment: Live in a good neighborhood.	6	0	0
Health: Have good health	0	0	7

labelled "Low H. Hill" refers to those teenagers in very poor circumstances and in trouble with the police. The figures in these tables come from the content analyses of the free responses and represent the percentage of persons who gave answers that fell within the categories listed.

Considering first the attributes of the ideal life, it appears that the Low Hickory Hill group is less concerned about holding a job than is either the other Hickory Hill group or the Suburban group. At the same time, the Low group is as concerned as the other two about having enough money and material goods. The same pattern is observed in responses to the question about the worst life (Table 2). There is no mention at all from the Low Hickory Hill group of the loss of a job or dissatisfaction with a job as being a condition of the worst life. The Medium group sees such an occurrence as the most salient aspect of such a life. The Low group continues to be concerned, however, about not having enough money to live on. The latter group also is unique in its salient concern for avoiding trouble with the law — being arrested, going to jail. It begins to appear that while the Low Hickory Hill group wants material benefits, enjoyment, and perhaps a family, the saliency of a job as the means of obtaining these goals is not strong. The Medium Hickory Hill group and the Suburban youth are more saliently concerned with work; these two groups look more like one another than like the Low group.

The fact that work is of low saliency in the life picture of the Low Hickory Hill group does not necessarily mean that this group sees no necessity to work. When asked explicitly about the best ways of getting enough money to live on, 87 per cent of the Low group mention jobs. This figure is essentially the same as those of the Medium and Suburban groups. However, 20 per cent of the Low group also mention illegal activities as one of the best ways. Only 4 per cent of the Medium

Table 2

Attributes of the Worst Life as Seen by Hickory Hill and Suburban Males

(*presented in percentages of persons responding*)

	SUBURB. MALES N = 17 AGE 16	MEDIUM H. HILL MALES N = 28 AGE 18	LOW H. HILL MALES N = 15 AGE 19
Economic: Not have enough money, to live in poverty.	18%	11%	33%
Job: Not have a job, be dissatisfied with job.	18	25	0
Social environment: Bad neighborhood, live in a slum.	30	7	0
The law: In trouble with the law.	6	4	20
Failure: Be a failure, not succeed.	12	10	13
Health: Have poor health, die young.	0	7	13

group and 6 per cent of the Suburban group give that response. Members of the Low group may desire a combination of legal and illegal means of income maintenance. As one respondent says about the best ways of getting enough to live on, "Working and having a good job and being able to take things on the side — stealing." It also must be kept in mind that the groups involved in this study are very small. Twenty per cent of 15 in the Low group is only three persons. It is necessary to look at other responses in order to determine whether these findings are part of a distinct trend.

Another question asks whether a person would continue to work if he inherited enough money to live comfortably.[8] Table 3 presents responses to this query along with the reasons given for working or not working. A clear pattern emerges. Only 20 per cent of the Low group say that they would continue to work whereas over 80 per cent of the Medium and Suburban groups give that response. Five out of 15 members of the Low group explicitly state that they feel work is an undesirable activity. Another four members say that they would not work if they inherited enough money because there would be no reason to do so. No members of the Low group mention that they like to work.

These results do not necessarily mean that the Low group would leave the workforce if guaranteed a poverty-level income of $3,000 a year. When asked how much income they would need to live comfortably, the median response is $10,500 a year, and the lowest income mentioned is $5,200. The median income figures for the Medium and Suburban groups are $10,200 and $13,700 a year, respectively.

Table 3

Responses to Question of Whether Person Would Continue to Work if He Inherited Money, and Reasons For Responses

	SUBURB. MALES N = 17 AGE 16	MEDIUM H. HILL MALES N = 28 AGE 18	LOW H. HILL MALES N = 15 AGE 19
Per cent of persons who would work if they inherited enough money to live comfortably[a]	81%	82%	20%
Reasons for continuing to work[b]			
Like to work.	31%	14%	0%
Want more money.	13	43	7
Would be bored otherwise.	31	11	7
Want to help others.	6	11	7
Reasons for not continuing to work[b]			
No reason to work.	20%	3%	27%
Work is undesirable.	0	14	33

[a] The original study in which this question was asked showed that over 90 per cent of male workers in their late twenties said they would work. See fn. 8.

[b] Presented in percentages of total number of persons responding.

While the work orientation of the Low group may differ from that of the other groups, the extent of its monetary aspiration is similar.

The response pattern of the Suburban and Medium groups differ from each other as well as from the Low group. Almost half of the Medium group say that they would continue to work in order to earn more money. Only 14 per cent of them explicitly mention a liking for work, and none of them say that work is undesirable. The possibility of three distinct patterns of work orientation is suggested by these data. The Low Hickory Hill group is oriented towards work only because it is a means of obtaining material goods, and then this orientation is weakened by alternative, illegal ways of obtaining such goods. The Medium Hickory Hill group maintains a much stronger linkage between work and the attainment of material goods, with some indication of work providing other sources of satisfaction as well. The Suburban group shows the most interest in work for non-economic reasons. An even clearer delineation of these patterns is gained by considering the group ratings on the agree-disagree items.

Responses to the Agree-Disagree Items

Examination of responses to these items has been facilitated by carrying out a factor analysis of the ratings given on a ten-point scale by all persons who responded to the questionnaire.[9] A factor analysis reveals the extent to which certain items cluster together and are highly correlated with a common factor.[10] Five psychologically meaningful factors were obtained. The definitions or titles given the factors come from the author's interpretation of what is the common element expressed by each set of items. For brevity, only the item most strongly correlated with each factor is considered in the present analysis.

Table 4 presents the mean values of the several groups of respondents for the five items that have the highest loadings for each of the five factors. Along with the ratings of the teenage groups, there is included for comparison the rating of a national sample of male workers for the same items. The first point to note from the table is that the highest score of each group occurs for Item 22 which represents the factor of personal recognition. The desire for recognition is especially strong in the Low Hickory Hill group. This is the group that gives the lowest rating to Item 29 which represents the factor of giving high priority to work. An interpretation that offers itself is that the Low Hickory Hill group has a strong need for recognition, but that work is not the most important way of getting it.

The Medium Hickory Hill group shows a need for recognition and gives a high priority to work. This group also sees work as an important means of relating to other people. The Low group gives less importance to such a matter. With respect to material benefit, both Hickory Hill groups show a comparatively high concern. This result is consistent with their earlier emphasis on economic matters in describing the ideal life and on their both requiring more than $10,000 a year to live comfortably.

When one turns to the Suburban youth, a paradox appears. The Suburban males appear to give work even less priority than the Low group, and far less than the Medium group. Indeed, if one were to consider the ratings of the Suburban males without knowing their socioeconomic status, one might conclude that they come from the poorest group with the least work motivation. How can this strange pattern of ratings be accounted for? One might attribute the pattern to chance fluc-

Table 4

Significance of Work as Seen From Ratings on Key Items[a]

	AMER. MALE WORKERS[b] N = 853	SUBURB. MALES N = 17	MEDIUM H. HILL MALES N = 28	LOW H. HILL MALES N = 15
Work as related to other people				
11. To me, almost the only thing that matters about a job is the chance to do work that is worthwhile to society.	5.6	5.7	9.1	7.2
Work as providing material benefit				
28. To me, work is nothing more than a way of making a living.	4.2	5.2	7.8	7.8
Work as providing recognition for self				
22. Getting recognition for my own work is important to me.	7.7	8.3	9.3	9.8
Work as an ethical activity				
15. It is better to be poor than to making a living illegally.	—	5.9	7.5	6.9
Work as of high priority in life				
29. Work should be the most important part of a person's life.	5.6	5.5	8.2	6.6

[a] The higher the rating on the ten-point scale, the more the agreement.
[b] These data come from the national study carried out by F. P. Kilpatrick, *et al.*, *Source Book of a Study of Occupational Values* (Washington: The Brookings Institution, 1964).

tuations within a small number of respondents. Or perhaps the Suburban youth chosen were highly atypical. These possibilities become less convincing when the responses of the national sample are reviewed. Ratings of American workers follow the same pattern exhibited by the Suburban teenagers.

The greatest difference between the Suburban and Low Hickory Hill groups in Table 4 is with respect to Item 28. The middle-class youth are relatively little concerned with work as a means of providing material goods. This does not mean that middle-class youth reject material comforts. Economic goods are salient matters in life as seen in responses to the open-ended questions. The more likely meaning is that Suburban youth take for granted the attainment of material comforts and also the attainment of good jobs. Such an interpretation is bolstered by the previous finding that most of the Suburban group would work even if they inherited sufficient money. The Low Hickory Hill group, on the other hand, does not take material comforts or good jobs for granted. Rather than striving for jobs, however, this group tends to adopt a negative orientation towards work. As mentioned earlier, only 20 per cent would work if they inherited enough money, and one-third said that working was undesirable.

The results thus far lead to the hypothesis that it is the upwardly mobile poor teenager who takes work most seriously, who sees it as a very important part of life and as the means of getting highly desired material goods. The middle-class youth and the youth most removed from middle class society take work less seriously, but for opposite reasons. For the former, work and a good job are assumed; for the latter, work and a good job are marginal activities. There are a few further strands of data from interviews that add to these tentative insights.

Expectations About Getting Ahead

After each person responded to the open-ended questions about the best and worst life, he was shown a picture of a ten-rung ladder. He was asked to indicate where on the ladder he would place his present life if the top represented the ideal life and the bottom the worst life. He also was asked to rate his life five years ago and five years hence. The results appear in Table 5.

The most striking result in Table 5 is the extremely high rating of the Low Hickory Hill group for goal fulfillment five years hence. It is necessary to remember that each group is giving its ratings in terms of its own goals. The relatively low rating of the Suburban youth for the future may reflect the greater difficulties they see in achieving their more extensive goals. But even taking account of the goals expressed by the Low group, it seems unrealistic for them to expect to obtain the house, the car, and the money they hope for.

Turning to the means by which the Hickory Hill groups expect to get ahead, consider responses to the question, "What kinds of things do you need to do in order to move up the steps toward the top?" While 67 per cent of the Medium group mention the need for more education, only 36 per cent of the Low group mention that need. About 30 per cent of the Low group mention the need for jobs,

Table 5

Extent of Fulfillment of Life Goals by Hickory Hill and Suburban Males[a]

	SUBURB. MALES N = 17	MEDIUM H. HILL MALES N = 28	LOW H. HILL MALES N = 15
Five years ago	5.3	5.7	6.0
Present	6.7	6.1	6.5
Five years hence	7.6	8.6	9.2

[a] Ratings made on a set of ten steps where the higher the rating, the greater the goal fulfillment.

and 30 per cent mention the need to "push myself harder." The Medium group appears to believe more strongly than the Low group in education as the means of advancing in life and in work.

The future life rating given by the Low group, in light of their lack of interest in education (67 per cent are dropouts), seems unrealistically high. While some members may be able to obtain substantial sums of money through illegal activities, other members face continued arrests and a decline in income. Are the life ratings of the Medium group any more realistic? Even if they have a positive work orientation at the present time, will they be able to obtain the further training and opportunity needed to rise in the work world? How effective are the antipoverty programs in this respect? Are there special programs that could be designed to help members of the Low group forge the link between material desire and a positive orientation towards work? These questions define the challenge for current efforts to help deprived young men rise in the world of work.

CONCLUSIONS

Findings from the pilot study, of course, must be regarded as highly tentative. Nevertheless they point up issues that need to be given further consideration by researchers and policy makers. It may be important to think of having different kinds of job training opportunities for teenagers with different orientations. The kind of program that draws in persons who already have a strong positive orientation towards work may have little impact on those persons with a negative orientation. The Hickory Hill data, moreover, support the proposition that teenagers with differing work orientations tend to cluster in different peer groups. It perhaps is wise to think of work training more in terms of involving whole peer groups rather than unrelated individuals.

The apparent lack of extreme commitment to work on the part of the middle-class teenage sample and the regularly employed men in the national sample should serve as a caution in judging the behavioral significance of work orientation. Continuing participation in the workforce is likely to be a function of social position as well as psychological orientation. Middle-class males pursuing their normal day-to-day activities, including normal peer group relations, are likely to find themselves on the way to college and good jobs, even though a number of them may hold weak commitments to work. Ghetto youth pursuing their normal activities are likely to find themselves dropping out of school and being able to obtain only low paying jobs. It may be that only those ghetto youths with extremely strong work motivation can overcome the disadvantages of their social position and enter the mainstream of American economic life. If these comments have some validity, it becomes all the more important to think of job training and job opportunities being designed to meet the different psychological and social positions of young males living in poverty.

The limited data in the present report do not permit any deeper analysis of the suppositions and questions that have been raised. When the two-year study of work orientations is completed, a more sophisticated examination of the issues can be carried out. Interviews will have been completed with a large sample of welfare mothers and their sons and with a comparison group of middle-class mothers and sons. A definitive statement then could be made about the strength of work orientations of these two groups of women and the orientations of their sons. An extensive study of the participation of male and female welfare recipients in the new Work Incentive Program will illuminate the relationship between work orientation and performance in training and job situations. It will be possible, in particular, to compare the feasibility and effectiveness of training males and females with varying orientations towards work.

As noted earlier, a person's orientation towards work is only one determinant of the extent of his participation in the workforce. An understanding of this orientation, nevertheless, is crucial to the adequate training and placing in the workforce of persons who otherwise would find themselves underemployed and poor. Ideally, of course, the study of work orientation should be part of a broader effort to show the inter-relation of psychological, social, and economic factors influencing the workforce participation of poor people.

REFERENCES

1. The high level of satisfaction and concern about work among American workers is seen in the national study of the workforce carried out earlier by the Brookings Institution. See Franklin P. Kilpatrick et al., *Source Book of a Study of Occupational Values* (Washington: The Brookings Institution, 1964), p. 403.
2. A recent report of the Labor Department gives a more realistic picture of employment in the slums by computing a "subemployment" index as against the traditional "unemployment" index. The new index shows subemployment to be over 33 per cent in ten urban ghettos. See W. Willard Wirtz, *A Sharper Look at Unemployment in U.S. Cities and Slums* (Washington: U.S. Department of Labor, 1967).
3. For one of the few studies of the relation of work satisfaction to community satisfaction, but only for a select group of regularly employed persons, see Frank Friedlander, "Importance of Work Versus Nonwork Among Socially and Occupationally Stratified Groups," *Journal of Applied Psychology,* 50 (December 1966), pp. 437–41.
4. See Elliot Liebow, *Tally's Corner* (Boston: Little, Brown, 1967), pp. 29–71; William L. Yancey, "Intervention Research: A Strategy of Social Inquiry," presented at the 1965 meeting of the American Sociological Association; and Helen Safa, *An Analysis of Upward Mobility in Low Income Families* (Syracuse: Youth Development Center, 1967).
5. See *Intergenerational Comparisons: Codebook Mobilization for Youth* (New York: Research Center, New York School of Social Work, no date), mimeo; and *Study of the Meaning, Experience, and Effects of the Neighborhood Youth Corps on Negro Youth Who Are Seeking Work* (New York: Center for the Study of Unemployed Youth, Graduate School of Social Work, New York University, 1967), pp. 144–65.
6. Kilpatrick, *Source Book.* . . .
7. For discussion of the self-anchoring scale, see F. P. Kilpatrick and Hadley Cantril, "Self-Anchoring Scaling, a Measure of Individuals' Unique Reality World," *Journal of Individual Psychology,* 16 (November 1960), pp. 1–16.
8. For results from earlier use of this question, see Nancy C. Morse and Robert S. Weiss, "The Function and Meaning of Work and the Job," *American Sociological Review,* 20 (February 1955), pp. 191–98.
9. The total number of persons was 183, including 43 from Hickory Hill, 17 Suburban males, 36 mothers and 36 sons from Baltimore, and 51 males and females in work training programs. Responses of the Baltimore persons and the 51 males and females in work training programs are not evaluated in this report.
10. For a discussion of the meaning of factor analysis, see Jum Nunnally, *Psychometric Theory* (New York: McGraw-Hill Book Co., 1967), pp. 288–347.

9 Differences Between Economically Disadvantaged Students Who Volunteer and Do Not Volunteer for Economic Opportunity Programs

EDSEL L. ERICKSON
Western Michigan University

ALBERT RITSEMA
Wisconsin State University

WILBUR B. BROOKOVER
Michigan State University

LEE M. JOINER
Southern Illinois University

Economically disadvantaged students who volunteer for work training programs are apt to be students whose "life chances" are slight — in terms of their academic achievement levels, support from parents and friends, self-images, and aspirations. They know that they are at the bottom of the socioeconomic ladder — and they are desperately anxious to move up.

Among the economically disadvantaged, there are students who are high academic achievers, have high occupational plans and educational aspirations, and have the normative support for high levels of academic achievement from family, friends, and teachers. For these economically disadvantaged students, "life chances" are, perhaps, better as compared to other economically disadvantaged students. For other economically disadvantaged students, "life chances" are not so good. These students achieve at lower levels, have lower occupational plans and educational aspirations, and do not receive high levels of academic support from others. Apparently, it is this latter group for whom "life chances" are relatively low which motivated the development of several federally sponsored poverty programs.

The Work Training Programs, for example, conducted under Title I-B, and The Economic Opportunity Act of 1964, are programs designed for high school stu-

From Edsel L. Erickson, Albert Ritsema, Wilbur B. Brookover, and Lee M. Joiner, "Differences Between Economically Disadvantaged Students Who Volunteer and Do Not Volunteer for Economic Opportunity Programs," *The Journal of Human Resources,* Volume I (© 1967 by the Regents of the University of Wisconsin), pp. 76–83.

dents, 16 to 21 years of age, who have economic need and who have the qualifications for the specific jobs made available to them. These jobs, in the program investigated by the authors, were made available within the school system and consisted of part-time work of 5 to 15 hours per week under the direct supervision of various school personnel (e.g., teacher-aids, office-aids, laboratory-aids, etc.). The general purpose of the Work Training Program was ". . . to provide useful work experience opportunities for unemployed young men and women . . . so that their employability may be increased or their education resumed or continued. . . ."[1] A sub-objective of this program was that these jobs should facilitate and encourage greater interaction between disadvantaged students and responsible school adults.

Many eligible economically disadvantaged students, however, do not avail themselves of these economic opportunities in the school. It is important, therefore, to determine who among the economically disadvantaged are likely or not likely to volunteer for a Work Training Program. Are the volunteers likely to be those for whom "life chances" are better, or worse?

In view of the fact that the Work Training Program studied required participating students to have relatively high contact with school adults — and that these lower class students are often said to be alienated from the school and its values — it was assumed that among the disadvantaged, the nonvolunteers would be characterized by lower academic achievement, lower educational aspirations and occupational expectations for the future, lower self-concepts of academic ability, and lower academic achievement expectations from parents, friends, and teachers than would the volunteers for programs involving high contact and involvement with the school. In other words, it was generally assumed and hypothesized that the "life chances" of volunteers were likely to be better than the "life chances" of nonvolunteers as indicated by achievement levels, aspirations and plans for the future, self-conceptions, and the perceived academic expectations of others.

It was further hypothesized that disadvantaged students who volunteer for economic assistance programs do not differ appreciably from disadvantaged students who do not volunteer, in terms of academic ability as measured by standardized intelligence tests. It was assumed that whether a student availed himself of economic opportunities involving added interaction with school staff personnel would be primarily a matter of norms and student conceptions of self and would not be accounted for by performance on academic aptitude measures. In accord with common knowledge that socioeconomic status is highly correlated with IQ, however, it was expected that both groups of economically disadvantaged students, volunteers and nonvolunteers, would exhibit lower IQ scores than the rest of the school population.

PROCEDURES

In order to test these hypotheses and be certain that the student data collected were in no way an effect of whether disadvantaged students volunteered or not, it was decided to collect the information prior to an awareness on the part of the school staff or the students that there would be a Work Training Program. In order to accomplish this, the school administration in the spring, 1965, held back the announcement that there would be a program until all were tested who were in the public schools of the city who were to become 16 years of age during a six-month period prior to the beginning of the program in the fall. It was felt that by testing all students, there would be no recognition of a focus upon disadvantaged students and that data from those students who were more economically advantaged would serve as a norm group to compare and assess the validity of findings on the disadvantaged. However, since no predicted differences between advantaged and disadvantaged students (except for IQ) were made prior to the observation of findings, statistical tests were not employed. Inasmuch as observed differences were just the opposite of predicted differences between volunteers and nonvolunteers, no statistical tests were needed to reject our hypotheses. Further research in progress, with a focus on school behavior and dropout characteristics, will provide an opportunity to appropriately test the unpredicted observations of their study.

In order to determine who were the economically disadvantaged, school personnel (primarily counselors) were given the economic criteria set up by the Office of Economic Opportunity for participation in Work Training Programs. Using the economic criteria, the school personnel then rated all 16-year-old students in six public high schools of the city as "eligible" or "ineligible" for the Work Training Program. Originally, the eligible (referred to as the "economically disadvantaged") were classified as (1) volunteers for WTP; (2) nonvolunteers who worked elsewhere — had jobs outside of school; and (3) nonvolunteers, did not work elsewhere. The ineligible group was classified as the "advantaged population." Since, however, no differences were noted on any of the major variables for nonvolunteers who worked elsewhere and nonvolunteers who did not work elsewhere, these categories were combined.

The authors wish to point out that the primary reason for the collection of these data is to establish "bench mark" data from which to assess the impact of the Work Training Program. In this paper, however, only findings relevant to volunteers and nonvolunteers prior to establishment of the Work Training Program are presented.

The population on whom data are presented in this report is composed of males only. Data on females (which will be reported later) are in accord with the findings presented here, except with reference to occupational plans and aspirations. Females in all categories tended to share a common aspirational level and occupational plan level (i.e., housewife). No differences were noted on the basis of racial identification; hence, white and nonwhite students are included together in this report.

Instruments previously developed under USOE Cooperative Research Projects[2] were used to assess the following social-psychological characteristics of students: (1) self-concept of academic ability; (2) educational aspiration level; and (3) occupational plans.

The self-concept of academic ability scale is made up of eight multiple choice questions which ask the student to indicate his ability to achieve in school tasks in contrast to his classmates. Reliability estimates were obtained with another student population.[3]

The items formed a Guttman scale with coefficients of reproducibility of .95 for males and .96 for females for 1,050 seventh grade students. In the eighth and ninth grades, random samples of 35 males and 35 females indicated that these items retained scale forms with reproducibilities of .96 and .97 for males in the two years and .92 and .93 for females in the same two years. In the tenth grade with random samples of 100 males and 100 females, reproducibilities were .86 and .91, respectively.

Educational aspiration level was assessed by asking the students: "If you were free to go as far as you wanted to go in school, how far would you like to go?" Six possible responses ranged from "I'd like to quit school right now," to "I'd like to do graduate work beyond college."

Occupational plan level was assessed by asking the students to respond to the open-ended question: "Sometimes the job you get is not the job you wish for. What kind of job do you think you will get after you finish school?" The responses were coded using Duncan's Socio-Economic Status Values.[4]

The normative support of family was assessed by asking the student to respond to the question: "What would be the lowest grades you could get and still have your parents satisfied with you?" There were nine possible responses ranging from "Mostly A's" to "Mostly E's" with the additional possible response of, "My grades do not make any difference to my parents." This question was repeated with reference to best friend and to favorite teacher.

Academic achievement was defined as the average of a subject's semester grades in English, mathematics, social studies, and science. In the tenth grade, however, where a student did not have one of these, subject grades were used.

The reliability of GPA for four subjects, computed by Hoyt's analysis of variance, was .91 for males and .93 for females in the seventh grade. In the eighth grade reliabilities by the same method were .93 for males and .93 for females. These reliabilities were calculated on random samples of 35 males and 35 females.[5]

Reading achievement level for each category was obtained by averaging the student percentile ranks on national norms on standardized reading tests (Iowa SS).

FINDINGS

As indicated in Table 1, both groups of disadvantaged students have a mean IQ of about 94 in contrast to the mean IQ of 105 for the economically advantaged population. This is in accord with other findings concerning measured intelligence and social class. It is important to notice, however, that there were no significant differences in measured intelligence between economically disadvantaged students who volunteered for the Work Training Program and nonvolunteers.

For the semester prior to announcement of a Work Training Program, volunteers appear to have achieved at a lower level in school, as measured by grade point average and standardized reading achievement tests, than did nonvolunteers. In contrast to nonvolunteers, volunteers also indicated lower levels of educational aspiration, lower occupational plans, and lower self-concepts of academic ability. Volunteers, in addition, also indicated that their parents and friends would be satisfied with lower levels of academic achievement on their part than did nonvolunteers. These findings are just the opposite of what was hypothesized by the authors.

The only contrast to the above findings, and which was in accord with the direction of differences predicted, was that volunteers indicated teachers normatively supported higher levels of academic achievement than did nonvolunteers.

Since hypothesized directional differences favoring volunteers in contrast to nonvolunteers were just the opposite of observed differences in every case except that of teacher support, tests of significance were not needed to reject research hypotheses. While the support of the teachers is in the direction hypothesized, merely by chance one would expect to be supported at least one out of eight times even if that one case were statistically significant. Hence, the authors are reluctant to take this one predicted outcome out of eight as supportive of their original general hypothesis that volunteers are likely to have better "life chances" than nonvolunteers.

Table 1

Characteristics of (I) Economically Disadvantaged Students Who Volunteered for Federally Sponsored Work Training Programs; (II) Economically Disadvantaged Students Who Did Not Volunteer for These Programs; and (III) Economically Advantaged Students

(16-year-old males in four public high schools of a Midwestern city)

VARIABLES	I ECONOMICALLY DISADVANTAGED VOLUNTEERS* (N = 19) $\overline{X}$	II ECONOMICALLY DISADVANTAGED NONVOLUNTEERS* (N = 31) $\overline{X}$	III ECONOMICALLY ADVANTAGED (N = 202) $\overline{X}$
Measured intelligence (K.A.)	94.35	94.29	105.48
School achievement variables			
1. Grade point average (semester previous to WTP)	1.52	1.55	1.97
2. Reading achievement level (mean percentile, Iowa SS)	37.14	41.26	56.22
Social-psychological characteristics			
1. Self-concept of academic ability	24.58	27.13	27.85
2. Educational aspiration level	5.19	5.40	5.57
3. Occupational plan level	51.56	61.37	57.32
Norms: Lowest academic achievement levels satisfying to			
1. Parents	4.61	5.00	5.46
2. Best friends	4.27	4.71	5.07
3. Favorite teacher	5.19	4.60	5.84

* Classified as economically disadvantaged according to criteria of eligibility for WTP established by the Office of Economic Opportunity. All data, except volunteer status, obtained prior to the public announcement that there would be a Work Training Program conducted by the schools.

CONCLUSIONS

The findings of this study are not supportive of the major hypothesis of this study. On the contrary, the authors accept the fact that their general hypothesis was not borne out. Among the economically disadvantaged those who sought to avail themselves of economic assistance in the form of jobs involving high interaction with school personnel were apparently those who had the poorest "life chances." One could argue that they were the students who most needed this type of school involvement.

In light of these findings, the favored position is that those who most need economic and academic assistance will avail themselves of opportunities when presented to them even when those opportunities involve high levels of contact with school personnel after school hours. Perhaps, the authors had mistakenly adopted a view analogous to the view that "slaves enjoy being slaves"; that the most educationally handicapped among the poor will not attempt to take advantage of opportunities afforded them. Perhaps we would have been on sounder theoretical ground if we had utilized a theoretical approach stating that where legitimate means to a general social goal are presented, individuals will tend to take them. It is also possible that there were no other jobs available for meeting the economic needs of the volunteers, while the nonvolunteers were able to find economic support elsewhere. At any rate, the rationale for the Work Training Program is supported by the evidence of this investigation. Those who sought to avail themselves of economic and educational opportunities were indeed those for whom "life chances" seem poorest. These people are certainly the ones for whom compensatory programs should be developed.

REFERENCES

1. Section III, Part B, Public Law 88–452, 88th Congress, S. 2642, August 20, 1964.
2. Wilbur Brookover, Edsel Erickson, and Lee Joiner, *Self-Concept and School Achievement in High School,* Vol. III (East Lansing: Bureau of Educational Research Services, Michigan State University, 1967); Wilbur Brookover, Jean LaPere, Don Hamachek, and Edsel Erickson, *Self-Concept of Ability and School Achievement,* Vol. II (East Lansing: Bureau of Educational Research Services, Michigan State University, 1965); Wilbur Brookover, Ann Paterson, and Shailer Thomas, *Self-Concept of Ability and School Achievement* (East Lansing: Office of Research and Publication, Michigan State University, 1962).
3. Brookover *et al., Self-Concept of Ability* . . . , 1962.
4. Wilbur B. Brookover, Edsel Erickson, and Lee M. Joiner, *Self-Concept of Ability and School Achievement,* Vol. III, U.S. Office of Education Cooperative Research Project No. 2831 (East Lansing: Michigan State University, 1967).
5. *Ibid.*

B
Housing

Housing problems are a keystone of almost every other urban problem — of poverty, unemployment, discrimination, transportation, learning attitudes and aptitudes, tax mechanisms. Although, since World War II, housing conditions have improved significantly, the supply of America's housing is inadequate to meet the requirements of the American people — especially in cities.

Most housing is built and sold to consumers by private industry, though much of it is financed by government loan guarantees. Private industry has been uncommonly successful in providing high cost homes for middle-income and upper-income groups but has not provided directly for lower-income groups. The poor live in the cast-off housing of the more fortunate who, in increasing numbers, move to new homes in the suburbs. The cast-off housing — old, deteriorated homes near the central city core — soon become known as slums. An urban blight spreads.

The federal government has taken the position that housing needs must be met by government action. Since 1934, a bewildering array of federal housing programs has been enacted — programs to create jobs, to clear slums, to improve the tax base of cities, to alleviate poverty. Some of these programs have been, in sum, not only bewildering but contradictory. The Urban Renewal Program's slum clearance attempts, for instance, actually have harmed the poor by forcing them out of the only housing they could afford. By 1968, the President's Committee on Urban Housing stated that some 7.8 million households were unable to afford decent housing, even after the flurry of federal programs. Indeed, the entire history of federal housing activity shows that only some 800,000 units of federal housing have been produced — or, only one-tenth of the needs has been met.

In urban ghettos the housing market is at least as poorly organized as the labor market. Location is decisive in housing decisions since the neighborhood effects of residential actions are regarded as extremely important, especially by higher-income people.

There is not merely one large housing market in an urban area; there are many. And, in small neighborhoods, balance between demand and supply does not always exist. Basic factors that affect the demand for and supply of housing include transport cost, job location, and the quantity and quality of public services available. Additionally, neighborhood environment is influenced by zoning laws, the urban form and density patterns generated by urban growth and change, and the segregation and discrimination (especially racial) which divide neighborhoods and the buyers and sellers of houses so effectively. Finally, urban renewal and other forms of government housing programs can have a powerful impact on the quantity and quality of housing in a neighborhood.

At the macroeconomic level, there has been, and continues to be, a repeated call for more housing for low-income people — albeit, in point of fact, housing conditions have improved significantly over the past twenty years, even for many poor people. Rising incomes and latter-day prosperity have raised the level of housing that many "affluent" families can afford, but since the existing stock is judged inadequate, housing subsidies, low-interest loans, and other government assistance to housing have been urged.

In order to simulate the housing process, residential matching systems are written into mathematical models which are designed to take account of residential preferences, work location, social stratification, moving behavior, and other factors. In the segregated ghetto housing markets, black and other minority housing patterns (especially home ownership patterns), physical characteristics, neighborhood effects, and quantity and quality of local public services are built into simulation models. Results of these analytical efforts have begun to yield some understanding of housing market fragmentation and segregation patterns in urban centers — and to provide a basis for policy recommendations aimed at greater coherence within the urban housing market as a whole.

Much planning has gone into the field of urban housing, and careful benefit-cost analyses of policies to combat slums and racial discrimination have been made. Welfare payments, income guarantees, federal and local rent supplements, and other programs have been planned — and sometimes implemented — to meet housing needs. The phenomenon of "blockbusting" in the real estate sales process is worthy of study — and has been studied — in detail.

10 Population Pressure, Housing, and Habitat

JOSEPH J. SPENGLER
Duke University

Population growth is creating intolerable conditions in the cities — particularly in the largest ones. Unless some method of control is found, cities will continue to expand, creating macro-environments which may restrict — indeed stifle — the micro-habitat, the home. One answer: new cities, with size limits.

> For life to run smoothly, for the living organism to remain healthy in the highest degree, the environmental complex must be made as perfect as possible.
> — J. W. Bews, *Human Ecology* 79 (1939).

> Woe unto them that join house to house, that lay field to field, till there be no room.
> — Isaiah 5:8.

> Very few people, indeed, want to be better than they are; or . . . hunger and thirst after righteousness.
> — T. S. Eliot, *Essays, Ancient and Modern* 115–16 (1936).

INTRODUCTION

A house is not a home. This aphorism is usually held to possess validity only in the demimonde. Brief consideration suggests, however, that the validity of this aphorism is not so confined. It fits other worlds as well; in particular, the world of housing upon which the current issue of this journal is focused.

It may still be true in this age of insecurity, anti-privacy, and emerging police states, that "the house of everyone is to him," as Sir Edward Coke declared four centuries ago, "as his castle and fortress, as well for his defense against injury and violence as for his repose." It is also true that a man's house means a great deal more, even to those who agree with Samuel Butler that occasional absence from one's house enhances its attractiveness.

In this article I argue (a) that the subject of housing must be examined in terms of the large set of *gesellschaftliche* and *gemeinschaftliche* relations within which the house, together with its occupying household, is situated; (b) that this set of relations and hence the role of housing is significantly affected by the growth and concentration of population, control of which is essential to the easing of the so-called housing problem.

Reprinted with permission from a symposium, Housing (Part I), "Population Pressure, Housing, and Habitat," appearing in *Law and Contemporary Problems* (Volume 32, Number 2, Spring 1967), published by the Duke University School of Law, Durham, North Carolina. Copyright, 1967, by Duke University.

The underlying issue is clearly recognized by architects such as Doxiadis who see in the expansion of the impersonal city and the associated elimination of nature a process that is destroying neighborhood and community units and making of man a building-occupying troglodyte subject to "instructions issued from the peak of the pyramid." He suggests that we once again create human communities in our cities, "operating neighborhoods, downtown shopping centers where people can walk freely, can come into natural contact, can enjoy quiet surroundings and create and admire art. These human communities should become the cells which will be interconnected by mechanical means of transportation and communications to form major systems and major cities."[1] While Doxiadis is here referring mainly to communities within large cities he recognizes the interrelation of housing and community and the importance of how man can spend his time, especially in a modern world in need of a moral equivalent to work.

I
HOME VERSUS HOUSE

How the Greeks, Aristotle in particular, viewed housing may be suggestive since concern for the eudaemonic aspect of life played a very important role in their view of housing — a concern honored more in the breach than in the observance in the United States.[2] Aristotle approaches housing in terms of the overall community and the pursuit of the "highest good." The polis, or city state, as he conceived of it, was a community which, embracing all other communities, aimed at the "highest good." The elemental community of which the state was composed was the household, to whose management Aristotle and those influenced by him devoted attention.[3] Aristotle, defender of simplicity in a simple age, pointed to the smallness of the number of instruments needed within a household to make the "good life" possible.[4] Presumably he agreed with Hesiod that a house was the "first and foremost" requisite of a household[5] and with the statement that "a house must be arranged both with a view to one's possessions and for the health and well-being of its inhabitants." A house must, therefore, "be airy in summer and sunny in winter"; whence it needs to face "north" and be longer than wide.[6] These and other aspects of a house were stressed several centuries later by the architect Vitruvius, a contemporary of Nero, who designed and situated several types of houses to meet specific occupational and climatic requirements.[7]

Aristotle looked upon a house as one of a triad of interrelated elements: house, household, and organic urban community. The house sheltered the members of the household and afforded them access to a good and healthy life. The household itself was relatively self-sufficient, as a rule. The head of a household was united with other household heads in that network of reciprocity which undergirded the state or urban community.

The problems confronting a household in Aristotle's day were fewer and simpler than those confronting a household in the affluent present. Cities usually were small and relatively free of congestion, even of that congestion of which Juvenal was later to complain in Imperial Rome. Getting to work, to recreational and religious centers, or to political responsibilities, presented no serious difficulties. Aristotle wanted to keep the Greek city that way. Not only did he insist that a city not be large, since "a very populous city can rarely, if ever, be well governed." He even suggested that its population not exceed "the largest number which suffices for the purposes of life, and can be taken in a single view."[8] Had he anticipated today's opulent society, he would have found it wanting, along with its conception of housing.

The observations made by Aristotle or imputable to him call attention to the fact that a house is not a solitary, autonomous, self-subsisting unit, even when occupied by a household, but rather a locus in many partially overlapping environments or complexes. It is a locus in the spatial economy of the household; it is a locus in a social environment; it is a locus in a physical environment that varies in salubrity and conduciveness to health. In the parlance of today, we may conceive of a house as a micro-habitat within a larger but highly relevant macro-habitat. The householder may be said to dwell in the former and carry on his extra-dwelling roles and functions in the latter. It is quite evident, therefore, that his well-being and the extent to which he can attain the good life depend in large measure upon the quality of each of these two habitats. This inference is borne out by data assembled on the amounts of time spent by various types of families, upon in-home and extra-house activities, respectively.[9]

Since a house is a micro-habitat within a macro-habitat, it is improper to conceive of housing independently of and in isolation from the macro-habitat within which houses are situated. To do so is on a par with conceiving of Gettysburg in terms of Edward Everett's prolix but forgotten oration. That housing often is so conceived of is a result of the absence of order, or even of ordering values, from the determinants of the growth, organization, and construction of cities. The outcomes resulting are accepted as parts of the scheme of things, with the result that the fundamental significance of the macro-habitat for the quality of housing is underestimated. In consequence, the impact of the growth and concentration of population upon man's macro- and micro-habitats receives little attention.

II
THE MACRO-HABITAT

The macro-habitat, within which household, house, and micro-habitat are situated, embraces a number of environments. For purposes of illustration we need discuss only a few. Perhaps the most important is the set of spatial economies within which the individuals composing a household seek the good life, directly and/or indirectly through pursuit of material means. Almost equally important are the social, physical, and health environments of the micro-habitat. It is sometimes said, of course, that modern man has become largely free of his external environment.[10] This exaggerated view suggests a modern Daedalus who pretends to have risen above his physical environment. One must, therefore, agree with Dubos' comment: "As happened to Antaeus of the Greek legend, his [man's] strength will probably wane if he loses contact with the biological ground from which he emerged and which still feeds him, physically and emotionally."[11]

A house is always a locus of household activities and a base from which members of a household operate. The household is situated in a net of activity-loci interrelated from the vantage point of members of a household even if not always connected by exchange as are interrelated markets. Each member of a household moves from his house to a locus of activity and back to his house either directly or via a path connecting diverse activities participated in sequentially. The problem confronting each member of a household is that of minimizing time utilized in moving from house to activity, from activity to activity, and from activity to house. His capacity to minimize time thus expended is quite limited, however, since the loci of these activities, together with the house, are not easily modified.[12]

Economy of time must be mainly sought, therefore, via economy of space, though some economy of time is achievable through reducing the actual time cost if not also the pecuniary cost of traversing space. Economy of space in turn must be sought through optimizing the spatial arrangement of relevant activities in the urban environs of the house and household.[13] When this is done a house begins to be viewed as a home, as the focus of man's search for the good life. This outcome is not likely to be emphasized, however, until both social scientists and those who manage the allocation of resources become space-minded — concerned about terrestrial and urban space rather than about mere lunar and martian space. For, as Isard observes, excessive emphasis upon time in economic analysis long made for neglect of the role of space in the theoretical and empirical structures of Anglo-Saxon economists.[14]

What constitutes a satisfactory social environment is not easy to define or to realize empirically. It is evident, however, that occupants of micro-habitats or neighborhoods are not likely to agree upon what makes a social environment satisfactory unless they agree on many things. This condition is overlooked, of course, in much of the discussion of housing that involves the intermingling of households which are quite dissimilar in tastes and conduct-determining norms. Even within a household common standards of value must be present to permit passage from the preference patterns of its individual members to a preference pattern representative of the household as such.[15] At the neighborhood level where the tastes of individuals must be sufficiently similar to permit the construction of "suitable social welfare functions,"[16] a minimal though not excessive degree of similarity of tastes is essential to insure agreement on what constitutes a satisfactory social environment. The degree required is less when there is agreement both on the need for day-to-day decisions and on the mechanism or process whereby these decisions are reached.[17] The market mechanism alone is unlikely to bring about this minimal degree under all conditions, though it can be enabled to do so if certain conditions are met.[18] It is true, as a rule, therefore, that a considerable though variable degree of homogeneity in the tastes of those inhabiting a neighborhood or macro-habitat is essential to their settling upon what makes a social environment good. When this degree is not fully attained, whether because of class or other differences, the macro-habitat becomes instable.[19] It can become instable also if the inhabitants and their children become too standardized.

While it appears to be true that whatever unduly reduces the degree of homogeneity of any particular neighborhood or macro-habitat affects it unfavorably, this inference does not support the view that cultural differences *between* macro-habitats should be reduced. There must be room in the all-inclusive community for a sufficiency of diversity which, while a characteristic of individuals, is in part a concomitant of differences between macro-habitats.[20] It may be well, therefore, that the overall community resemble a sea dotted with islands which differ culturally from one another.[21] Unfortunately, the "formal elegance of welfare economics" does not tell us how much homogeneity is essential to a people's happiness.[22]

It may be noted parenthetically that economic as well as social factors have to be taken into account if the current housing shortage confronting nonwhites is to be greatly reduced. For, while housing values in nonwhite areas tend to lie below those for comparable housing in nearby white areas,[23] and while block-busting can enlarge nonwhite housing areas, urban renewal programs tend to raise the price of affected urban land above the level at which it is economically attractive to most nonwhites.[24] Emphasis upon residential desegregation, it is said, is retarding the construction of low-income housing.[25]

The degree of attractiveness of the physical environment of a macro-habitat enveloping a dwelling unit depends upon many circumstances, some of which seem to have been taken into account even in ancient ghetto-ridden Egypt.[26] Among these circumstances are absence of disorder and traffic congestion, the availability of private and public space, and general attractiveness, now usually lacking within as well as outside American urban centers.[27] Closely related is the healthfulness of this environment and its freedom from noise and pollution both of which are inimical to good health.[28]

An environment's healthfulness usually depends, at least in advanced countries, upon its freedom from pollution, especially chemical pollution of the water and the atmosphere. "[T]he few facts available demonstrate," René Dubos states, "that pathological states can be caused by exposure to concentrations of pollutants of the order of those which exist in the urban atmosphere. On the basis of these results, it can be surmised that pollution can also have deleterious and lasting effects on human beings."[29] "The possibility of delayed and cumulative effects is not limited to any particular class of agent."[30] Dubos, therefore, stresses the "need for *striking information*" because "environmental pollution will not be controlled until physicians and scientists take an active part in its study."[31] Response to this same need on the part of students of urban and housing environments will help place efforts to solve housing problems in a more general context than is common at present; it will help men recognize that since, as Commoner shows, the elements of nature constitute an integrated totality,[32] it must be dealt with as a whole and not in a piecemeal fashion.[33]

III
POPULATION TRENDS

The rate of population growth has fallen below 1.5 per cent per year, at which rate it increased in 1960–64 when natural increase accounted for eighty-seven per cent of the total growth. Natality has since descended enough to reduce the current rate of natural increase nearly to one per cent per year. In the years just ahead, however, the large increase in the number of females aged 20–29, an echo of the upsurge of natality after the war, should push natality up somewhat. It is likely that the nation's population, nearly 198 million at the beginning of 1967, will number over 250 million by 1985 and 300 million or more by the close of the century. Should this population continue thereafter to grow 1¼ per cent per year it would number a billion or more by the year 2100, by which time population density might exceed 350 per square mile in the conterminous United States. Acres of all sorts per person would then average less than two.

The nonwhite population will increase somewhat faster than the white population, rising from twelve per cent of the total at present to about 13.5 per cent by 1985. At that time the rate of natural increase of the nonwhite population may be somewhat in excess of two per cent whereas the white rate will be about 1⅓ per cent. Should that rate differential persist, around one-fourth of the nation's population would be nonwhite by 2085.

While the farm population has continued to decline, from 32 million in 1920 to less than 12 million, increase in population concentration has been extensive rather than intensive. The population formerly defined as rural has continued to increase, though only about half as fast as the nation's population — in 1940–60 about sixteen per cent instead of thirty-five per cent as in the aggregate. The urban population increased more rapidly, of course, about fifty-two per cent; that in places under 100,000 increased about seventy-one per cent while that in places of 100,000 and over grew about thirty-four per cent. Even so, the proportion which the population in places of over 100,000 constituted of the total population changed only slightly.[34] The data just presented do not, however, fully reflect the implosion and megalopolitanization of population in process. But they do reveal how a shifting urban frontier has replaced that westerly moving rural frontier in terms of which some seventy years ago Frederick Jackson Turner interpreted the course of American history up to the 1890's. For a real sense of the change we must turn to metropolitan data.

Continuing population growth may intensify population concentration and urban crowding in two ways. First, it may simply add to the population situated in places of all sizes. Second, should the population-attracting power of cities increase more than in proportion to their numerical size, the rate of growth will be greatest in larger centers and the fraction of the nation's population concentrated therein will increase. This did happen between 1900 and 1930 when the rural fraction of the population fell from 60.3 per cent to 43.8 per cent and when the population in places of 100,000 and over rose from 18.7 to 29.6 per cent of the total population and from 47.1 to 52.7 per cent of the urban population. Then the process slowed down. Between 1930 and 1950 none of these percentages changed markedly. More recently some dispersion has set in. Between 1950 and 1960 the fraction of the nation's population situated in places of both above 500,000 and above 100,000 declined. This increase in dispersion may reflect in part a forty-two per cent increase in 1940–60 in the number of places under 100,000 — of which nearly three-fifths were added in 1950–60.[35]

Whether an increasing fraction of the nation's population does become concentrated in the larger centers turns on the strength of the stochastic process apparently underlying what Kendall, describing the work of Zipf and others, calls "a kind of the-higher-the-fewer rule." This rule "says, in effect, that for certain kinds of activity with a measurable size x, the number y of individuals greater than or equal to x is given by

$$y = A/x^p$$

where p is a constant which is often quite close to unity."[36] Here y stands for the rank of a particular city in size of population, x for its size, and p and A are constants, with A denoting the population of the largest center and p approximating unity. Now if A grows faster than a nation's population it will, after the manner of a Saturn eating his own children, increase at the expense of other communities, especially the smaller ones;[37] but if the number of communities grows rapidly enough, the population will tend to become more dispersed.[38]

It is within the metropolitan population that we find changes taking place of great significance for housing and its macro-habitats. First, the population of metropolitan areas is growing much faster than that lying outside these areas — 2.3 per cent per year in the 1950's and 1.9 per cent per year in 1960–65 when the corresponding rates for the nonmetropolitan population were 0.8 and 0.7 per cent per year. The fraction of the nation's population living in metropolitan areas rose from about 60.5 per cent in 1950 to about sixty-three per cent in 1960 and sixty-four per cent in 1965. The metropolitan population in 1960 already approximated nine-tenths of the urban population and it could easily rise to seventy-five per cent of the nation's total population within 40–50 years. Second, while the proportion of the nation's population growth taking place in metropolitan areas is greater than before the Second World War, the proportion taking place in central cities situated within metropolitan areas is declining, especially in those with over a million inhabitants.[39] In sum, while the nation's population is becoming more concentrated, within the larger areas of concentration a redistribution of population is taking place and thus changing or threatening to change many of the macro-habitats within which housing is located. The rate of change underway can be especially significant because it is made up of net in-migration as well as of natural increase. For example, between 1950 and 1960 about thirty-five per cent of the increase in metropolitan population was due to in-migration.[40]

The long continued migration of the Negro to the city in search of better economic opportunity and housing, coupled with the decline in foreign immigration, is bringing about a redistribution of population within metropolitan centers.[41] This redistribution is of very great significance for housing problems since in 1965 about sixty-four per cent of the white population of the United States and about sixty-eight per cent of the nonwhite population lived in metropolitan areas. This redistributive process reflects forces affecting both concentration and congestion as well as the passage of a city's racial composition beyond a so-called tipping point.[42] First, the population outside the central cities has been growing much faster than that in these cities, four per cent per year in 1950–60 and 3.3 per cent per year in 1960–65 compared with annual increases in central cities of one per cent in the 1950's and 0.6 per cent in 1960–65. Second, the nonwhites are displacing the whites in central cities with the result that if this process continues, by 1980 seven or more large cities will be predominantly nonwhite (mainly Negro) and perhaps thirty more about one-third nonwhite. Of the top ten cities in the United States only Houston and Los Angeles will be predominantly white thirty-five years from now.[43]

Illustrative of current redistributive tendencies are those of 1960–65 when the nonwhite population of metropolitan areas increased 2,508 thousand, of whom 2,096 thousand settled in central cities. Meanwhile, the metropolitan white population increased 8,982 thousand, *all* of whom settled outside central cities, together with about 470 thousand who migrated there on balance from central cities. The nonwhite fraction of the total central-city population thus rose from about eighteen per cent in 1960 to nearly twenty-one per cent in 1965; in 1950 it was only about thirteen per cent.[44] Meanwhile the nonwhite fraction of the metropolitan population in the ring of areas outside central cities, about 5.5 per cent in 1950, had declined to five per cent by 1960. An unpublished study of eleven central cities, by my colleague Reynolds Farley, indicates that residential segregation is again increasing.

So alarmed has the present administration apparently become at the current drift and its implications for desegregation of the school system that what amount to legislative and administrative efforts to countervail or reverse the drift are being initiated.[45] This approach not only is unmindful of potential boomerang effects;

it overlooks the advantages to be had from the proposal made below to multiply the number of urban centers to which Negro and white can migrate and through which the problem of concentration can be greatly alleviated, though not solved altogether.

IV
POPULATION EFFECTS

The effects of the population trends described in the preceding section are of two sorts, sequelae to population growth and sequelae to population concentration. Four sequelae to population growth may be noted. The first of these, the accentuation of population concentration or density, has already been touched upon. The second, increase in overall population, is treated largely under the head of population concentration, of which it is a source. Of course, enlargement of areas of population density outside areas of heavy concentration do produce effects of the sort discussed below, though less intense than those found in areas of heavy concentration.

The third effect of population growth is the absorption of inputs which might otherwise have been used to improve the material condition of the existing population and its replacement. Here we may indicate only the order of magnitude of this cost which may then be compared with fixed investment in residential construction that has been running about $22 billion a year. If we conceive of capital only in terms of hard goods and suppose it costs about four per cent of the national income to support a rate of population growth of one per cent per year, then the cost of America's population growth has been in the neighborhood of $30 billion a year since 1964. If we include under the head of "capital" all expenditure which serves to increase the stream of income in the future and allow as well for the adverse effect of population growth upon the age composition of the population, we may raise this figure to around $45 billion. Another way of arriving at an estimate is to suppose that the cost of adding a cross-sectional thousand people to the nation's population costs between $10 and $20 million. On this supposition, adding about 2.5 million persons a year to the population costs between $25 and $50 billion a year. Whatever be the correct estimate, it represents an annual expenditure far in excess of the current rate of expenditure upon residential construction. Of course, even should fertility fall to the replacement level, it would take a few years for the benefits to materialize fully and then they might be utilized in part in the form of leisure.[46]

The fourth effect is associated with the continual change in city size produced by population growth and discussed earlier. Let us suppose that a country's population is stationary. Its population distribution will then be fairly stable, affected by changes in technology, incomes, and the composition of tastes and amenities, but *not* by the main source of distributive change operative in the past — namely, increase in the nation's population. The urban problem would then become mainly one of keeping particular cities and their macro-habitats intact; it would thus resemble maintaining a stationary economy's capital intact.[47] Financial provision for the maintenance of all components of a city including its housing and macro-habitats could then easily be put on an orderly basis. Planning for changes could be carried out readily since almost any particular change would be but a wave in a sea of stability. Short and long time-horizons would differ less than now. The remaining changes would be small enough so that, were they met sub-optimally, corrective action would be easy and not very costly. Under these conditions demographic metabolism, the replacement of old families nearing or beyond retirement by younger families, would entail little unfavorable change in the quality of the environment.

Population concentration and density produce a number of somewhat distinct effects, all of which, when intensified beyond a critical point, outweigh the advantages associated with a lesser amount of population agglomeration. These effects are incident on some or all the macro-habitats constituting a community, though in varying degree, and they reduce the contribution that housing can make to welfare. "Welfare," in other words, may be viewed as a joint "product" of (*inter alia*) that which a household's housing and macro-habitat make possible and that which the larger, all-inclusive community makes possible. Agglomeration of population continues to increase the latter contribution after it has begun to diminish that of housing and habitat, until a point is reached where the positive effect is offset at the margin by the negative effect. This is the optimum point; it varies with household, of course, and this variation affects how population distributes itself within urban or metropolitan space.

It is not possible here to catalog and describe all the effects associated with excessive population growth and concentration, but the main ones may be touched upon in order to illustrate the theme of this paper. These effects are contraction of space, pollution, congestion, unproductive use of time, and sub-optimal distributions of population.

Population concentration reduces the ratio of space available per person for household and/or other activities and thus diminishes the contribution of space to the city-dweller's standard of life. In 1960 about twenty-eight per cent of the nation's population occupied only 0.23 per cent of its land-area, and about forty-five per cent occupied just under one half of one per cent of this area. Population density ranged from 13,870 persons per square mile in places of a million or more to just over 3,900 per square mile in places of 50–100 thousand and about 2,290 per square mile in places of 10–25 thousand. Expressed in terms of acres per person, ground space per person ranged from about one twenty-fifth of an acre in places of over a million to one-sixth of an acre in places of 50–100 thousand and nearly three-tenths of an acre in places of 10–25 thousand. Even if we allow four persons per household, the pinch of space is pronounced, for part of this average land quota is required for streets, structures other than housing, and very rarely for parks. Moreover, since the daytime population of cities is much greater than their nighttime population, density within the city in daytime is more pronounced than our data suggest.

Second, population concentration increases the exposure of housing and macro-habitats to pollution of all sorts. Most of it is ultimately of human origin and therefore is in greatest amount where men are concentrated and live, work, and consume, and hence manufacture debris, pollutants, and contaminants of all sorts. Moreover, the impact of this unwelcome product is hard to cushion. For example, since about nine-tenths of United States air pollution "consists of largely invisible but potentially deadly gases," air conditioners cannot defoul the atmosphere; at best they can remove particles.[48] It is doubtful, therefore, if man's natural right to breathe clean air can be made realizable in megalopolitan or other large centers.

Indeed, he may find himself hard pressed even to dispose of his refuse and get a sufficient supply of usable water.[49]

We may state the problem generally and in terms of a set of hypothetical flows. Modern life is subjective and objective; it consists largely in symbolic communication and in the flow of men and matter. The volume of each stream tends to increase faster than population, especially in urban settings. Indeed, an urban center, above all, a megalopolis, may be thought of as a network of channels for the conduct of men and matter, together with information, within that center and between it and the world outside its environs. Channel capacities are limited and so are the number of channels actually or potentially available. Let R_e represent the rate of flow of effluent e and C_e the capacity of channels existing for the conveyance and disposal of e into the atmosphere, into waters, and elsewhere, but always in keeping with the health and good life of all concerned. If $R_e > C_e$, portions of e must be destroyed at points of origin, or stored until R_e falls below C_e. Otherwise e will accumulate within the population center and perhaps in areas immediately nearby. Presumably R_e grows at least as fast as $(p' + g')$ where p' denotes the rate of population growth of an urban center and g' denotes the rate of growth of per capita consumption and/or production of output which gives rise to various forms of effluent within the urban center. Since C_e has upper limits, it is inevitable that as a center's population grows, the probability of pollution of the macro-habitats of housing increases.

Third, congestion of channels for the conveyance of people and perhaps also of those for the conveyance of information tends to increase with population growth and concentration. Consider for example the movement of traffic through the center of a metropolitan area; it can grow nearly as the square of the population. "To keep the degree of traffic congestion constant, road traffic capacity must rise far more than in proportion with the rate of increase of population, and sheer problems of geography and land availability practically preclude such a possibility. Of course, the fact that population tends to cluster and is not spread evenly throughout the city only adds to these congestion problems."[50] This congestion, together with the accompanying noise and disorder, tends to accentuate two interrelated forces which generate the cumulative deterioration of local environment and macro-habitats — namely, urban blight and flight to the suburbs.[51] Dense traffic is not the only form of congestion that inflicts uncompensated costs upon a large fraction of the population. There is also, as Colin Clark points out, a second type, "zonal congestion," the dearth of open space for recreational and other purposes.[52] Oddly enough, another British author argues for the "concentration of future population growth in a limited number of major cities as opposed to a balanced and uniform expansion of all existing urban centres."[53] Such concentration will economize on land and thus preserve more land for agriculture and the amenities.[54] He has in mind England where overall population density is very high, greater even than in Japan.

Fourth, two further concomitants of population concentration may be noted, each of which may affect man's macro-habitat adversely. First, a population and its activities may become sub-optimally dispersed within a metropolitan region and then perpetuated because the totality of public and private fixed capital outlays undergirding this distribution is so great as to render modifications very expensive. Herein, it is to be noted, we find support for careful anticipational urban planning, together with emphasis upon the preservation of flexibility and the retention of options realizable in the future. Since urban decisions tend to become frozen in steel and concrete as well as in transport systems, they should not be taken and acted upon until and unless the future is relatively clear. Second, a sub-optimal distribution of population and activities makes for high consumption per capita of modern man's most precious possession, time that might otherwise be discretionary and hence contributive to his well-being. Perhaps increasing education will result in countervailing measures. Did not Dante write: "Who knows most, him loss of time most grieves."[55]

V
POLICY IMPLICATIONS

Certain policy implications may be derived from what has been said. First, it is unlikely that the housing problem can ever be solved satisfactorily so long as population continues to grow and with it the excessive size of cities. For the impact of growth, unless carefully planned for and counterbalanced, will make for continual decay of parts of cities and hence of macro-habitats. Not only central cities but suburbs as well will continue to be subject to this process of decay which steals in unobtrusively, not as a fast-working pestilence that comes in the night but as a slowly working mutagen which produces a bodily change that in time metastasizes. It will probably be many years, however, before population growth ceases, or, in the absence of nuclear war, becomes negative.

Second, contemporary tax and subsidy systems conduce to the deterioration of many macro-habitats, together with housing, by putting a premium on deterioration or by shunting its costs from those responsible to non-responsible third parties. (a) Buildings and land need to be differentially taxed in order that taxation of real property, usually a deterrent to its maintenance and improvement, will cease to be so.[56] (b) Every business firm or organization must be made to bear all congestion and related costs to which it gives rise, costs currently borne in part by others. (c) Impose the entire cost of urban expansion upon those responsible for this cost, instead of partly upon non-responsible parties as at present.

Third, current financial arrangements for maintaining housing and other forms of urban capital are inadequate to keep this capital intact through repair and/or replacement. Two approaches seem indicated. (1) Requiring the accumulation of adequate, earmarked liquidable assets to permit repair or replacement as it becomes necessary. (2) Require architects to plan construction in much greater measure than now in terms of easily replaceable parts, a point insisted upon by A. Spilhaus in his plan for an experimental city of about 250,000.[57]

Fourth, many problems associated with urban growth and housing flow from inattention to the need to balance *total* costs and benefits at the margin; and this form of inattention tends to grow faster than the size of urban centers. Pollution, congestion, and related costs are among those that need to be offset. A variety of measures is available for this purpose, some of which are better suited than others to particular cases.[58]

Fifth, several implications follow from the irreversible character of decisions or processes determining urban growth after it has taken place. It sometimes happens, as Lösch has pointed out, that production, having been initiated in the wrong place, will be continued there.[59] For such mislocation imperfectly planned investment is responsible. Urban growth and extension entail heavy fixed-capital investment the sacrifice of which, along with that of economy-yielding business connections, makes decision-makers loath to shift location. Given this heavy *ex-post* anchor, should not *ex-ante* decision-making be forced to take into account all expected costs as well as all suppositious advantages? Should not the set of forces currently shaping city growth be brought under more effective control, at least so long as these forces resemble those governing the growth of polyp colonies? Of course, city size could be explicitly limited, and the ownership of all urban land could be vested in cities. Such controls might, however, run counter to economic flexibility and American ideology. The same objectives could probably be achieved through use of a system of taxes and subsidies, calculated to influence population distribution and provide compensation to those on whom discretionary decision-makers imposed unrequited direct and indirect costs. These tax and subsidy arrangements would be reinforced if a rent-absorbing tax in keeping with, say, the *zonal* opportunity cost of land were imposed on all *land* in and around cities.

Sixth, perhaps the greatest promise lies in the development of an adequate number of additional cities of such size — say, 100–200 thousand — as provides adequate communal opportunity, together with near-optimum conditions for housing and macro-habitats as well as abundant access to amenities and recreational space. Suppose that 600 such cities were established during the next thirty-five years. They could absorb 60–90 million or more inhabitants, or something like 60–80 or more per cent of the prospective population increase, most of which will settle in urban centers. If, say, as much as one-fourth of the population absorbed into these cities were nonwhite, it is possible that more than the anticipated increase in the nonwhite population would be settled there; then the current drift into central cities and ghettoes would be checked and perhaps reversed. Should such cities not be established, the population of most cities now over 100,000 would be greatly increased, for the next thirty-five years will witness the addition of 100 or more million to this nation's population and perhaps that of an equal number to the urban population, which in 1960 already numbered 113 million on the old census definition and 125 million on the new definition.

That this promise is realizable is suggested by two facts: (a) the relevant Key Decisions regarding location and many other matters are made by a very small number of businessmen; (b) big businessmen and corporations are becoming increasingly interested in the development of attractive, rationally-organized cities. We may divide a working population into Primary Job Makers and Job Takers, in which category may be placed Secondary Job Makers. The Primary Job Makers establish and locate the basic enterprises and employments. Around these gather Secondary Job Makers whose enterprises service and meet the needs of the Primary Job Makers and their employees as well as those of all persons who fall in the Job-Taker category. The heads of some but not all governmental agencies and foundations belong in the Primary Job-Maker category as they make Key Decisions affecting location of activities.

(a) That the making of Key Decisions respecting location is highly concentrated is suggested by the following data. In 1965 twenty-one out of each 100 persons employed in the United States were employed by 750 companies, many of which are describable as Primary Job Makers. About 55.1 per cent of all industrial workers were employed by 500 industrial companies.[60] Brian Berry reports that in the area around Chicago the location decisions of about twenty retailers control those of about 20,000 lesser retailers respecting where they will carry on for the next twenty-five years.[61] It is evident, therefore, that the Key Decisions essential to locating basic employment in new cities may be made by a small number of business firms. The implementation of such locational decisions would entail a redistribution of "brains," now most unevenly distributed because of unequal distribution of economic activities and educational institutions.[62] For "brains" have not merely replaced muscle; they now constitute the most strategic form of mobile and creative capital. "Brains," however, insist on access to cultural and other amenities as well as to good housing and attractive macro-habitats. Of this Key Decisions Makers are becoming increasingly aware even if the current urban power structure is not.

A Key Decision Maker or two can launch a new city destined to number 100–200 thousand inhabitants by establishing an economic base capable of multiplying and expanding into around 40–80 thousand jobs.[63] If such base is established, say by introduction of manufacturing plants that employ 10–20 thousand persons, the labor force will expand sympathetically to something like 40–80 thousand gainfully employed. Manufacturing is not, of course, the only possible source of an initiating economic base, particularly in the United States where the ratio of employment in manufacture to all employment is falling. Other activities, among them collections of services, may provide a base; they need only to supply the exports that enable the community to purchase goods and services not supplied locally.

(b) A Key Decision Maker may be interested in doing more than locating activities at a point in space where, he believes, a city with attractive environs will come into being. He may want to establish a more complete city, one providing not only basic employment but also ordered and abundant space for all ancillary activities and amenities (including even such activities as amateur theatricals and similar activities which seldom yield returns even equal to private monetary costs). In such a city far more than in those described under (a) high priority must be given to housing and its macro-habitats and to averting the diverse costs and dissatisfactions associated with both life in central cities and life in isolated suburbs. Otherwise the collection of houses and macro-habitats constituting this city will not prove convertible into a community that generates a degree of loyalty and collective responsibility. It is probable that planned cities of this sort, together with those referred to under (a), can absorb most of the prospective increase in urban population. Illustrative of the planned type of community is that near Clear Lake, Texas, sponsored by the Humble Oil Company and the National Aeronautics and Space Administration, and intended to evolve over a fifteen-year period into a city of some 140,000 residents living in some 40,000 houses situated in an area of twenty-four miles square that includes a 365 acre town center and a 1,000 acre research park.[64] Somewhat similar cities are planned by General Electric Company, Goodyear Tire and Rubber Company, Westinghouse, and other large corporations. Several are well along — Robert Simon's Reston, Virginia, intended to house about 75,000 people, and James Rouse's Columbia, Maryland, intended to house about 110,000 people. All follow Secretary Udall's advice that "city planning should put people first."[65]

The types of towns referred to have a localized primary base, supplemented in several instances by the activities of inhabitants destined to work in nearby metropolitan centers. The housing problem is solved, though sometimes at the expense of considerable cost in potentially discretionary time. This time-cost must be borne also by some of those who live in small planned communities (other than retirement communities) situated near metropolitan centers to which many must journey daily for employment. Again, however, the housing problem is solved.

CONCLUSION

The argument permeating this essay is that the housing question must be examined and carried toward resolution through a systematic approach rather than through the piecemeal approaches of speculators and others who neglect the fundamental importance of macro-habitats and their relations to each other and the larger urban unit. This approach is of increasing significance in an age when discretionary time is increasing and the challenge of the inept may be undergoing intensification, perhaps with Toynbeean implications.[66] It is not inferred that improvement in housing or even in macro-habitats will solve the ills of the day though it may contribute to solutions under appropriate conditions. It is suggested, however, that we are in need of innovation of systematic though diverse arrangements suited to the housing, habitat, and related needs of communities of varying size and situation. It is emphasized finally that our capacity to meet these needs is likely to be inversely related to our rate of population growth.

REFERENCES

1. Doxiadis, "Topics: Of Inhuman and Human Cities," *N.Y. Times*, March 11, 1967, at 28, col. 5. *See generally* on *gemeinschaft and gesellschaft*, T. Parsons, *Structure of Social Action* 686–94 (1937).
2. *See, e.g.*, R. E. Wycherly, *How the Greeks Built Cities* (2d ed. 1962).
3. *Politica* 1:2. *See generally Oeconomica* 1:1, a work partly Aristotelian and partly reflective of the influence of Xenophon and others.
4. *Politica* 1:8–9.
5. *Oeconomica* 1:2.
6. *Id.* at 1:6.
7. Vitruvius, *The Ten Books of Architecture* 24–26, 38–41, 170–92 (M. H. Morgan transl. 1960).
8. *Politica* 7:4.
9. *E.g.*, the excellent account given in J. N. Morgan, I. A. Serageldin & N. Baerwaldt, *Productive Americans* (1966).
10. For example, R. W. Gerard writes: "Man has, in fact, largely cut himself off from the external environment and created a hothouse internal environment of culture in which he lives in remarkable physical comfort. . . . Our lives are spent overwhelmingly at the symbolic level, and we live in a man-made sea of meanings. And the sea is still rising more or less exponentially." Gerard, "Intelligence, Information, and Education," 148 *Sci.* 762, 763 (1965).
11. R. Dubos, *Man Adapting* 279 (1965).
12. An extended inquiry into the relationships between time, space, and activity is being conducted by G. C. Hemmens. A recent progress report is available: The Structure of Urban Activity Linkages, 1966 (mimeo., Center for Urban and Regional Studies, University of North Carolina, Chapel Hill).
13. W. Isard, *Location and Space-Economy* (1956).
14. *Id.* at 24–27.
15. K. J. Arrow, *Social Choice and Individual Values* 9 n.1 (Cowles Comm'n for Research in Economics Monograph No. 12, 1951).

16. *Id.* at 81. "[I]t must be demanded that there be some sort of consensus on the ends of society, or no social welfare functions can be performed." *Id.* at 83.
17. Arrow concludes that "we may expect that social welfare judgments can usually be made when there is both a widespread agreement on the decision process and a widespread agreement on the desirability of everyday decisions." *Id.* at 91.
18. The market mechanism does not always take into account all relevant matters, although it can be manipulated to this end. *See* Arrow's discussion, *id.* at 81–86.
19. For example, a retirement city built outside Sacramento for retired military personnel proved a flop. "[I]t turned out that retired colonels did not like to live beside retired sergeants, and neither liked the idea of living on streets named Billy Mitchell Boulevard and Hap Arnold Court." *Fortune,* Feb. 1966, at 158.
20. *See generally* Platt, "Diversity," 154 *Sci.* 1132 (1966), for a discussion stressing the importance of cultural and other diversity.
21. In the United States, for example, though unifying common values are present, there are also many local communities which, though they include diverse elements, have evolved each into a somewhat unique constellation of values and institutions. *See, e.g.,* R. E. Engler, Jr., *The Challenge of Diversity* (1964).
22. Mishan, "A Survey of Welfare Economics, 1939–59," in 1 *Surveys of Economic Theory* 154, 211–13 (American Economic Ass'n & Royal Economic Soc'y 1965).
23. Bailey, "Effects of Race and of Other Demographic Factors on the Values of Single-Family Homes," 42 *Land Econ.* 215 (1966).
24. *See* J. Rothenberg, *Economic Evaluation of Urban Renewal* (1967); Bailey, "Note on the Economics of Residential Zoning and Urban Renewal," 35 *Land Econ.* 288 (1959); Nourse, "The Economics of Urban Renewal," 42 *Land Econ.* 65 (1966).
25. "The Achilles heel of housing programs has been precisely our insistence that better housing for the black poor be achieved by residential desegregation. This ideal glosses over the importance of the ethnic community as a staging area for groups to build the communal solidarity and power necessary to compel eventual access to the mainstream of urban life. . . .

    "If group conflict is at the root of past failures, strategies must be found to improve ghetto housing without arousing the ire of powerful segments of the white community." Piven & Cloward, "Desegregated Housing, Who Pays for the Reformers' Ideal?," *New Republic,* Dec. 17, 1966, at 17, 21. That this proposal for the improvement of ghettos is not impractical is suggested by the actions of a number of large building supply companies that are rebuilding parts of slums, to be turned over to nonprofit sponsors, and by plans to establish corporations that can produce housing competitive with public housing. *See* Ridgeway, "Rebuilding the Slums," *New Republic,* Jan. 7, 1967, at 22.
26. Perhaps the world's first model village for workmen was that built in Amarna in Egypt in the 14th century, B.C. *See* E. Wells, *Nefertiti* 162–63 (1964).
27. *See* L. Halprin, *Freeways* (1966); Faltermayer, "How to Wage War on Ugliness," *Fortune,* May 1966, at 130; Larremore, "Public Aesthetics," 20 *Harv. L. Rev.* 35 (1906). *See generally* R. Starr, *The Living End: The City and Its Critics* (1966); Spengler, "*The Aesthetics of Population,*" 13 *Population Bull.* 61 (1957).
28. *See generally* on the adverse effects of noise, Beranek, "Noise," *Scientific Am.,* Dec. 1966, at 66; Kryter, "Psychological Reactions to Aircraft Noise," 151 *Sci.* 1346 (1966); "Silence at Less than $35 an Ounce," *Fortune,* Dec. 1966, at 191; "When Noise Annoys," *Time,* Aug. 19, 1966, at 24, and on the destructiveness of the "sonic boom," offset only by an increase in the egg-hatching rate among chickens, *The New Yorker,* Dec. 18, 1965, at 41.
29. Dubos, *supra* note 11, at 209–10. *See generally* Environmental Pollution Panel, President's Science Advisory Committee, *Restoring the Quality of Our Environment* 1–9, 91–111 (Report of the Environmental Pollution Panel, 1965).

30. Dubos, *supra* note 11, at 221. *See generally* B. Commoner, *Science and Survival* (1966); "Ecology," *Time,* Jan. 27, 1967, at 48.
31. Dubos, *supra* note 11, at 225. (Emphasis added.)
32. Commoner, *supra* note 30.
33. *See, e.g., Committee on Pollution, National Research Council, National Academy of Sciences,* Pub. No. 1400, *Waste Management and Control* (1966); Subcomm. on Science Research, and Development, House Comm. on Science and Astronautics, 89th Cong., 2d Sess., *Environmental Pollution — A Challenge to Science and Technology* (Comm. Print 1966).
34. In 1940, 28.8 per cent of the total population and 51 per cent of the urban population lived in places of 100,000 and over. The corresponding percentages in 1960 were 28.4 and 45. I have used the former census definition of "urban" in order to make the data of 1940 comparable with those of 1950 and 1960.
35. U.S. Bureau of the Census, Dep't of Commerce, *Statistical Abstract of the United States 1965,* at 15 (1965); C. Taeuber & I. B. Taeuber, *The Changing Population of the United States* 114–15, 118 (1958).
36. Kendall, "Natural Law in the Social Sciences," 124 *J. The Royal Statistical Soc'y* (ser. A) 1, 4 (1961). *See generally* Isard, *supra* note 13, at 55.
37. G. K. Zipf, *National Unity and Disunity* 55 (1941). In the United States the ratio of New York's population to that of the nation rose between 1880 and 1930 and thereafter fell. *Id.* at 56. I have computed the ratios for 1950 and 1960.
38. The ratio of places to population rose from 100 in 1900 to 115 in 1930, 118 in 1940, and 126 in 1960.
39. W. S. Thompson & D. T. Lewis, *Population Problems* 141–48, 156 (5th ed., 1965).
40. *Id.* at 151–52.
41. *See* Newman, "The Negro's Journey to the City" (pts. 1 & 2), 88 *Monthly Labor Rev.* 502, 644 (1965).
42. *See, e.g.,* Grodzins, "Metropolitan Segregation," *Scientific Am.,* Oct. 1957, at 33; Tauber & Tauber, "White Migration and Socio-Economic Differences Between Cities and Suburbs," 29 *Am. Sociological Rev.* 718 (1964); Winsborough, "An Ecological Approach to the Theory of Suburbanization," 68 *Am. J. Sociology* 565 (1963); Winsborough, "City Growth and City Structure," *J. Regional Sc.,* Winter 1962, at 35.
43. *U.S. News & World Report,* Feb. 21, 1966, at 72–73; *U.S. News & World Report,* March 6, 1967, at 58–62.
44. The fraction that was Negro was slightly smaller than the nonwhite. *See generally* on the suburbanization process, Winsborough, "An Ecological Approach to the Theory of Suburbanization," *supra* note 42.
45. *See U.S. News & World Report,* Feb. 27, 1967, at 68–69.
46. When families earn less than $6,000 per year they tend to put forth extra effort. *See* Morgan, Serageldin, & Baerwaldt, *supra* note 9, at 191. *See generally* on choosing between more work and more leisure, *id.* at 198–202.
47. *See generally* on "maintaining capital intact," A. C. Pigou, *Economics of Welfare* 43–49 (4th ed. 1932).
48. "Ecology," "Time," Jan. 27, 1967, at 48, 49–50; *See generally Restoring the Quality of Our Environment, supra* note 29, at 1–9, 62–69.
49. New York's garbage dumps will be filled in eight years. *N.Y. Times,* Feb. 20, 1967, at 27, col. 1. *See generally* on the water problem, Wolman, "The Metabolism of Cities," *Scientific Am.,* Sept. 1965, at 179, 181–85.
50. Baumol, "Urban Services: Interactions of Public and Private Decisions," in *Public Expenditure Decisions in the Urban Community* 1, 7–8 (H. G. Schaller ed. 1963).
51. *Id.* at 11–14; G. Neutze, *Economic Policy and the Size of Cities* (1965).
52. Clark, "Industrial Location and Economic Potential," *Lloyds Bank Rev.,* Oct. 1966, at 1, 3–4.

53. Bellan, "The Future Growth of Britain's Cities," 37 *The Town Planning Rev.* 173, 183 (1966).
54. *Id.* at 183–84. *See generally* G. P. Wibberley, *Agriculture and Urban Growth* 201–29 (1959).
55. *Purgatory,* Canto I.
56. M. M. Gaffney writes of building taxes as distinguished from land taxes that "It would be hard to contrive a tax calculated to throw more risk onto the builder in proportion to the revenues raised." Gaffney, "Property Taxes and the Frequency of Urban Renewal," in *Proceedings of the Fifty-Seventh Annual Conference on Taxation* 272, 284 (National Tax Ass'n 1964). The builder responds by not making improvements since the assessment of his land moves with the assessment of the structure on it. If, however, land is assessed and taxed at its true opportunity cost, it can no longer be economically allocated to sub-optimal uses. *See id.* at 272–85. *See generally* Woodruff & Ecker-Raoz, "Property Taxes and Land Use Patterns in Australia and New Zealand," *The Tax Executive,* Oct. 1965, at 16.
57. Spilhaus, "The Experimental City," *The News and Observer* (Raleigh, N.C.), Jan. 22, 1967, 3, at 1.
58. *See, e.g.,* Ogden, "Economic Analysis of Air Pollution," 42 *Land Econ.* 137 (1966).
59. A. Lösch, *The Economics of Location* 258, 330–31 (1954).
60. "Big Business in American Society, Is It Really Taking Over?," *Business in Brief* (Chase Manhattan Bank), Oct. 1966.
61. North Eastern Illinois Planning Commission, *Metropolitan Planning Guide Lines, Commercial Structure* 94, *cited in* Clark, *supra* note 52, at 3.
62. *See* Lapp, "Where the Brains Are," *Fortune,* March 1966, at 154.
63. In 1960, 40% of the population was in the labor force. Given lower fertility this fraction might rise slightly.
64. "The Birth of a City," *The Humble Way,* No. 4, 1963, at 1–3.
65. S. L. Udall, *The Quiet Crisis* 170 (1963).
66. *See* Goode, "The Protection of the Inept," 32 *Am. Sociological Rev.* 5 (1967). *See generally* on the internal proletariat, 5 A. Toynbee, *A Study of History* 58–194 (1939).

11 The Tenement Landlord: Lessons from Newark

GEORGE STERNLIEB
Rutgers University

The problems associated with residential property ownership in slum areas are enormous: buildings are old; city building codes, out of date; speculators' requests for ruinous zoning changes, a constant threat. Some city fathers have considered

From *The Tenement Landlord,* by George Sternlieb, New Brunswick: Rutgers University Press, 1969, pp. 225–235. Reprinted with permission.

stringent regulation of landlords through code enforcement or licensing systems. Almost all agree that, unless they implement a wide range of programs to assist, as well as regulate, landlords, they can expect little progress.

The entangled mesh of ownership patterns, of changes in the form and function of the older city and the folkways of its inhabitants, the great migration patterns which have dominated the demographic considerations in and about the United States metropolitan areas, the rising standards of expectation, all provide the matrix within which . . . data (on tenement landlords) must take form. Any efforts at improving attitudes toward slum maintenance and rehabilitation must in turn take this matrix into account, or prove unsuccessful.

The present market situation is one of virtual stagnation in the hardcore slum areas. The combination of risk, decreasing profitability, and loss of potential for capital gains has substantially restricted the kinds of professional owners who are willing to invest in slum properties. It takes a highly insensitive individual to become a professional nonresident owner of slum property, in the light of present societal attitudes. This is not an individual who is easily influenced to invest his money unless an appropriate return can be secured. Given the relative weakness of the slum apartment market, a weakness which has been aided in Newark's case by substantial amounts of public housing, as well as the shifts out of the central city . . . the professional landlord has been faced with the choice of basically two alternatives: to stand pat and not increase his investment, or to attempt to improve his parcel in order to secure higher rentals.

The pattern that was observed in the course of this study indicates that the choice substantially has been the former. The observer cannot fail to be struck by the "heads you win, tails we lose" nature of this phenomenon. When the apartment market is very strong the landlord need not improve; when the apartment market is very weak the landlord fears for his investment and does not improve. What can municipal authorities use to break this impasse? Code enforcement is the usual reply. Code enforcement, however, must be, as will be noted later in more detail, accompanied by financing help and tax reassurance. Without this accompaniment it will merely lead to wholesale evasion and corruption. Before pursuing these matters in more detail, it is essential that the basic question be resolved — what the city, as a reflection of society, is or should be doing with slums and their occupants.

WHAT IS, OR SHOULD BE, THE CITIES' ATTITUDE TOWARD SLUMS AND SLUM DWELLERS?

If this writer may be permitted a gross oversimplification, the problem of the slums is one both of plumbing and morale. It has largely been viewed in the past as consisting solely of plumbing. This is not to denigrate the former; but the provision of appropriate housing amenities is certainly an essential step toward improving the outlook and aspiration level of slum dwellers. However, the morale problem cannot be cured merely by providing physical amenities. The relatively limited success of public housing bears testimony on this point.

Government policy towards the slums must have as its primary aim the improvement of the aspiration level and capacity for goal realization of the slums' inhabitants. Tax policy, code enforcement, financing aid, and municipal services; all of these must be viewed within the context of the overall objective.

The community must face the realities of the slum situation fairly, without self-deception or romanticism, and at the same time move for change. A review of slum conditions as they exist is in order.

1. In Newark, as in many other Northern industrial cities, the overwhelming majority of hard-core slum area residents are Negroes. The whites, who continue to decrease in number, are typically an elderly remnant of earlier immigration.
2. There is little evidence of a substantial return of the white middle class to the slum areas of the city.
3. A substantial proportion of slum tenements are owned by absentee white owners. These owners are not merely absentees from the slums per se, they are also absentees, at least as residents, from the city in which they own property.
4. The factor of ownership is the single most basic variable which accounts for variations in the maintenance of slum properties. Good parcel maintenance typically is a function of resident ownership.
5. Dependent upon major programs of land clearance for purposes of urban renewal and/or highway construction, a population vacuum will develop in the slums. The tidal wave of Southern Negro migration has slowed down and is substantially bypassing some of the Northern cities which were its traditional goals.[1] With virtual stability in the Puerto Rican population size, there is no new depressed group on the horizon to fill the older slums.
6. While this population decrease makes the problem of relocation much simpler, it also tends to limit the landlords' capacity and will to improve parcels.
7. Given a substantial dependence upon land taxes in the face of increased demands upon the municipality for services, taxes have become a major inhibitor of entrepreneurial activity in the central city. Both in terms of their impact, and in terms of the uncertainty which surround their administration, current municipal tax policies are leading to further degeneration of the slums.
8. The relationship of client and patron, which plays a dominant role in the dealings between government, both municipal and federal, and the poor population of the slums, is deleterious to the morale of the individuals concerned.

Within these parameters are there policies which would improve present slum conditions, both in terms of buildings and of people? Over the past year a whole armory of enabling legislation has been passed by Congress. Local authorities have been given the essential weapons for the fight against blight and for better housing conditions. The Housing and Urban Development Act of 1965 is indicative of the growing sophistication of government policies in rehabilitation. From a direct loan program, which provides long-term 3 per cent loans, to the rehabilitation grant procedure under section 115 of Title I of the 1964 act, and to the demolition grant and aid to code enforcement divisions, a vast armory has been supplied to local authority.[2]

It should be stressed that the enabling legislation mentioned above is strictly that — enabling legislation. It remains for local authority to take the initiative in implementing programs which will take advantage of this legislation. There are certain to be many difficulties on the road to implementing this legislation. There is no new legislation that does not require some degree of experience in its utilization. Certainly, however, the community is better armed for rehabilitation than has ever before been the case.

The discussion which follows will focus first on the development of resident landlords, and the ancillary elements which this will require, such as guidance and financing arrangements, as well as tax policy. From this the discussion turns to the question of municipal services and the problem of the hard-core slum and code enforcement.

BOOSTING THE PROPORTION OF RESIDENT LANDLORDS IN SLUM TENEMENTS

. . . *There is no question of the significance of landlord residence, particularly of single-parcel landlords, as insurance of proper maintenance of slum tenements.* Given the priority accorded by multiple-parcel owners to tenant problems as an inhibitor . . . the lack of feeling on this score by resident landlords, coupled with their good record in maintenance, is most significant. *It is the resident landlord, and only the resident landlord, who is in a position to properly screen and supervise his tenantry. No one-shot wave of maintenance and paint-up sweep-up campaign can provide the day-to-day maintenance which is required in slum areas.* Given the relatively small size of Newark tenement units, and others like them, this can only be accomplished by a resident landlord. The record of these landlords, as we have indicated, is such as to inspire confidence in their future behavior on this score.

By making it feasible for more residents to become owners, we further encourage the development of local leadership which is so sorely lacking in most slums. The role of resident owners as guides and creators of life patterns for the youth of the slums to follow is clearly evident.[3]

How could this type of development be stimulated? There are several prime requirements. The first of these, obviously, is financing help. In Exhibit 1 is presented a table which indicates cash flow requirements as a function of mortgage term and interest rates. As can be noted in the Exhibit, the term of mortgages is much more significant from a cash flow point of view than are interest rates. For example, a mortgage at 6 per cent which is written for a fifteen-year period imposes a smaller cash flow burden than an equivalent size mortgage for ten-year period at 3.5 per cent. Given the dearth of available financing, which is currently the case in the slums, there is obviously no alternative but to provide something in the way of longterm FHA guaranteed mortgages for slum tenement purchases *by residents.* The analogy with the early Homestead Act springs readily to mind. In that case, government lands were provided at relatively reasonable rates and with liberal financing to those who would live on them. The same thing must be done in the slums. The 1965 Housing Act is a beginning on the road.

With this must be coupled inexpensive fire and liability insurance for resident owners in slum areas. The expense and difficulty of securing these necessities is rising rapidly and it strikes hardest upon the poor landlord who has limited leverage with an underwriter.

Financing, however, is merely one of the several steps which is required. . . . (Consider) the *storm window syndrome.* This is . . . one symptom of the frequent victimization of relatively innocent new resident buyers of slum tenements by a variety of home improvement services. The pride of these people in ownership makes them easy marks for "pay later" operators. The point raised by a money lender interviewed in the course of this study should be kept in sight here.

Exhibit 1

Monthly Level Payments Required to Amortize $1,000 over Various Terms and at Various Interest Rates

Interest Rate (per cent)	Term (in Years)						
	10	15	20	25	30	35	40
6.0	$11.10	$8.44	$7.16	$6.44	$6.00	$5.70	$5.50
5.5	10.85	8.17	6.88	6.14	5.68	5.37	5.16
5.0	10.61	7.91	6.60	5.85	5.37	5.05	4.82
4.5	10.36	7.65	6.33	5.56	5.07	4.73	4.50
4.0	10.12	7.40	6.06	5.28	4.77	4.43	4.18
3.5	9.89	7.15	5.80	5.01	4.49	4.13	3.87

Source: Ernest M. Fisher, *Urban Real Estate Markets: Characteristics and Financing* (N.Y.C.: National Bureau of Economic Research, 1951), p. 71.

He pointed to the fact that commonly when he has to repossess a parcel, the typical cause is that the owner has burdened the parcel with two or more home improvement loans. Just as the Agriculture Department provides a variety of advisory services for the farmer, so the city and/or the Federal Government must provide equivalent advisory services for the new home owners in the slum areas. These advisors must be competent not merely in home improvements, but also in financing and appraising parcels. It would seem entirely possible that among the ranks of senior savings and loan people, as well as within the ranks of the present FHA personnel, such individuals could be found. Technical competence, however, must be linked with a basic sympathy with the aspiration level of the new owner and with none of the *deus ex machina* attitude that so often exists in government relations with the poor.

The question of tax policy is a most significant one on this score, as it is in terms of the general problem of slums. It may well behoove the city to continue its policy of full assessment based upon market values. Obviously, where broad-based taxation is available on a basis other than land, it may reduce some of the strain. Reassessment policy, however, must be more clearly defined than is presently the case. The landlord should have no reason to fear city reassessment merely because of painting the outside of his house.

It is essential that the city not merely adopt a more reasonable attitude toward taxation, but also *sell* the facts of this attitude to those who may be influenced by misconceptions as to its reality. In addition, in the long run it may very well pay the city to provide the equivalent of homestead rebates for resident landlords. This is a format (which will be recognized by those readers who are familiar for example, with tax policy in a city such as Miami Beach) in which the homesteader, i.e. the resident landlord, receives either a reduction or a rebate in his real estate taxes. This might well be coupled with a stipulation that the rebate be employed in the improvement of the parcel in question. The area of uncertainty and suspicion which surrounds current taxing procedures must be clarified. Its existence clearly inhibits improvements . . . (We must remember) the fears of landlords on municipal tax policy. *This fear has been justified frequently in fact because* of the financial bind of a municipality dependent on realty taxes in the face of expanding needs and a static base. In these circumstances, pressure on the landlord's pocket is a constant. While . . . tax relief in itself will not generate improvement — it is an essential step toward fostering it. Alternative means of financing municipal needs, therefore, must be found.

MUNICIPAL SERVICES

There seems to be ample evidence that the level of municipal services required by the slum areas is higher than that required by nonslum equivalent areas. At the same time there is reason to believe that the actual delivery level of these services is reversed with poorer areas being slighted. The comments of a Negro owner on this subject are most apropos.

> Parcel #330 was purchased in 1935. "You know the neighborhood has really changed terribly since we moved in here. At first it was mostly German and Jewish, and the police in the city took care of things. No trucks parked overnight in the streets and no noise or anything like that. Now there is mostly Negro and they don't seem to come any more. If you complain they want to put you in jail. — Many of the owners here would like to stay, but the neighborhood is run down so that most of them sell just to get away. Since Negroes have become predominant, the city has allowed things that they would not allow when I just first moved here."

One should notice that the parcel was very well maintained. The owner commented that he was sure that continued municipal surveillance would have saved the neighborhood regardless of who moved in. The backyard of this parcel which has a very handsome garden, looks out upon a sea of debris. The owners complain that they have had to screen their back porches to keep the rats out. Another Negro landlord made the following comment:

> "When I went to complain to the police department about overnight truck parking and teenage hoodlums on the block, the cops made me feel like a criminal. I was glad to go home and kind of hide myself behind the door."

These comments mirror attitudes which are most common among current resident landlords.

Every effort must be made by the city to provide an optimum level of services within the slums. Such functions as police protection, street lighting, parking restrictions, garbage collection, and a host of others could be named here. Not least among these is the question of educational facilities. While this is a subject whose depth is beyond the scope of this study, it cannot be omitted. Without substantial efforts on all of these fronts, the efforts at rehabilitating the slums must falter.

THE FUTURE OF THE HARD-CORE SLUM

. . . There are clear-cut indications that new resident buyers are unwilling to move into an area which is . . . (already seriously blighted). The dominance of large-scale absentee landlordism in that area is a tribute to the fact that they are the only landlords who are willing to invest in such problem situations. One can seriously question the potential of such an area for rehabilitation. Given the relatively loose housing market, which presently exists in center-city Newark, the bulldozer approach to such hard-core areas would seem to be the only answer. This should not wait upon redevelopers. The existence of such hard-core blight (. . . the area in question has less than 25 per cent sound housing on the basis of the 1960 Census) can only serve to drag down the neighborhoods peripheral to it.

The loss of tax revenue to the municipality through this process of demolition must be accepted as surgery essential to preserve the surrounding areas from the spread of deep-seated blight. Obviously, the scale of this blight will require considerable discretion on the part of municipal authorities on the phasing and speed of demolition. Given the present functioning of the market, as has been indicated earlier, private enterprise cannot be depended on to remove buildings which are no longer usable. Again, new urban renewal legislation to ease this process was adopted in 1965, it must be vigorously utilized.

There is some question whether a change in tax policy to encourage demolition might not be in order. The needs of the city for more open space, the potential of already assembled and cleared substantial size tracts in encouraging further development, must be depended upon to generate future use for the areas in question. The maintenance of the hard-core blight areas, given the facts of alternative housing availability, cannot be justified upon tax income reasons alone.

CODE ENFORCEMENT

Parallel with all of the suggestions above is the requirement that code enforcement be made much more rigorous. But prior to this, there is required a much more adequate definition of just what the code should be. For example, the requirement of central heat is observed least in some of the better housing areas. . . . It is not uncommon, particularly among members of earlier immigrant groups, that cold-water flats with suitable decentralized heating facilities are preferred to those whose heat supply is subject to the administration of the landlord and of the vagaries of the heating system. *Adequate insect and rodent control, plumbing that works, paint, and general cleanliness may be much more significant to the inhabitants of a tenement both physically and spiritually than the existence of central heat or plaster walls.* Whether the studs used in a repair are 16 inches on center or are 20 inches on center may be completely irrelevant to a tenant. A building which is completely satisfactory on the basis of existing codes, may be completely unsatisfactory in terms of its effect upon its occupants.

Code enforcement, therefore, must require a much more subjective approach than has previously been the case. This is particularly the case with those buildings in the hands of landlords who cannot afford repairs. In these cases, it may be necessary to work out a long-term plan of rehabilitating the parcel in question, with major emphasis being given to the paint and cleanliness functions, those most easily encompassed by "sweat equity." Good maintenance and resident landlordism are much more significant than mechanical adherence to a mechanical code. With the legality of multiple housing codes clarified, the city has a new avenue of creative action.

The responsibility of social workers to appreciate the fact that the loose housing market does enable them to move their clients "up" into better quarters is clear, though far from universally acted on. At least one of the major owners interviewed for this study is upgrading his parcels for welfare tenants whose housing allowances have been "opened up" slightly and who have alert social workers as guides.

NO FALSE ROMANTICISM!

The self-help capacity of the poor is limited. Some resident landlords are elderly, others are uneducated, and some lack an appropriate aspiration level. The fact remains, however, that as a group, they are presently the best landlords in the slums, and provide probably the major hope for better maintenance in the future. It will require a talented and understanding guidance operation to help generate landlord enthusiasm while restraining over-expenditure. The problems here should not be underestimated. It is essential if this operation is to be truly successful, particularly from a morale standpoint, and also from the standpoint of securing *long-run* improvement, that the advisory service be a guide and an inspiration, not a directorate.

The present and future strains on the municipalities' budget, coupled with limited increases in revenue, will make it most difficult to pay for the services which are required. The alternative, however, of increasing degeneration is all too clear-cut. From a fiscal point of view, the program outlined above is a most burdensome one; this point should not be evaded. There is no other answer, however, from the city's point of view.

Tax policy must be directed toward aiding the good landlord, and penalizing those owners who do not properly maintain their properties. A tax policy based on sales value can easily have the reverse effect. The potential of homestead exemption, of rigorous code enforcement, and of self-help stimulating devices, must be rigorously exploited.

REHABILITATION AND RENT INCREASES

There is a well-founded fear on the part of the tenantry that rehabilitation leads to rent increases. This must be accepted as a fact of the market. Although tax policy can somewhat relieve this factor, particularly when coupled with more adequate financing, this fact should be faced. *The potential of rent subsidies for the underincomed with which to pay better rents is quite clear here. There is no substitute for this approach. This is not to underestimate the value of code enforcement — but rather to add a carrot to the stick. There is more positive achievement by making rehabilitation profitable than in attempting to secure it through punitive measures.* The reward in terms of the aspiration level and general morale of the slum dweller will, I think, outweigh the cost. This is particularly true when the cost/benefits are contrasted with those of institutionalized public housing.

The key to improving the slums from a "people" point of view, is the creation of a resident responsible middle class within those areas— not a middle class which while physically in the area does not belong to it, as is the case with the efforts to create new middle class housing within slum areas cleared by urban renewal. This has no organic unity with the tenements per se, and can only provide frustration rather than leadership and emulation. These goals can best be accomplished and living conditions within the slum areas most enhanced by increasing the number of owner residents of slum tenements. This will require a highly coordinated effort in terms of tax policy, financing help, code enforcement, and advisory services. The rewards of a successful program are very great. The cost of present policies are equally evident.

REFERENCES

1. The nonwhite population of the United States is continuing to leave the South, but the outflow has been slowed considerably. Out-migration of Negroes from the South has averaged little more than seventy thousand per year in the period from 1960 to 1963, or only half that of the 1950 to 1960 period. This is based on a study done by the Metropolitan Life Insurance Company. See MLIC, *Statistical Bulletin*, April 1965, p. 3.
2. See H.H.F.A., *Local Public Agency Letters* 340, 341, 342, 343, 345, & 349 [Washington, 1965].
3. Given the lack of a masculine image which has been commented on as a not unfamiliar shortcoming of family upbringing among the poor, the significance of a resident owner *peer unter pares* to slum youth as a potential goal setter is clear-cut.

12 Urban Renewal:
Weapon Against Slums

MAXWELL STEWART
Public Affairs Committee

A definition of, and some of the "ground rules" for, urban renewal.

The 1949 Housing Act provided federal encouragement for . . . (slum clearance programs). Title I of the Act authorized grants totaling $500 million to local authorities for urban redevelopment. The aid was limited to projects for the clearance of residential slums, where families were relocated, or new housing. After an extensive study in 1953 by a President's Advisory Committee, this program was enlarged and strengthened by passage of the Housing Act of 1954. This Act emphasized as its central concept the task of "urban renewal," a term used for the first time. This involved clearance, conservation, and rehabilitation. And the Act authorized the use of 10 per cent of a new appropriation for non-residential projects. The figure was later raised in stages to 30 per cent. To supervise the broadened program, an Urban Renewal Administration was created as a part of the Housing and Home Finance Agency.

A new program of FHA mortgage insurance was also set up by the 1954 Act to be used in rehabilitating older housing and building new housing inside and outside urban renewal areas.

The basic idea developed in these two pieces of legislation was a new one in this country. To make urban renewal possible, the federal government under-

---

From *Can We Save Our Cities?*, by Maxwell Stewart, New York: Public Affairs Committee, Inc., 1965, pp. 5–14. Reprinted with permission.

took to pay two-thirds of the net cost of the project, including the cost of purchasing the slum property, the provision of sewers, streets, and other needed improvements, and the clearance of the land for resale in accordance with a carefully worked-out plan. The buildings on the slum property are torn down. Then the land is sold at fair value to private developers who will build according to the plan or it is converted to public use. Credits were later provided for such uses as expansion of hospital or university facilities. After the project is completed, the city may benefit financially from sharp increases in tax assessments on the revitalized area.

In 1961, at the urging of President John F. Kennedy, Congress further broadened the urban renewal program and increased the amount of money available to our cities for low and middle income housing. Greater emphasis was placed on rehabilitation of sound older buildings as well as on revitalizing the business sections of the central cities and on planning for whole metropolitan areas, including both the city and the suburbs.

In 1964 the existing relocation payments available under urban renewal were supplemented to include a rent subsidy to help displaced families after they move into new quarters. Then, in March, 1965, President Lyndon B. Johnson sent a special message to Congress urging the use of urban renewal and public housing funds to aid low income families by repairing homes, and the payment of a new federal rent supplement to lower and moderate income families so they can afford decent housing.

HOW URBAN RENEWAL WORKS

The key to the whole urban renewal program lies in the use of federal funds to stimulate communities to tackle the problems of blight by enlisting private financial resources. The initial impetus may come from civic-minded local citizens. Anyone can start the ball rolling. It may be a local banker, a neighborhood group, a citizen's committee organized by the chamber of commerce, or a social work team. The emphasis on local initiative and local planning has been one of the greatest strengths of the program.

SELECTION OF PROJECTS

The conditions under which an area in a city may be selected for redevelopment have been clearly set forth by state law and the regulations of the Urban Renewal Administration. It must be an area in which blighted conditions predominate; there must be a plan for re-use of the land; and the plan for use of the land must be consistent with the general plans of the community or city. The land may be used for housing, for commercial buildings or for industry, or for institutional purposes, if consistent with a city's overall urban plan and zoning ordinances.

The local governing body must formally declare that the area selected is a slum, a blighted, deteriorated, or deteriorating area, and support its statement by specific information on the buildings and as much information as possible on the neighborhood. This information is submitted to the Urban Renewal Administration in a preliminary application and, if it is approved, specific planning is begun by a "local public agency" created for this purpose. Such agencies have various names, the most common being "redevelopment agency," "planning board," or "housing authority." Or the local government may handle the task itself.

WORKABLE PROGRAM REQUIRED

Since 1954, the cities have been required to submit a Workable Program for Community Improvement before renewal funds can be appropriated. This comprehensive document is intended to give reasonable assurance of the success of the renewal project by making certain that the community has a program to back up the project. The Workable Program must include evidence that local housing codes and ordinances setting up standards of health and safety have been enacted and are being enforced together with an analysis of the neighborhoods in the community, identifying those which are blighted. There must also be a comprehensive plan for land use, thoroughfares, and community facilities. Zoning ordinance and subdivision regulations must be submitted. Required also are: estimates of the financial resources that can be tapped for renewal; information on the cost of the properties to be acquired; a description of the local government's administrative setup; assurance that all groups within the community have been informed of and, so far as possible, participate in the renewal planning; detailed data on housing resources available for displaced families.

STANDARDS FOR RELOCATION

The federal authorities have been particularly insistent on adequate planning for relocation of displaced families. This necessitates not only interviews with the families concerned, but a survey of the vacant housing that might be used. Local standards must be established for decent, safe, and sanitary housing for the displaced families. If there are not enough satisfactory housing units available, plans must be made to provide them. Experience has shown that help in relocating business concerns dislocated by the project is also extremely important.

If the local agency wants to rehabilitate rather than clear the area, a building-by-building study is required. It is also necessary to study the financial situations of the owners to determine their ability to make the necessary investments, and to find out whether local financial institutions can provide needed funds.

If the area is to be cleared, estimates must be prepared on the costs of demolition and grading and the provision of new streets and utilities. With this and such other information as may be necessary, the local agency must draw up a formal Urban Renewal Plan. This must be submitted to the local governing body and approved before submission to the federal government.

FEDERAL FINANCING

Several types of federal financial assistance are available for an urban renewal project. (1) *Advances* may be made for the preparation of the project plan. Subsequently, the planning costs are absorbed in the overall cost of the project. (2) *Temporary Loans* provide working capital for carrying out the project. These funds may be obtained through the sale of federally-guaranteed notes to fiscal institutions. (3) The federal government will make *grants* to cover two-thirds (three-fourths in small communities) of net cost (including administration) of slum property purchased by local authorities, torn down, and subsequently sold. The local community is expected to cover the remainder. (4) The federal government bears the entire cost of *relocation grants* to reimburse dislocated families and businesses for the expense of moving or for loss of property.

Two and a half billion in federal funds have been committed in urban renewal and another two billion reserved, but the federal contribution is dwarfed by the private investment that has been attracted. Thus far, excluding the land, approximately $6.90 of private investment has been made for every $1 of federal grants.

GETTING UNDER WAY

After the Urban Renewal Plan has been approved and the financial arrangements made, the project is well underway. The next task is the acquisition of the properties in the project. This is done by negotiation and purchase when possible, but condemnation proceedings are used if necessary. A relocation service is set up as soon as possible to find homes for displaced families.

The demolition is normally carried out by private contractors, and the site may be prepared either by a contractor or a public agency. When the site has been cleared, work on the planned improvements is started, and the renewal agency advertises the availability of the land for private construction in accordance with its basic plan. Potential developers must then raise funds from private sources to finance the actual construction. Mortgages must be available for the long haul since few projects will be immediately profitable.

HOUSING USES

Since private investment funds are not likely to be forthcoming if there is no definite prospect of sizable profit, it is understandable that many of the early plans envisioned luxury housing, or commercial or industrial use. Thus, except for a few public housing projects, comparatively few new housing units were provided for the dispossessed families. Many of these families did, however, obtain space in neighboring public housing projects. Unfortunately, Congress has never been willing to appropriate enough funds for the Public Housing Administration to subsidize all the low-cost housing units that are needed.

MIDDLE-INCOME HOUSING

Under a program authorized by the Housing Act of 1954 — intended primarily to promote construction of moderate income housing for relocation of families from urban renewal areas, but also for similar construction in renewal project areas — 163,312 dwelling units had been underwritten by the FHA as of the end of 1964.

The Housing Act of 1961 went a step further and provided for low-interest federal mortgage insurance to nonprofit organizations for the construction of middle income housing on or off renewal sites. Some sites that otherwise might have temporarily remained idle because of lack of demand for luxury housing were thus utilized.

REHABILITATION

Originally, most urban renewal sites were completely cleared to make way for new buildings, but by the middle of the 1950's it became apparent that complete clearance was not always necessary in many of the areas selected for renewal. Some "blighted areas" were in such dilapidated condition that there was little choice but to tear down the old buildings and use the cleared areas for new projects. However, there were also numerous areas in which the older and deteriorating homes were still basically sound and could be repaired and refurbished. In many instances these were sections where neighborhood feeling was strong and the residents — often of a single nationality — were deeply attached to their homes. Such families usually were interested in fixing up their homes but believed it hard to obtain long-term mortgage funds to do so. Many of them simply did not know what was needed or how to go about getting the job done.

The 1954 Housing Act opened up a way of rehabilitating such areas without destroying all existing housing, although much remains to be learned. Later, with more flexible rehabilitation standards on the part of the Federal Housing Administration, long-term loans for rehabilitation were made available to the owners in renewal areas. As part of a program motivating neighborhood improvement and services, the owners also receive skilled guidance with respect to design and construction.

Adequate financing is the key to this rehabilitation program. Fortunately, many of the homes in the older parts of our cities were financed many years ago, and their mortgages have only a short period to run. So it is possible in these instances to arrange a moderately substantial new loan and provide for it to be repaid over a period of years by payments no larger than have been carried in the past. FHA mortgage insurance has also been an important factor in enabling owners to refinance their mortgages and thus pay for substantial property improvements. But it is still a fact that many low income families simply do not have the resources for the necessary rehabilitation, and federal funds have thus far been made available only on an experimental basis.

In addition, under the Housing Act of 1961, nonprofit organizations may apply to the FHA for loans to finance the rehabilitation of apartment houses for rental to middle income families.

MAGNITUDE OF PROGRAM

Because of its complexity, the urban renewal program was slow in getting started. Only large cities were interested at first, and even these lacked the experience in clearance and relocation to overcome all the obstacles that had to be overcome. Urban renewal was, in a sense, a new industry. It took years to tool up, organize adequate staff, obtain the necessary supporting state legislation, and deal with the varied roadblocks thrown up by the opposition. But following the 1954 revision of the Housing Act, and particularly after the passage of the much improved 1961 Act, urban renewal projects multiplied rapidly and many more smaller cities began submitting proposals. By the middle of 1964 some 1,500 urban renewal projects were underway or completed in nearly 750 towns and cities. More than 67,000 dwelling units had been completed on urban renewal sites and 100,000 more were being built.

Rehabilitation projects have also been speeded up in recent years. By the middle of 1964 some 187,000 dwelling units had been scheduled for rehabilitation in urban renewal areas; rehabilitation of about 39,000 had been completed.

These figures reflect the *direct* effect of urban renewal. Statistics are meager on the indirect effects. Any visitor to a neighborhood where an urban renewal project has been completed, however, will notice that many of the buildings on the periphery have been rehabilitated as well. Property values in adjacent areas have been considerably enhanced, and there has frequently been a considerable amount of new construction. It is, of course, one of the basic assumptions of the urban renewal program that the use of government funds to eliminate the worst blight will, like a pebble thrown in the water, gradually spread in ever-widening circles to improve living conditions in surrounding areas.

13 Housing Segregation, Negro Employment and Metropolitan Decentralization: An Alternative Perspective

JOSEPH D. MOONEY[1]
University of Michigan

The explosive growth of our cities has led to the expansion of attractive suburbs for white people and to old and crowded city areas for blacks and other minorities. Unfortunately for male minority workers, most of the factory jobs move along with the suburbs — to the outer fringes of metropolitan areas. At the same time, service jobs, likely ones for female minority workers, increase in the central city. Conclusion: if these trends continue, a matriarchal society, already emergent, will dominate the central city ghettoes.

I. INTRODUCTION

In the May 1968 issue of this *Journal* (*Quarterly Journal of Economics*) John Kain wrote a pioneering article on a subject which had concerned me for some time.[2] Although the objectives of our separate and independent research efforts were the same, the mode of testing similar hypotheses is quite different. Whereas Kain examines only Detroit and Chicago, this study examines the twenty-five largest Standard Metropolitan Statistical Areas (SMSA's). The reader who examines both articles will note many other substantive and methodological differences as well. In those instances where our research objectives were the same, my results generally support Professor Kain's results. My paper, however, does contain additional results not included in Kain's paper. In sum, this paper is presented not as a critique

From "Housing Segregation, Negro Employment and Metropolitan Decentralization: An Alternative Perspective," by Joseph D. Mooney, *The Quarterly Journal of Economics,* Volume 83, Number 2, May 1969, pp. 299–311. Reprinted with permission.

of Kain's research, but as a piece of empirical research on an important topic from an alternative perspective.

Over the past four years, the United States has witnessed a tragic succession of devastating riots and civil disturbances in the predominantly Negro neighborhoods of many of our largest cities. The causes of the riots have been examined in a number of reports.[3] Causes aside, one possible effect may be a further acceleration of the exodus of employers out of the central city to the suburbs. For a variety of reasons, the post World War II period has witnessed a decline in the role of the central city as a *situs* of employment relative to the surrounding metropolitan ring. For an even longer period, the central city has been the major "haven" for large numbers of Negro in-migrants, particularly from the rural South. As a result of their low incomes and a certain degree of racial discrimination in the housing market, urban Negroes (migrants and "natives") have been largely constrained in their choice of residences to particular areas of the central city. There are some exceptions to this latter generalization (e.g., Mt. Vernon outside New York City and Chester, Pennsylvania outside Philadelphia have substantial Negro populations), but they are few in number. The central city concentration of Negroes has to some extent isolated them from growing employment centers — namely the suburbs and ring areas of metropolitan regions. How much effect has this geographic separation had on the employment conditions of Negroes in the ghettos? The latter is the basic problem analyzed in this paper.

Section II briefly describes the major employment changes in twenty-five of America's largest cities during the postwar period. Section III outlines the salient aspects of Negro population changes in these cities. Section IV presents the model used to test for the existence and magnitude of the effects of decentralization of urban unemployment on Negro employment opportunities. Section V contains the empirical results, and Section VI is a discussion of the major implications and conclusions of these results.

II. CHANGES IN EMPLOYMENT PATTERNS

The twenty-five metropolitan areas chosen for analysis in this paper are those cities with the largest Negro populations in 1960 *for which all the relevant data were available*. For all practical purposes, they constitute the twenty-five largest SMSA's in the country.[4]

The shift of employment out of central cities to the suburbs is a phenomenon that has been recognized by previous investigators — particularly the change in location of the manufacturing sector.[5] This primarily descriptive section brings the decentralization story up to date (i.e., through 1963) and it includes data on certain employment sectors which do not appear to be following the decentralization pattern to the same degree as certain others.

Table 1 gives an aggregate picture of employment changes within central cities and fringe areas for four major sectors for the period, 1948–63.[6] Briefly, the highlights of Table 1 are as follows:

(i) Generally, there has been a decline in central city employment in every sector except selected services.

(ii) More specifically, the sharpest declines in central city employment were registered in the manufacturing sector ($-338,952$) and retail trade ($-249,798$).

(iii) Conversely, the sectors in the fringe areas which exhibited the most dramatic increases were manufacturing (+959,458) and retail trade (+539,487).

(iv) In 1948 the percentage of all jobs in the twenty-five SMSA's which were located in the central city was 67.8. By 1963 this percentage had fallen to 59.2.

Probably the most disturbing statistic in Table 1, as far as the economic outlook of our largest central cities is concerned, relates to the decline of the manufacturing sector. The decline of the retail trade sector in the central cities can largely be explained as the result of the large growth in suburban and fringe area populations. To some extent the latter explanation pertains to the wholesale trade sector also. The shift in the location of manufacturing employment, however, needs to be explained by a more complex set of factors. Cheaper and more available land, changes in plant design, expansion of the urban highway system, available labor supply, and increased utilization of trucks relative to railroads as the major means of interurban transportation have all contributed to the rise of fringe areas as sites for manufacturing plants and the concomitant decline of central cities.

The aggregate figures in Table 1, however, mask a variety of employment patterns for individual cities. The fraction of SMSA total employment which is located in the central city has remained quite high in a number of southern cities such as Dallas, Houston, and Atlanta as a result of inner city growth and annexations. Certain other cities such as Boston and Pittsburgh have experienced decentralized employment patterns for several decades now. Still others, such as Cleveland, Chicago, Detroit, Baltimore, and St. Louis have witnessed a very sharp decline in the percentage of total SMSA employment located in the central city during this postwar period.

Table 2 provides data on employment changes in the *central counties* of the same twenty-five SMSA's from 1948 to 1964. The figures in Table 2 pertain only to the following areas — finance, insurance and real estate, contract construction, and public utilities. Central counties rather than central cities are used as the geographic base because these data are taken from the *County Business Patterns* publications prepared by the Social Security Administration (SSA). This latter survey covers only insured employment and does not break down the data by central city. For "historical" reasons, the *Census of Business* does not survey the employment sectors listed in Table 2.

Although the geographic boundaries of the central counties often do not coincide exactly with the boundaries of the central cities, the data in Table 2 depict one important change in the employment pattern of the urban core areas.[7] The finance, insurance and real estate sector has shown a very marked increase in total employment of 442,789 in the postwar period. Cyclical and seasonal factors make it difficult to interpret the increase in construction employment. The rise in public utilities employment is probably highly correlated with the general population increase. It is noteworthy that the two (selected services, and finance, insurance and real estate) employment sectors within or around the central city which have exhibited the most impressive increases in employment are to a large extent employers of female help. Of all industrial sectors, these two industries have by far the largest percentages of female employees. Succinctly, it would appear that central city labor markets are becoming in relative terms more likely sources of employment for females than for males. I shall return to this point in a later section.

Table 1

Employment Totals in 25 Major SMSA's, 1948–1963, by Sector

SECTOR OF EMPLOYMENT	TOTALS CENTRAL CITIES	FRINGE AREAS	CENTRAL CITY EMPLOYMENT AS A % OF SMSA EMPLOYMENT
Wholesale Trade			
1948	1,138,735	116,414	(90.7)
1963	1,103,250	370,268	(74.8)
Selected Services			
1948	823,721	214,221	(79.4)
1963	1,125,353	454,652	(71.2)
Retail Ttrade			
1948	2,049,691	901,835	(69.4)
1963	1,799,893	1,390,290	(56.4)
Manufacturing			
1948	3,969,988	2,552,016	(60.9)
1963	3,631,036	3,066,359	(54.2)
Totals			
1948	7,982,135	3,784,486	(67.8)
1963	7,659,532	5,281,559	(59.2)

Sources: U.S. Department of Commerce, Bureau of the Census: *Census of Manufactures: 1947*, Vol. III, *Area Statistics; Census of Manufactures: 1954*, Vol. III, *Area Statistics; Census of Manufactures, 1958*, Vol. III, *Area Statistics; Census of Manufactures: 1963*, Vol. III, *Area Statistics; Census of Business: 1948*, Vol. III, *Retail Trade — Area Statistics; Census of Business: 1947*, Vol. V, *Wholesale Trade — Area Statistics; Census of Business: 1948*, Vol. VII, *Selected Services — Area Statistics; Census of Business, 1954*, Vol. IV, *Wholesale Trade Area Statistics; Census of Business: 1954*, Vol. VI, *Selected Services — Area Statistics; Census of Business: 1958*, Vol. II, *Retail Trade — Area Statistics; Census of Business: 1958*, Vol. IV, *Wholesale Trade — Area Statistics; Census of Business: 1958*, Vol. VI, *Selected Services — Area Statistics; Census of Business, 1963*, Vol. II, *Retail-Trade. Area Statistics; Census of Business, 1963*, Vol. V. *Wholesale Trade — Area Statistics; Census of Business, 1963*, Vol. VII, *Selected Services — Area Statistics*.

III. NEGRO POPULATION CHANGES IN THE URBAN AREAS

The concentration of Negroes in the central cities of our largest metropolitan areas is an amply documented fact. A recent report indicates that between 1950 and 1968, the Negro population in all metropolitan areas increased by 6.6 million.[8] Of this total increase, 5.4 million or 81 per cent of the total increase occurred within the central cities of the metropolitan areas. The aforementioned report notes that there was a slight decline in the central city Negro population between 1966 and 1968.

The Negro population changes in the twenty-five SMSA's encompassed by this study can be summarized very briefly. From 1950 to 1960, the Negro population in these twenty-five SMSA's increased by 2,538,376—from 5,063,065 to 7,601,441. Note, however, that 2.2 million of the overall 2.5 million increase occurred in the central cities. In 1960, 83 per cent of all Negroes living in these twenty-five SMSA's

Table 2

Employment Changes in 25 Central Counties Within SMSA's, 1948–1964, by Sector

SECTOR OF EMPLOYMENT	TOTALS	CHANGE
Finance, Insurance and Real Estate		
1948	896,197	+442,789
1964	1,338,986	
Contract Construction		
1948	675,082	+107,408
1964	782,490	
Public Utilities		
1948	1,085,851	+122,394
1964	1,208,245	
Totals		
1948	2,657,130	+672,591
1964	3,329,721	

Sources: U.S. Department of Commerce, Bureau of the Census *County Business Patterns*, 1948–1964.

lived in their respective central cities. The proportion for the white population was only 41.4 per cent.

There would seem to be little point in elaborating further on the fact that the urban Negro population has become concentrated in the central cities of these SMSA's.

IV. A MODEL OF DECENTRALIZATION OF EMPLOYMENT AND ITS IMPACT ON THE URBAN NEGRO'S EMPLOYMENT PROBLEM

To reiterate, the aim of this study was not merely to describe the changes in employment patterns within these major urban areas but to estimate the impact of the decline of the central city as a place of employment on the Negroes presently residing there. Since the poorest ghetto areas within the central cities would be most likely to be affected by this decentralization phenomenon, I decided to concentrate on these areas. The first task was to isolate these communities. This was done by means of two arbitrary but reasonable assumptions. Using the 1960 *Census Tract* data for these twenty-five central cities, I designated as poverty tracts those tracts for which the median family income in the tract was less than two-thirds of the median family income in the entire SMSA. This relative definition of poverty eliminates the problems associated with using an absolute level of income for different geographic areas. Secondly, I then selected central city tracts which had a nonwhite population greater than 50 per cent of the tract's total population. Although some whites were thus included in this analysis, it is a minor distortion since the vast majority of these tracts had nonwhite populations which were 75 per cent or more of the total population of the tracts.[9] It was then a simple but time-consuming exercise to compute the employment-population ratios for Negroes over fourteen years of age who lived in these areas. Employment-population ratios for the poorest Negroes in each of these cities were thereby constructed. To explain the variation in these ratios across cities in terms of the "decentralization of employment" model was the objective of this study.

Any regression model which attempts to explain the variation in a variable such as the employment-population ratio in a particular geographic area has to include a variable depicting the degree of "looseness" or "tightness" in the regional labor market. The logical candidate for this variable was the SMSA unemployment rate during the census month of 1960. The SMSA unemployment rate was used because we are implicitly viewing the entire metropolitan region as one big labor market.

Constructing a meaningful index of decentralization presented somewhat more difficult problems. The only sources of data known to me from which such indices could be devised, were the *Census of Business* and the *Census of Manufactures* conducted in 1948, 1954, 1958, and 1963. In these censuses, employment data are collected for four sectors — wholesale trade, retail trade, selected services, and manufacturing — by SMSA and central city. Thus, it is possible to calculate the ratio of all jobs in these four sectors in the central city to all jobs in the SMSA. Just such an overall index was used in this study. The same ratio of jobs in the central city to those in the SMSA can be constructed for each of the sectors individually. Since the manufacturing sector is still the largest sector of employment for Negro males and has experienced the largest absolute shift out of the central cities to the fringe areas, an index for the manufacturing sector was also used. For similar reasons, an index for selected services was also constructed in an attempt to explain the variation in the employment-population ratio of Negro females. The ratio of all jobs in the central city to all jobs in the SMSA and the same ratio for the manufacturing sector were plotted for the four years, 1948, 1954, 1958, and 1963, and interpolated for 1960. Since a trend line characterized the time path of these ratios in virtually every city, it was simple and justifiable to interpolate them for 1960.

Finally, it was necessary to devise a variable which measured at least crudely the accessibility of the fringe areas to the central city ghetto residents. Differences in the size of geographic areas covered by particular metropolitan regions and in the comprehensiveness of the public transportation systems mean that the fringe areas and the jobs there are more accessible for the Negro residents of some cities than for others. Unfortunately, it was not possible to devise a variable which could be used as a proxy for the public transportation system. Consequently, I was forced to use a variable which reflects the accessibility of the fringe areas rather than measures it.

In the *Journey to Work* volume of the *Census of Population, 1960* there is information on the place of work and the place of residence of the nonwhite population by sex in each of these twenty-five SMSA's. It is thus possible to ascertain how many nonwhites worked in the ring area and lived in the central city. The variable which I used to measure accessibility of the ring area for nonwhites was the ratio of nonwhites who worked in the ring and lived in the central city to all nonwhites living in the central cities. This variable was constructed for all Negro males and females over fourteen years of age. It is admittedly a rather crude measure of accessibility but its insertion into the regression greatly improved the specification properties of the model.

If the decentralization of employment trends was having the hypothesized effects, the signs of the coefficients for the independent variables can be easily predicted. The higher the ratio of all jobs (or manufacturing or selected service jobs) in the SMSA located in the central city, the higher would be the employment-population ratio of Negroes in the ghettos. Also, the higher the ratio of all nonwhites living in the central city *who work in the ring area*, the higher would be the employment-population ratio of Negroes. Finally, a negative relation between the employment-population ratio and the SMSA unemployment rate would obviously be predicted.

Since the size of the Negro population in the ghettos of the twenty-five cities varied from approximately 221,000 nonwhite males in New York City to 6,400 in Milwaukee, it was deemed necessary to correct for heteroskedasticity by multiplying all observations on all variables by $\sqrt{P}$ (where P equals nonwhite male (female) population which was fourteen years of age or over and lived in the ghetto census tracts). When using this procedure for weighting regressions, $\sqrt{P}$ is introduced as an additional variable.[10]

V. THE REGRESSION RESULTS

Glossary of Variables

Dependent Variable

$\left(\dfrac{E}{P}\right)$ = Employment-population ratio of nonwhite males or females in the "poorest" census tracts of each city for census week 1960.

Independent Variables

(1) U = SMSA total unemployment rate (census month 1960)

(2) $\dfrac{E_{cc}}{E_{SMSA}}$ = Ratio of jobs in wholesale trade, selected services, retail trade, and manufacturing in the central city to all jobs in the four sectors in each SMSA (interpolated for 1960)

(3) $\dfrac{M_{cc}}{M_{SMSA}}$ = All manufacturing jobs in the central city divided by all manufacturing jobs in the SMSA (interpolated for 1960)

(4) $\dfrac{S_{cc}}{S_{SMSA}}$ = All selected service jobs in the central city divided by all selected service jobs in the SMSA (interpolated for 1960)

(5) $\dfrac{R_{M(F)}}{CC_{M(F)}}$ = All nonwhite males (females) over fourteen years of age who work in the "ring" and live in the central city divided by all nonwhite males (females) over fourteen years of age who live in the central city and work in the central city or ring (for census week 1960)

When the employment-population ratio of Negro *males* is used as the dependent variable, the regression results are as follows:

(1) $\left(\dfrac{E}{P}\right)_M = .63 \quad -2.86U+ \quad .19 \left(\dfrac{E_{cc}}{E_{SMSA}}\right) + .24 \left(\dfrac{R_M}{CC_M}\right)$
$\qquad\qquad\quad (.052) \quad (.56) \quad (.06) \qquad\qquad\quad (.06)$
$R^2 = .95, F = 13.5, n = 25.$

$$(2) \quad \left(\frac{E}{P}\right)_M = \underset{(.05)}{.68} \underset{(.58)}{-3.08U} + \underset{(.05)}{.14} \left(\frac{M_{cc}}{M_{SMSA}}\right) + \underset{(.06)}{.24} \left(\frac{R_M}{CC_M}\right)$$
$$R^2 = 94, F = 12.6, n = 25.$$

All the coefficients have the "correct" sign and are significant at the .01 level. Although the model "works" in the sense that the decentralization variables $\left(\frac{E_{cc}}{E_{SMSA}}\right)$ and $\left(\frac{M_{cc}}{M_{SMSA}}\right)$ and the proxy variable for accessibility to the ring area from the central city $\left(\frac{R_M}{CC_M}\right)$ have the predicted signs and are significant, the reader should not lose sight of the fact that the size of the coefficient of the unemployment rate is substantially higher than the size of the coefficients for either of the other variables. Thus, although the geographic separation of the central city Negro from the metropolitan fringe areas reduces to some extent his employment opportunities, relative to aggregate demand conditions in a particular metropolitan area (as represented by the unemployment rates), the factor of geographic separation does not seem to be too important.[11] Finally, caution should be employed in interpreting the proxy variable for measuring the accessibility to the fringe areas on the part of Negroes. It is possible that this ratio is higher in particular metropolitan areas not because the suburbs are more accessible to Negroes in some physical sense but rather because the occupational skill mix of suburban jobs tends to work to the relative advantage of Negroes in some metropolitan areas but not in others. It was impossible to check this possibility with existing data. However, it is quite likely that the relationship between Negro employment (E/P) and U asymptotes at an unemployment rate much lower on the average than that observed in 1960, a year of rather high unemployment.

It is interesting and illuminating to compare the results for Negro females with those above for Negro males.

$$(3) \quad \left(\frac{E}{P}\right)_F = \underset{(.07)}{.38} \underset{(.79)}{-3.3U} + \underset{(.08)}{.15} \left(\frac{E_{cc}}{E_{SMSA}}\right) + \underset{(.01)}{.03} \left(\frac{R_F}{CC_F}\right)$$
$$R^2 = .65, F = 11.8, n = 25.$$

$$(4) \quad \left(\frac{E}{P}\right)_F = \underset{(.10)}{.44} \underset{(.81)}{-3.8U} + \underset{(.10)}{.08} \left(\frac{S_{cc}}{S_{SMSA}}\right) + \underset{(.01)}{.025} \left(\frac{R_F}{CC_F}\right)$$
$$R^2 = .63, F = 11.5, n = 25.$$

Measured by the goodness of fit and the significance of the coefficients for the decentralization variables, the regression model for Negro females fares rather badly relative to that for Negro males. The size of the coefficient for the proxy variable designed to measure accessibility to the fringe areas on the part of Negro females is on the order of one-tenth the size of that for Negro males. In the next section, some of the possible reasons for these differences in the model as it pertains to males and females will be examined.

VI. CONCLUSIONS AND IMPLICATIONS

The effects of residential segregation of Negroes on various socioeconomic indicators such as academic performance, family stability, housing conditions, and crime rates have been examined by previous researchers. This paper, and that of Kain, represent the first attempts to measure the impact of housing segregation on the employment opportunities of segregated Negroes. On the basis of these preliminary results, it might be concluded that although the geographic separation of the ghetto Negro from the burgeoning job areas in the fringe areas reduces to some extent his employment opportunities, aggregate demand conditions, characterized by the unemployment rate in a particular SMSA, play a more important role. It was also found that the geographic separation of inner city Negro females from growing job centers in the suburbs had an almost negligible effect on their employment opportunities.

Our results seem to indicate that federal fiscal and monetary policies which affect the unemployment rate may have a disproportionate effect on central city employment. The rationale for this may be somewhat as follows. During periods of high unemployment, such as from 1958 to 1963 when the annual average unemployment rate never fell below 5.5 per cent, the existence of underutilized factors is likely to have had an important effect on the distribution of employment which worked to the disadvantage of central cities. In slack periods, firms tend to remove their least productive plants from production first. The rapid growth of employment in the suburbs prior to the high unemployment of the late 1950's suggest that the average age of capital in suburban locations was probably much lower than in central cities, and consequently suburban plants were probably more efficient. Consequently, the suburbs could be expected to gain employment relative to the cities during a period of high unemployment.

If the above argument is valid, then one would expect the performance of the central cities in terms of jobs to have been relatively better since 1963, during which time the unemployment rate fell from 5.7 to 3.8 per cent in 1966. Unfortunately, a serious attempt to test this hypothesis must await publication of the 1968 *Census of Business* and *Census of Manufactures*. On the other hand, the devastating riots of recent years in many of our largest cities may have been enough to offset this possibility.

The second major finding of this study is that the growing employment sectors in the central cities are large female employers (selected services and finance, insurance and real estate). Many occupations in the service sector (including finance, insurance and real estate) do not require physical strength. This means that women can compete more equally with men for the available jobs. In July 1967 women held approximately 52 per cent of all service jobs compared with only 25 per cent of those in the manufacturing sector.[12] In addition, the service industries are attractive for women because they provide more opportunities for part-time work. Almost one-fourth of all selected service industries employees were part-time employees on a voluntary basis. Only 2.9 per cent of all manufacturing workers were part-time workers on a voluntary basis.[13] Lastly 20 per cent of all female nonagricultural workers were employed on a voluntary part-time basis. Approximately 7 per cent of all male nonagricultural workers were on a voluntary part-time basis.[14]

In sum, changes in the composition of jobs within central cities bode badly for the Negro male in the ghetto who aspires for a high-wage "regular" blue-collar job. If present trends continue, i.e., Negroes remain heavily concentrated within the central city, it is likely that the Negro female will become even more important as an earner in the typical urban Negro family.[15] The nature of the jobs remaining in America's cities tends to favor a female, Negro or white.

What policy conclusions can be drawn from such preliminary results? Surely, the importance of maintaining a low unemployment rate for the purpose of aiding the inner-city Negro (male or female) cannot be overemphasized. Some have urged a complete revamping of our urban transportation system in order to facilitate the movement of central city Negroes to suburban job centers.[16] In fact, the Department of Housing and Urban Development has already undertaken demonstration projects along these lines in Los Angeles, St. Louis and several other cities.[17] The preliminary findings of this study would seem to indicate that major increases in total Negro employment, should not be expected from these experiments. However, they can help alleviate some unemployment and some hardship — and at a relatively low cost. They are a visible manifestation of public concern and action. Of course, a comprehensive federal open-housing law, rigidly enforced, might represent a more genuine and effective manifestation of public concern and action.

REFERENCES

1. I should like to thank Saul Hymans, Harvey Brazer, and George Johnson for their helpful comments on an earlier draft of this paper.
2. See John Kain, "Housing Segregation, Negro Employment, and Metropolitan Decentralization," in this *Journal,* LXXXII (May 1968), 175–98.
3. E.g., the *McCone Commission Report* dealing with the Watts riot, and the more comprehensive *Report of the National Advisory Commission on Civil Disorders.*
4. The Standard Metropolitan Statistical Areas are: Atlanta, Baltimore, Birmingham, Boston, Buffalo, Chicago, Cincinnati, Cleveland, Columbus, Dallas, Detroit, Houston, Indianapolis, Kansas City, Los Angeles, Louisville, Miami, Milwaukee, New Orleans, New York, Philadelphia, Pittsburgh, St. Louis, San Francisco, and Washington, D.C.
5. See John Kain, "The Distributions of Jobs and Industry," in *The Metropolitan Enigma,* ed. James Q. Wilson (Washington, D.C.: Chamber of Commerce of the United States, 1967), pp. 1–31; and John R. Meyer, John F. Kain, and Martin Wohl, *The Urban Transportation Problem* (Cambridge, Mass.: Harvard University Press, 1965), Chap. 3.
6. It should be noted that the geographic boundaries of the cities have not been corrected for annexation during this period. If this correction could have been made so that employment totals in the annexed areas could have been accurately subtracted, the decline of the central city (with 1948 boundaries) as the main location of urban employment would have been even more pronounced. Meyer, Kain, and Wohl, *op. cit.,* adjust for this shortcoming by assuming that job annexations as a percentage of total employment are equal to population annexations as a percentage of total populations. However, they present no compelling reason for making this particular type of adjustment.
7. The central counties are coterminous with the central cities in Baltimore, New Orleans, Philadelphia, St. Louis, San Francisco, Washington, D.C., and New York City. In these seven central counties (i.e., central cities), employment in the finance, insurance and real estate sector increased by 141,236 or almost 30 per cent from 1948–64. The other two employment sectors (contract construction and public utilities) in these central cities followed the same general pattern for all twenty-five central counties. These findings lend support to the contention that employment changes in the central county generally reflect employment changes in the central city.
8. See U.S. Department of Labor, Bureau of Labor Statistics, Report No. 347, *Recent Trends in Social and Economic Conditions of Negroes in the United States* (Washington, D.C.: July 1968), p. 4.
9. For a more complete discussion of the characteristics of the people residing in these poverty tracts, see Joseph D. Mooney, "Urban Poverty and Labor Force Participation," *American Economic Review,* LVII (March 1967), 104–20.

10. See E. Malinvaud, *Statistical Methods of Econometrics* (Chicago: Rand McNally, 1966), pp. 254–58.
11. Further support for this finding was derived by examining the beta coefficients of each independent variable. The beta coefficients are the regression coefficients of the normalized variables. The beta coefficients estimate the change in the dependent variable (E/P) from its mean measured in standard deviations, that would occur as a result of a change in the independent variable from its mean by one standard deviation. For equation (1), the beta coefficients for (U), $\left(\dfrac{E_{cc}}{E_{SMSA}}\right)$ and $\left(\dfrac{R_M}{CC_M}\right)$ were .65, .40, and .36 respectively. All were significant at the 5 per cent level. Clearly, the unemployment rate is the most important variable in explaining the variation in (E/P). The results were very similar for equation (2).
12. See U.S. Department of Labor, Bureau of Labor Statistics, *Employment and Earnings and Monthly Report of the Labor Force*, Vol. 14, No. 5 (Nov. 1967), Table 13.3.
13. *Ibid.* p. 27, Table A–22.
14. *Ibid.* p. 28, Table A–23.
15. It is interesting to note that increases in Negro female employment in the service in these twenty-five SMSA's between 1950 and 1960 were almost entirely concentrated in the subsector — professional and related services. Total Negro female employment in this latter subsector rose from 89,357 in 1950 to 215,461 in 1960. Negro female employment in total private households (largely domestics) remained almost stable over the 1950–60 period in these twenty-five SMSA's at around 300,000. Clearly, Negro females in urban areas are moving into the better paying service jobs at a rapid rate. (Source: U.S. Census Bureau, *Census of Population, 1960.*)
16. For example, see *Detroit Free Press*, Sept. 2, 1968, where a front-page article calls for a large-scale subsidized system of buses to transport inner-city Detroit Negroes to suburban employers.
17. See Charles Haar, "Transportation and Economic Opportunity," in *Traffic Quarterly*, XXI (Oct. 1967), 521–26 for a complete description of these demonstration projects.

14 The Housing Market in Racially Mixed Areas

DAVID McENTIRE
University of California, Berkeley

Arguments for and against open housing — as the question relates to residential property values in formerly all-white neighborhoods.

Two studies undertaken for the Commission on Race and Housing deal specifically with the impact of racial mingling in residence areas on local housing markets. One is an inquiry into the effects on residential property values of nonwhite entry

From "The Housing Market in Racially Mixed Areas," *Residence and Race*, by David McEntire, Berkeley: University of Southern California Press, 1960, pp. 157–171. Reprinted with permission.

into formerly all-white neighborhoods.[1] The second study is an analysis of demand for housing in racially mixed areas of one large city.[2]

PROPERTY VALUES AND RACE

According to traditional and widespread opinion, Negroes, and other minorities as well, are dangerous to property values when they seek housing, as they must, outside established minority residence areas. Underlying this belief are two basic propositions: first, that whites will not live in areas entered by nonwhites, and second, that nonwhite demand for housing is not sufficient to replace the vanished white demand and hence, prices must fall.

To many, these propositions seem self-evident, but in recent years both have been challenged. Not only have proponents of racial equality endeavored to demonstrate the error of the "property values myth," but in the real estate appraisal profession, increasing doubts have been expressed about the validity of the traditional doctrines under present-day conditions.

The importance of the problem needs no emphasis. Fear of financial loss gives every property owner in white neighborhoods a direct personal stake in excluding minorities, at least up to a point. Convictions that racial mingling injures property values influence business decisions to build, finance, and sell in ways that restrict the opportunities of nonwhites to acquire housing and limit them to certain districts. In acting on the assumption that values in an area are going to fall, the housing industry and property owners may help to bring about the anticipated result. If major lenders act together to reduce their loans in an area, they may be not merely recognizing but making a shift to lower prices, by eliminating a part of the demand. Similarly, when homeowners in an affected area hasten to sell before the expected price decline occurs, the resulting oversupply of houses may push down their selling prices.[3]

The motive, moreover, of preserving capital, an eminently respectable purpose, often provides moral justification for racial discrimination. People may consider themselves not merely justified but even obligated to exclude minorities for the sake of maintaining values. The real estate board in one large city took this ground in a public statement of policy:

> It is a matter of fact and experience that when a Negro or Chinese or Japanese or Filipino moves into a white district, the house values drop . . . *We don't look at this as a social problem. To us this is an economic problem.* Looking at it this way, the Board has asked that its members not introduce into a residential district any occupancy or race which will have the effect of lowering values.[4]

In a similar vein, a savings and loan association executive said in an interview: "There are lots of things we would like to do personally, such as treating everybody equally, . . . but we are responsible for millions of dollars. . . . We will lend on properties up to three blocks away from colored areas but not closer . . ."

Twenty years and more ago, real estate authorities asserted the adverse effect of nonwhite occupancy on values straightforwardly and with few qualifications. Fisher (1923), McMichael and Bingham (1923), Babcock (1932), Hoyt (1933, 1939), and other authors of standard texts and treatises pronounced a common judgment, accepted apparently without dissent.[5] Property appraisal standards of the Federal Housing Administration incorporated the accepted doctrine.

Since World War II, differing theories have been advanced by professional appraisers and others. According to one contemporary theory, the price depression associated with nonwhite entry is only temporary. House prices weaken in areas anticipating a racial change and may continue depressed during the early stages of transition, but after transition, prices rise again.[6] Myrdal espoused this view in the *American Dilemma* (1944).[7] More recently Charles A. Benson, chief appraiser of a leading mortgage-finance institution, reporting on a study of price changes in two Chicago areas — one all-white and one in racial transition — concludes:

> ... prices of residences are depressed from 30 per cent to 55 per cent when an area is threatened by transition. As soon as transition becomes a fact, prices tend to rise ... After transition has been accomplished, prices in the then Negro area compare favorably with prices in the city as a whole and are controlled by supply and demand.[8]

Some appraisers hold that nonwhite occupancy may actually enhance real estate values in certain conditions. According to the authorities just mentioned, active movement of nonwhites into an area is better for values than the continued threat of entry. Thurston Ross writes that "in poor and slum sections racial encroachment sometimes raises the economic standards of the neighborhood." He reports "instances where obsolescence has been arrested and additional years of useful life given a neighborhood by racial encroachment, particularly when older people are displaced by younger groups of the encroaching race."[9]

The newer theories differ from the old in recognizing a variety of conditions under which nonwhite movement into an area can take place, and consequently a range of possible effects on values. Weaver especially emphasizes variation. Reviewing the evidence available in 1948, he wrote:

> The effect of Negro occupancy upon property values varies from one section of the city to another and from one time to another. ... The arrival of a few Negroes may be the signal for a great decline in selling prices or it may lead to an appreciable increase. Much depends upon the state of the total housing market and the manner in which colored people enter an area ... *There is no one universal effect of Negro occupancy upon property values.*[10]

Weaver's view is reiterated by Abrams, who finds a complex of factors at work and "no fixed rules as to when minority neighbors raise or lower values."[11]

Appraisal policies of the Federal Housing Administration reflect the change in appraisal thinking. Where once the FHA flatly asserted the value-destroying tendency of mixed neighborhoods, in successive editions of the *Underwriting Manual* provisions touching race and property values have become steadily more qualified. References to "social and racial classes" have been deleted in favor of the more neutral "user groups," and the *Manual* now states,

> If a mixture of user groups is found to exist it must be determined whether the mixture will render the neighborhood less desirable to present and prospective occupants. If the occupancy of the neighborhood is changing from one user group to another, ... any degree of risk is reflected in the rating ... Additional risk is not necessarily involved in such change.[12]

These judgments of real estate and housing authorities have been based mainly on professional experience and observation rather than on research, for few factual studies have been made of what actually happens to house prices when nonwhites move into new areas. Difficult problems of method confront the study of this question. Merely to observe the course of prices in a neighborhood experiencing racial change tells little, for the movements observed might well be caused by factors other than the racial change. The measurement of racial influence on values is especially complicated by the tendency of minority groups to concentrate in slum and deteriorating sections affected by various adverse influences. To attribute the lower rents and prices in such areas solely to the presence of nonwhites would be obviously misleading.

To isolate the price effects of racial mixture, the price performance of racially mixed areas must be compared with some standard that is free of the racial influence being investigated. Laurenti's research for the Commission on Race and Housing attempts to do this. Twenty neighborhoods, recently become racially mixed, in San Francisco, Oakland, and Philadelphia were chosen for study. Each neighborhood, called a "test area," was matched with a "control" neighborhood which had remained all white. Each pair of neighborhoods was chosen according to criteria to ensure that the two would closely resemble each other in major factors affecting house prices. Criteria for matching included the age, type, and market value of houses, topography, location, land-use pattern, income and broad occupational class pattern, income and broad occupational class of residents, and the character of neighborhood development. A large number of areas were sifted in the search for matching pairs. Comparability of the paired neighborhoods was checked with local real estate brokers, appraisers, lenders, and assessors familiar with the histories of the areas. Informed local judgments were followed in fixing the area boundaries, usually marked by topographic features, arterial streets, or subdivision limits. All areas chosen were away from the central city districts and built up largely with single-unit, owner-occupied houses in the middle-value range. This collection of neighborhoods, therefore, represents the residences of the home-owning middle class in the cities studied. Within this category and subject to the limitations of matching, neighborhoods were selected to give as much diversity as possible in price class and degree of nonwhite occupancy.

The data consist of prices paid for houses in test and control neighborhoods during a period beginning before the entry of nonwhites into the test area and ending in the latter part of 1955. In most of the test areas the first nonwhite buyers arrived during the early postwar years. Sources of price data were the multiple listing services in San Francisco and Oakland, information from real estate brokers, and a real estate directory in Philadelphia, generally considered a reliable source of data for real estate transactions. Approximately ten thousand sales prices were collected, representing about half of all transactions in the San Francisco-Oakland areas and total sales in the Philadelphia areas during the periods studied.

For each neighborhood the collected prices were averaged by quarter years. In some areas with a wide range of prices, ratios of selling price to assessed valuation were computed and averaged by quarters. Using these quarterly averages, the movement of house prices in the neighborhoods entered by nonwhites was compared with price movements in matching allwhite neighborhoods. Some of the twenty test areas were sufficiently similar to more than one control area to permit multiple comparisons. In all, thirty-four paired comparisons were made. Analysis yielded the following principal findings:

1. In fourteen of the forty-four comparisons (41 per cent), test prices stayed within 5 per cent, plus or minus, of control prices during the observation period. This is considered to mean no significant difference in price behavior.
2. In fifteen comparisons (44 per cent), test prices ended relatively higher than control prices, by margins of more than 5 to 26 per cent.
3. In the remaining five comparisons (15 per cent), test prices ended the observation period relatively lower than control prices, by margins of 5 to 9 per cent.
4. From the date of first nonwhite entry to the end of the observation period, twenty of the thirty-four comparisons showed larger per cent increases each quarter for test prices than for control prices.

At the end of the observation period (fall, 1955) the proportion of nonwhite residents in the twenty test areas varied from less than 2 per cent to more than 70 per cent. The data were examined to determine whether the extent of nonwhite entry affected the comparative performance of test and control area prices, with results given in Table 1.

As shown in Table 1, test areas in all ranges of nonwhite occupancy manifested both superior and inferior price performance as compared with control areas, but in every category, the majority of significant differences favored the test areas.

Distribution of test areas by per cent of population nonwhite corresponds approximately to their distribution by average house value. The three neighborhoods

Table 1

Paired Comparisons of Test and Control Area Prices by Per Cent of Nonwhites in Test Area Populations

TEST AREAS BY PER CENT OF POPULATION NONWHITE, 1955	PAIRED COMPARISONS OF PRICE MOVEMENTS			
	TOTAL	NO SIGNIFICANT DIFFERENCE	TEST AREA HIGHER	CONTROL AREA HIGHER
30 to 75 per cent; 8 areas	16	10	5	1
14 to 28 per cent; 6 areas	9	3	4	2
6 to 7 per cent; 3 areas	5	...	4	1
3 per cent or less; 3 areas	4	1	2	1

Source: Luigi Laurenti, *Property Values and Race,* Special Research Report to the Commission on Race and Housing (Berkeley and Los Angeles: University of California Press, 1960), chaps. vi, vii, and viii.

with very limited nonwhite entry are of the exclusive type with houses considerably more expensive than any of the other areas. It is most unlikely that these neighborhoods can become all or mainly nonwhite within the foreseeable future, in contrast to the eight areas at the other end of the scale which were well on their way toward complete racial transition. It is significant, therefore, that in both classes of neighborhoods, nonwhite entry was more often associated with strengthening than with weakening house prices.

The facts of this study contradict the theory that nonwhite entry into a neighborhood must produce a fall in property values. The findings are consistent with newer theories emphasizing a diversity of price outcomes according to circumstances; however, for the areas and time periods studied, the entry of nonwhites into previously all-white neighborhoods was more often associated with price improvement or stability than with price declines.

In assessing the significance of these findings, several factors must be borne in mind. The time period — end of the war through 1955 — was one of unprecedented Negro demand for housing generated by large population movements to northern and western cities, by the new economic position of Negroes, and by the increasing availability of mortgage credit. A great backlog of Negro demand had accumulated, and the persistence of exclusion barriers through most of the better housing supply served to concentrate this pent-up demand on the areas open to Negroes.

In the neighborhoods studied, the behavior of white residents seemed to be quite different from the traditional response of whites to nonwhite entry. Although some of the areas showed considerable disturbance, there was almost complete absence of the panic flight of whites which in the past has characterized many zones of racial transition. In many of the neighborhoods, the white residents were anxious to sell but waited until they could get adequate prices from incoming buyers. Under the existing conditions, the nonwhite market offered sufficient demand to move the properties without price weakening — in fact, at prices generally somewhat higher than prevailed in comparable areas not affected by racial change.

These considerations may account for the maintenance of an orderly market and stable or rising prices in those areas heavily entered by nonwhites and evidently destined for complete racial transition. They do not explain the favorable price movements in the neighborhoods with low nonwhite proportions, for these depended upon continuing demand from whites. The conclusion must be that in these relatively expensive and desirable neighborhoods, a sparse scatter of nonwhites, almost imperceptible to most residents or prospective residents, did not noticeably affect the attractiveness of the areas in the white market.

HOUSING DEMAND IN RACIALLY MIXED AREAS

The second study to be considered goes behind the facts of price movements to analyze the components of demand for housing in areas undergoing racial transition. This study analyzed all house sales recorded during 1955 in four areas of Philadelphia. Two of the areas contained relatively good housing, and in two the housing was mainly poor. Each quality pair further consisted of one area undergoing rapid racial transition and one where the Negro population was growing slowly. In all four areas, Negroes occupied 20 to 30 per cent of the dwelling units.

A racial transition zone is commonly pictured as one where whites are leaving and nonwhites coming in. The Philadelphia study found the process to be considerably more complex. Among some two thousand home buyers, 443 or more than one-fifth were whites. Although outnumbered more than three to one by Negroes, the presence of white buyers in substantial numbers is, nevertheless, a significant fact from several points of view. It refutes the notion that whites will not buy in an area once entered by Negroes, and calls for inquiry into the conditions under which whites will continue to buy in such areas. Whether any area can maintain a racially mixed composition depends, of course, on its ability to attract new white residents.

Investigation of the trend of house prices in one area (good housing, rapid transition) revealed a substantial price advance from 1948 through 1955, of approximately the same magnitude as occurred in the city as a whole. The rise appeared most pronounced in the sections of heavy Negro entry and rapid departure of whites. This is further evidence that racial change is not necessarily associated with depressed prices.

Mortgage lenders often take a dubious view of racially mixed areas, but this was not true in Philadelphia. Financing was liberal and played a key role in sustaining demand and prices. Ninety per cent of the white buyers and practically all the Negroes depended on mortgage financing to acquire their homes. The loans came almost entirely from established institutional sources. Negroes obtained mortgage terms more liberal than those advanced to whites. A third of the Negro buyers borrowed the entire purchase price and another third received 90 per cent or more financing. Only 43 per cent of the whites received 90 per cent loans or better. Negro borrowers also received more favorable interest rates. Four-fifths of them paid less than 5½ per cent, as compared with three-quarters of the whites. The superior terms obtained by Negroes are explained by the higher percentage of VA and FHA loans made to this group. In addition to interest, "points" were generally charged, especially on VA loans, the typical charge being 5 per cent. Point charges were usually paid by the seller but, in the judgment of informed observers, passed on to the buyer in the form of higher prices permitted by liberal VA appraisals. The role of easy financing in supporting the price rise is thus doubly apparent. Down payments of 10 per cent to zero enabled large numbers of Negroes to buy who could not have met the down payment requirements of conventional loans.

The liberal policies of Philadelphia lending institutions toward these mixed-occupancy areas are a departure from the general practice of mortgage lenders. It should be noted that the loans were both safe and profitable. Nearly all were government insured or guaranteed. The willingness of sellers to pay point charges permitted lenders to combine the safety of guaranteed loans with the higher interest rates associated with conventional mortgage loans. Lenders were also influenced, undoubtedly, by the abundance of mortgage funds available in 1955. Whether they would take the same view of transition-area risks in a period of credit stringency is problematic.

Negro and white buyers paid virtually identical average prices for the homes they acquired except in one area of poor housing and rapid transition, where Negroes paid substantially more than whites, on the average, and presumably acquired better dwellings. Negroes and whites received about the same value for their housing dollar, paying substantially the same prices for similar houses.

Analysis of the spatial distribution of Negro and white purchases reveals a marked tendency toward racial separation. Among the study areas, the ratio of Negro to white buyers was three to one in the area of good housing and rapid change, but twenty-seven to one in the area characterized by poor housing and fast change. In a third area, where the housing is good but change slow, Negroes were outnumbered by white buyers two to one.

Within the areas some blocks have become wholly Negro occupied, others are mixed, still others have not yet received a Negro resident. In the two areas accounting for the great majority of white purchases, about a third of the blocks were white, but they were the location of the large majority of all purchases by white families.

To measure more strictly the spatial relationship of Negro and white purchases, two calculations were made including the proportion of white purchases made in a mixed block or adjacent to a mixed block,[13] and the per cent of white families who purchased homes on the same street front or directly across the street from Negro residents. The second measure, obviously, is a more critical test of residential proximity, since residents in the same street between intersections are likely to encounter each other frequently in the course of ordinary comings and goings. In the study areas, moreover, the predominant row-type single-family houses are highly homogeneous on any given street, allowing no symbolism of status differences among the residents.

The two measures yielded a striking result. Nearly three-fourths of the white purchases were found in a mixed block or adjacent to a mixed block, that is, within a maximum of three linear blocks from a Negro resident. But only 27 per cent of the white buyers acquired homes on the same street front or facing a street front on which Negro families lived, whereas the remainder purchased on all-white street fronts and facing street fronts. Thus, it seems that the closer the proximity of Negroes, the smaller will be the proportion of white purchasers in any mixed area. This result was, of course, not unexpected. However, the significant finding may not lie in the sharp drop-off in proportion of white purchasers, but in the fact that 119 white families chose to buy homes on mixed streets. The other white families, moreover, by purchasing in an area of transition, exposed themselves to the likelihood of having near Negro neighbors in the not distant future.

White families who choose to buy homes in the same areas with nonwhites, because they go against a behavior norm, may be thought to have some unusual characteristics or motivations which account for their actions. The present study searched for such characteristics but was unable to find any which significantly differentiated the group from the white home-buying population at large. In many ways the white purchasers resembled the resident white population in the areas into which they bought.[14]

As in the general home-buying population, a large proportion of these purchasers were young families. Two-thirds of the family heads were less than forty-five years old. Three-fourths had children less than eighteen and half had children of school age — percentages somewhat higher than among all home purchasers in Philadelphia during 1955 and 1956.[15] About half of the purchasers had attended high school; their educational attainment was similar to that of the resident population of the study areas in 1950. Occupationally, the purchaser family heads showed no unusual concentration in professional or other groups which might be associated with special views on race. Their family incomes, from available scanty evidence, were somewhat lower than those of all recent Philadelphia home purchasers, but averaged about the same as white family incomes in the city as a whole. Two-thirds of the purchaser families were Catholic, a proportion somewhat higher than in the Philadelphia white population but similar to the composition of the study areas.

The Negro purchaser group was quite similar to the white buyers, only somewhat younger, with fewer children, slightly lower family incomes, and a smaller representation in the white-collar and skilled-craftsman occupations.

The white purchasers did not have unique or impelling motives for buying in the mixed areas. Most, in interview, gave commonplace reasons for their choice, mentioning such factors as convenience to work, school, friends and relatives, suitability of the house, or simply, "I'm accustomed to the neighborhood and I like to live here." Familiarity with the neighborhood and attachment to it evidently played an important role in the housing choices of these purchasers, for more than 60 per cent of them had lived in the area before buying their homes.

As to racial attitudes, the fact that this group of home purchasers decided to buy in mixed areas implies that they were at least comparatively receptive to the presence of Negroes. However, in interviews, they did not express attitudes of unusual tolerance. If any were motivated by a desire to give a personal example of racial democracy, they were few in number. More than a third of those interviewed expressed varying degrees of dissatisfaction with the presence of Negroes, but strongly negative sentiments were rare. Attitudes of acceptance or rejection were markedly correlated with the degree of hypothetical proximity. Sixty per cent of the respondents expressed approval or indifference to the residence of Negroes in the neighborhood; 40 per cent to residence on the same block; and 31 per cent to residence in an adjacent house. Only 4 per cent of the respondents voiced strong disapproval of Negro residence in the neighborhood, but 31 per cent were strongly negative toward having Negroes next door.

The racial attitudes expressed by these white home purchasers are fairly consistent with their observed behavior in choosing locations. All of them bought in a general area of mixed occupancy. But as the proximity of Negroes increased, in passing from area to zone to block to street, the proportion of white purchasers contracted.

CONCLUSIONS

During the time period covered by the present studies, surging Negro demand, supported by growing availability of mortgage credit and concentrated at certain points, was sufficient to maintain and to strengthen house prices in many areas of racial transition. Market stability was helped by the apparently changing attitudes of white property owners which led them generally to refrain from flooding the market with houses on the appearance of Negroes. To an appreciable extent, whites continued to buy into some racially mixed areas, and this too, of course, helped to keep prices up.

In the future, it is certain that Negroes and other minorities will continue to enter many neighborhoods that are now all-white. But some of the conditions which in the recent past generated strong Negro demand for housing in transitional areas are disappearing. Consequently, predictions from recent experience for the future must be heavily qualified. The pent-up housing demand of Negroes which accumulated during the war and early postwar years has by now been satisfied in large part. The increasing market freedom which minorities are gaining, together with the growing social differentiation of the groups, means undoubtedly that their housing demand will be more dispersed and more varied in the future than in the past. Nonwhites are apt to enter more areas than the nonwhite population can fill, and for some areas complete racial transition will be impossible. As noted, this is already true in some higher-priced neighborhoods. Hence there is likely to be an increasing number of neighborhoods where the maintenance of a sufficient market for houses will require white as well as nonwhite buyers in adequate numbers.

The Philadelphia study found white buyers in numbers which may be thought impressive yet were not sufficient to maintain for long the mixed-occupancy pattern. Where four-fifths of the purchasers in a particular area are non-white and only one-fifth white, the outcome is plain. The one area where only a third of the purchasers were Negro does have the prospect of a stable interracial balance, if the present ratio is maintained.

The Philadelphia white buyers did not come from any special group in the population nor were they characterized by unusually favorable attitudes toward Negroes. Their motivations for purchase were those of home buyers generally. Similar findings concerning white purchasers in new interracial housing developments are reported. This absence of distinctive traits coupled with the acknowledged general lessening of racial prejudice in the white population during the past twenty years suggests the existence of considerable potential demand by white families for housing in racially mixed areas.

At present, most mixed neighborhoods compare unfavorably with all-white areas in quality of housing, community facilities, or social conditions. But as minority groups gain more freedom in the housing market, an increasing number of good-quality residence areas will be brought into the mixed category. Urban renewal programs may continue to rehabilitate some of the existing deteriorated mixed areas.

The critical racial factors limiting the number of both prejudiced and unprejudiced white buyers who will purchase in mixed areas are the actual or expected number and proportion of nonwhites in the mixed community, and the spatial distribution of nonwhite residences in relation to the homes which white buyers contemplate acquiring. The two factors are related; however, the Philadelphia data show white purchasers to be more accepting of Negroes a short distance away than in the immediate vicinity. An increasing proportion of Negroes in a mixed area is reflected in a shrinkage of white demand, but the behavior of white buyers seems to be related more to the anticipated than to the actual proportion of Negroes.

The level of white demand and consequently the prospects for achieving *both* a stable racial mixture and stable or rising prices in an area depended primarily, therefore, on the expectations of white buyers. In the past, it has been the most common expectation that a neighborhood once entered by nonwhites would become wholly occupied by them, and in most cases events have justified this anticipation. The present outlook, however, is for an increasing number of neighborhoods where this expectation cannot be fulfilled. What this implies for demand and prices in those areas is problematic. If white demand for housing in a given area shrinks in anticipation of racial transition, but Negro buyers do not appear in the expected numbers, the prices of residences may well decline. But present trends may lead to a revision of expectations of white buyers, and to the extent that this occurs, race will tend to lose its importance in the housing market.

REFERENCES

1. Luigi Laurenti, *Property Values and Race: Studies In Seven Cities.*
2. Chester Rapkin and William G. Grigsby, *The Demand for Housing in Racially Mixed Areas: A Study of the Nature of Neighborhood Change.*
3. This type of collective behavior, akin to panics, bank runs, and hoarding sprees, has been termed by Merton, the "self-fulfilling prophecy." Robert K. Merton, "The Self-Fulfilling Prophecy."
4. Statement on behalf of the San Francisco Real Estate Board, reported in "The Negro in San Francisco," *San Francisco Chronicle,* November 6, 1950. Italics supplied.
5. The relevant professional writings are reviewed in Laurenti, *Property Values and Race,* ch. ii.
6. George W. Beechler, Jr., "Colored Occupancy Raises Values," *The Review of the Society of Residential Appraisers,* XI, no. 9 (September, 1945). See also Stanley L. McMichael, *McMichael's Appraising Manual,* p. 169.
7. Gunnar Myrdal, *An American Dilemma,* p. 623.
8. Charles A. Benson, "A Test of Transition Theories," *The Residential Appraiser,* Vol. 24, no. 8 (August, 1958), 8. Quoted with permission of the Society of Residential Appraisers.
9. Thurston H. Ross, "Market Significance of Declining Neighborhoods."
10. Robert G. Weaver, *The Negro Ghetto,* p. 293. Italics in original.
11. Charles Abrams, *Forbidden Neighbors,* pp. 286, 292.
12. Housing and Home Finance Agency, Federal Housing Administration, Underwriting Manual, Rev. April, 1958, sec. 1320.
13. The unit of measurement consisted of five contiguous blocks in the shape of a cross in which the house acquired by the white purchaser was in the central block. If any of the five blocks was mixed in occupancy, the whole unit was classified as mixed.
14. Data for this phase of the study were obtained by interviews with 194 white families who purchased homes during 1955 in mixed blocks or adjacent to a mixed block, 100 white renter families in mixed blocks, and 196 Negro home purchasers in the study areas.
15. U.S. Bureau of the Census, *1956 National Housing Inventory,* Philadelphia Supplement (unpublished).

C
Transportation

Rapid transit for residents of large and teeming urban areas is a highly controversial subject. Some city planners, for instance, regard rail rapid transit as absolutely essential to rational land use — claiming that it is impossible to move people rapidly enough by automobile or bus to avoid congestion and a plethora of street and highway problems. Other planners claim that the American's preference for his Ford, Chevy, or jalopy is so strong that he is willing to make many accommodations in order to continue using it — move to the suburbs, pay high prices for the car, gasoline, taxes, and arrange his schedule around traffic flow.

More than ninety per cent of all travel in American cities is in private automobiles. The controversy between rail rapid transit and private automobiles continues only because of the congestion of our freeways during the hours when most people are going to or from work, particularly to and from the central business districts of major cities.

The controversy arises, in part, over the methods we use to pay for transportation facilities. All automobile drivers, whether they use their cars to go to work or not, must share in paying for the streets and freeways, which are built from gasoline tax, property tax, and general tax revenue. Usually, there is no special charge for peak-hour use. Thus, families who already have invested in a car and must invest in taxes anyway feel that the extra cost of peak-hour use of the car is slight. Families who ride public transit, however, must pay fares each time; so, for them, the extra cost is significant. It is significant, even though subsidies by cities and states cover at least twenty per cent of the total cost. In effect, the peak-hour motorist is subsidized heavily — in the costs that accrue to society as a whole for, say, congestion — by taxes collected from off-peak hour motorists; the rapid transit user is subsidized only lightly by the population in general.

Writers, legislators, and public policy makers who favor a form of rail rapid transit emphasize the undesirable neighborhood effects of, in a metropolitan area, an excessive number of automobiles. Congestion is a factor. Increasingly, the environmental pollution caused by gasoline fumes and the internal combustion engine is another, and frightening, factor.

Microeconomic analysis of the demand for and supply of transportation deals not only with automobile and rail rapid transit, but with helicopter and other forms of local transportation and with major air terminal connections. Urban and regional aspects of the analysis involve study of residential, job, and industrial location within a metropolitan area. Subsidies to peak-hour auto commuters, smaller subsidies to peak-hour rail commuters, and the high costs assessed off-peak travellers of all kinds are regarded as substantial market imperfections.

Macroeconomic analysis reflects the continuing prosperity experienced since World War II, and the resulting strong preference for automobile over other forms of transportation. It is high and rising incomes that have made it possible for consumers to express such a preference — one to which the decline and disappearance of other forms of urban transit attests. Although talk about the need for rail rapid transit often is loud and clear, political leaders and planners have been unable to muster broad popular support for their cause.

In the study of urban transportation, simulation models have been effective, particularly origin-destination studies, which have provided detailed analyses of the factors which influence transportation decisions, and in the process have shed much light on housing decisions and labor market imbalances. Planners have been involved in the programming of freeways and rapid transit facilities, using benefit-cost analysis to decide among alternative methods of providing transportation in an urban community.

15 Urban Transportation in Summary and Perspective

JOHN R. MEYER
Yale University

J. F. KAIN
Harvard University

M. WOHL
The Urban Institute

In this view, the extremely high cost of rail rapid transit makes such transit undesirable for most cities — certainly as long as consumers continue to demonstrate a strong preference for private automobiles.

Reprinted by permission of the publishers from John R. Meyer, John F. Kain, and Martin Wohl, THE URBAN TRANSPORTATION PROBLEM, Cambridge, Mass.: Harvard University Press. Copyright 1965 by The RAND Corporation.

An array of technological, economic, and social forces has altered the structure and character of American cities in recent decades. The particular form, mode, or even presence or absence of public transit facilities in a city is only one of these forces, and apparently one of limited importance. In fact, the patterns of land use, population growth, employment locations, and residential choices recorded in recent years by the most transit-oriented American cities have essentially mirrored those of other cities with very strong highway orientation. At least the broad outlines, though probably not the details, of land use in urban areas seem to be independent of the availability of public transit. With or without mass transit, American cities have been decentralizing.

This trend implies that the urban transportation problem in most American cities will change in character. Continued decentralization could ameliorate the single most difficult aspect of urban transportation: moving people during the morning and evening rush hours into and away from areas of high population and workplace density. In fact, even now, with *both* public and private transportation taken into account, it is not at all clear that the quality of urban transportation has been declining in most major cities. On the contrary, it seems to have improved in the last five years, if such quantitative measures as the number of transit route miles or the time required to complete commuter trips of a certain length or to clear a central city of people going home in the evening rush hours are applied.

Public transport and private transport are, of course, highly interdependent. Better highways into a city, especially limited-access facilities, not only speed up the movement of a specific number of people out of central areas by private automobile, but also usually reduce demands on public transport by diverting people to private modes. If service offerings on the public facilities are not reduced correspondingly, their quality of service will improve by reducing numbers of standees and thus congestion inside transit vehicles. Even if some service is curtailed, quality can still improve because higher performance speeds may be possible. This improvement can ensue, moreover, even if public transit vehicles do not operate over new express highways, since limited-access highways usually improve performance on parallel neighboring streets by reducing their congestion. In fact, new expressways are sometimes called inadequate because they speed up rush hour traffic from 25 to only about 35 mph on *both* the expressways and neighboring streets, rather than achieving the maximum expressway design speeds of 55 to 60 mph. Grumbling about the "failure" of new urban expressways is often traceable to this gap between expectation and reality.

In some important senses urban transportation did deteriorate, though, immediately after World War II. During the immediate postwar years, the stock of private automobiles expanded much more rapidly than did urban highway facilities. Throughout the postwar period, moreover, the quality of public transit has declined, at least as measured by frequency of service. This decline is heavily attributable to the negative interaction between public transit and private transportation. As more and more people used private transport, transit services were curtailed for economy reasons. This was particularly true for non-rush-hour periods, because the abandonment of public transportation for noncommuter purposes was much greater than for trips to or from work. The increased specialization of public transit in commuter work-trips mainly reflects its disadvantage for shopping, social, and recreational trips in comparison with the private automobile. In fact, an outstanding feature of urban passenger travel demands is a strong preference for the private automobile for virtually all noncommuter trips.

The private automobile is also increasingly used for commuter trips. Private automobile commutation, by eliminating transfers and supplying greater privacy and schedule flexibility (where car-pooling is limited), is unquestionably a superior economic good in the minds of many urban commuters. Therefore, as income levels have increased, it is hardly surprising that more and more commuters have taken to the automobile. In short, there is considerable evidence that consumers may prefer an "automobile" solution to their urban transportation needs, even if it is a costly solution.

Another important postwar phenomenon is the increasing prevalence of cross-haul and reverse commuter trip patterns in urban areas to the point where non-CBD trips are now more than twice as numerous as those to and from the CBD. In the past, it was common to find a high concentration of urban travel demands along a few corridors originating in the CBD and radiating outward to residential neighborhoods. The cross-haul pattern results from an increase in the number and geographic dispersion of trip origins and destinations, which in turn are a function not only of lower residential densities but of decentralization in manufacturing, transportation, shopping, and recreational facilities. The CBD-oriented, corridor pattern remains important only in a few of the largest cities, notably New York, and even then accounts for far less than a majority of regional trips.

One especially important problem has been intensified by the increase in cross-haul trips. This is the long-standing phenomenon of rush hour traffic which is not bound for the CBD area but is merely passing through. Ironically, this kind of traffic, which becomes entangled with CBD rush hour congestion against its will, often accounts for a remarkably high percentage of the rush hour demand pressure on downtown highways and streets. The solution advocated by highway engineers is to bypass this through traffic by creating "inner" or intermediate belt highways at the outer edges of downtown districts or slightly beyond.

In a different vein, the development of lower-density residential neighborhoods in American cities and suburbs is hardly attributable solely or even strongly to the automobile. Rising incomes have enabled households to consume more space; and at the same time, dispersion of workplaces has made it easier and cheaper for families to find desirable housing within commuting range of their workplaces. Tax concessions favorable to home ownership, and Federal programs to make housing credit cheaper and more available to low-income families, have also contributed. In general, commuter transportation and suburban land, particularly for new housing with private yards, are highly complementary economic goods; any policy or undertaking that promotes the demand for one is likely to do the same for the other. In the postwar period there has been a remarkable convergence of public policy and economic and demographic developments which has increased the attractiveness of both suburban housing and private transportation.

There is also limited evidence that transit facilities are suffering from a failure to adapt to a peculiar bifurcation apparently emerging in the demand for urban public transit. Specifically, the relative increase in the importance of office and control functions as a source of downtown employment has apparently resulted in relatively more demands for trips to downtown areas originating from professional groups and other office workers; these are superimposed on the trip demands of low-income employees in the service and retail industries that have remained in the central area. The future demands for transportation into downtown areas, therefore, may come from opposite poles in the spectrum of social and economic classes, and past experience suggests that it may be difficult to get these contrasting groups to accept the same quality of transportation service, or in some cases to travel together.

Little is known about how extensively opposition to social or racial integration causes declines in transit patronage, but there is at least some suggestive evidence that desegregation in parts of the South has caused transit patronage to decline. In the same vein, public transit has recorded some of its strongest recent performances in certain Northern areas where social and racial segregation is a function of geography. The Shaker Heights Line in Cleveland and the Chicago and Northwestern Railroad's North Shore operation in Chicago continue to enjoy considerable popularity, and it seems possible that some of this popularity is a result of a geographically built-in selection process that guarantees unusual social and economic homogeneity in the clientele. More information with which to test the validity of these and related hypotheses would at least contribute to a more realistic discussion of the basic problems involved in trying to develop mass public transit as an alternative to private automobile commutation. Furthermore, the problems created by this cleavage in the urban transportation market are intensified by racial segregation in housing. This restricts both the opportunity and the willingness of some people to reside closer to their workplaces and forces others to live closer than they might otherwise desire. As a consequence, the demand characteristics for urban transportation services are altered.

More explicitly, reverse-hauls running against the direction of major commuter flow in the morning and evening and long commuter trips are mostly made by three groups: multiple-wage-earner families; minority groups with restricted housing opportunities; and high-income families. Multiple-wage-earner families obviously find it difficult to select a residential location that minimizes transportation time and cost for their two or more wage-earners, while still meeting other family requirements. Minority groups commonly are limited to housing in older residential areas near the CBD, thus experiencing shorter trips for central-area jobs, but longer ones where suburban employment is involved. As suburban employment becomes increasingly important, minority groups could experience increasingly longer work-trips — assuming a continuance of geographical segregation as it now exists. High-income groups, on the other hand, commute to the CBD from outlying residential areas where they can satisfy high space demands and more easily find other housing amenities they desire.

These few observations on urban transportation demand patterns, while useful, are still notably incomplete. Much more needs to be known about patterns of demand, particularly demand elasticities and cross-elasticities for the different urban transit modes.

By contrast, considerable information is available on the costs of providing urban transportation. In fact, by making a few simplifying assumptions, reasonable estimates can be made of the relative costs of performing urban transportation by various modes. In making these cost analyses it is useful to differentiate among the three basic urban transportation functions: the line-haul, residential collection and distribution, and downtown collection and distribution.

The line-haul to the CBD is usually the most costly (and longest) part of the over-all urban transportation operation, though its relative importance diminishes as workplaces and residences disperse. A striking feature of line-haul cost comparisons is that a highway-oriented system is almost always as cheap as or cheaper than rail alternatives. Rail transit remains economically attractive for the line-haul only where population densities are extremely high, facilities are to be constructed underground, or rail roadbed structures are already on hand and can be regarded as sunk costs. It is therefore significant that most American cities with enough population density to support a rail transit operation, or even with prospects of having enough, usually possess rail transit already.

A surprising aspect of the line-haul cost comparisons is that a private automobile system even with a car occupancy of only 1.6 persons will usually be cheaper than either bus or rail transit when specific channel or corridor demands fall much below 10,000 persons per hour — a level well within the range of maximum channel or corridor demands in many American cities.

Highway vehicles are particularly well suited for residential collection and distribution. To be most efficient, residential collection requires flexible and preferably continuous (or nontransfer) transportation — more easily supplied by the bus and automobile than by rail transit. In recognition of this fact, all pending proposals for new rail transit incorporate a heavy reliance on feeder buses and private automobiles to bring passengers to suburban rail stations, and contain plans for large numbers of parking spaces at outlying points along the rail facility. Park-and-ride, however, is a very costly mode for residential collection and distribution. The least expensive approach to residential distribution is to incorporate residential operations into the line-haul by extending line-haul express bus or automobile trips whenever feasible. In fact, where trip origination densities and line-haul volume levels are low, extension of the automobile trip is about the only inexpensive recourse — unless the housewife can be pressed into chauffeur duty in a kiss-and-ride operation. Bus operations, either as extensions of line-haul express runs or restricted to residential collection and distribution, become attractive, though, when trip origination densities reach a moderate level.

Collection and distribution in downtown or other high-density employment districts is much more complicated. Designing an efficient system for this particular function is made difficult by the fact that no available technology is well suited to the existing structures and plans of many older American cities. This is particularly true where streets are narrow and little offstreet parking is provided. Every city, moreover, is likely to have a number of special geographic and other traits that will offer obstacles.

Some general principles can be laid down, however. First, extending rapid transit facilities into downtown areas by tunnel or elevated structure is costly. This expense is likely to be justified only if corridor volumes are very high or street capacity is very limited, or if passenger travel time or convenience is highly valued. Generally, the cheapest solution (except at very high corridor volumes) to the downtown distribution problem is simply to extend via surface streets line-haul trips made by automobile or bus. Also, it rarely becomes attractive to think of having virtually *all* line-haul express facilities terminate at the edge of the CBD, with travelers transferring to specialized surface vehicles for the last part of their journeys. A special CBD secondary distribution system may be helpful on a limited basis, though, as a means of tying peripheral parking to the CBD and facilitating shopper and other short-hop movement during the day.

Frequently the key to choosing an efficient CBD distribution system is whether downtown street capacity will be sufficient to handle collection and distribution by surface modes. This, in turn, can depend on the availability of a belt highway around the CBD since such highways reduce congestion by diverting through traffic. Available street space can be further expanded by providing more offstreet or peripheral parking facilities, especially for all-day parkers. A good downtown collection and distribution system also can make peripheral parking more attractive.

In very-high-density employment districts, especially with little surface street area, the simplest and most economical solution for downtown collection and distribution usually will be rail or bus transit operating either in subways or on elevated structures. The choice between elevated and subway is largely an aesthetic question, the answer depending on whether burying the facility is worth in beauty the extra cost. If long tunnels are required or deemed desirable, rail transit has a substantial cost advantage for the downtown distribution function in being able to carry much larger volumes in a small bore than other modes. It is in this quality more than any other that rail has a particular or special advantage.

Obviously, the optimum over-all transportation system for a city will depend on a large number of factors: the age of the city, the existing supply of wide avenues and rail transit rights-of-way, the geographic density of its workplaces and residences, the income level and tastes of its population, and its future prospects and patterns of population and employment growth. At present, only a handful of American metropolitan areas seem to have enough rush hour CBD cordon crossings or sufficiently optimistic prospects for the future to justify even serious consideration of elaborate grade separated transit system investments, whether bus or rail. For American cities of moderate size, efficient urban transportation seems most readily obtainable by using private automobiles, complemented by various amounts and types of bus transit using common rights-of-way. In many ways the most crucial transportation question facing these cities is whether they can achieve the self-discipline required for coordinated, efficient use of their highway facilities, particularly during rush hours.

This coordination might be achieved in several ways. One would be to levy tolls on the use of important urban highway facilities and to charge substantially more for use during the peak commuter hours where differential costs are common; the same objective also might be achieved by special licensing or related schemes. A number of political and technical obstacles complicate the implementation of such price rationing schemes; they do, though, have appeal on the basis of economic considerations alone, particularly if the marginal costs of additional peak-hour costs are very high.

A more strictly technical solution to the highway coordination problem — one without so many obvious difficulties — would be to monitor flows and limit expressway access to levels that could be expeditiously accommodated, that is, that made full use of the highway capacity and did not overtax and thereby coagulate the traffic flow. The technical means exist for such schemes and actually have been applied in a few experimental cases. If monitoring and controlled access of major urban expressways were coupled with priority access for public transit buses, a simple and quite inexpensive form of rapid transit would be quickly available in most American cities. At a minimum, it would be sensible to experiment with these priority access schemes for buses before committing large sums to rail rapid transit installations. The fact that priority access for buses might be put into effect almost immediately, rather than in the five or more years often required to build a rail transit system, only heightens the appeal. Indeed, a good argument might be made for giving buses priority access to urban expressways as an interim measure even if a rail system is to be constructed.

Useful changes also could be made in transit operating and scheduling practices that would both cut costs and improve service in many instances. Very often today's operating practices represent a slavish adherence to meeting past needs rather than a rational assessment of how best to serve present needs. For example, simple modifications in door, seating, and terminal arrangements in many cases could do much to improve the quality and cut the costs of transit operations.

Several institutional changes, some of them quite minor in character, could also contribute to improving urban transportation. If differential pricing of highways for use at different times of the day and by different vehicles is ruled out as impractical, it still seems conceivable that much could be done to rationalize urban transportation by making parking charges more reflective of costs. In particular, the present trend toward offering cost-justified rate concessions for parking smaller cars in crowded downtown areas could encourage greater use of small cars as commuter vehicles. Any step in this direction is likely to be beneficial, not only in terms of reducing parking costs but also by permitting somewhat more intensive use of highway and street capacity, cutting operating costs, and even alleviating smog problems by reducing gas consumption in urban areas.

A general reduction in market controls and government regulations on urban transit and taxi operations also seems in order. Free entry into the taxi business and the availability of private or rented automobiles would provide a more than sufficient competitive check on any "monopolistic tendencies" in which modern transit companies might be tempted to indulge. As a promotion of public transit, less regulation and more flexibility in pricing and service offerings, including the possibility of earning a positive return on invested capital, might be just as salutary as direct government subsidy.

It is difficult, in fact, to build many strong justifications for subsidizing urban transit on economic grounds alone. In general, economic theory offers little direct help in defining policy objectives for urban transportation. The theory provides only some loose guidelines in the selection of policies for achieving objectives stipulated by the political process. For example, alternative pricing and subsidy policies can be evaluated for their technical feasibility, their probable effects on efficiency, their applicability to urban transportation markets, and probable implications for income redistribution. Many times, it seems, currently proposed urban transit subsidies, when subjected to careful economic evaluation, appear to be internally inconsistent, ill-conceived, and often in conflict with other goals of government policies in urban areas.

16 Planning Adequate Transportation for Southern California: a Case Study

JOSEPH E. HARING
Occidental College

A balanced view of transportation — one which supports the need for rail rapid transit as well as for numerous improvements in local street traffic (for instance, off-street parking, one-way streets, center-city malls). As one of a series of proposals, this article helped lead to the establishment of a new government organization to manage the rapid transit of Southern California.

No less than twelve official, sometimes conflicting governmental reports about transit in Southern California have been published since 1953. And interested individuals' public pronouncements and proposals are legion. The result is a considerable amount of confusion and indecision on the part of responsible civic leaders.

The Southern California Research Council has taken on the task of sifting the millions of words to define a rational approach to transportation planning in Southern California.[1] "An Orderly and Efficient Transportation System for the Southern California Metropolis" is the title of the report to be published later this year.[2]

SCRC BEGINS RESEARCH

The need for such a study became imperative recently because of: (1) the confusing flood of reports about monorail and freeways; (2) the rapidly increasing automobile congestion on the freeways and streets of Southern California; and (3) the fear of economic strangulation if the roads, streets and other transport facilities of the area become too congested to permit efficient movement of goods and people.

SCRC began its research work by comparing carefully all the available public and private reports on transportation in Southern California. Monorail reports, freeway extension statements, plans for new freeways and new street facilities, and national and statewide policy statements on transportation planning were studied.

This mass of printed material prompted an interview survey of the top businessmen and government planners in the area and at the national level. Civic leaders

---

From "Planning Transportation for Southern California," by Joseph E. Haring, *Traffic Quarterly,* Volume 14, October 1960, pp. 474–487. Reprinted with permission of *Traffic Quarterly* and Eno Foundation.

were asked to consider the strengths and weaknesses of Southern California's transportation system and transport planning, and then were solicited for recommendations about improvement.

The third step was to condense the collected information into concise statements of fact and policy recommendations.

The council's findings can be grouped under three headings: (1) Southern California's expected growth; (2) Southern California's transport requirements; and (3) public planning and organization.

SOUTHERN CALIFORNIA'S EXPECTED GROWTH

Southern California is expected to nearly double its population between 1960 and 1980, increasing from nine million to seventeen million in the next two decades. By far the largest portion of this increase will be absorbed by Los Angeles County, which is to receive nearly four million persons in addition to its present six million. Adjacent Orange County is expected to have the largest relative increase — nearly two million residents are to join the present 700,000.[3]

Residential living habits are expected to reflect dispersion tendencies as in the last two decades: single-unit dwellings will house most of the expected population increase. Outlying areas, where the cost of housing is cheaper, are likely to develop rapidly.

There are several reasons for the growing dispersion of residences, commercial establishments, and industrial facilities. The primary cause is the desire and ability to pay for suburban-type living. Midwesterners who come to Southern California are accustomed to single-unit homes, and immigrants from the densely populated eastern seaboard may relish the opportunity to avoid apartments.

A widely dispersed labor force requires large parking lots at factory sites; so industrial planners are placing their new establishments in the outskirts of cities, where land is cheap enough to permit adequate parking lots. That is a second reason for dispersion.

Third is the huge land requirements of many of the leading manufacturers of Southern California: aircraft, missile, and some electronics firms find single-story buildings with long production lines by far the most efficient. These firms cannot afford to locate in high-priced central business or manufacturing districts.

Finally, dispersed factory locations often provide congenial working facilities for valuable workers, and industrial firms allow this factor to influence their choice of site.

Growth patterns are expected to continue to reflect concentric expansions around the central business cores of Los Angeles, San Diego, and San Bernardino-Riverside, with the circles meeting and crossing as the outer reaches of one community melt into the outer reaches of another. Figure 1 illustrates this pattern of expansion in graphic form.

The three population centers of the area are alike in that dispersion of population and industry is likely to continue in a concentric pattern, but Los Angeles is different in that it is growing up (in population density) as well as out because of the growth of centralized commercial and financial facilities in the central business district and along the Wilshire Corridor.[4]

The Wilshire Corridor, extending from the center of Los Angeles (CBD) westward along Wilshire Boulevard, appears to be developing into a business and

Figure 1

The Southern California Metropolis

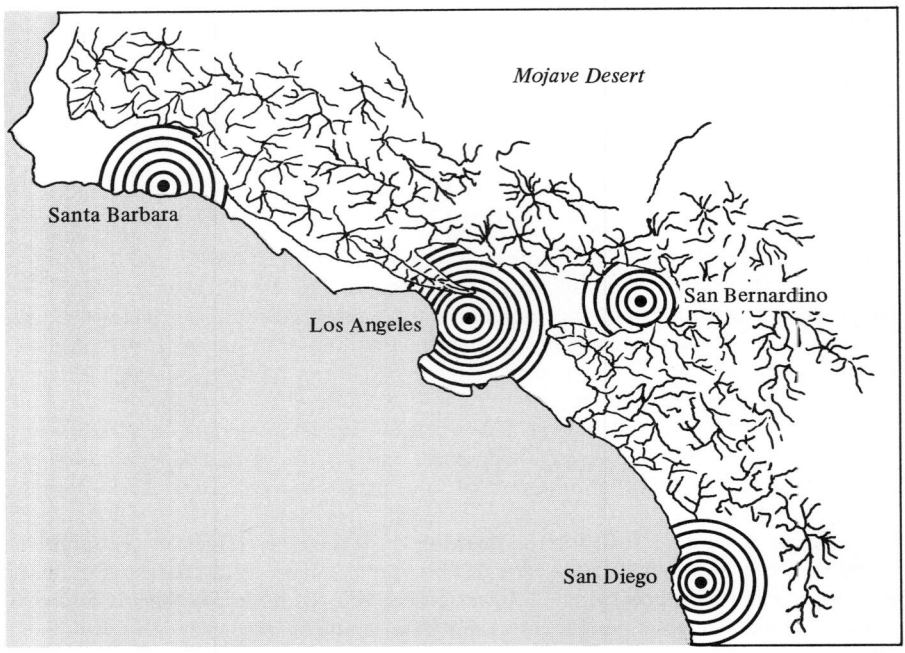

finance center for the area. Multi-unit apartments a block or two to either side of the Boulevard provide residences for many of the white-collar workers employed in businesses on Wilshire. Population densities along the corridor are increasing rapidly, making the area a major exception to the general growth pattern in Southern California. Other areas of relative high density are Santa Monica, southwest of the Wilshire Boulevard and Western Avenue intersection; and to a lesser extent, Pasadena, some twelve miles northeast of the central business district.

Southern California has developed considerable engineering technology in its aircraft, missile, electronics, and research industries, among others. Further growth is expected to occur in the same types of "sophisticated" industries widely scattered in the area.

TRANSPORTATION REQUIREMENTS

Because of growing dispersion of population and industry, automobiles will continue to provide the most economical mode of transportation in the region's foreseeable future. The freeway system, the central portion of which is outlined in Figure 2, has provided transport links to the outer reaches of the Los Angeles Basin. Its planned expansion (indicated by dotted lines) is designed to become a transport grid that will greatly increase the potential growth of the area.

Financing for the freeway program is assured by the State of California through gasoline tax and automobile registration fee laws. Divisions VII, VIII and XI of

Figure 2
Rapid Transport Corridors and Transport Centers in Southern California

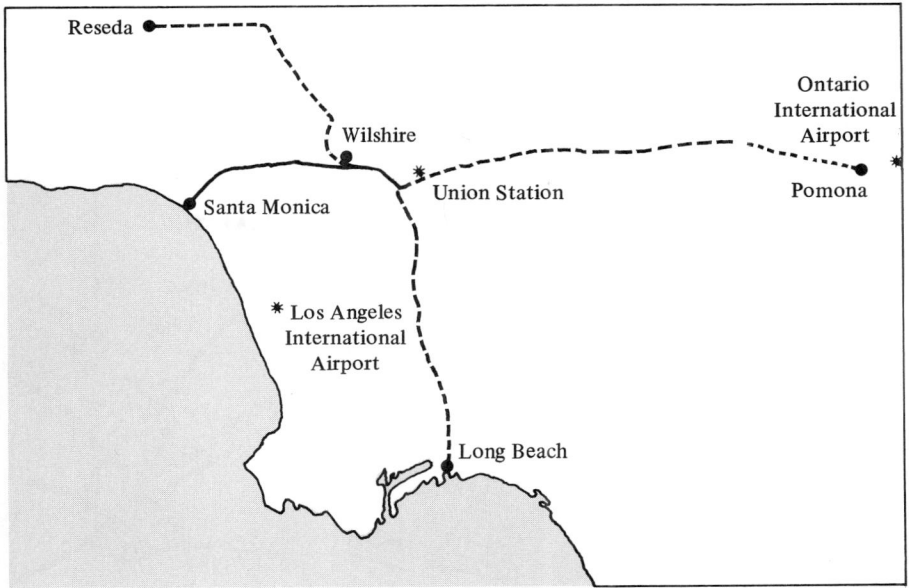

the state division of highways are charged with planning and constructing the freeway system as tax monies become available. The freeway system is expensive in both land and construction costs, but for widely-dispersed populations it is still more economical than any other form of travel known in Southern California today.

Mass rapid transit for the Los Angeles Basin is being studied by the Los Angeles Metropolitan Transit Authority (LAMTA), a public corporation created by the state legislature to provide mass transit in Los Angeles and Orange Counties. LAMTA has engaged engineering firms to make detailed recommendations for fixed-location (rail) transportation of passengers. The most recent proposal recommends a four-armed, seventy-five-mile system feeding the Wilshire-CBD commercial corridor. Figure 3 indicates the proposed routes. Consulting engineers estimate that the system, an overhead duorail, would cost $529.7 million. Estimates of expected revenues are yet to be developed.

However, preliminary origin-destination studies by engineering consultants to LAMTA indicate that the Santa Monica-Wilshire-CBD corridor has a larger number of potential riders than any of the other suggested transit routes. Land values along this corridor are relatively high, so an overhead rail system, using relatively little land, may be capable of providing cheap transportation. Further studies of expected demand-and-cost schedules should provide more accurate evaluation of the economic feasibility of rail transit in this and other corridors.

LAMTA is now operating a single-rail transit line (to Long Beach), and several bus lines. Ninety-five per cent of Los Angeles commuters find the present facilities

Figure 3

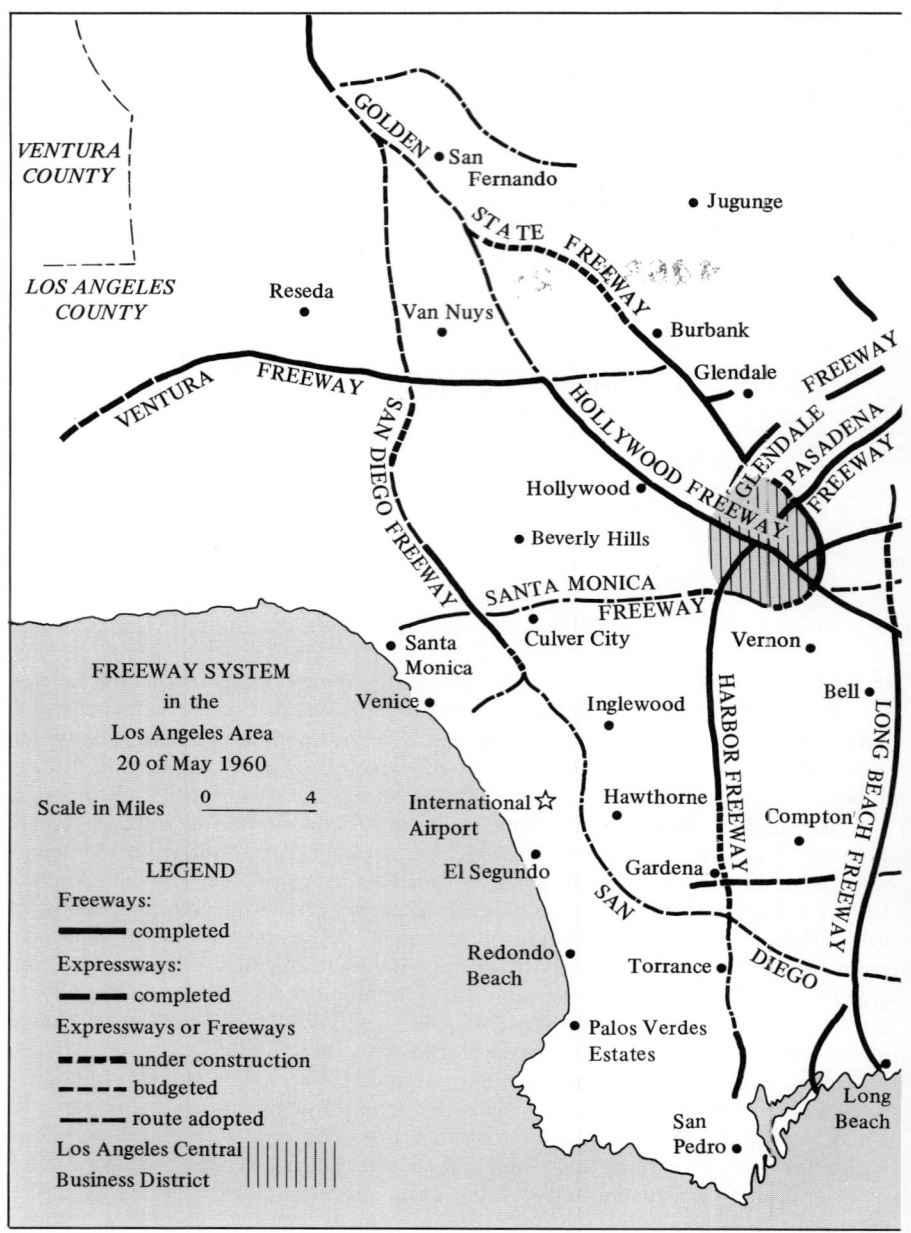

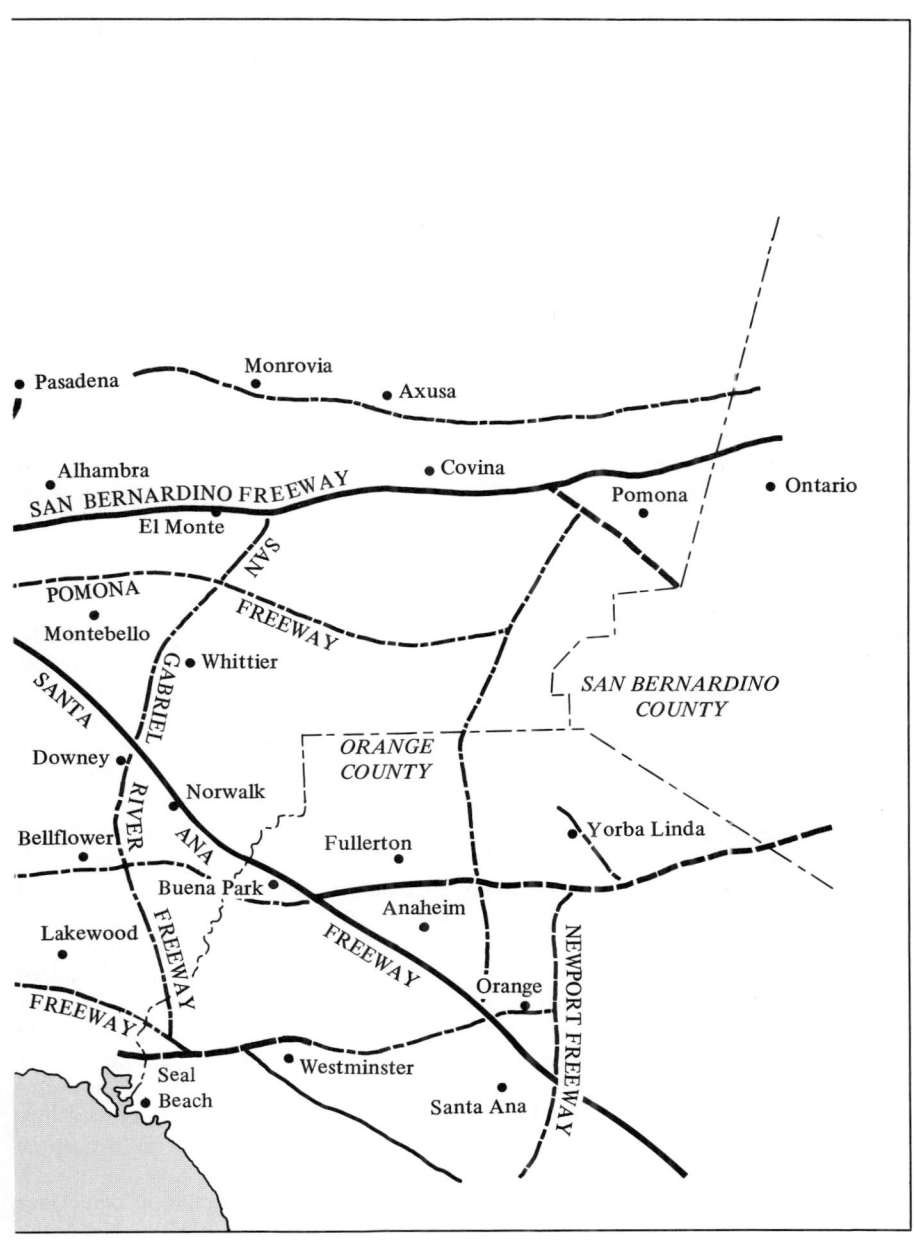

unattractive, though the "Freeway Flyer" express bus service to the San Fernando Valley is gaining in popular acceptance, according to LAMTA.

Buses are by far the most flexible and convenient form of public mass transit, but their widespread use will require a special function of roadways for buses. One possibility is the construction of special new freeways for buses, on which express bus service could be provided for commuters. For example, buses could use local streets in suburbs to pick up passengers, proceed to the bus freeway, and then at high speed go directly to the business district.

The reverse pattern could be used for homeward trips in the evening. This service could be as fast as any proposed form of rail service, and would be much more convenient to passengers not living or working near rail stations.

Bus freeways might be built (by LAMTA or some other suitable agency) almost as cheaply as the "metro" duorail suggested by the Authority's consulting engineers.[5] Many new LA freeways cost half, or less than half, of the $5.9 million a mile of the proposed duorail. Special bus freeways are more versatile than rail facilities because they can be rented to motorists on a toll basis as well. Rush-hour commuters may be willing to pay a toll of one-half cent a mile or more for the privilege of getting home thirty minutes sooner by using bus expressways; weekend vacationists might save considerable time and expense by paying for the privilege of driving on them.

TRANSPORT CENTERS NEEDED

Strategic to the development of satisfactory mass transit is a system of multipurpose transport centers. Area transport centers could serve as collecting points for people and goods en route to more distant parts of Southern California by a variety of travel modes. Such centers would be economical where rail mass transit is to be used, because parking lots and feeder bus-connections required for adequate rail service provide a natural nucleus of cooperative service units. Adding helicopter and taxi service to the bus, parking, and freight-forwarding facilities around a rail terminal would increase the economies realized from joint solutions to transport problems.

A system of bus expressways, on the other hand, would tend to reduce the need for transport centers; a large one in the CBD (at Union Station, for example) might be able to serve the whole area for both passenger and freight purposes. Bus expressways would make it possible to tailor service to the many locations required without frequent changes.

In any case, the chief center is likely to be in the CBD hub, with auxiliary centers at transit extremities, as indicated on Figure 3. Union Station in downtown Los Angeles is already functioning in a small way as a hub, and Pomona has a multipurpose transport center that might serve as a pilot operation for later developments. Los Angeles International Airport has great potential as a multi-purpose transportation center.

Central to this analysis, of course, is the assumption that population dispersion will continue to keep travel densities low, except along the CBD-Wilshire-Santa Monica corridor.

Sufficient population and industry dispersion tend to eliminate parking space problems, though Los Angeles' CBD-Wilshire corridor will continue to require considerable commercial parking space. Although a law has been passed requiring parking allocations according to expected occupancy of new buildings, there is little evidence that new buildings are being planned without express consideration of parking requirements. Destruction of old buildings is in fact encouraged by real estate tax reductions on land so converted.

Freight movements in and around Southern California are largely handled by private firms. Rail, truck, ship, airplane, and pipeline companies compete with one another for the available business, though each mode of transport is constrained by a different set of regulations and subsidy patterns.

Railroad freight movements are constrained by Interstate Commerce Commission rate-change policies, labor union make-work schemes, and unimaginative management policies on the part of the railroads themselves.[6] Some truckers are regulated (interstate lines), but many are not; some truckers pay low fuel taxes by using diesel engines, some do not. Shipping is heavily subsidized by the United States government in some cases, and protected in others (coastwise shipping). There appears to be no consistent national policy regarding air freight; pipelines are also subject to ICC policy.

National policy changes regarding freight movements are required to correct many of the inconsistent practices found in Southern California as well as around the nation.

Los Angeles International Airport handled nine million passengers in 1959 and is expected to serve twenty million passengers in 1970, plus a considerably greater relative increase in air freight. The area will need another large airport early in the 1970's, and plans need to be laid now. No official action is being taken at the moment, but several interested private groups are exerting pressure toward this end.

PUBLIC PLANNING AND ORGANIZATION

The Council's findings on public transport planning fall into three categories: (a) some of the area's transport planning has been thorough, though primarily concerned with only one transport medium; (b) a sizeable portion of the planning seems to have been uncoordinated and short-sighted; and (c) much needed planning was not being done at all.

The state division of highways, the Los Angeles metropolitan transit authority, certain county officials, the railroad companies with regard to property for industry, and the Long Beach and Los Angeles Harbor Departments have attempted thorough, long-range planning.

The state division of highways has developed a master plan for freeways and some local streets in Southern California, under provisions of the Senate Current Resolution 26 and subsequent legislation. Some 190 miles of freeways have already been constructed by this agency, which is financed in large part by gasoline tax and vehicle registration revenues collected by the state. More than 1,000 miles of additional freeways are planned for District VII of California which includes Los Angeles, Orange, Ventura, and parts of Riverside and San Bernardino counties.

In cooperation with the traffic department of the City of Los Angeles, the state highway engineer for District VII is currently engaged in an area-wide origin-destination study of transport needs. "The Los Angeles Regional Transportation Study" is expected to be completed early in 1962. Representative state (including LAMTA), county and city officials of the area have been invited to act as an advisory committee to this project.

The planning of the state division of highways concentrates on freeways and major expressways — its chief responsibility. Limitation of its responsibilities in the past has precluded detailed consideration of the role of mass rapid transit, rail, monorail, or other transport modes.

The Los Angeles metropolitan transit authority concentrates exclusively on the problem of mass rapid transit for Los Angeles and its immediate environs. The Authority foresees considerable development of mass transit in and around the central business district, with spurs going some distance into the suburbs. Financial and legal limitations prevent LAMTA from making an extended overall plan of freeways, freight movements, pipelines, and air travel. By choice it has not examined bus expressways as rapid transit possibilities.

Planning by county officials has been forward-looking but under-financed. Los Angeles County has by far the most promising planning unit in its regional planning commission which attempts to study land use for regions within the county. Inter-county cooperation has been promoted by the Los Angeles regional planning commission, with but sporadic success. In 1958, an inter-county planning group engaged in a regional recreational study for eleven counties in Southern California,[7] but study has lagged because of insufficient funds.

The three major railways in Southern California — Santa Fe, Southern Pacific, and Union Pacific — have purchased or leased land adjoining their rights-of-way that would be suitable for industrial sites. This is a thoroughly desirable form of land-use planning. It is not, unfortunately, being integrated into the rapid transit or freeway system development plans made on a continuing basis by LAMTA and the state division of highways.

Planning by the Long Beach and, to a lesser extent, the Los Angeles Harbor Department, has been comprehensive. Their plans integrate growth of freight and passenger movement with the expansion of the freeway system in Southern California. By connecting the Port of Long Beach and the Southern California freeway system, cargoes can be moved from any pier in the part area directly onto the Long Beach Freeway and to all points in Southern California. The Los Angeles Harbor is attempting to develop similar facilities.

RESULTS OF UNCOORDINATED PLANNING

Examples of apparently uncoordinated planning include: (1) that done for the roads around the new International Airport; and (2) the placement of freeway entrances and exits in the downtown area of Los Angeles.

Los Angeles International Airport is a giant $200 million installation that will be expanded and completed in 1961. The runways and hangars are excellent and the passenger and freight-handling facilities will be the most modern in the world. Traffic patterns beyond the edge of airport property are another matter, however. City officials have pointed out that in 1965 more than ten million cars are expected to move in and out of the new airport — almost 30,000 cars a day.

Unless new plans are developed, however, nearly all of these cars will have to pass the Sepulveda-Century intersection near the airport entrance. This intersection is already the busiest in Southern California by actual count. The city Department of Airports predicts a 350 per cent increase in air traffic by 1970, but that department has no authority beyond the airport to alter street, freeway, or land transport around the airport.

At first blush one may be tempted to blame the airport planners. But the basic reason for this lack of planning is that no single agency has the authority for providing facilities to handle traffic to and from the expanded airfield. Federal, state, and city highway and road officials all are responsible for moving traffic from the airport.

Congestion on the downtown freeways in and around the famous four-level interchange is compounded by an excessive number of exits and entrances in close proximity. Traffic officials estimate that the flow of traffic could be substantially increased by eliminating or closing some of these exits and entrances, which were built for the convenience of those living or working nearby. Increasing acceptance of the idea that freeways are for long-distance (six miles or more) travel — not for local movements — will probably preclude similar planning errors in the future.

We come now to public transport planning that has been neglected: public regulatory agencies and most small towns and cities are outstanding examples of important economic forces which, by their own admission, do little or no long-range planning.

Public regulatory agencies (the Public Utilities Commission or the Interstate Commerce Commission) report that they have neither the staff nor policy responsibility required to make decisions about railroad tariff rates, pipeline transport rates, and the like, except on a day to day *ad hoc* basis that fits into no particular long-range transport plan at all. The federal government itself has complained about this lack of policy and authority, but as yet no action has been taken.[8]

Planning commissions for the 125 small towns and cities in Southern California spend from eighty-five to ninety per cent of their time on changes in zoning and variance regulations, and have neither time nor authority to do long-range planning. In some of the communities the voting public has authorized them only to live with and maintain the status quo.

It seems apparent that, operating all by themselves, many government units cannot afford the comprehensive planning needed for long-term growth in Southern California. A multitude of these small local governments exist in Southern California. Some 600 local government districts must make plans and decisions about transportation in the area. But by and large they have not been able to work together.

POLICY RECOMMENDATIONS

The transportation system in Southern California must, if it is to function adequately, provide transportation flexible enough to meet the needs of widely scattered population, businesses, and industrial plants and at the same time prevent congestion in the densely populated CBD-Wilshire corridor. Accomplishment of this goal will require close cooperation by state, regional (LAMTA has regional authority over Los Angeles and Orange Counties), county and city officials of the area.

Because the disjointed governmental machinery so far employed has not produced integrated planning, a need exists for a regional transport coordinating authority, similar to those provided for the San Francisco Bay area and the Port of New York area.

The regional transport coordinating authority should be required to perform two major functions. First, it should be charged with the responsibility of assuring adequate highway, rail, airplane, pipeline, and water transportation, consistent with the high rate of economic growth in the basin. This means that various forms of transportation must be jointly designed to complement each other in such a way as to provide the necessary transport at the lowest possible cost.

The second responsibility of the regional transport authority should be to arrange for the proper spacing of residential, industrial, commercial, and recreational areas so as to minimize unnecessary travel.[9]

REFERENCES

1. The Council, jointly sponsored by Occidental and Pomona Colleges and thirty-five distinguished business firms in the area, has published seven reports since 1953 on subjects concerned with specific problems of the Southern California economy. Its latest report, entitled "The Southern California Metropolis — 1980," was released early this year. SCRC is affiliated with the College-Community Research Center Program and is in part financed by the Committee for Economic Development and The Fund for Adult Education of the Ford Foundation.
2. Los Angeles, Orange, Ventura, Santa Barbara, San Bernardino, Riverside, San Diego, and Imperial Counties make up Southern California for purposes of this study.
3. The population and income projections of this section have been developed by the Council in its "The Southern California Metropolis — 1980," Southern California Research Council, Los Angeles, 1959, pp. 8 ff.
4. More than seven million square feet of new office space have been constructed in the Corridor during the last six years.
5. These engineers estimate that the 74.9 miles of duorail system, exclusive of rolling stock, would cost $443.7 million, or $5.9 million a mile. The Colorado Freeway extension to the Golden State Freeway, perhaps typical because it transverses both densely and sparsely populated areas, is costing about $6 million a mile, or about as much as "metro," according to District VII of the California Division of Highways. Precise comparisons, of course, must await detailed engineering studies of the proposed routes and the available rights-of-way. *Cf.*, E. T. Telford, "Freeways in District VII," *California Highways*, Vol. 39, January–February, 1960, pp. 3–19.
6. *Cf.*, J. R. Meyer, *et al*, *The Economics of Competition in the Transportation Industries*, Cambridge, Harvard University Press, 1959, Chapter III, and *passim*.
7. Including Kern, Inyo and Mono Counties in addition to those under discussion in this article.
8. *Cf.*, U.S. Department of Commerce, *Federal Transportation Policy and Program*, Washington, D.C., March, 1960, pp. 4 and 5 and *passim*.
9. SCRC is developing a recommended administrative structure for the proposed transport authority, and will publish their recommendations in a comprehensive report later this year.

D
Public Health and Education

High population densities and serious misuse of land and space contribute to poor health and inadequate education in our large cities — through crowded homes, congested streets, overburdened schools, understaffed public hospital and clinic staffs.

The central city schools seem closer to nightmares than to the American dream of the "melting pot." As the now famous Coleman Report tells us, the schools are no longer narrowing the gap between minorities and the white majority; indeed, the longer children stay in school, the wider the gap. Overall, the Coleman Report makes a convincing case for the view that student achievement depends, crucially, on forces external to the schools — on forces which the schools cannot control.

In central cities, the health needs of the middle-income and low-income groups are met only haphazardly, if at all. Such groups receive little, if any, information about diet, exercise, venereal disease, the risks of drug use, and the subject of mental health. (The National Institute of Mental Health estimates that mental illness and emotion-related illnesses cost American business $10 billion each year; that eighty-five per cent of all industrial accidents and seventy per cent of all dismissals are caused in large part by mental or emotional disturbance. Yet *The Wall Street Journal* estimates that the federal government, since 1963, has spent only some $400 million on John F. Kennedy's program of federal provision for neighborhood health centers.)

Added together, public health and education budgets in American metropolitan areas seem meaningful. On the average, some ten per cent of local government expenditures are for public health; some thirty-five per cent for public education. State and federal governments spend additional amounts. In the late 1960's, local, state, and federal spending for these services, totaled more than $60 billion per year.

Benefit-cost studies can help in evaluating the public health and education budgets — the programs which are put forth by planners. Program budgeting, made famous by Robert McNamara, former Secretary of Defense, is a complete and rational method of synthesizing all of the demand, supply, and financing matters that bear on public decisions. Now being applied to health, and especially to education, planning-programming-budgeting systems (PPBS) illustrate the expansion of the field of economics to vital areas of urban life.

Since public health and education are both important in rural areas as well as in cities, heretofore they have not been considered part of urban and regional economics. But high population densities have created severe problems of mental and physical health. The educational system developed in rural and small-town America has proved particularly ill-equipped to cope with the education and training of children in densely populated areas. Furthermore, the labor market imbalances so evident in the blighted areas of metropolitan regions can be corrected in part by public provision of better health and higher skills for the labor force. Finally, physical health and educational achievement are used as screening devices in admitting individuals to employment.

Conventional microeconomic theory has been extended to the fields of health and education by considering them to be forms of human capital — capital which can be increased by "investment" expenditures on better health or more education. Similarly, the stock of health and education with which a person begins economic activities may deteriorate if not properly maintained and renewed.

Economists have described the supply of health and education in the form of human capital as a response to the relatively high rates of return that may be expected from this kind of investment. Statistical studies of rate of return on health and educational capital indicate that investment in both can be very profitable, and that some types of health and education expenditures are much more profitable, of course, than other types.

17 Physical and Mental Health in the City

E. JAMES LIEBERMAN
Howard University
and *Harvard University*

LEONARD J. DUHL
University of California, Berkeley

Urban health needs can be met by no single program; only by the concerted use of many disciplines and the concerted action of many groups.

Health is related to everything that affects human beings, including all of urban life. This does not make health professionals experts on city planning, but it does

---

From "Physical and Mental Health in the City," by E. James Lieberman and Leonard J. Duhl, *The Annals of the American Academy of Political and Social Science,* Volume 352, March 1964, pp. 13–24. Reprinted with permission.

make them necessary collaborators in planning and imposes upon them the responsibility of working with and learning from experts in welfare, education, labor, business, architecture, economics, and so on. A whole host of persons and professions is concerned with the improvement of urban life; all have comprehensive ideals, and limited knowledge and skills. Rational co-ordination of our efforts, without arbitrary restriction, will make a tremendous difference in our contribution to society. It is part of our job to share concerns and to pool our skills to find approaches which are generally acceptable and, therefore, workable. The contemporary health worker must be practitioner, planner, politician, and, not least, scientist.

THE SCOPE OF THE PROBLEM

The manifest complexity of the urban condition demands responsible, rational planning which respects the intricate dynamic balance of ecological systems. Uncertainty will always be present, adding to the burden of responsibility, not to excuses for inaction. As we acquire knowledge and experience, quality of planning will assume its important place among criteria for judging health programs.

One way of judging the quality of a public health program is the amount of preventable disease and disability which occurs in a community. Another is the attainment of optimal levels of function in the population. In more positive terms, the merit of a public-health program rests on its ability to close the gap between the advances in medical science and their optimal application in the community.

It is often difficult to assign causes even in significant relationships, and the urban condition is no exception. Diseases are distributed in the population differentially by age, sex, occupation, education, income, ethnicity; all these and more factors, separately and in combination, provide clues to the epidemiologist and, hopefully, indicators of need to practitioners. Health services are distributed in the population differentially, but all too often, regardless of such indicators, in a pattern determined by wealth and counterproductive political factors. Our purpose is to include these factors in our thinking and planning in the most constructive way possible at the same time we work wholeheartedly for necessary changes.

In most parts of the world prior to this century, urban health was inferior to rural. Public health and other social services, along with technological changes, have now reversed the picture. Water supply and sewer systems more than compensate for the bodily needs of human aggregates. Rapid transportation brings the clinic within reach of many. Schools provide at least some surveillance and education in regard to health. While some areas of the city still concentrate and intensify pathology, the urban center also provides the miracle work of modern medical specialties. Early diagnosis and treatment mean limitation of disability to the individual and limitation of contagion where that is a concern. Of course, the same factors which keep us within reach of medical care contribute to higher totals of morbidity and mortality due to accidents, air pollution, and, perhaps, anxiety. The educational and cultural assets of the city bolster the sanity of many who are sorely tried by density, dirt, and the stresses of modern urban family life.

In health, as with other matters, the great cities have often fared poorly because of stronger rural representation in state legislatures. With massive urban-renewal programs, the federal government is deeply involved in many aspects of city life and planning. Metropolitan government is notoriously fragmented all across the country. Suburbs and cities have grown and coalesced across county and even state lines, making traditional jurisdictions functionally absurd. Here, as in some other matters, Americans are quick to respond to a crisis but are slow to adopt the less dramatic, stable approach of planning and prevention.

Only forty-five years ago, our population was 50 per cent rural. Now more than two-thirds of the populace resides in cities, and metropolitan areas are absorbing 80 per cent of population growth and, with it, the bulk of health problems. The city's nature is also changing: the center decays, becoming a slum; many with means move to the suburbs, taking with them tax support and social skills so sorely needed by the city's institutions; urban renewal comes, replacing and dispersing a slum, but rarely using this crisis as an opportunity to rehabilitate people or to prevent further decay. City planning and urban renewal is very well motivated, but have we learned from experience? What is the social price we pay in health and other social services when we adopt this program? In isolation from social planning, it is ineffective and even damaging. We are concerned too often with the mechanics and give inadequate attention to the city dweller as a person. What is the gain from a project which clears a slum only to displace the tenants to other blighted areas where rents are within their means? What will become of the best-laid city plans when archaic tax laws deter competent developers and only encourage abandonment of the central city for the suburbs?

People develop attachments to their neighborhoods — and legislators to their statutes — old and poor as they may be, and "improvements" which disrupt these ties will often boomerang. This is not cause for resignation, however. While we can understand that slum tenants might want to stay where they are rather than move to better housing, we cannot shrug off those neighborhood conditions and resistances to change which block improvements in health, schooling, and delinquency. A program of planning which is less concerned with blueprints and which more fully involves the people being planned for in the process of planning, utilizing the multiplicity of social, economic, physical, and health skills, will permit us to match our increasing understanding of human behavior with increasingly effective courses of action.

HEALTH IN THE UNITED STATES

Before turning to the relationship of health to the broader problems of urban communities, it is well to look at some of the indices now available to measure the incidence and prevalence of disease.

The United States is increasingly an urban country. The evaluation of needs and planning of services must be done less and less in the archaic political jurisdictions and more on a regional functional basis. National statistics, which we present here, reflect urban trends, but there are great discrepancies within each city: this is a primary concern.

Causes of death and morbidity in the United States are typical of the Western industrial nations generally and very different from the developing countries where infectious and nutritional diseases are still the major problem. Infections still take their toll from infants under one year, and it is also true that tuberculosis and venereal disease rates are beginning to increase after a steady decline over some years. The leading killers, however, are the so-called degenerative diseases whose toll mounts up enormously with longer life spans, in the later decades of life.

LEADING CAUSES OF DEATH
(Rate per 100,000 population)

Over-all	939
Heart disease	363
Cancer	147
Cerebro-vascular lesions	108
Accidents	52

As expected, the chronic conditions — with varying amounts of disability — are as follows:

PREVALENCE OF CHRONIC ILLNESS
(Rate per 100,000 persons)

Diagnosis	
Heart conditions	3,000
Hypertension	3,100
Ulcer	1,400
Arthritis and rheumatism	6,300
Asthma and hay fever	5,400
Mental illness (hospitalized)	324

Efforts to establish the number of nonhospitalized mentally ill persons are fraught with difficulty. A common estimate is that 10 per cent of the population is in need of psychiatric treatment. There is no evidence that city life itself is a cause of the high rates of pathology in certain groups: it may be that susceptibles are concentrated in the city or that factors such as poverty, social mobility, and changes in family life account for heightened risk of illness. Some observers in newly industrializing nations report an increase in psychoneuroses accompanying urbanization. Doctors in London and New York see a large amount of psychosomatic illness among West Indian and Puerto Rican immigrants, respectively. Mental illness, according to Social Security Administration figures, is the largest single cause of disability among United States workers under fifty years old (28.3 per cent of those compensated in 1960).

Accidents are the leading cause of death among all persons between the ages of one and thirty-six. For youths aged fifteen to twenty-four, accidents claim more lives than all other causes combined; five-sixths of these are males. Obviously, accidents are a public health concern: they take a high toll in death and disability and ostensibly are preventable. Note that accidents became a major concern because of the effectiveness of "death control" in the age groups between infancy and the onset of heart disease: the over-all death rates are lowest between one and thirty-six, hence accidents stand out. Before we can move effectively to prevent this tragic toll, we must understand much more about the meaning of these data and their relation to many other phenomena: intoxication, suicide, homicide, adolescent aggression, automobile design, law enforcement. Accidents may be symptomatic of a number of other processes which may or may not be amenable to benign intervention. Here, as elsewhere in public health — and city — planning, the effects of intervention must be thoroughly weighed, continuously; good intentions are no substitute for this responsibility.

That we can be concerned about accidents, schizophrenia, and geriatrics reflects the relative excellence of health in the United States as compared with many parts of the world. We need not be ashamed of relatively high rates of diabetes or geriatric disease if these rates reflect good case-finding and treatment which keeps more people alive longer. If it represents preventable disease, or the results of inadequate medical care, that is another matter. Diseases which occur predominantly after age fifty have proved very resistant to control measures. Infant mortality, by contrast, is dropping off very sharply in response to modern health practices; it is this phenomenon which has contributed most to the remarkable increase in present-day life expectancy at birth, and, of course, it accounts for the rapid net increase in population growth.

Infant mortality deserves our special attention because the United States ranks eleventh among the nations of the world in the measure, and we are falling farther behind. Here we can only touch briefly on the significance of this, keeping in mind that the problem, like that of accidents, has a complex of causes, none of which can be attacked in isolation from the social phenomena of which they are a part.

Currently, 25 of each 1,000 live births in the United States die within the first year of life. While this is an improvement over the past, it compares poorly with the rate of 15.3 registered in Sweden and the Netherlands. Our nonwhite minority suffers from an infant mortality rate double that of the white population: 44 against 23.2 This discrepancy is largely a reflection of the low socioeconomic status of our nonwhites: 11 per cent of the population, they comprise 25 per cent of those living in poverty. In most of the countries with lower rates, midwives under medical supervision perform normal deliveries! The United States has a higher ratio of physicians to population than countries which, in this important respect, must be judged healthier. Factors related to infant mortality include prematurity, extent and quality of perinatal care, and infant morbidity, including anomalies and mental deficiency.

President Kennedy brought national attention and legislation to bear on the last-mentioned problems as a preventive of mental retardation by means of improved maternal and child health care. There is a dearth of such care for low-income groups, and many obstacles stand in the way of full utilization of them: lack of transportation and costs of medical care, long waits, poor quality of service, fragmented services, ignorance about health matters and health services, and, by no means least, lack of birth-planning advantages with consequent hostility or indifference toward many an unborn child. Without attention to family planning, we cannot expect to deal effectively with the situation. This factor is rarely mentioned in this context, although it evidently plays an important part in other countries. For example, the countries doing well with regard to infant mortality either have low birth rates — northwestern Europe — or are less densely populated — Australia, New Zealand. Conversely, in our country, birth rates are highest among the group having greatest infant mortality, the Negroes. Infant mortality is a crude way to keep population growth down. Birth control is evidently necessary to reduce infant mortality further, especially in the cities, where a large family is usually no advantage but, rather, the opposite.

The reduction of infant mortality is more than a health problem — as are so many other categories of pathology. Its solution will require good data collection and research, a multitude of skills — medical, social, teaching, administrative, political — including sensitivity to and respect for resistances; in short, it will require an ecological approach. There will be no panacea: no matter how good we think a measure is, whether birth control, fluoridation, or seat belts in cars, it has to be "sold" to a distributor first and then to consumers — and often compromised on the way. Some consumers, in fact, will never buy it. Only the naive would suppose that the introduction of any of these programs will quickly and easily change the situation. Here, as with every other social innovation, we are confronted with a complexity of biological, psychological, social, and historical factors.

SOME GOALS AND IDEALS

It is useful to think about some specifications of an ideal urban community in order to recognize the limitations upon translation of the ideal to anything real. Goals and ideals are not blueprints; they, like any plans, can only set directions for the complicated processes which must be set in motion to improve a community's health. Even those who have the rare privilege of starting a city from scratch must build it within some existing political jurisdiction which, chances are, will have many limiting aspects. These features, like the more ideal ones, are manmade, and it is man with whom we — physicians, city planners, politicians — are concerned. A fictional construct labeled "man" or "city," taken as a blueprint, will only lead us astray. But a plan without some notion of the directions in which we should aim would be as unrealistic as a good plan considering only physical amenities and not human ones. Many of these goals are untested by research and reflect values of many concerned with the human condition. We need not wait for research if such values are important.

People need sunlight, heat, water, air, and food to live. There can be no healthy community without these. We can be equally sure, though less precise, about space, recreation, education, and protection from contagious diseases and other environmental hazards. In addition, we must include concerns for human relationships and creative endeavor; politics, art, science; specialization and interdependence. Here again, for these most important factors, we lack hard data, but let us not repeat the error of considering most what we can measure best — bricks, census tracts, and dollars.

Let us postulate a location with climate favoring a variety of outdoor activities, breezes enough to disperse the gathering smog, and water for hydration, cleanliness, electric power, and recreation. Parks and playgrounds will make space in neighborhoods and green belts to freshen the landscape and the air. More important, though, may be the aesthetic pleasures of green areas; no research can measure its importance. If grass is important to people, we do not need research as much as vocal constituents.

Safe, efficient transportation will put physical and cultural amenities close at hand. Regulations based on the most advanced engineering techniques will reduce environmental pollution to a minimum. Automobile traffic will be rationally governed to reduce chaotic competition with pedestrians and other forms of transportation. Housing will meet aesthetic as well as structural and health criteria; youngsters must have fit places to play, toddlers their protective enclosures, the elderly some place to walk and rest outdoors. Resources for physical maintenances and renewal of the city shall be included from the beginning.

What about the city's size and population balance? The city, like our planet, cannot hold an infinitely expanding populace. More important than specifying size is regulating growth. Unless we do so, we face a time in the future when parenthood itself will have to be restricted. Right now, the United States family averages 3 children or more; an average of 2.7 would replenish the population. The difference between 2.7 and 3 accounts for an annual rate of population increase of 1.7 per cent — very substantial, especially when one considers the state of our schools, the unemployment picture, and the fact that those with highest fertility are hardest pressed by poverty.

Another factor of balance is age distribution: how much of the population is productive in economic terms, and how much dependent? Our population has been expanding not only with new babies but with more surviving senior citizens. We must somehow increase production, education, and geriatric services. We cannot keep them apace of an indefinitely growing population, and hopefully we will achieve some balance before the physical environment compels it: by that time, our already substantial problems of health, education, welfare, employment, and recreation will be overwhelming.

The sociopolitical part of our ecological ideal is hardest to define, although there has been an increasing amount of helpful study and discussion.[1] Poverty, ignorance, and crowding are associated with high morbidity and mortality from tuberculosis, malnutrition, maternal and child disorders, and untreated psychosis. Socioeconomic status has proved to be a frequent correlate of health and illness, with the brunt of pathology falling on the poor.

Recent National Health Survey statistics reveal a direct relationship between poor health and poverty — and not only among the elderly, who comprise a disproportionate fraction of the poorest. Obviously, sparkling new clinics and expensive drugs will not make a dent upon illness related to substandard living conditions. We will have to diminish the amount of poverty, which today affects an estimated 40 million Americans.[2]

As matters now stand in most cities, even those who stand to benefit greatly from existing services may have a jurisdictional obstacle course to run to obtain them. Multiple screenings and diagnostic evaluations, splitting up of family services, and arbitrary eligibility requirements are all too common. The ideal city would offer co-ordinated — not bureaucratically stultified — services addressed to human needs and potentials rather than proof of income, length of residence, and moralistic judgment. Political jurisdictions would coincide rationally with the metropolitan area: the fragmentation of city governments into traditionally sacred but totally outmoded districts is a menace to public health practice, among its other liabilities. Organization of certain services at regional, national, and international levels is essential to the health of the modern city.[3]

There would be places for newly arriving migrants to live and to learn how to manage in an urban world. Much of the housing would be owner occupied, and health, building, and tax codes would be designed to motivate residents and owners toward maintenance and improvement of neighborhoods. Social and health services would be accessible in neighborhoods and also through functional groups such as unions, schools, clubs.

The threat of financial ruin by illness would be removed by programs of insurance which soundly and equitably distribute the financial risks. Provision of medical-care benefits in lieu of wage and salary increases will continue, putting health programs even more under the scrutiny of consumers — and powerful consumers such as labor and industry. The results should be an improvement in both quality and distribution of services, including preventive services, but it will require a good deal of learning and adjustment on the part of physicians and consumers alike. It appears certain that both private and governmental programs will be increasingly necessary to insure adequate medical services for those who bear the highest risk of illness or who are not adequately protected through existing channels.

The university and medical school will be judged by their community services as well as their academic and research achievements. Students, now taught in run-down city hospitals and in ivory towers devoted more to the rare diseases than the common man, will, instead, find a new balance between everyday needs of the community and the exotic clinical syndrome. Medical students themselves cannot provide adequate care, but it is true that their questioning presence definitely bolsters the quality of medicine provided by their elders. These facts argue for distributing students — and their teachers — more widely in the field of medical practice. Of course, doctors would organize their practices consistent with high standards of quality and ethics. In training institutions, bed space and personnel would be allotted to community services, teaching, treatment of selected populations or diseases, and research. In short, health facilities should carry their own weight in the community. It makes no sense, say, to invest in surgical repair of rheumatic heart valves at the expense of preventive programs against rheumatic fever. Certainly it is more dramatic to restore an invalid to health than to prevent the invalidism in the first place. Our "ideal city" planners and health officials may be expected to devote much effort to dramatizing prevention or redirecting public fervor.

Mental-health programs should also have a neighborhood orientation, with appropriate facilities, co-ordinated within a larger community. This means early diagnosis and prompt treatment, with no waiting list: the timing of intervention in crises and the rational use of resources must be weighed along with depth and duration of treatment. Mental-health workers will, through consultation, assist and learn from those community care-givers who are close by in many situations of emotional distress: physicians, clergy, police, teachers, scout leaders, and bartenders. There will be facilities for night or day care in addition to regular inpatient services so located that the mentally ill will not be removed from their families and the community as now often happens. There will also be halfway houses and similar arrangements for patients who need to return to the community gradually and independently. Vocational training and sheltered workshops will provide opportunities for rehabilitation. Mental-health manpower will be bolstered from the ground up with recruitment of persons with human relations aptitude from the increasing roster of unemployed workers. They will assist in case-finding, group work, and community organization, counseling and leadership, and rehabilitation. Thus we will draw upon tremendous resources of care-giving power, at the same time providing education and dignified, challenging work to those facing social and health crises, diminishing social dependence and increasing their ability to cope with problems of an urban world. The special capabilities of women must be considered. No city should countenance the breakup of a family because of a mother's illness; an ever-ready homemaker service would be available in such an emergency.

Untreated psychosis among lower socio-economic groups is notoriously prevalent. More vigorous and equitable approaches to treatment will doubtless help, but, again, prevention is a key word. On this score, we are far from the solution; there are no vaccines or nutriments to be administered and tested as preventives of most mental illness. It is difficult to know what aspects of poverty, for example, are most damaging to health; we cannot alter factors one by one so easily as in the search for the causes of heart disease in executives. Undoubtedly, the elimination of poverty must precede the prevention of many diseases — and, inevitably, will lead to increasing occurrence of others. Some of the strengths peculiar to poverty-stricken people will be lost also, as they become more affluent, unless new challenges emerge as their horizons extend farther and farther beyond the next meal and the next day. In our quest for solutions to health as well as other problems, we must be wary of substituting one sickness for another.

Public health services have altered the world's ecology, made some of our worst maladies bad dreams from the past, though the changes have not been inevitably for the better. We can assume that a number of new conditions, many of which are malignant, will occur. Hopefully, a well-planned city will improve human health and growth. It is a false picture of life, however, which omits conflict and compromise, and so we conclude our discussion of ideal health goals with a reminder of its unreality.

THE ATTAINMENT OF URBAN HEALTH

The problems faced by metropolitan areas in planning for comprehensive health services is indeed a difficult and complex one. We have pointed out that the development of model programs in any one of many areas, though needed, cannot answer the total needs of the community. Similarly, we propose that attempting to achieve an ideal state of health is unrealistic. We have posed, therefore, a comprehensive ecological model relating health to almost all the other problems faced by metropolitan areas. This model relates health to poverty, to education, to planning and architecture, to transportation and population control, among many others. In view of this complexity, it is obvious that no program in health can achieve its goals unless it fits into other activities and programs related to it in a host of other areas. Thus the utilization of health facilities is related to the availability of information, transportation, baby sitters: what is critical is understanding something about these complex interrelated processes.

When faced with such complexity, one can be completely overwhelmed because one sees innumerable obstacles in the way of success. Another reaction to the enormity of the task is to propose a program of saturation of all services which presumably will bring to bear the best of all programs on the problem. Such an approach is unrealistic from various points of view. No one seriously argues the feasibility of saturation programs in all the metropolitan areas. We do not have the manpower or the resources to achieve this end. What is needed is a way of conceptualizing the total problem relating health to other areas and determining what the key critical leverage points may be which will achieve the goals desired by the community. Following the ecological model, such leverage points, for health, may be in fields such as education, research, physical planning, or even economics and law. Conversely, achievements in some of these fields may only be accomplished with the development of programs in the health field.

If one's leverage points are ascertained, it is possible to anticipate what the effect of such actions would be on a host of related fields in achieving the goals indicated. Having done this, it becomes clear that one can then make a choice between interventions, making only those that are most necessary and those which will have the maximum effect at minimum economic and social cost in achieving the goals desired. The role of planning should be primarily the reconceptualization of the problem, the collection of information and ideas, and the ability to set a process in motion. The actual determination of goals must be decentralized, and the implementation of all programs must meet the specific needs of total populations and of the various geographic and functional groups in the community. This is a tall order, for we are asking for an increased responsibility on the part of the citizens to participate in the planning for their own future.

One might easily say that they are inadequately prepared to assume such a role because they do not have the skills and technical abilities of the experts. It is our contention that our responsibility in developing the process of planning is to set as the highest priority the learning by the people who are being planned for how to participate in the planning process and to take a place in the political arena. If, through a variety of processes, such as community organization and education, we can achieve the goal of the people knowing how to organize, to evaluate, and to play a role in determining their own future, they can then make use of the expert knowledge available.

Perhaps we are stating too idealistic a goal, but we feel this is the direction that we must take. The essence of democracy is the political participation of its citizens for its own welfare. The essence of education is learning how to do so. The critical problem in the field of health, as it is in the whole field of general welfare, is to bring together our current skills, knowledge, and ability with current practice. As we narrow this gap and as we meet the needs of people who know how to make choices, we will achieve a much more healthy situation.

With this as our primary goal we cannot lose sight of the need for dealing with specifics. Services are necessary for treatment. In this country, services will continue to be given by a variety of means, both private and public. No single system of health services will ever be attained. However, what is critical is the need for persons in the community who can see to it that, whatever people desire in terms of service, they can get and make use of the available resources. There has been much talk about multipurpose workers or urban agents in the community. Their job is seeing to it that the consumer and services are brought together and that, in fact, use is made of the array of services we now have. In fact, the services that we have are very diverse, and, if they could be utilized well, we might have a coordination by means of the urban agent where we cannot get it on the administrative level.

It is clear that, in this broad ecological model, no matter how good the planning or how much we achieve, solutions to problems beget new problems. As one medical philosopher suggested, the health professional's main function is to help the patient choose the most socially acceptable set of symptoms. Another way to put this is that, as we solve the problems of infectious disease, we are left with problems of the chronic ones. As we deal with problems of nutritional defect, we will encounter problems of vitamin poisoning.

The problem of health, viewed in an ecological framework, is a never-ending process. Each time society achieves new values, produces new devices, we will have new problems. It is critical, therefore, since we are a nation in favor of progress, to develop organizations capable of meeting unforeseen problems. This means flexibility, rather than bureaucratic scleroses. This means the ability to let organizations die and new ones be created.

At this moment, in the field of health, the technical advances have been so great that physicians and the technical experts too often are concerned with the hardware and the science and too little with the needs of the human being and the population. In this instance, the problem of health is like the problem in many other areas. Technology has moved fast, leaving the human being at the wayside. It is important, therefore, to create new organizations, such as the Peace Corps, which offer the opportunity for work on a person-to-person basis. To have similar organizations on the domestic scene, either nationally or in the form of local voluntary groups, seems to us to be of highest priority. The need to maintain the human touch with children in institutions, as homemakers in homes where parents are sick, or in hospitals where the patient is waiting to recover from an operation, or even waiting to die, is essential. One of the most important things about our country is concern for the individual. In our technological advance, we cannot forget that, and, therefore, within the metropolitan area, we need more programs encompassing the human dimension.

Thus, it is important that our health concepts and vital statistics grow in subtlety as well as completeness, so that we can determine the interrelationships of ulcer, hypertension, accidents, suicide, crime rates, poverty, in large and small population groups. Fortunately, this has begun in some areas where urban centers are gathering information data banks on many related problems. Failing this kind of effort, our action programs, like some examples of urban renewal, may push down one ugly head of pathology only to have another pop up somewhere else.

Our suggested approach, rather than utopian, is an ecological one. We look at the available measures, but, before launching the attack on a particular disease entity — as though such a thing really existed — we examine the functional universe in which the phenomenon exists and address ourselves to what we find. By focusing narrowly on particular diseases, we alter the ecological balance anyway and perhaps create new problems. We believe that the particular diseases will yield more completely and finally to this broad environmental approach, just as the symptoms of an illness yield to treatment of its many causes. This is a tentative approach, not a dogmatic answer. It will be useful if it makes us as respectful of socio-economic facts of life as we are of the biological and as skillful in community planning as we are in opening the heart.

Epidemiologic studies repeatedly point to socioeconomic factors in illness. Medical-care studies indicate vast differentials both of quality and quantity of services utilized by our city dwellers. To reduce the high levels of sickness occurring among the poor will require far more than the noblest efforts of men and women in white. A planful, energetic, humane attack on the phenomenon of poverty will necessarily go hand in hand with reduction of its many accompaniments: disease, social incompetence, apathy, and illiteracy. While illiteracy is primarily an educational problem, it is hard to conceive of an illiterate being healthy in the terms we have used. Mental health, especially, brings into focus the need to include education, labor, leisure, economics, and social history into proper relationship. The ability of our cities to integrate relevant disciplines in the area of health services will be another qualitative criterion of achievement.

In this paper on health and urbanization, we offer no blueprint. We have pointed to some critical issues in urban health, perhaps with a new perspective for those who have tended to look at health in more usual terms. We have not forgotten that in the field of health it is often necessary to treat symptoms. We have not suggested that there is any lack of need for *ad hoc* programs to deal with emergencies and with the many ills of our urban society, but we do hope that, as more knowledge comes and with information, we can come up with a new conceptualization, a diagnosis, and perhaps an understanding of the very complex etiology of the disorder. By doing so, we will be able to go beyond the symptoms of our urban ills and with the combined resources and skill of the health and other professions as well as the people who are being planned for, we may be able to develop ongoing solutions.

While the process of urban planning and coping with problems of health is a complex one involving social, economic, political, as well as health problems, the health worker, modest but unabashed, ought to be in the thick of it.

REFERENCES

1. L. Duhl (ed.), *The Urban Condition* (New York: Basic Books, 1963); Alvin Schorr, *Slums and Social Insecurity* (Washington, D.C.: U.S. Department of Health, Education, and Welfare, 1963); Lowdon Wingo, Jr. (ed.), *Cities and Space* (Baltimore: Resources for the Future, Inc., The Johns Hopkins Press, 1963).
2. Dwight MacDonald, "Our Invisible Poor," Sidney Hillman Reprint No. 23 (adapted from *The New Yorker*), 1963; and Michael Harrington, *The Other America: Poverty in the United States* (New York: Macmillan, 1962).
3. World Health Organization, *Urban Health Services*, Techn. Rep. Ser., 1963, p. 250.

18 Neighborhood Health Centers

SEYMOUR S. BELLIN
Tufts University

PETER KONG-MING NEW
Tufts University

In the field of public health, poverty programs — for instance, the "negative income tax" — cannot do enough for the poverty-stricken. Indeed, health programs are inadequate for middle-income as well as low-income groups and will remain inadequate until both groups are organized to voice their demands for adequate ones.

"Issues in the Development of Neighborhood Health Centers" by Drs. Goldberg, Trowbridge, and Buxbaum[1] . . . has raised a series of important issues in the cur-

From "Neighborhood Health Centers," by Seymour S. Bellin and Peter Kong-ming New, *Inquiry*, Volume 6, June 1969, pp. 62–63. Reprinted with permission of Universitetsforlaget, Oslo.

rent method of delivery of health care to the poor.[2] . . . We would like to take issue with a general misconception which they have unwittingly perpetuated. They say:

> It can be argued that health care in the United States is divided into two systems, one for those who can pay and another for the poor. Those able to pay can select and insist on care that meets with their satisfaction. In this way, their consumer voice is heard. The poor generally have no financial leverage. They could acquire such leverage through mechanisms such as guaranteed annual income, negative income tax, and generalized extension of Medicaid, Medicare, or other medical payment subsidies. (p. 46)

We would argue that in the present system of delivery of care, the middle class are actually no better off than the poor in trying to have a voice in insisting on good care. The scarcity of physicians has created an "asymmetrical" supply and demand situation in which physicians can say what patients they are willing to see. One need to look only at middle-class persons who have chronic conditions, alcoholic problems, or mental illness or mental retardation problems, and ask: Where are they getting care? They have money, but they are not receiving proper care. There does not exist in every community the full spectrum of needed curative and preventive services. Nor are the various services and agencies — at the neighborhood, community, state and national levels — coordinated in such a way as to afford the ultimate consumer comprehensive continuous, personal and family-centered health care. Community medicine — a more comprehensive perspective — remains more a concept than a reality in the suburbs as much as in the central cities or rural areas.

Money alone is *not* the solution. We feel that sophistication in organizing to demand medical service is more central, and Dr. Lashof has properly touched on this in her comment. As far as the poor and medical care are concerned, help must be rendered to organize and involve them in all sectors that touch on health: political spheres, health agencies, social welfare agencies, public health, medical and other health schools, and even insurance. Through various consumer health associations in neighborhood health centers, the poor are rapidly organizing to have a voice in their health care. However, the neighborhood health center is only one small part in the spectrum of health care. Through the vehicle of the neighborhood health center, we feel it is urgent that the consumers must also know the broader implications of health care.

For instance, Dr. Lashof raised a fundamental question concerning the way medical schools and hospitals currently view neighborhood health centers as "outposts" for teaching and training. It is precisely because of this that the poor need to know more of the way decisions are made in this particular sector of health care. They should be on the boards of medical schools and hospitals as well, so that they could have a say in the policies that are made regarding *their* care. Many hospitals which are right in the middle of ghetto areas somehow feel they are "serving" the poor, when in reality, the hours certain clinics are open are only suitable to the middle class. Some physicians who are single-handedly running small neighborhood health centers have run into a stone wall when it comes to obtaining cooperation from the hospitals and medical schools in their areas.

Financial leverage can be a very potent weapon in bringing about effective consumer influence upon the health care services, but only if the consumer can mobilize this through the creation of effective collective organization and direct representation on decision-making bodies. Of course, organization and representation will afford the consumer other kinds of potent leverage in addition to money. The consumer needs to have a voice in all parts of the health care system, in ambulatory as well as inpatient health care facilities, and at all governmental levels of health care administration and planning. This applies to the middle classes as much as to the poor.

As wealthy a nation as we are, we still have not brought about effective controls over automobile safety, pricing of drugs, air and water pollution — all presumably within the capacity of the middle class who can have some say. We have not learned the mechanisms, poor and rich alike, to organize and become involved. We feel that Goldberg, *et al.*, need to broaden their perspectives to include other parts and pieces of the health system; they are certainly aware of this when they say, "Health care is but one system among many in a democracy." (p. 46) However, to say that and then turn right around and adopt a more limited view by saying that only if the poor had more money can they have more of a voice in bringing about changes in medical care seems contradictory. Why not go the whole way?

REFERENCES

1. This article appeared in *Inquiry*, March 1969, pp. 37–47.
2. In addition, Dr. Lashof ("Comment," same issue, pp. 47–48) has focused on other crucial points regarding consumer participation or control and the place of the hospital and medical school in providing continuity of care. We realize Goldberg, *et al.*, could not possibly go into great detail on the points they raised.

19 Academic Motivation and Equal Educational Opportunity

IRWIN KATZ
University of Michigan

The Coleman Report revealed strikingly the close tie between the academic achievement of black pupils and the social environment of the classroom. Here, the author advances a theory of racial differences in the early socialization of academic moti-

From Irwin Katz, "Academic Motivation and Equal Educational Opportunity," *Harvard Educational Review*, 38, Winter 1968, 57–85. Copyright © 1968 by President and Fellows of Harvard College.

vation to account for some of the favorable effects on blacks of (1) teachers' and classmates' competence and (2) attendance at predominantly white schools.

In some ways the most intriguing data in the Coleman Report are those that reveal the marked sensitivity of Negro pupils to the social environment of the classrooms.[1] Beyond the earliest grades, the scholastic achievement of Negro children when compared with that of whites is much more closely related to the intellectual proficiency of both teachers and classmates. About a year ago I wrote elsewhere about the possible meaning of these findings from the standpoint of what was then known about social-class and racial differences in the early socialization of academic motivation.[2] More recent research has further illuminated the subject.

The earlier paper suggested that in lower-class Negro homes children's language and problem-solving efforts were not adequately encouraged and reinforced so that children failed to acquire the internal mechanisms that were requisite for autonomous achievement striving — namely, realistic standards of self-evaluation and the capacity for intrinsic mediation of satisfaction through self-approval of successful performance. In white middle-class children, on the other hand, internalization of the achievement motive presumably is relatively well advanced at the time of entering school. Therefore, for disadvantaged students but not for their more affluent age peers, the development of the will to learn should depend heavily upon the behavior of social models in the classroom — that is, upon the extent to which teachers and fellow students exhibit suitable standards of performance and reward individual accomplishment with genuine approval and respect. Moreover, in predominantly Negro schools were low attainment levels prevail, most pupils should be largely incapable in the absence of external cues of realistic self-appraisal or intrinsic mediation of achievement satisfaction.

RECENT RESEARCH ON THE MOTIVATION OF NEGRO PUPILS

To test this last proposition, Reuben Baron, Gloria Cowan, and I recently carried out exploratory research in a northern, *de facto* segregated elementary school.[3] Fourth- through sixth-grade children were taken individually from their classrooms for testing. During a self-evaluation phase, a series of simple tasks (picture assembly, or construction of four-letter words) was presented to each child, who was seated alone at a table and surrounded by partitions. Near the child on the table was a metal box with three buttons which activated small light bulbs of different colors labelled "Good," "Poor," and "Don't Know."

The instructions were in part as follows: "We think you will enjoy doing these things more if you can tell yourself how nice a job you think you did. So after you finish each one you can press the button which shows how you feel about the kind of job you did. . . . No one will know which button you pressed." The experimenter left the room after explaining the procedure. Hence, the self-evaluations were ostensibly private, unobserved, and for the child's own amusement. But the setup was deceptive: the button pressings were mechanically recorded by counters concealed in the box.

In another phase of the testing, the extent to which the child's self-evaluations had affective consequences was investigated by ascertaining whether the colored lights used in the self-evaluation box had acquired positive or negative incentive value by virtue of being associated with self-criticism or self-approval. Two techniques of assessing acquired reinforcement value were tried at different times. One involved the introduction, after the self-evaluation phase, of a toy-like gadget that the child was permitted to play with unobserved for a few minutes. It had three levers which activated bulbs when depressed. The bulbs corresponded in size, color, and position to those on the self-evaluation box, but were not labelled. The index of acquired reinforcement value was the number of times each lever was depressed as recorded by concealed mechanical counters. The second technique required the child to fill in an outline with colored crayons both before and after the self-evaluation series, from which quantitative measures of the use of critical colors were obtained.

To date we have tested seventy-nine Negro children. Two types of subjects were used: those whom teachers regarded as high achievers and those regarded as low achievers. Of the total sample, only ten were girls. Girls who were good and poor students showed little difference in their self-evaluations; hence they were temporarily dropped from the research. *Among boys, the poor students engaged in more self-criticism and were less favorable in their total self-evaluations than the good students.* That the differences between groups were not created by a few extreme scores is evident from the data on thirty-six boys who evaluated their performance on the picture assembly tasks: only three out of seventeen good students, but fully sixteen out of nineteen poor students, used the "Poor" button at least once out of a total of six self-evaluations. Another male sample of roughly equal size that evaluated their constructions of simple words showed similar differences between high and low academic achievers.

As a check on the possibility that the self-evaluations were reasonably accurate appraisals of actual performance, judges who were unacquainted with the experimental procedures were asked to rate subjects' productions. *They detected no differences in quality of performance associated with academic achievement or self-ratings.*

With respect to mediation of affect, quantitative results did not reach levels of statistical significance, but *there were suggestive tendencies on both the lever-pressing and crayon-coloring tests for boys who had been highly self-critical to avoid exposing themselves to the color that had previously been associated with the critical label "Poor."*

What are the implications of the foregoing findings? First, it should be explained that the great majority of the children, particularly of the boys, in the school where the testing was done were in the "low achiever" category. The teachers who selected the subjects were hard put to come up with thirty-six boys whom they could call "high achievers" — that is, whom they regarded as clearly competent in school work — and they were drawing on an aggregate pool of about two hundred male pupils. Hence, it is fair to say that the typical boy in the school was both academically weak by teachers' standards, and critical of his own achievement efforts. Yet, relative to pupils in other predominantly Negro schools in the urban North, these boys were no worse than average.

What is intriguing about the results is the suggestion that among northern Negro children academic failure is not necessarily associated with low or unstable standards of self-evaluation. If standards are to be inferred from a predisposition to criticize oneself, then the low-achieving Negro boys had very high standards indeed. Conceivably, their standards were so stringent and rigid as to be utterly dysfunctional. They seem to have internalized a most effective mechanism for self-discouragement. In a sense, they had been socialized to self-impose failure. I use the term socialization deliberately, believing that what is involved is not merely a lack of prior rewards for achievement efforts, but also a history of punitive reactions by socializing agents to such efforts.

The home socialization experiences of subjects were investigated by means of a *Reinforcement History Questionnaire* devised by Reuben Baron. It contained twenty-one items dealing with characteristic reactions of the father or mother to the child in a variety of situations.[4] *We found both low academic achievement and self-criticism related to children's perceptions of low rewardingness and high punitiveness on the part of both parents.*

THE ANXIETY-REDUCTIVE FUNCTION OF SELF-CRITICISM

Two theories of children's self-critical behavior point to an anxiety-reductive function. First, consider Aronfreed's model for the socialization of self-criticism as a response to transgressions.[5] Aronfreed is concerned mainly with accounting for the internalization of moral self-control, but his concepts are sufficiently general to apply to achievement situations as well. He defines self-criticism as the most common form of a class of reactions to transgression in which the child imitatively reproduces components of the punishment to which he has been previously exposed. Aronfreed's conception is basically quite simple. *Once a child has had some contact with punishment for a particular type of behavior, he will experience anticipatory anxiety in the intervals which occur between subsequent enactments of such behavior and the occurrence of punishment.* Certain of the stimulus components of punishment can then acquire value as signals for the attenuation of the child's anticipatory anxiety, since they mark the end of the interval of anticipation. Thus, young children can sometimes be observed to verbalize self-criticism aloud and to make the anxiety-reducing function of these responses quite transparent when they show signs of distress following a punishable behavior and then apparent relief after they have overtly censured themselves. Very likely, the extent to which self-criticism is acquired by a child as a technique for reducing anxiety — rather than avoidance, withdrawal, or outwardly-directed hostility — will be governed to some extent by his dependency on adults for emotional security.

A theory of emotional blocks to learning that deals explicitly with the conflict between emotional dependency and hostile impulses has been formulated by Sarason and his associates at Yale in connection with their investigations of test anxiety.[6] Like Aronfreed, the Yale group offers an anxiety-reduction interpretation of self-blame. They regard the test-anxious child as one who typically reacts with strong unconscious hostility against teachers and others whom he thinks are passing judgment on his adequacy as a person. Because of his dependency on adults, the child does not express his feelings openly but instead turns them inward upon himself in the form of self-derogatory attitudes. This is as far as the theory goes with regard to the adaptative function of self-blame. I would simply add that when inward-directed hostility expresses itself as self-criticism, the resultant discharge of the displaced impulses tends to be cathartic, hence anxiety-reducing.

The theoretical linkage between self-criticism and anxiety made it desirable to administer the Yale group's *Test Anxiety Scale for Children* to the Negro boys who were used in our experiments. When this was done, test anxiety scores were found to be higher among the low academic achievers than among the high achievers, and to be directly related both to propensity for self-criticism and to perception of parents as punitive rather than rewarding. *Thus the likelihood that self-imposed failure operates as an anxiety-reducing mechanism in disadvantaged male pupils is clearly indicated.*

Impressive support for the contention that Negro pupils in racially isolated schools are the victims of inordinately high levels of anxiety has very recently come to my attention through an unpublished report by Sheila Feld and Judith Lewis.[7] These investigators administered the *Test Anxiety Scale for Children* to the entire second-grade population of a suburban school system in the eastern part of the United States. Over eight hundred Negroes and sixty-five hundred whites attending *de facto* segregated schools were tested. Negroes were found to have substantially higher anxiety scores not only on the total scale but also on each of four subscales which were derived by means of factor analysis: test anxiety, remote school concern (e.g., "When you are in bed at night, do you sometimes worry about how you are going to do in class the next day?"), poor self-evaluation, and somatic signs of anxiety. Interestingly, a group of 105 Negro children in racially mixed schools obtained scores about midway between those of the segregated Negro and white samples. However, the meaning of this comparison is not entirely clear, since the Negro children in desegregated schools came from homes of relatively high socio-economic status, a factor found to be associated with low anxiety. Sex differences appeared for white pupils — white boys obtained lower anxiety scores than white girls — but not for Negroes.

THE ROLE OF NEGRO PARENTS

Paradoxical as it may seem, an important source of school anxiety in Negroes is probably the inordinately high demands for academic achievement that are made by minority-group parents — demands that are higher even than those imposed by white middle-class parents. Several investigators, for example Bell in Philadelphia and Keller in New York City,[8] have found that a majority of Negro parents who have attained an economic status above the very lowest levels of poverty desire a college education for their sons, and majorities or near-majorities want them to enter professions. These aspirations are so discrepant with the amount of effort lower-class parents actually devote to their children's educational needs (for example, helping with homework), and so unrealistic in view of the typical lower-class child's academic retardation, as to suggest that they are merely empty statements made for the benefit of the interviewer or expressions of fantasies that have nothing to do with real events. In my opinion, the parents' aspirations are indeed in the nature of wishful fantasies, in the sense that the parents do not know how to implement them, but the aspirations have consequences in that they somehow get conveyed to the child as expectations he is supposed to fulfill. This hypothesis helps explain why the low-achieving Negro boys in our study appeared to be harshly over-critical of their own achievement efforts rather than easily satisfied or indifferent. It is also consistent with research that has shown higher educational aspirations among Negro children than among white age-peers of comparable economic levels. In the Coleman survey, Negro twelfth-grade students reported higher levels of academic motivation, interest, and aspiration than whites. For example, when asked about whether they wanted to be good students, a higher proportion of Negroes than any other ethnic group — over half — reported that they wanted to be one of the best in the class. Negroes reported also more studying outside school than any group except Oriental-Americans.

There is, I daresay, a large element of defensiveness or wishful thinking, or both, in the Negro responses. This becomes apparent with regard to college aspirations, for while more Negroes than whites in the Coleman study reported a desire to go to college, lower proportions of Negroes had seen a college catalogue or written to a college. *But having a need to overstate the degree of one's educational interest on an anonymous questionnaire is in itself a fact of much significance. It reveals that one holds achievement values and achievement standards that do not get reflected in actual achievement efforts.* Values and goals have been internalized, but not the behavioral mechanisms requisite for attaining them. The disjunction of cognitions and behaviors is not difficult to understand, for verbal attitudes are relatively easy to acquire through mere imitation of verbalizations observed in adult or peer models. If the attitudes expressed are the "correct" ones, i.e., are held by socializing agents — and I have mentioned research which shows that Negro parents verbalize high educational goals for their children — they will tend to get reinforced either directly or vicariously. But performing the behaviors that are instrumental for attaining the goals is a more difficult feat than the acquisition of verbal attitudes about the goal, especially when there are no models of competency to imitate, and when achievement strivings are not socially recognized and reinforced. Apparently, the typical Negro mother tries to socialize her child for scholastic achievement by laying down verbal rules and regulations about classroom conduct, coupled with punishment of detected transgressions. But she does not do enough to guide and encourage her child's efforts at verbal-symbolic mastery. Therefore, the child learns only to verbalize standards of academic interest and attainment. These standards then provide the cognitive basis for negative self-evaluations.

The foregoing analysis can explain why Negro students do not express *less* scholastic interest than whites, despite lower achievement levels, but it does not satisfactorily account for the finding in the Coleman survey of *greater* scholastic interest in Negro twelfth graders. I suspect that as part of his adjustment to failure, the low-achieving Negro student learns to use expressions of interest and ambition as a verbal substitute for behaviors he is unable to enact. The effect is probably double-edged: anxiety is *reduced* in situations where verbal expressions are enough, yet by emphasizing the discrepancy between real and ideal performance, anxiety is *raised* in actual achievement situations. Hence, as the Negro student falls increasingly behind in his school work, the expression of high verbal standards contributes to a growing demoralization.

Implicit in my analysis is the proposition that *when high standards are adopted, but not the behavioral mechanisms necessary for attainment, the relationship between verbal expressions of the standards and actual performance will tend to be an inverse one.* The Coleman data for Negro students nationally are not inconsistent with the proposition. At the sixth-grade level, the relationship between expressed interest in school work and achievement test scores is very small and positive, at ninth grade it is zero, and at twelfth grade it is extremely small but *negative*.[9] Since I do not contend that Negro students *totally* lack the positive self-reinforcement mechanism, I find the reversal trend with increasing age an encouraging indication that my substitute-value hypothesis may be correct for certain types of Negro students.

SENSE OF CONTROL AND OTHER ATTITUDES

In all, Coleman and his associates measured three types of student attitude relevant to academic motivation: interest in school work, self-concept as regards ability, and sense of control of own rewards.[10] For Negro students, sense of control was clearly the most important attitude, contributing at different grades from two to several times as much to the accounted-for variance of verbal achievement as either of the others. Moreover, the relation of Negroes' sense of control to achievement was considerably stronger than that of any family-background factor. Finally, comparing races reveals that among older children sense of fate control accounted for about three times as much test variance among Negroes as among whites.

Since the Coleman findings represent merely empirical correlations, the causal connections between sense of internal control and other variables can only be surmised. Nonetheless, there are strong suggestions in the data regarding the relative importance of home and school determinants. The Report indicates that for Negroes sense of control was little influenced by home factors or objective school characteristics, but one factor apparently affected it strongly: as the proportion of white students in school enrollments increased, Negroes' sense of internality grew stronger. Their self-concept of ability, however, declined as proportion white increased. Since Negro achievement in fact was higher in majority-white schools, it would appear that *a modest self-concept is not detrimental to Negro academic performance, provided children can depend upon the environment to dispense rewards in a fair and equitable way.*

Thus, a fascinating implication of the Coleman Report is that relatively realistic perceptions of one's ability relative to classmates of higher ability need not produce discouragement in the disadvantaged pupil — indeed, it may have the opposite effect — provided the child has a secure awareness of opportunities for social and material reward commensurate with his own efforts and capabilities. The research described earlier in this paper on self-criticism and anxiety provides support for the above interpretation of the Coleman findings — that is, debilitating anxiety in minority-group students may be more a function of perceived isolation and exclusion from the main American opportunity structure than of awareness of one's intellectual limitations relative to classmates. Future research should be addressed to this question.

REFERENCES

1. James S. Coleman, *et al.*, *Equality of Educational Opportunity* (Washington: U.S. Government Printing Office, 1966); *Harvard Educational Review*, Vol. 38 No. 1 Winter 1968.
2. Irwin Katz, "Some Motivational Determinants of Racial Differences in Intellectual Achievement," *International Journal of Psychology,* II (1967), 1–12.
3. This research is reported more fully in the following publication: Irwin Katz, "The Socialization of Academic Motivation in Minority Group Children," in D. Levine (ed.), *Nebraska Symposium on Motivation* (Lincoln, Neb.: University of Nebraska Press, 1967).
4. The *Reinforcement History Questionnaire* is described in Katz, "The Socialization of Academic Motivation in Minority Group Children," *op. cit.*
5. J. Aronfreed, *Conduct and Conscience: The Socialization of Internal Control Over Behavior* (New York: Academic Press, 1968).

6. S. B. Sarason, *et al., Anxiety in Elementary School Children* (New York: John Wiley & Sons, 1960).
7. Sheila Feld and Judith Lewis, "The Assessment of Achievement Anxieties in Children" (Mental Health Study Center, National Institute of Mental Health, 1967, MS).
8. R. R. Bell, "Lower Class Negro Mothers' Aspirations for their Children," *Social Forces*, XLIII (1965), 493–500; Suzanne Keller, "The Social World of the Urban Slum Child: Some Early Findings," *American Journal of Orthopsychiatry*, XXXIII (1963), 823–31.
9. See Table 3.26.2 in Coleman *et al., op. cit.,* p. 322.
10. To assess sense of control, students were asked to respond to three statements — that "good luck is more important than hard work for success"; that "every time I try to get ahead something or somebody stops me"; and that "people like me don't have much of a chance to be successful in life."

20 Educational Vouchers:
An Overview

CENTER FOR THE STUDY OF PUBLIC POLICY

The voucher program would give to the parents of each American child a voucher to be used in payment of school fees — either private or public.

THE CASE FOR COMPETITION AND CHOICE

Conservatives, liberals, and radicals have all complained at one time or another that the political mechanisms which supposedly make public schools accountable to their clients work clumsily and ineffectively. Parents who think their children are getting inferior schooling can, it is true, take their grievances to the local school board or state legislature. If legislators and school boards are unresponsive to the complaints of enough citizens, they may eventually be unseated, but it takes an enormous investment of time, energy, and money to mount an effective campaign to change local public schools. Dissatisfied though they may be, few parents have the political skill or commitment to solve their problems this way. As a result, effective control over the character of the public schools is largely vested in legislators, school boards, and educators, not parents.

If parents are to take responsibility for their children's education, they cannot rely exclusively on political processes to let them do so. They must also be able to take *individual* action in behalf of their own children.

From *Education Vouchers*, Report to the U.S. Office of Economic Opportunity, by the Center for the Study of Public Policy, Cambridge, Mass.: Center for the Study of Public Policy, 1970, pp. 1–17.

At present, only relatively affluent parents retain any effective control over the education of their children. Only they are free to move to school districts with "good schools" (and high tax rates). Only they can afford non-sectarian private schooling. The average parent has no alternative to his local public school unless he happens to belong to one of the denominations that maintains low-tuition church schools. Only a few denominations do.

The system of education vouchers proposed in this report will, we believe, encourage the development of many new alternatives, open to *every* parent. This would make it possible for parents to translate their concern for their children's education into action. If they did not like the education their child was getting in one school (or if the child did not like it), he could go to another. By fostering both active parental interest and educational variety, a voucher system should improve all participating schools, both public and private.

Under the proposed voucher system, a publicly accountable agency would issue a voucher for a year's schooling for each eligible child. This voucher could be turned over to any school which had agreed to abide by the rules of the voucher system. Each school would turn in its vouchers for cash. Thus, parents would no longer be forced to send their children to the school around the corner simply because it was around the corner. If the school was attractive and desirable, it would not be seriously affected by the institution of a voucher plan. If not, attendance might fall, perhaps forcing the school to improve.

Even if no new schools were established under the voucher system, the responsiveness of existing schools would probably increase. But new schools will be established. Some parents will get together to create schools reflecting their special perspectives or their children's special needs. Educators with new ideas — or old ideas that are now out of fashion in the public schools — will also be able to set up their own schools. Entrepreneurs who think they can teach children better and cheaper than the public schools do will also have an opportunitiy to do so.

None of this ensures that every child will get the education he needs, but it does make such a result more likely than at present.

All these arguments have, of course, been used over and over to justify the maintenance of free markets and competition in areas other than education. Why, then, have virtually all American communities allowed elementary and secondary education to remain a monopoly or at best a duopoly?[1]

Monopoly situations are usually justified by one of three arguments:

Competition would be technologically inefficient in this field.

Consumers are not competent to distinguish between good and bad products in this field, so competition would lead only to more imaginative forms of fraud.

Competition in this field would encourage consumers to maximize their private advantages in ways that are inimical to the general welfare.

Let us examine the applicability of these three arguments to education.

The "technological" argument for educational monopoly may have had some relevance in the days when most Americans lived in sparsely settled rural areas. It was hard to get enough children together in one place to pay a single teacher's salary. Competition could (and sometimes did) prevent *any* school from being established. Today, however, most Americans live in densely populated areas, where it is perfectly feasible to maintain several competing schools within reasonable distance of any family. Logistical arguments against diversity, competition, and choice in education have therefore become irrelevant.

Proponents of public monopoly also talk a good deal about economics of scale, especially at the high school level. There is, however, no solid evidence that such economies are real. Big schools can provide certain resources (a physics lab, a Spanish teacher, a swimming pool, etc.) at less cost than small schools. But nobody knows whether these resources increase the likelihood that a school will turn out competent, civilized adults. Recent disorders in many big high schools suggest that massing large numbers of adolescents together in the same place may actually be dysfunctional. The possibility that competition might result in smaller schools need not, then, be viewed with alarm. It could be very healthy.

The "gullible consumer" argument for educational monopoly is only slightly more persuasive. There are instances (e.g., prescription drugs) where consumers really cannot judge the products offered them. Rather strict regulation seems appropriate in these areas. In order to justify governmental regulation, however, it is necessary to show that the government is harder to gull than the individual consumer. This is fairly easy to do in the case of drugs. The government presumably has access to scientific evidence about the effects of each drug, and this evidence is not readily available or comprehensible to laymen. Analogous arguments with respect to schooling seem more tenuous. The government can obtain "expert" opinions about the effects of any given school on various types of children, whereas the average parent cannot obtain such opinions. But there is no evidence that "experts" really know any more than parents about the likely effects of specific schools on specific children. There is no consensus about what causes what in education, much less any scientific evidence to back a consensus. This makes it hard to argue that the government should protect children from their parents' naiveté by denying the parents choice about their children's schooling and imposing what the government's experts happen to think "best."

Even if we were to accept the argument that "experts know best," it would not follow that the best solution would be to make education a public monopoly. We do not, after all, have a public monopoly on the production or distribution of drugs, even though we assume that "doctors know best." Instead, we have a publicly regulated market, in which the patient is free to choose both a doctor and a druggist. It would be perfectly possible to establish a similarly regulated market in education. Indeed, such a market already exists — but only for the affluent. The state establishes certain basic rules about what a school has to do before opening its doors to the public. These rules cover physical safety, teacher qualifications, and the like. But in most respects affluent parents are free to send their children to any kind of school they want. It is hard to see why affluent parents should be judged competent to select their children's schools from a wide range of alternatives while poorer parents are given no options.

The final argument against competition and consumer sovereignty is that if parents are encouraged to make educational choices strictly in terms of private advantage, the cumulative result of these choices will be at odds with the general welfare. Unlike the two previous arguments, this one is in some ways persuasive. Creating a completely free market for schooling would almost certainly result in more segregation by race, income, and ability. It would also result in a redistribution of educational resources from disadvantaged to advantaged children. Taken together, these changes would probably leave students from low-income families further behind students from high income families than they are now. This increase in inequality would in turn tend to widen the gap and intensify conflict between racial groups, between economic groups, and between political interests.

But monopolistic control over educational choices is not the only way to avert these evils. Proponents of smog control, for example, argue that so long as the choice is left to individual consumers, not many auto purchasers will elect to pay for expensive exhaust systems whose benefits go largely to other people. But few proponents of smog control claim that the only alternative is to nationalize the automobile industry. Most simply urge legislation which forbids the sale of automobiles that pollute the air. Similarly, we can ensure integration and equitable resource allocation in education without having the state operate 90 per cent of the nation's schools. It would be perfectly possible to create a competitive market and then regulate it in such a way as to prevent segregation, ensure an equitable allocation of resources, and give every family a truly equal chance of getting what it wants from the system.

CRITERIA FOR REGULATING THE EDUCATIONAL MARKET

Those who want to give parents more voice in shaping their children's educational destinies can be found almost everywhere on the political and educational spectrum. Their objectives are almost as diverse as the objectives of education itself, and their proposals for breaking the present public monopoly therefore cover an extraordinary range of alternatives.

In recent years many advocates of competition and choice have united around a single slogan: "education vouchers." The idea of an education voucher is relatively simple. The government issues the voucher to parents. The parents take the voucher to the school of their choice. The school returns the vouchers to the government. The government then sends the school a check equal to the value of the vouchers. As a result, government subsidies for education go only to schools in which parents choose to enroll their children. Schools which cannot attract applicants go out of business.

Beyond this, however, differences of opinion begin. Who would be eligible for vouchers? How would their value be determined? Would parents be allowed to supplement the vouchers from their own funds? What requirements would schools have to meet before cashing vouchers? What arrangements would be made for the children whom no school wanted to educate? Would church schools be eligible? Would schools promoting unorthodox political views be eligible? Once the advocates of vouchers begin to answer such questions, it becomes clear that the catchphrase around which they have united stands not for a single panacea, but for a multitude of controversial programs, many of which have little in common.

These diverse voucher schemes can be viewed merely as different approaches to the regulation of the educational marketplace. Some schemes propose no regulation at all, counting on the "hidden hand" to ensure that the sum total of private choices promotes the public good. Others involve considerable economic regulation, aimed at offsetting differences in parental income and at providing schools with incentives to educate certain kinds of children. Still other schemes involve not only economic regulation, but administrative regulations aimed at ensuring that schools which receive public money do not discriminate against disadvantaged children. Finally, some schemes would establish extensive regulations to ensure that schools provided the public with usable information about what the school was trying to do and how well it was succeeding in doing it. . . .

In order to deserve support from the Office of Economic Opportunity, a voucher plan should have two objectives: (1) to improve the education of children, particularly disadvantaged children; and (2) to give parents, and particularly disadvantaged parents, more control over the kind of education their children get.

These two objectives are not identical. For the most part we will assume that they are compatible, but this will not be true in every instance.

These broad generalizations require some elaboration. First it is important to decide whether "improving the education of the disadvantaged" means improvement relative to the education offered advantaged children today. We believe that, at least in education, closing the gap between the advantaged and the disadvantaged is of paramount importance. This conviction is central to our proposals for regulating the educational marketplace, so the reasons for it require explanation.

A generation ago the average American finished school with roughly eighth-grade reading competence, while the bottom quarter of the population was at about sixth-grade level. Mass circulation newspapers, being aimed at the "middle majority" of the population, also assumed something like eighth-grade reading competence. This meant that most people in the least competent quarter of the population could, with some difficulty and a bit of misunderstanding, follow a daily newspaper. Today the schools have boosted the average reading competence of people finishing school to the twelfth-grade level. They have boosted the average competence of the bottom quartile to the ninth-grade level. The gap between the bottom quartile and the average for the population has thus widened. A comparison of today's mass circulation newspapers with yesterday's indicated that they too have raised their standards, using larger vocabularies and more complex prose than before. The net result could easily be that the least competent quarter of the population is less likely to read the same papers as the "middle majority." If this were in fact the case, the cultural, political, and social isolation of the bottom quarter would have increased, even though their absolute competence had risen.

Man is indeed a social creature. His capacity to do most of the things he cares about depends on his relationship to his fellow men. If he is less competent than they, he will find himself frustrated at every turn. If he is more competent than they, he will be in a good position to get what he wants from life. In a society of illiterates, a man who knows the alphabet is a scholar and a gentleman. In a society of college graduates, he is an illiterate. Translated into practical terms, this means that a man's satisfaction in life depends more on relative advantage than absolute attainment. We judge that this is particularly true in education. It follows that the well-being of American society depends less on its wealth, power, and knowledge than on the way these things are distributed among the population.

We recognize that many Americans reject this view. Nonetheless, if the upheavals of the 1960's have taught us anything, it should be that merely increasing the Gross National Product, the absolute level of government spending, and the mean level of educational attainment will not solve our basic economic, social, and political problems. These problems do not arise because the nation as a whole is poor or ignorant. They arise because the benefits of wealth, power, and knowledge have been unequally distributed and because many Americans believe that these inequalities are unjust. A program which seeks to improve education must therefore focus on inequality, attempting to close the gap between the disadvantaged and the advantaged.

Having said that regulatory machinery ought to help close the gap between the advantaged and the disadvantaged, we must also say something about how this might be done.

First, America must *reallocate educational resources* so as to expose "difficult" children to their full share of the bright, talented, sensitive teachers, instead of exposing them to less than their share, as at present. Merely equalizing expenditures will not suffice to achieve this. Teachers are human, and most of them instinctively prefer children who learn quickly and easily over children who learn slowly and painfully. In order to change these values, society must make working with disadvantaged children a prestigious and highly paid career. This means that if schools that enroll disadvantaged children are to get their share of able teachers, they must be able to pay substantially better salaries and provide substantially more amenities (e.g., smaller classes, more preparation time) than schools which serve advantaged children.

Second, America must alter *enrollment patterns* so that disadvantaged children have more advantaged classmates. A student's classmates are probably his most important single "resource," even though they do not appear in most calculations of per-pupil expenditure. Children learn an enormous amount (both for better and for worse) from one another. Equally important, a student's classmates determine how much, if anything, he will get from his teachers. If, for example, a disadvantaged child attends a school in which most children never learn algebra, his teachers will not expect *him* to learn algebra, even if he is perfectly capable of doing so.

All this implies that a competitive market is unlikely to help disadvantaged children unless it is regulated so as to: provide substantially more money to schools that enroll disadvantaged children than to schools which enroll only advantaged children; and prevent an increase in segregation by race, income, ability, and "desirable" behavior patterns.

The second general requirement of a regulatory system is that it gives parents more control than they now have over the kind of education their children receive. We assume that increasing parents' sense of control over their environment and over their children's life chances is an end in itself both because it makes parents' lives less frustrating and because it makes them more effective advocates of their family's interest in non-educational areas.

Increasing parents' control over the kind of education their children receive should, however, also increase the chances that their children get a good education. The more control parents have over what happens to their children, the more responsible they are likely to feel for the results. This could easily make them take a more active role in educating their childern at home. In addition, parents tend to care more than public servants about making sure that their child gets whatever he needs. The intensity of the typical parent's concern is, of course, often partially or entirely offset by his naiveté about what would actually be good for his child or by his inability to get what he thinks the child needs. Nevertheless, we think that on the average parents are unlikely to make choices that are any worse than what their public schools now offer.

For parental choice to make a difference, however, genuine alternatives must really be available. "Good" education will always be in short supply, even if the parents are given money to buy it. Most (though not all) disadvantaged parents will want the same kinds of education as advantaged parents. When the two groups apply to the same "good" schools, disadvantaged children will not normally get their share of places. If disadvantaged parents are to feel that they also have control over the kinds of education their children receive, the market must be regulated in such a way that disadvantaged children have a fair chance of being admitted to the school of their choice.

The foregoing criteria do not exhaust the possible yardsticks for evaluating alternative regulatory systems. Before presenting our proposals it may therefore be useful to review the principal objections that others have raised to vouchers as a device for promoting competition and choice.

First, integrationists fear that vouchers would make it harder to achieve racial integration. This might result in a voucher system being declared unconstitutional, as has already happened in four Southern states. Even if the system were not declared unconstitutional, it would be undesirable if it intensified rather than alleviated racial separation.

Second, civil libertarians fear that vouchers would break down the separation of church and state. Again, this might result in a voucher scheme being declared unconstitutional. Even if it did not, it could unleash a series of bitter political struggles from which America has in the past been relatively exempt.

Third, egalitarians have emphasized that an unregulated market would increase the expenditures of the rich more than it increased those of the poor, exacerbating present resource inequalities instead of reducing them.

Fourth, public school men have feared that the public schools would become the "schools of last resort" and hence dumping grounds for students no other schools wanted.

Finally, some educators have argued that parents are not qualified to decide how their children should be educated and that giving parents a choice would encourage the growth of bad schools, not good ones.

The next sections show how these problems might be solved.

A MODEL VOUCHER SYSTEM

In order to understand the proposals made in this report, the reader must begin by reconsidering traditional definitions of the terms "public" and "private" in education. Since the nineteenth century we have classified schools as "public" if they were owned and operated by a governmental body. We go right on calling colleges "public" even when they charge tuition that many people cannot afford. We also call academically exclusive high schools "public" when they have admissions requirements that only a handful of students can meet. And we call whole school systems "public" even though they refuse to give anyone information about what they are doing, how well they are doing it, and whether children are getting what their parents want. Conversely, we have always called schools "private" if they were owned and operated by private organizations. We have gone on calling these schools "private" even when, as sometimes happens, they are open to every applicant on a non-discriminatory basis, charge no tuition, and make whatever information they have about themselves available to anyone who asks.

Definitions of this kind conceal as much as they reveal, for they classify schools entirely in terms of *who* runs them, not *how* they are run. If we are to understand what is really going on in education, we might well reverse this emphasis. We would then call a school "public" if it were open to everyone on a non-discriminatory basis, if it charged no tuition, and if it provided full information about itself to anyone interested. Conversely, we would call any school "private" if it excluded applicants in a discriminatory way, charged tuition, or withheld information about itself. Admittedly, the question of who governs a school cannot be ignored entirely when categorizing the school, but it seems considerably less important than the question of how the school is governed.

Adopting this revised vocabulary, we propose a regulatory system with two underlying principles: (1) no public money should be used to support "private" schools; and (2) any group that starts a "public" school should be eligible for public subsidies.

Specifically, we propose an education voucher system which would work in the following manner:

1. An Educational Voucher Agency (EVA) would be established to administer the vouchers. Its governing board might be elected or appointed, but in either case it should be structured so as to represent minority as well as majority interests. The EVA might be an existing local board of education, or it might be a new agency with a larger or smaller geographic jurisdiction. The EVA would receive all federal, state, and local education funds for which children in the area were eligible. It would pay this money to schools only in return for vouchers. (In addition, it would pay parents for children's transportation costs to the school of their choice.)

2. The EVA would issue a voucher to every family in its district with school-age children. The value of the basic voucher would initially equal the per pupil expenditure of the public schools in the area. Schools which took children from families with below-average incomes would receive additional payments, on a scale that might, for example, make the maximum payment for the poorest child double the basic voucher.

3. In order to become an "approved voucher school," eligible to cash vouchers, a school would have to:

    a. accept a voucher as full payment of tuition;
    b. accept any applicant so long as it had vacant places;
    c. if it had more applicants than places, fill at least half these places by picking applicants randomly and fill the other half in such a way as not to discriminate against ethnic minorities;
    d. accept uniform standards established by the EVA regarding suspension and expulsion of students;
    e. agree to make a wide variety of information about its facilities, teachers, program, and students available to the EVA and to the public;
    f. maintain accounts of money received and disbursed in a form that would allow parents and the EVA to determine whether a school operated by a board of education was getting the resources to which it was entitled on the basis of its vouchers, whether a school operated by a church was being used to subsidize other church activities, and whether a school operated by a profit-making corporation was siphoning off excessive amounts to the parent corporation;

g. meet existing state requirements for private schools regarding curriculum staffing, and the like.

Control over policy in an approved voucher school might be vested in an existing local school board, a PTA, or any private group. No governmental restrictions would be placed on curriculum, staffing, and the like except those established for all private schools in a state.

4. Just as at present, the local board of education (which might or might not be the EVA) would be responsible for ensuring that there were enough places in publicly managed schools to accommodate every school-age child who did not want to attend a privately managed school. If a shortage of places developed for some reason, the board of education would have to open new schools or create more places in existing schools. (Alternatively, it might find ways to encourage privately managed schools to expand, presumably by getting the EVA to raise the value of the voucher.)

5. Every spring, each family would submit to the EVA the name of the school to which it wanted to send each of its school-age children next fall. Any child already enrolled in a voucher school would be guaranteed a place, as would any sibling of a child enrolled in a voucher school. So long as it had room, a voucher school would be required to admit all students who listed it as a first choice. If it did not have room for all applicants, a school could fill half its places in whatever way it wanted, choosing among those who listed it as a first choice. It could not, however, select these applicants in such a way as to discriminate against racial minorities. It would then have to fill remaining places by a lottery among the remaining applicants. All schools with unfilled places would report these to the EVA. All families whose children had not been admitted to their first choice school would then choose an alternative school which still had vacancies. Vacancies would then be filled in the same manner as in the first round. This procedure would continue until every child had been admitted to a school.

6. Having enrolled their children in a school, parents would give their vouchers to the school. The school would send the vouchers to the EVA and would receive a check in return.

We believe that a system of the kind just described would avoid the dangers usually ascribed to a tuition voucher scheme.

It should increase the share of the nation's educational resources available to disadvantaged children.

It should produce at least as much mixing of blacks and whites, rich and poor, clever and dull, as the present system of public education.

It should ensure advantaged and disadvantaged parents the same chance of getting their children into the school of their choice.

It should provide parents (and the organizations which are likely to affect their decisions) whatever information they think they need to make intelligent choices among schools.

It should avoid conflict with both the Fourteenth Amendment prohibition against racial discrimination and with First Amendment provisions regarding church and state.

The voucher system outlined above is quite different from other systems now being advocated. It regulates the educational marketplace more than most conservatives would like, and contains far more safeguards for the interests of disadvantaged children. We recognize that such restrictions will be considered undesirable by some people. But we believe that a voucher system which does not include these or equally effective safeguards would be worse than no voucher system at all. Indeed, an unregulated voucher system could be the most serious setback for the education of disadvantaged children in the history of the United States. A properly regulated system, on the other hand, could inaugurate a new era of innovation and reform in American schools.

REFERENCE

1. Public subsidies are normally available for a child's education only if he attends a school managed by the local board of education. In most cases the child's family has little or no choice about which school this will be.

    Church subsidies are available in many communities if the child attends a parochial school, but there is seldom much competition between public and parochial schools. This reflects the fact that neither the public nor the parochial system has any economic incentive to expand. On the contrary, when either the public or the parochial system increases its share of the market, it must either decrease its expenditures per pupil or increase its tax or tithing rate. Additional students thus mean more financial problems, not fewer. The result is that both systems have a vested interest in the other's continued survival and popularity.

    The incentives affecting independent schools are somewhat more effective, since most independent schools charge enough tuition to cover the marginal cost of adding a student. Independent schools therefore have an economic incentive to broaden their appeal and please more parents. But their share of the market remains limited by the fact that they get no outside subsidy. As a result, they have little impact on the range of alternatives open to the majority.

E
The Economics of Crime

Millions of dollars are spent each year on crime detection and on the apprehension of criminals by police forces. Two or three times the amount spent by police forces are spent on crime prevention by social workers, churches, and schools. Added to these millions are the costs of jails, prisons, and courtroom procedures — for a grand total which is probably in excess of $25 billion each year.

Most crimes are committed by people from the lower socioeconomic classes against others from the very same classes and in the areas where the poor live. Criminal activity is a part of the syndrome of slum behavior and common to every large city in the United States. Undoubtedly, it is related to poverty, isolation, lack of a favorable self-image — to the characteristics of people in blighted urban areas. Police activity in the field of crime has been almost as futile as the activity of educators in the schools: for all of the millions of dollars spent on both activities, few criminals are caught and few students are educated. One sociologist, Walter B. Miller, argues that neither the "tough-minded" approach of the policeman nor the "tender-hearted" approach of the social worker exerts a significant influence on juvenile crime, for instance, among the lower socioeconomic classes.

For economists crime is a new field. Only in the last ten years has much economic analysis been attempted. Growing population densities have greatly increased visible crime rates, and the big city riots of the 1960's have convinced many observers that the police, when most needed, are ineffectual. Earlier, the problems of deciding how much money to spend for detection and apprehension of criminals were treated as negligible.

Most of the economic analysis of crime detection and prevention begins with benefit-cost analysis: police budgets are examined and compared with police effectiveness. Dissatisfaction with police achievement has not led simply to increased budgets but to the endeavor by economists, politicians, and planners to find out *what* should be done in the field and *who* should do it. It seems apparent that policemen have been asked to do many things unrelated to crime detection and prevention and that in fact other institutions in our society may be able to do such things more effectively. Studies of the marginal productivity of police effort are now being made — comparing the effort's probability of apprehension with its costs.

Simulation models of criminal behavior and of the process of detection and apprehension are needed — for these are complex matters indeed. No doubt the basic tools of microeconomics (especially) will be built into these models as the work proceeds, though clearly this is the place for interdisciplinary analysis.

21 The Economics of Defense Against Crime in the Streets

MARTIN T. KATZMAN*
Harvard University

Society faces trade-offs in allocating resources to crime deterrence and to other goals. The internal economy of a police department is affected by trade-offs among expenditures, programs, crimes to be deterred, neighborhoods to be protected. Our quantitative knowledge of trade-offs, at all levels, is slight indeed.

Economists have had relatively little to say about the deterrence of crime.[1] In other problem areas, such as the business cycle, economic thinking has been a generation ahead of the public in visualizing solutions. Public concern about crime, on the other hand, highlighted by the report of the (1967) President's Commission on Law Enforcement,[2] catches the economist either unconcerned or unprepared to contribute to the discussion. Detachment on the part of economists is unfortunate and untimely because the federal government is preparing to spend considerable sums on local police forces.[3] This essay is an attempt to clarify some of the important trade-offs and economic choices which confront a society in deterring crime. In this essay, we shall first sketch the systematic relationships among the activities of the public, the criminals, and the police. We shall then focus on the behavior of the police as an economic activity. Hopefully, the discussion compensates for its relative lack of elegance by its relevance.

CRIMINAL BEHAVIOR AND THE PUBLIC

Typology of Criminals

We distinguish among three types of criminals, who differ by type of crime, responsiveness to punitive threats, and by rationality.[4] The first, the "organized criminal," is a member of a business engaged in providing illegal services (such as gambling), often using illegal means (such as violence and extortion).[5] The or-

---

From "The Economics of Defense Against Crime in the Streets," by Martin T. Katzman, *Land Economics*, Volume 44, November 1968, pp. 431–440. Copyright © 1968 by the Regents of the University of Wisconsin (*Land Economics* Magazine). Reprinted with permission.

ganized criminal is fairly well acquainted with the law relevant to his own enterprise, and may engage in profitable bargains with the police to encourage the enforcement of the law in his favor. Of all types of criminals, he is probably most affected by changes in police methods of detection because his crimes often have no victims — e.g., gambling and prostitution. The "unorganized professional," the second criminal type, tends to commit crimes against property — e.g., larceny, forgery, or counterfeiting. While not necessarily adverse to committing violence, the professional sees the end of his criminal activity as mostly economic. Furthermore, this activity is a full-time vocation, which requires considerable rational calculation for survival. By far the largest number of crimes are committed by the third criminal type, the "amateur." The amateurs comprise the would-be professionals who lack the skill of avoiding arrest and also individuals who commit criminal acts in moments of passion or irrationality. The murderer, the rapist, and the joyrider are involved in crimes whose ends are not basically economic or whose costs and benefits have not been carefully evaluated. It is the amateur, responsible for most of the crime in the streets, upon whom this essay focuses.

The Supply of Criminals

Perhaps the major explanation for differences in the rate and type of crime in the various neighborhoods of a metropolis is the supply of criminals. The supply of criminals in a neighborhood is related to the sex, age, class, and ethnic composition of its residents, and those who have easy access to it.[6] For example, neighborhoods with large numbers of lower-class teen-agers tend to have high crime rates. Despite journalistic tales of increasing middle class crime, most crime is committed *by* lower-class people, *against* other lower class people, *in* lower class areas.[7] Especially in crimes of violence, such as murder, assault, and rape, the victim and offender are not only of similar lower class background, but they are often acquaintances.

The Opportunities for Crime

The opportunities for criminal activity are affected by three factors. First are the alternative costs to the potential offender for criminal activity. In times of heavy unemployment, when the most crime-prone class and age groups are also the least likely to hold a job, legitimate economic activity does not compete with criminal activity.[8] Similarly during the evenings and summers, the peaks of crime cycles may result from increased opportunities for leisure. Second are the perceived costs and benefits of engaging in criminal activity. The land use pattern of a metropolis delimits the areas in which crimes of different types are likely to occur. In commercial areas, where the wares of an affluent society are alluringly displayed, the opportunities for as well as the benefits from larceny are at their peak. In residential areas, where people have the leisure to commit violence on one another, murders and rapes attain their peaks.[9] Third are factors which affect the probability of successfully consummating a crime. These are the private crime detecting and deterring mechanisms. Jane Jacobs cites as an inadvertent crime deterrent: the "eyes on the street" of her "slum" neighbors when chatting from their windows or doorways.[10]

Perhaps a considerable amount of crime might be deterred by action on the part of the victim. For example, more than 40 per cent of all stolen cars had keys left in the ignition; an even larger percentage of such cars were left unlocked.[11] Theft victims on the whole act as if the nuisance of locking one's car outweighed the value of the increased security. Even if they were fully informed of the probable losses associated with locked versus unlocked cars, theft victims might in their private calculus rationally prefer negligence. Private calculus, however, does not consider the social costs of recovering the stolen vehicle, the costs to the usually youthful offender who was led into a criminal career by a misperception of easy gains, and costs to others who may become more prone to victimization, and a process discussed below. Business can similarly affect its chances of being victimized. Omitting the tellers' cages in new suburban banks and providing self-service retailing increases the probability of being robbed.[12] Bankers and retailers may rationally choose to suffer pilferage when more than offset by increases in business. Clearly, individuals and firms do expend considerable sums on private police forces, common to factories, department stores, and universities. Although an individual may perceive benefits from his private crime deterrence activities, the very existence of housebreaking or shoplifting attests to the fact that at a point with a positive crime rate, the private costs of crime deterrence are greater than the private benefits. The private cost-benefit calculations may have serious spill-overs. An amateur auto thief might be deterred from attempting to rob a particular car, whether or not it had an alarm, if from his past experience most other cars had burglar alarms. One might argue that all car owners would be better off if unlocked cars were ticketed, with especially heavy fines for those with keys left in the ignition.

While there is some evidence that individuals avoid victimization by foregoing certain desired activities, this is a costly though somewhat effective means of deterrence.[13] For example, not walking at night or avoiding the subways or parks, may effectively reduce the chances of being mugged, but the inconvenience of these private activities is what prompts the public demand for protection against "crime in the streets."

POLICE AND THE PUBLIC

One popular image of the police is of their prevention of crime by vigilance against evildoers. Actually, the relationship between the police and crime is extremely complex, involving the populace and the courts. At best, the police have a very indirect role in deterring crime — a role mediated through the public. . . .

Police Activities: Detection

Far from being omnipresent or omniscient, police rarely catch a criminal in a violent act.[14] More often, police detection of crime depends upon a report by the victim, the public, or even the criminal. Because he may be vulnerable to prosecution himself (e.g., for carrying a weapon, for suspicion of some other crime), a victim often will not report a crime. Similarly, the public may not wish to get involved by reporting a crime, and may accept crime as one of the risks one must take in life, or settle accounts themselves.[15] Quite often a criminal himself will report a crime although his motives may not be those of crime deterrence.[16]

Another influence on the detectability of a crime by the police is the public's evaluation of the gravity of the crime. Organized crime such as prostitution or drug addiction lacks an outraged victim to report the crime. Either because the public is disinterested or unaware, there is rarely a third party to report the offense.

Often the victim does not perceive his misfortune as resulting from a criminal act. For example, if two men engage in a barroom brawl, at least one of them has technically committed assault and battery. Were the brawlers lower class, they are unlikely to consider their behavior criminal. If the combatants were middle class, the loser would undoubtedly report a case of assault. A final influence on the detectability of crime by the police is the probability of restitution to the victim. The robbery of small, uninsured items is less likely to be reported than the loss of a valuable, identifiable insured item.

The one set of "crimes" which the police detect themselves, the attitudes of the victim notwithstanding, are traffic violations. These violations are generally visible outdoors and little information is needed for their detection except for that given on the instruments of the police. The detectability of various crimes can be summarized by comparing official rates of the uniform crime reports to the rates determined by surveys. In general, less than half of all property crimes and about half of all crimes of violence are reported, as shown in Table 1. These estimates of reported crimes are conservative in using the victim's rather than the police's judgment as to whether an event was a crime. Most auto thefts were reported, because loss is insurable and the auto is recoverable. If crimes without victims — e.g., traffic offenses and vice — were enumerable, they would prove to be the least detectable.

Investigation and Apprehension

If a crime has been detected, say if a victim reports a robbery, the next function the police may attempt to perform is to discover and to apprehend the criminal. How long and hard the police will search for an offender depends upon the chances of finding him and the gravity of the crime. The probability of apprehension in-

Table 1

Comparison of Actual Versus Reported Crime, 1965–1966
(per 100,000 population)

CRIME	ACTUAL	REPORTED	% REPORTED
Traffic offenses	N.A.	N.A.	N.A.
Abortion	N.A.	N.A.	N.A.
Vice	N.A.	N.A.	N.A.
Forcible Rape	42.5	11.6	27
Burglary	949.1	299.6	32
Larceny ($50+)	606.5	267.4	44
Aggravated Assault	218.3	106.6	49
Robbery	94.0	61.4	65
Auto Theft	206.2	226.0	110
		Total Traffic	N.A.
		Total Vice	N.A.
		Total Property	45
		Total Violence	52

Source: President's Commission, p. 22.

creases with the speed with which the police arrive at the scene of the crime or with the degree to which the victim can identify the offender. The willingness of the public to provide the police with information, hence the ability to investigate, may increase with the seriousness of the crime. Aside from crimes without victims, there is a remarkable consensus among the public of all classes, the police, and judges as to the seriousness of various crimes.[17] For example, most people agree that murder is more serious than assault, which is more serious than auto theft. There may be some disagreement, however, among the public of different classes and between the police and the public as to whether an assault against a lower class Negro woman is as serious as an assault against a middle class white woman.

Recovery

If the police were able to recover the criminal's benefit from the crime and provide restitution to the victim, the police might deter criminals and compensate victims. Even if the police "get their men," restitution is often impossible, as in cases of personal violence. For some property crimes, the stolen goods may have been consumed or damaged. Since the benefit to the auto thief is generally the joy of riding in a stolen car, the auto is returned to its rightful owner in about 80 per cent of thefts.[18]

Retribution

Although the police are not officially society's arm of retribution, police contact may be the only punishment a criminal may experience since only a small percentage of those arrested ever serve in jail. Apprehension *per se* may be punishing if it leads to time consuming and costly incarceration and litigation, even if one is declared innocent. The costs of litigation may be so high that, in cases where the punishment is minor such as traffic offenses, individuals may pay a fine in lieu of a trial. The direct administration of "curbstone justice" by the police, however, seems to be declining as a form of retribution.

Deterrence

While retribution may be of benefit to some members of society, most people view deterrence as the most important output of the institutions of law enforcement and the administration of justice. In other words, the public believes that the police can and ought to decrease "crime in the streets." Before discussing the deterrence of crime by police protection, we discuss the kinds of economic trade-offs the police can make in combatting crime.

Allocation of Police Resources

Police administrators have developed rules of thumb for the deployment of their resources.[19] Framed in terms of "desirable" patrolmen/street mile, or patrolmen/population ratios, they provide no insight into the kinds of trade-offs the police face in their internal allocation of resources nor provide a method of evaluating the productive efficiency of a particular allocation.

Budget Constraint

The first economic choice involving the police is the level of their budget. Given the method of operations of the police, what is the marginal output of the force in terms of crimes deterred or criminals apprehended for an additional $X of expenditures? How are given police resources disbursed among neighborhoods, program, and items of expenditures?

Choices Among Neighborhoods

Because policemen in one neighborhood cannot quickly respond to a reported crime in another neighborhood, there may be trade-offs in deterring crimes among different neighborhoods. Allocative choices among neighborhoods are simultaneously distributive; that is, *who is protected* is determined.[20]

Choices Among Crimes

Which crimes the police try to detect and investigate are a matter of discretion. While a patrolman may produce the joint products of simultaneous vigilance against murder, arson, robbery, traffic violations, etc., the investigator has to choose which offenders at large are worth pursuing. Often the choice among crimes is quite explicit. A patrolman may deliberately not detect a petty criminal — e.g., a drunk or vagrant, who in exchange might provide information about more serious crimes in the future. The existence of many people vulnerable to arrest in a neighborhood can be a valuable resource to the policemen who can stock up on "potential arrest." The effect of mutual exchanges in police-community relations is discussed below.

Choices Among Programs

There are trade-offs between detective and apprehensive programs. Total commitment of resources to detection leaves little manpower for apprehending criminals not caught in the act. Total commitment to investigation leaves many crimes undetected. Just as there cannot be consumption without some investment, there cannot be apprehension with detection, and there are trade-offs to consider in trying to maximize the number of criminals detected *and* apprehended.

Choices Among Items of Expenditure

The police budget is expended on several classes of inputs in pursuit of crime-fighting programs among the several neighborhoods of a big city. The major items are manpower (patrolmen, investigators, administrators); vehicles (automobiles, motorcycles, scooters, and often helicopters and horses); and the communication network (alarm boxes, two-way radios, telephone lines).

Besides cost trade-offs, there are output trade-offs in choosing among items of expenditure. For example, a patrolman on foot is less mobile than one in an auto but he may have greater contacts with the public on his beat. His closer contact with the public may facilitate their cooperation in crime detection and investigation or, on the other hand, provide more opportunities for "brutality." From the point of view of police administration the foot patrolman is less communicative with headquarters, hence less controllable than an auto patrolman with constant access to a two-way radio.

Other types of trade-offs among inputs are not hard to understand: a one-man patrol car with a finer spread of manpower and higher capital costs versus a two-man car with doubled manpower for any emergency and perhaps higher morale; widespread public alarm boxes facilitating both the reporting of crimes and false alarms, etc.

Normative Constraints

An important exogenous influence on police allocation decisions is the normative proscription on police technology and behavior. As articulated by the courts, these norms proscribe, among other actions, wire-tapping, random searches of citizens, arrests without warrant, and the extraction of confessions through torture, all of which may possibly increase the ability of the police to detect and investigate criminal behavior.[21] While such constraints may facilitate detection and investigation, it is not clear that they affect the police's ability to *deter* crimes by amateurs, or even more rational professionals. Most likely these constraints proscribe the ability to deter organized crime without victims. Although it is not clear how the criminal behavior of amateurs, who commit most crimes on the street, would be affected by a less constrained police force, it is quite clear that inconvenience to the public would be increased. Just as there is the cost of tasting bitter pills in fighting disease, there is the cost of police inconvenience to third parties in fighting crime.

Choices Between Criminal and Noncriminal Activities

Although police view themselves as "protectors of law and order," they often perform functions usually associated with social work in the public mind. The range of noncriminal services performed depends upon both the socio-economic composition of the population and the willingness of the police to engage in such "nonprofessional" services. In Boston the police locate missing persons, get raccoons out of cellars, provide information about parking regulations and baseball scores, converse with lonely people, and mediate domestic disputes. While the Boston police routinely offer first aid and drive people to hospitals, the Los Angeles police generally refuse involvement with medical problems.

Clearly all types of service demands do not emerge randomly from the population. Middle-class people are less likely to request all kinds of services than do lower-class people.[22] Older, less nimble and mobile individuals often require medical assistance or emergency household repairs. Females heading households often request assistance in disciplining children. Solitary people are most likely to call the police just to talk.

Although these services may seem unprofessional to some police administrators, they provide considerable benefit to the public *per se* and enhance the police image among the groups whose cooperation may be extremely important in detecting and investigating crime. Rather than being a pure drain on police resources, "community relations" activities may serve as an intermediate input to the crime deterrence process by increasing the public's willingness to cooperate with the police.

In an economic sense the provision of many social services is nearly costless. Because criminal activity tends to be cyclical the police have considerable periods of slackened "demand." For men in the communications department, giving information and advice is nearly a free good, both helping the public and freeing the policemen from demoralizing inactivity. Service work by men on patrol is economically cheap, too. While it may reduce their vigilance on the beat, the patrolmen, like radiomen, learn to judge when the slack periods on their beats will occur. During peaks of criminal activity, not only do the police hesitate to answer social service calls, but the public often hesitates to ask.[23] For other social services, such as police athletic leagues, there are real manpower costs to improving community relations.

THE DETERRENCE OF CRIME IN THE STREETS

Interactions of Public, Criminals, and Policemen

In Figure 1 we summarize the systematic interrelationships in the behavior of the public, the criminals, and the police. We identify the final outputs (circles) and policy variables (triangles) of the system. Where relevant, the direction of the effects are indicated by pluses (direct variation) and minuses (inverse variation).

Two outputs of the system are negatively correlated. Specifically, policies which deter crime better also inconvenience the public more. Ideally, one would want to know the costs of changing any policy variable on the deterrence of crime, retribution, and inconvenience, all of which have their prices. In fact, pitifully little is known of the precise effects of any of these policy changes on any one output, e.g., deterrence. Rather than masking ignorance with mathematical rigor, we present below the kinds of economic trade-offs in crime deterrence.

1. Criminal activity increases with cyclical unemployment, which lowers the alternative costs to the criminal. What are the marginal costs in crime if the unemployment rate increases by X per cent? What are the costs, if any, of providing employment for the potentially criminal subgroups in society?

2. What are the trade-offs between public and private resources in the detection of crime? Considering the by-products of both private and public expenditures on crime fighting, what is the best mix of private and public protection?

3. What are the technological trade-offs between patrolmen and vehicles in detecting a given crime? Given the budget constraint, what combination(s) of patrolmen and vehicles detect the most crime, weighted by its gravity?

4. What are the technological trade-offs between patrol and investigative manpower in detecting a crime *and* apprehending a criminal? Given the budget constraint, what is the best combination(s) of patrol and investigative resources for apprehending the most criminals, weighted by the gravity of their crimes?

5. What effects do the detection of crime and the apprehension of criminals have on the rate of different crimes? Given the public evaluation of each type of crime, what is the deterrent value of police activity for different neighborhoods?

6. What are the shadow prices of policemen, investigators, and vehicles? In terms of crimes deterred, what are the benefits of easing the budget constraint on the police?

7. What are the effects of the normative constraints on police behavior? Do the courts really "handcuff" the police in their fight against crime? If the public were willing to tolerate the inconvenience of a less restrained police force, how much additional crime would be deterred?

8. What are the costs of providing social services to the public? What are the trade-offs in terms of crimes deterred between resources devoted to professional, direct anti-criminal activity, and maintaining community relations?

Figure 1

Interrelations Among the Police, the Public and Criminals

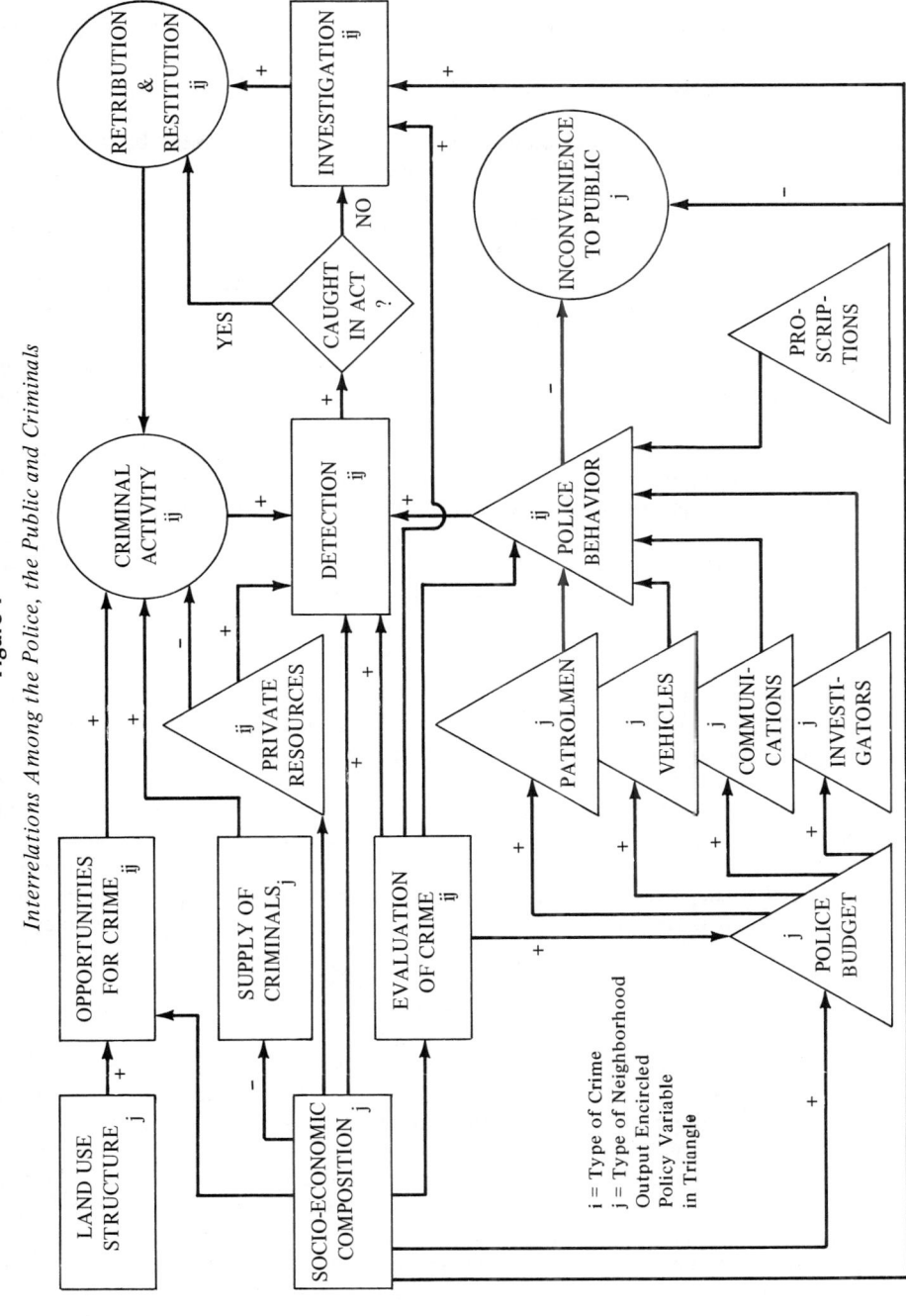

Distribution of Police Protection

Even if we were able to methodically trace out the effects of police protection on inconvenience to the public, recovery of stolen goods, retribution against criminals, and deterrence of future crimes, we are faced with the more difficult question of *who benefits from it?* While costs of inconvenience may be traced to those experiencing police contact and benefits of recovery may be traced to the victim, the benefits of retribution and deterrence are not so easily traced. All individuals do not evaluate retribution against a convicted offender similarly. At one extreme some may view him as an unfortunate creature of circumstance who may hopefully be rehabilitated. At the other extreme, others may view him as deserving to pay "an eye for an eye." For criminals who have no victims (gamblers, dope pushers, abortionists, bootleggers), there may even be remorse on the part of the clientele.

Aside from the obvious case of crimes without victims, all individuals do not benefit equally from the deterrence of a given crime. The simple reason is that we are not equally likely to be victimized.[24] The probability of coming to violence, as mentioned before, depends upon one's socio-economic status. The losses from property crimes are perhaps most sharply felt by owners of property, for example.

While the upper-middle classes are unlikely to be victims of any crime, much less organized crime, they tend to be outraged by vice and gangland killing. For this class, crime deterrence, regardless of the potential victim, is perceived as a public good and the police as the enforcers of their civic morality.

CONCLUSION

The main points of this essay are quite simple. First, society faces trade-offs in allocating resources to crime deterrence and other goals. In private decisions individuals trade off the expected losses from crime against the costs of taking safety precautions, self-service firms trade off the costs of salesmen against the losses due to crime, and banks trade security for attractiveness to customers. In public decisions, there are trade-offs between resources spent on police protection and those expended on other goals. Second, there are trade-offs in the internal economy of a police department among items of expenditures, programs, crimes to be deterred, and neighborhoods to be protected. The internal economic choices are somewhat constrained by public opinion and court edicts. Third, painfully little quantitative knowledge of the several trade-offs described is available. In the absence of such hard knowledge, it is difficult to evaluate alternative crime deterrent policies or efficiency of police operations.

In principle, the analysis of crime deterrence should be easier than that of nuclear deterrence, mainly because the output of police protection, a drop in the crime rate, is more palpable than the output of the Defense Department, a drop in the probability of war with Russia.[25] One must be intellectually prepared to accept a finding that the police have negligible effects on the crime rate, as some anthropologists argue.[26] If this were true, then millions poured into local police departments might be better spent on improving the economic conditions of potential criminals or on other social goals. Although frustrating to the political activist, one might find changing the criminal behavior of the lower class as difficult as changing their educational behavior.[27]

REFERENCES

* The author acknowledges the assistance of the Joint Center for Urban Studies of the Massachusetts Institute of Technology and Harvard University for providing the facilities and stimulating colleagues helpful in conceiving this essay. Werner Hirsch and the Institute of Government and Public Affairs of the University of California at Los Angeles provided a forum for some of the ideas in this essay. Deputy Superintendent William Bradley of the Boston Police provided the author the opportunity for uninhibited observation of police operations. Walter B. Miller and Martin Levin were extremely helpful in sharpening the analysis.

1. The notable exception is, Carl S. Shoup, "Standards for Distributing a Free Governmental Service: Crime Prevention," *Public Finance,* December 1954, pp. 383–401. While an interesting application of economic analysis, Shoup's article abstracts away the more interesting problems of choice among inputs and outputs to be of any policy implication. Belton Fleisher, *The Economics of Delinquency* (Chicago, Illinois: Quadrangle Books, 1966), elegantly shows the effects of income and unemployment on delinquency; however, his analysis provides little information about the effects of police.
2. The President's Commission on Law Enforcement and the Administration of Justice, *The Challenge of Crime in a Free Society* (Washington, D.C.: United States Government Printing Office, 1967).
3. James Q. Wilson, "Crime in the Streets," *The Public Interest,* Fall 1966, pp. 26–35, argues that intellectuals, especially liberals, have been unwilling to regard crime as a serious problem in its own right, but have tended to look to more macroeconomic causes such as unemployment or poverty.
4. I am grateful to Martin Levin for these distinctions among criminal types.
5. For a description of organized crime see, Thomas C. Schelling, "The Economics of Organized Crime," *The Public Interest,* Spring 1967, pp. 61–79.
6. For statistical evidence see, Donald R. Cressey, "Crime," Robert K. Merton and Robert A. Nisbet (eds.), *Contemporary Social Problems* (New York, New York: Harcourt Brace, 1961), pp. 21–76; also Albert K. Cohen and James F. Short, Jr., "Juvenile Delinquency," Merton and Nisbet *op. cit.,* pp. 77–126.
7. Cressey, *op. cit.;* Nesbit, *op. cit.;* President's Commission, Chapter 1.
8. Belton Fleisher, *op. cit.,* describes the coincidence of criminal and unemployment cycles.
9. The President's Commission, *loc. cit.,* discusses the spatial distribution of crime. Werner Z. Hirsch, "Factors Affecting the Level of Government Expenditures," John C. Bollens (ed.) *Exploring the Metropolitan Community* (Berkeley, California: University of California, 1961), pp. 317–352, shows the relationship between socio-economic and land-use patterns and the nature of police inputs.
10. Jane Jacobs, *The Death and Life of Great American Cities* (New York, New York: Random House, 1961), pp. 29–54.
11. President's Commission, pp. 29–30, pp. 264–65.
12. *Ibid,* Chapter 1.
13. *Ibid.,* pp. 50–51, finds that substantial proportions of residents of big cities consciously engage in crime-avoiding behavior: 82 per cent lock their doors at night, 37 per cent keep firearms, 28 per cent have watchdogs, and 10 per cent bar their windows. Patricia Cayo Sexton, *Spanish Harlem* (New York, New York: Harper and Row, 1965), describes how the residents live in chronic fear of being robbed, knifed, attacked, bullied or having their children injured.
14. President's Commission, p. 249, states that a patrolman will *observe* a robbery on the average of once every 14 years.

15. President's Commission, p. 20 ff., describes the many reasons people give for not reporting crimes. Herbert Gans, *The Urban Villagers* (New York, New York: Free Press, 1962), argues that, although lower-class people are more prone to be victimized than are middle-class people, they are more resentful of the outside interference represented by the police than are middle-class people.
16. Walter B. Miller, *City Gangs* (New York, New York: John Wiley and Sons, forthcoming), argues that the police have a respected adversary role in lower-class subculture. A youth may often confess a crime that the police had not heard of, to elicit their wonderment and praise for "pulling a clean job."
17. J. Thorsten Sellin and Marvin E. Wolfgang, *The Measurement of Delinquency* (New York, New York: John Wiley and Sons, 1964). The set of evaluations of crime forms a ratio scale — i.e., there is a zero point, and ratio comparisons of crimes can be made.
18. President's Commission, Chapter 1.
19. Orlando W. Wilson, *Police Planning* 2nd edition (Springfield, Illinois: Charles Thomas, 1957), and *Police Administration* (New York, New York: McGraw Hill, 2nd edition, 1963); G. Douglas Gourley and Allen P. Bristow, *Patrol Administration* (Springfield, Illinois: Charles Thomas, 1961), on rules of thumb for deploying manpower and machinery over time and space.
20. This is the major problem discussed by Shoup, *op. cit.*
21. William A. Westley, "Violence and the Police," *American Journal of Sociology,* July 1953, pp. 85–88 on the police attitude towards violence.
22. James Q. Wilson, "The Police and Their Problems: A Theory," *Public Policy,* 1963, pp. 189–216, argues that the only contacts most middle-class people have with the police are service calls.
23. Men on the Los Angeles switchboard during the Watts disturbance in 1965 claim that calls from other parts of the city diminished. Similarly, the officer in charge of police communications in Boston during the blackout in November 1965 claimed that fewer than usual calls were received. Apparently both criminal and noncriminal elements are hesitant to overload the police with burdens during extraordinary peak periods.
24. John Dollard, *Caste and Class in a Southern Town* (New Haven, Connecticut: Yale Press, 1937); and Michael Banton, *The Police and the Community* (London, England: Tavestock, 1964), argue that Negro communities in parts of the South are essentially without police protection. The apathy with which the police treat crimes with Negro victims and the vigor with which crimes against whites are investigated, they argue, encourages intra-Negro crime.
25. Charles Hitch and Roland McKean, *The Economics of Defense in the Nuclear Age* (Cambridge, Massachusetts: Harvard Press, 1960) is the pioneering study of the economics of deterrence.
26. Walter B. Miller, "Lower Class Culture as a Generating Milieu of Gang Delinquency," *Journal of Social Issues,* December 1957, pp. 5–19, argues that it is normal and desirable in lower class youth culture to engage in activities considered criminal and likely to involve the police; in *City Gangs* he argues that neither the hard-minded disapproval of the police nor the tender-hearted approach of the social worker have much impact on juvenile crime.
27. James Coleman *et al., Equality of Educational Opportunity,* (Washington D.C.: Office of Education, 1966), finds that variations in school inputs have little impact on the academic achievement of the children of lower socio-economic status.

22 The Clandestine Distribution of Heroin, Its Discovery and Suppression

SIMON ROTTENBERG
Duke University

A review of the potential profits and potential risks in heroin pedaling. Detection of peddlers is more meaningful at the wholesale than at the retail level, for the wholesaler may be able to provide information about both producers and retailers.

Heroin that is illegally consumed in the United States derives, for the most part, from opium produced in Turkey which is converted there or in Lebanon to morphine base and which is, in turn, shipped through Istanbul or Beirut to France. In France it is transformed to heroin in small laboratories and is transported to the United States, either directly or via Italy, Canada, or Mexico (Giorgano, 1966, p. 5; U.S. Senate, Permanent Subcommittee on Investigations, 1964, pp. 881 ff.).

A distribution system in the United States puts the product into the hands of consumers. There are said to be between 45,000 and 100,000 narcotics addicts in this country,[1] about half of whom are in New York City.

The trade is illegal, and various federal agencies (mainly the Bureaus of Customs and Narcotics and the Food and Drug Administration) and state and local law enforcement authorities are charged with the responsibility of the execution of the law.

The prevention of the contraband introduction of narcotics into the country is apparently very difficult because narcotics are easily transported and concealed and have great value relative to their weight and volume (Anslinger and Tompkins, 1953, p. 172). It is estimated that one and one-half tons of heroin are brought into the country illegally each year (President's Advisory Commission on Narcotics and Drug Abuse, 1963, p. 5); only a small fraction of this quantity is intercepted and seized by the authorities.

THE ORGANIZATION OF CLANDESTINE ENTERPRISE

Clandestine enterprises consist of two parts: one that produces the service or good which is the nominal product of the enterprise and another that conceals the activities done in the pursuit of the first object.

From "The Clandestine Distribution of Heroin, Its Discovery and Suppression," by Simon Rottenberg, *Journal of Political Economy,* Volume 76, January–February 1968, pp. 78–90. Copyright © 1968 The University of Chicago. Reprinted with permission.

Both activities consume resources. The firm will, in the fulfillment of the second object, choose among alternative strategies for security on optimizing principles. That is to say, it will seek to minimize security costs per unit of concealment achieved, and it will carry the security operations of the enterprise to a scale that will fulfil the condition that the marginal cost of that activity will equal its marginal revenue.

A unit of revenue in the firm's security operations is the magnitude by which the probability of detection diminishes times the "loss" suffered (the costs incurred) if detected. Thus 0.4 probability of detection may be reduced, by incurring additional security or concealment costs, to 0.3 probability. The incremental revenue derived from the additional expenditure would be 0.1 times, say, the negative value put on five years in prison — which might be lost earnings — net of consumption while in prison, plus the negative value put on the state of being shut away from society and being deprived of the freedom to move, both discounted, minus the capitalized value of the income stream produced by schooling in criminal business skills while in prison and by business associations formed there.

The probability of discovery of someone engaged in the narcotics trade is a partial function of the number of transactions in which he engages. Thus one kilo of heroin sold in a single one-kilo transaction is to be preferred by those engaged in the trade to one kilo sold in two half-kilo transactions.

This suggests that the risk of discovery is largest at the point in the chain of distribution where the quantum of heroin transferred in any given transaction is smallest at the mean and where, therefore, the number of transactions is largest.

Since the mean of the magnitude of transactions becomes successively smaller as heroin makes its way from importing to retailing, and the number of transactions engaged in by any operators becomes larger in the same process, the risks of detection are, other things being equal, smaller for the importer and larger for the retailer.

The narcotics distribution system may be long or short. In principle, the importer can do his own retailing; or his own wholesaling, selling to other retailers; or he may sell to jobbers who, in turn, sell to wholesalers who sell to retailers.

The length of the system will depend, in part, on the extent of the market, since this, in turn, affects the degree of specialization in the trade.

If the organization of the trade is managed — if, that is to say, a central director (say the importer or a factor) determines the number of transaction points — then the length of the system may be greater than that indicated by efficiency criteria. This is because the narcotics trade is illegal, and, therefore, those who engage in it operate clandestinely. A clandestine enterprise can be expected to be organized so as to minimize the probability of discovery of its organizer.

The larger the number of transaction points, the smaller the quantity of information possessed by any participant at any point. By elongating the chain, therefore, the organizer of the trade creates a buffer between himself and any point on the chain. The risk he runs of being discovered is inversely proportional to the number of informants who must be successively broken in order that he be found out.

The narcotics trade in some territory may be that of a single monopoly firm which organizes a chain of dealers of some number, or the trade may be carried on by a number of complementary monopolists (U.S. Senate, Permanent Subcommittee on Investigations, 1964).

If it were a single firm, then the organizer (manager) would determine the magnitude of the difference in prices of heroin between each pair of links in the chain of distribution. This magnitude would be just what is sufficient to attract the relevant number of people to the trade at each link. The compensation of the traders would be determined by the differences between their buying and their selling prices net of the costs of doing business, including the cost of being thought odious by the community and the cost of punishment for engaging in an illegal trade, in a probability sense.

If the trade is carried on by complementary monopolists, the price at each transaction link will be indeterminate, since this would simulate Edgeworth's classic duopoly case; the price would depend upon the relative shrewdness of the monopoly traders, within some range.

The magnitudes of differences in prices of narcotics between successive pairs of transaction points will be primarily affected by differences, between successive pairs of points, in the cost of doing business.[2] In this trade, the largest single cost is that associated with discovery, apprehension, conviction, and punishment. The quantity of law enforcement resources and its allocation along the distribution chain would seem to be the primary determinant of the structure of narcotics prices.

Sellers of drugs, when they hold inventories, possess commodities which, if they are discovered, constitute incriminating evidence (Eldridge, 1962, p. 53). There will be a strong incentive to "unload" rapidly and to refrain from holding inventories. As with other stored commodities, inventories may be held in expectation of a price rise; there is an optimal storage policy that takes account of the cost of storage. In the case of an illegal commodity (that is, one whose mere possession, or whose possession with intent to sell, is illegal), the cost of storage is pre-eminently the negative value associated with discovery.

Law enforcement would be advantaged by any change that induced sellers to hold larger inventories and for longer periods. Can enforcement policy be designed to bring this about? Would it be helpful in this connection if possession were not illegal, nor presumptive evidence of illegal activities accepted by the courts? If this induced illegal operators to hold inventories and, in turn, provided information to the authorities about the persons to watch (for *other* kinds of activities than possession — which activities *would* be illegal), would the incidence of discovery rise? But, if possession, even if legal, were found to have secondary adverse consequences, operators would still have an incentive to refrain from storing.

The distribution of opiates is apparently done by "organized criminals," and the distribution of LSD and marijuana is done largely by amateurs.[3] Presumably, this is because the rate of return, adjusted for the cost of doing business, is higher in the opiate trade than in the others. This must be because opiate traders are able to enforce a monopoly which produces rents for them. But why do they not also enforce a monopoly in the other drug trades? Is it because (*a*) opiate distribution is considered to be the more odious trade; therefore, "amateurs" are less willing to engage in it; therefore, "professionals" have a monopoly of "talent" and it is from this that their rents derive?

Or is it because (*b*) the costs imposed upon discovered and apprehended opiate distributors are higher than the costs put on traders in LSD and marijuana; these costs are differentially valued by different classes of persons; the amateurs believe a five-year prison sentence is a high price to pay for the monetary gains derived from the trade, but the professionals believe the price is not so high. Therefore, only a small number will engage in the trade (if there were no monopoly and given the relative, adjusted earnings in the opiate trade), and the enforcement costs of a monopoly — which must exclude only a small number of aspirants to the trade — will be low. The costs imposed upon LSD and marijuana distributors are lower (the prison sentences are shorter); therefore, for given rewards, more will engage in these trades; the enforcement of monopolies in these trades would require the exclusion of many disposed to enter; the cost of enforcement of the monopoly would, therefore, be high in them. Presumptively, since we do not observe monopolies in these trades, the cost of making a monopoly effective is high enough so that such an undertaking is not worthwhile.

What are the expected consequences of more energetic enforcement of the laws against the trade in narcotics?

Crimes are of three classes: (1) they may destroy part of the capital stock of society, as murder and arson; (2) they may involve coercive transfer payments, as theft; (3) they may involve the sale and purchase of commodities that society believes reprehensible, as prostitution and narcotics.

Some crimes damage society more than others. Society can affect the product mix of the crime industry by allocating law enforcement resources among crimes, thus determining the distribution among crimes of the costs of criminal activity paid by criminals.

It is assumed that criminals will choose that criminal career which will maximize their net revenues. If, other things being equal, some crimes are made more costly for those who perpetrate them, criminals will, at the margin, move to other crimes. The degree of enforcement of the law against the trade in narcotics will, therefore, enlarge the cost to society from other crimes.

Society's indifference curve between crimes can be assumed to be concave to the origin so that the increment of other crimes than the trade in narcotics that it is willing to suffer, in exchange for the reduction by one unit of the narcotics trade, will be small, if the narcotics trade is of relatively small volume and other crimes of relatively large volume; and it will be large if the volume of narcotics trade is relatively large and the volume of other crimes is relatively small.

Criminals now diversify their output to some extent. That is to say, they engage in a number of different criminal activities. This is a form of hedging. If one criminal activity is made relatively more costly to engage in, other things being equal, the quantity of that crime tends to shrink, and that activity becomes inferior, as a hedge, to what it had been before the cost change occurred. The failure rate of criminal enterprises will rise as a consequence.

As heroin moves forward toward the consumer in the distribution chain it is successively diluted, usually by milk sugar or quinine hydrochloride (U.S. Senate, Subcommittee to Investigate Juvenile Delinquency, 1963a, p. 3133). The consumer finally buys a combination of heroin and inert materials that may be 1.5–33.0 per cent heroin by weight.

Why does narcotics dilution take place? As with any other commodity, it is not necessary to dilute in order to effect a rise in price. Two alternative hypotheses are suggested: (1) Consumers will offer less resistance to a price rise produced by additional adulteration of the product and will be less likely to search out alternative sources of supply than if the price rise were outright and open. This seems like a questionable hypothesis, since users can apparently tell the intensity of their experience in the consumption of drugs and do adjust by increasing the number of bags used in a single dose when adulteration occurs. On the other hand, adulteration simulates the behavior of, say, the candy manufacturers who kept the price of candy bars constant while shrinking their sizes. (2) Adulteration is a rationing device employed when heroin is in short supply. This hypothesis would explain variance in the degree of dilution but not the apparent secular tendency for dilution to occur.

Another possible hypothesis is that dilution opens options for consumers. It permits users to choose between small (say one bag) doses and large (say three bag) doses. But this hypothesis gives no clue as to why the extent of dilution has increased with time; it suggests only that dilution will always occur in order to provide a lower "quality" product for those whose preference functions make it desirable to ingest small quantities. It is like explaining why Falcon automobiles will be manufactured, as well as Continentals, but would not explain why the fraction of Falcons rises and the fraction of Continentals falls.

THE MARKET FOR THE SERVICE OF POLICE INACTION

An increase in the probability of interception of illegally imported heroin would have the expected effects of raising its price and of shrinking the trade. These effects can also be achieved in other ways. Anything that increases the expected costs of engaging in this trade will have the same results. Thus, if the fraction of illegally imported heroin that is intercepted does not rise, but if there were an increase in the probability of discovery, apprehension, and/or conviction of smugglers, the trade would also tend to decline. Conversely, of course, anything that diminishes the expected cost of doing business in the trade will diminish the price of its product and enlarge the trade.

The narcotics trade, like many other criminal activities, is probably cartellized (U.S. Senate, Subcommittee to Investigate Juvenile Delinquency, 1963b, p. 3029), and it produces monopoly rents. Those engaged in the trade have earnings which are superior to those they could earn in alternative competitive employments, and they might be disposed to use these differential earnings to buy the 'services" of law enforcement officers (Maurer and Vogel, 1954, p. 230). Even if the trade were competitive, the earnings of the traders would be higher than those in alternative employments by some quantity just sufficient to compensate them for the higher risks they run of having fine, imprisonment, deportation, and other costs imposed upon them; these are risks they would not run in legal employments. It would pay them, therefore, to use part of their differential earnings to reduce, in a probability sense, the magnitude of the expected costs for which the differential compensates them. Competitive traders, too, therefore, would be disposed to buy law enforcement officers' services. They will do so only if the price of these services is less than the "value" of the fraction by which the risk of the trader is diminished.

The quantity of discovery and apprehension can be expected to be a function of the quantity of information that comes into the possession of the law enforcement officers charged with the execution of the narcotics laws and of the officers' willingness to use that information to proceed against violators of the law.

The information that comes into the possession of these officers may be suppressed. It is reported that "the importation and distribution at wholesale levels, and frequently at retail levels, is likely to flourish only under some form of police protection" (Maurer and Vogel, 1954, p. 207).

This protection can occur, however, only if the administration of law enforcement activity has the properties of a monopoly industry (Rottenberg, 1960, pp. 5 ff.). Law enforcement officers are employed in something like a competitive labor market. They are paid the market wage for performing the services of their craft. For this wage, they are expected, among other things, to receive information or to search it out, to develop information that will be acceptable in the criminal courts, and to report this information to their relevant superior officers. The officer may, however, be in a position to extract some of the monopoly rents of monopoly illegal traders or to share with them the differential earnings for superior risk of competitive illegal traders. The officer can do this only if he, himself, monopolizes access to the relevant information and the initial "right" to report information. If other officers "compete" with him in the performance of these services and if there are enough of them so that coalitions cannot be formed among them at low cost, then the officer is without monopoly power and has nothing to sell to the illegal trader. For if the trader should buy inaction from one officer, he still runs the risk of discovery and action by another.

This problem can perhaps be solved by contriving arrangements in the administration of the law enforcement function so that administrative monopolies of the kind here suggested do not exist, and administrative competition is substituted for it. Another possible solution is to install incentive-compensation systems for law enforcement officers that will pay off the delivery of information. There are, of course, problems associated with this form of the solution; the system may generate larger police earnings to patrols which are in crime-prone areas than others; and, if not done with care, it may produce the formation of coalitions of criminals and policemen whose object is the promotion of criminal activities which, in turn, produce incentive earnings.

A nominal rule of police administration is that officers will execute the orders of their superiors and, ultimately, that the police will be administratively responsive to the behavioral implications of the law — that they will do those things which they must do, if the law is to be effectively applied.

The law imposes costs upon criminals in some probability sense, but these costs can be diminished by purchasing inaction from a police officer. To the extent that these costs are reduced, the incidence of crime and the cost of crime borne by the community rises.

The propensity to sell the services of inaction varies among police officers so that some will fail to act (refrain from enforcing the law) if they are given, say, $100, while others would require $1,000 for the same (non)act.

If it were possible to identify the class with respect to which the propensity to be dutiful (to do only those things which are consistent with nominal and relevant rules or, perhaps, to do only those things which the community does not think odious) is high, police recruitment and selection procedures ought to be biased in favor of that class.

Given the magnitude of these propensities in a given police force, it should be possible to organize the activity of the police so as to minimize the quantity of police inaction.

If the probability of buying non-performance at a given price by one officer is 0.1 and by another also 0.1, then the probability of doing so for two independently deciding officers is the product of these probabilities, or 0.01. If these were the magnitudes involved, there would be great advantage in organizing the law enforcement machinery in such a way that inaction, to be effective in a given case (to have value to someone), would require that more than one officer be bought off.

If the individual propensities to sell non-performance were much larger than this, the advantage of such an organization would be much smaller. For example, if the corresponding probabilities were 0.9 for each officer, then the probability of securing inaction from two of them would be reduced to only 0.81, and there may be other costs associated with such an organization of police activity that would cause this arrangement to produce net disbenefits.

On the assumption that the probability numbers are small, the clear advantage associated with an organization such that inaction requires that non-performance be bought from more than one officer will occur, as has been mentioned, only if each officer makes his decision with respect to whether he will sell his (non)services independently of the decisions of other officers.

If the decision of one affects the decision of the other, the factor by which the joint probability is reduced is smaller. The organization of police activity ought, therefore, to take account, also, of joint decision effects. There is an advantage, that is to say, in refraining from establishing regular pairs or teams of officers that encourages the formation of coalitions among them.

Corrupt behavior by a police officer may be either known or not known to his colleagues on the force. If known, others who possess the knowledge may either divulge it to their superiors or they may not. Non-divulgence may imply the imposition of costs upon those who conceal information about the malfeasance of their fellow officers, and these costs may be of different magnitudes rising from the polar case of zero cost. Or divulgence may be rewarded, and the gains may be of different magnitudes. Whatever increases the cost of concealment or increases the gains from non-concealment will increase the quantity of information about corrupt behavior that passes to superior officers.

An increase in the quantity of information on the corrupt behavior of an officer that is transmitted to higher echelons of the force will increase the probability of discovery and punishment of the corrupt officer. This will increase the price of corrupt behavior. Corrupt behavior purchased from the police officer is an input of a criminal activity. If the price of this input rises, the cost of doing criminal business rises, and the price of the product (narcotics-selling services) also rises. If there is any demand elasticity, the quantity (of narcotics, and narcotics-selling services) transacted falls.

A bribe paid to a police officer is different in detail, but similar in effect, to the payment of an insurance premium. If one insures against disaster, he does not diminish the probability that the disaster will occur but reduces the cost of the disaster *to him* to the magnitude of the premium payments. Bribes paid to officers *do* reduce the probability of the occurrence of the disaster and, in doing so, reduce the disaster cost to the payer of the bribes. If the probability of occurrence is reduced to zero, then the disaster cost is the cost of its avoidance and is equal to the magnitude of the bribes paid. A criminal may self-insure by running the whole risk that disaster will strike and by bearing the whole cost associated with it. If he pays the bribe-premium instead, it is because his costs are lower this way.

The purchase of police inaction can be thought of in another context. If the state prohibits the sale of narcotics and executes, say, a punishment of three years of imprisonment or a fine of $500 upon offenders, it is saying, substantially, that the value of that punishment is the price for a license to engage in the trade. A police officer who accepts a private payment made to him for failing to charge an offender is selling the license — the right to enter the trade — for some other price. The officer's price must be lower than the state's or the offender would not consent to transact the license with him; he would prefer to purchase it from the state by paying the state's (punishment) price. The officer's behavior shifts traders' marginal cost curves to the right and enlarges the trade.

THE ALLOCATION OF POLICE RESOURCES

Even if corruption tends to be most common at the lowest level of police administration — with the man on the beat — it may be that the more uncommon cases at higher levels, when properly weighted, turn out to be more important in the aggregate. In any case, detected information tends to grow by a chain process, and the suppression of a seemingly trivial bit of information discovered "on the street" may forestall the coming into possession of more important pieces some links away.

A large fraction of law enforcement activity is that subset of activity which generates information. Information is of a number of classes, for example, information that a crime has been committed, information about the identity of the criminal and his whereabouts, and information of an evidentiary nature that will pass muster in a criminal court proceeding.

Information-generating resources are commanded by the police, and they are scarce goods that ought to be economized. The police have options in the allocation of these resources along the narcotics distribution chain. This allocation is optimal when the information outputs at every link, which are produced by the final units of information-generating resources employed at each link, are themselves equal. The fulfilment of this condition undoubtedly requires the use of more of the resources at some links than at others. It seems reasonable to suppose that a larger expenditure at middle links than at polar links is appropriate, since the former may produce information which, in turn, produces a second generation of information about occurrences both forward and backward in the chain of distribution, while information produced at the poles can have only unidirectional second-generation consequences.

This is complicated by the fact that the cost of acquiring a bit of information is less at the retail end of the chain than elsewhere along its length; concealment seems to be more difficult at the retail end (Shur, 1962, p. 58; Chein *et al.*, 1964, pp. 17 and 331). This is probably because retailers advertise their wares more than do distributors at other parts of the system.

If a large part of the cost of doing business is the imprisonment cost imposed upon discovered operators, this cost becomes successively larger. Margins between buying and selling prices can be expected to cover the full cost of doing business. This explains why margins become progressively larger as heroin moves toward the consumer (U.S. Senate, Subcommittee to Investigate Juvenile Delinquency, 1963*b*, pp. 3028–29).[4]

In seeking information that is necessary to law enforcement, it is appropriate that information-collecting resources be employed preferentially at the points (*a*) where information is concentrated and (*b*) where the cost of concealment of information is high.

Customs personnel and search resources are not sufficiently large to permit intensive inspection of all entries of persons and cargo (President's Advisory Commission on Narcotics and Drug Abuse, 1963, pp. 37–38; U.S. Senate, Subcommittee to Investigate Juvenile Delinquency, 1963b, p. 2989). If these resources *were* large enough for this purpose, intensive inspection would apparently prolong the time consumed in entry beyond permissible limits. Except for persons and cargo which are suspect because U.S. Customs possess incriminating information about them (all of which should presumably be intensively examined), Customs has the options of extensive examination of all entrants, or intensive examination of a sample of entrants, or some combination of these two. The sample that is examined intensively may be randomly selected. It is not clear whether there would be any advantage in the intensive inspection of a randomly selected sample of the universe of entrants.

Narcotics agents work overseas, infiltrating, producing information, standing at the ready to receive information, and offering payments for information. Is the price paid for information sufficient to draw forth the optimal quantity of it?[5] Information is non-homogeneous with respect to its value in enforcement of the law. Is the structure of rewards or payoffs to informers appropriate from the standpoint of maximizing information (adjusted for quality) received by the law enforcement agencies for given expenditures for this purpose?

The narcotics trade is now apparently a monopoly trade. We assume that, as in other monopoly cases, the net revenue position of the narcotics trader is maximized when the prices he charges are higher and the output he produces is lower than they would be if this were a competitive trade.

The enforcement authorities are in a position to re-enforce the monopoly or to make the trade more competitive. They do the former if they are more energetic in the enforcement of the law against new entrants than against the monopolist incumbent in the trade. They do the latter if they are equally energetic in enforcement against all.

If consumer expenditure for narcotics were of income earned from the performance of services or from the ownership of assets, it would clearly be in the community interest to re-enforce the monopoly on the ground that a smaller noxious industry is preferable to a larger one. Since it is known, however, that income spent for this purpose is derived largely from clandestine or coercive extraction of unwilling transfer payments from others (that is, from theft), it is not so certain that a smaller industry is always to be preferred. This is because the demand schedule for narcotics, if relatively inelastic, causes a smaller industry to impose higher larcenous transfer payment costs upon the community than would a larger industry.

The optimal allocation of enforcement resources will be affected by the mechanism by which addiction spreads. Two possible hypotheses are: (1) There are constant "returns" to scale, and (2) there are increasing "returns" to scale. If the first of these characterizes the world, one addict will infect x number of non-addicts (causing them to become addicts), and a cluster of ten addicts will infect $10x$ non-addicts. If the second is true, then if one addict will infect x non-addicts, a cluster of ten addicts will infect some number of non-addicts which is larger than $10x$.

If the second hypothesis is correct, it suggests that critical mass of some magnitude is necessary for infection to occur. The process would be analogous to the spread of fire. If a matchstick burns, the probability of neighborhood fires is less than if a house burns. Or if ten houses burn, each of which is separated from any other burning house by ten miles, the probability of disastrous spread of fire is less than if the ten burning houses were in the same neighborhood.

Suppose non-addicts experiment with drugs for a number of reasons, say: (a) they are told by an addict that it produces pleasurable experiences, or, by observing a user, they can see that it produces these experiences; (b) they admire another whom they know to be a user because of other qualities he possesses (he is an accomplished playwright, or poet, or musician); and (c) they desire to be a member of a community they believe to be congenial, and the consumption of drugs is a necessary condition of entry into this community.

Of this small catalogue of motivations for experimentation, (a) and (b) would be operative whether the observed addict is isolated or one of a cluster of addicts. However, (c) would be operative only when there were clusters. As long as there is one additional incentive associated with a cluster which is absent in the case of the isolated addict, the cluster will be a stronger focus of infection than the individual; and a cluster will have stronger infecting consequences than an equal number of isolated individuals.

This suggests that the quantity of enforcement per addict should be larger where clusters occur than where there are no clusters and addicts are isolated; that clusters should be broken up and their members diffused more thinly in the population and in space; that clusters, where they are not broken, should be isolated; that devices should be employed to cause that segment of the non-addict population which is on the margin of experimentation to believe, given the values they presently hold, that the addict cluster community is not congenial (this may require either the exposition of the truth, or systematic misrepresentation of fact, or some combination of them); and that devices be employed to alter the values of the sector that is on the margin of experimental drug consumption so that the probability diminishes that experiments occur.

Maximizing individuals seeking euphoric utilities will prefer those instruments for securing it that are cheapest.[6] Can the substitutes for dangerous drugs (either in the form of drugs that are not dangerous or other [non-drug] commodities) be ranked in the order of their goodness as substitutes? If so, policy can perhaps reduce their prices, relative to the prices of dangerous drugs.

The authorities charged with the enforcement of the narcotics laws are faced with a set of alternative strategies among which they exercise options. This paper has touched upon some of the variables that affect optimizing behavior by those authorities.

REFERENCES

1. Estimation methods in current use yield approximations that are subject to a large coefficient of error; the true number of addicts is not known (President's Advisory Commission on Narcotics and Drug Abuse, 1963, p. 4).
2. The U.S. Attorney for the Southern District of New York reported that the wholesale price of heroin rose greatly immediately after the arrest of two wholesale traders (U.S. Senate, Subcommittee to Investigate Juvenile Delinquency, 1963a).
3. The commissioner of the Food and Drug Administration reports that "a crude form of LSD could be produced by a college chemistry laboratory" (Giorgano, 1966, p. 15; Goddard, 1966, p. 4).

4. It is reported that, in the spring of 1966, the price of a gram of heroin (at 10 per cent purity) was a little less than $0.05 in Turkey (in the form of illegal opium), $1.40 at the point of importation in New York, $35 at wholesale in Chicago, and $295 at retail in Chicago.
5. It is reported that the U.S. Treasury Department pays $500 for information leading to the seizure of a kilo of narcotics; that this is less than the payment for information that leads to other kinds of contraband goods, where the payment is 25 per cent of the value of the contraband recovered and may be as much as $50,000; and that the Treasury's "standing offer" to informers of narcotics smuggling is a weak incentive for disclosure (U.S. Senate, Subcommittee to Investigate Juvenile Delinquency, 1963a, p. 3067).
6. Juveniles arrested in Los Angeles told the police there that they turned from marijuana to barbiturates "because they are cheaper" (U.S. Senate, Subcommittee to Investigate Juvenile Delinquency, 1963b, p. 2761). Some price information is available for various illegal drugs. Comparisons are meaningless, however, because the physical units of measure vary among them and because they differ in the properties, intensity, and duration of euphoric experience produced by their consumption.

Anslinger, H. J. and W. F. Tompkins, *The Traffic in Narcotics*. New York: Funk & Wagnalls, 1953.
Chein, Isidor, et al. *The Road to H*. New York: Basic Books, 1964.
Eldridge, W. B., *Narcotics and the Law*. Chicago: American Bar Foundation, 1962.
Giorgano, H. L., Statement before the Special Subcommittee on Juvenile Delinquency of the Senate Committee on the Judiciary, May 26, 1966 (duplicated).
Goddard, J. L., Statement before the Special Subcommittee on Juvenile Delinquency of the Senate Committee on the Judiciary, May 23, 1966 (duplicated).
Maurer, D. W., and V. H. Vogel, *Narcotics and Narcotics Addiction*. Springfield, Ill.: Charles C. Thomas, Publisher, 1954.
President's Advisory Commission on Narcotics and Drug Abuse. *Final Report*. Washington: Government Printing Office, 1963.
Rottenberg, S., "A Theory of Corruption in Trade Unions," *Series Studies in Social and Economic Sciences*. (Nat. Inst. Soc. and Behavioral Sci., Symposia Studies Series No. 3.) Washington: Nat. Inst. of Soc. and Behavioral Sci., 1960.
Schur, E. M., *Narcotics Addiction in Britain and America*. Bloomington: Ind. Univ. Press, 1962.
U.S. Senate, Permanent Subcommittee on Investigations, Committee on Government Operations, 88th Congress. Hearings pursuant to S. Res. 278. Part 4: *Organized Crime and Illicit Traffic in Narcotics*. Washington: Government Printing Office, 1964.
U.S. Senate, Subcommittee to Investigate Juvenile Delinquency, 87th Congress. Hearings pursuant to S. Res. 48. Washington: Government Printing Office, 1963. (*a*)
U.S. Senate, Subcommittee to Investigate Juvenile Delinquency, 87th Congress. Hearings pursuant to S. Res. 265. Washington: Government Printing Office, 1963. (*b*)

PART THREE

URBAN FINANCING

THE URBAN ISSUES, or most of them, which we have discussed will require government action: some governments will have to stop doing what they are doing and start doing other things; some things they cannot do at all will have to be done jointly by all elements of society. In some instances, the action required will be only the changing of rules or the passing of laws and thus may be inexpensive (additional salaries, additional equipment). In other instances, the government will have to invest in, let us say, capital goods.

How much money should government spend for all of its purposes and administration? Where should government get this money? The following table presents a summary of civilian public expenditure in the United States for the year 1966–1967, reflecting some one-half of total government expenditure, the balance going to war or war-related activities. It is clear, from the table, that most of the expenditures on urban problems are made by local and state governments. The federal government supplies minor supplements — or less than fifteen per cent of all local and state government expenditures are financed by federal aid.

Income redistribution activities — which involve taxing the whole population for the benefit of certain groups, primarily the poor — include health and welfare expenditures to the poor, retirement programs through the social security programs, and the token government housing programs.

One of the basic economic problems of the heavy load that local and state governments must bear is in the very inadequate tax base from which they can draw. Such governments lean heavily on the property tax, which is regressive in nature, particularly for school expenditures, but also for welfare expenditures, police and fire protection, water supply and water treatment.

With a huge income tax base on which to draw, the federal government is much less restricted. The resulting imbalance between local governments and the federal government is referred to as "fiscal imbalance." Due to their tax base, local gov-

Civilian Public Expenditure in the United States, 1966–1967
(in billions of dollars)

ACTIVITIES	FEDERAL GOVERNMENT EXPENDITURE[1]	STATE-LOCAL GOVERNMENTS EXPENDITURE	FEDERAL AID
All Civilian Programs[2]	52.0	102.7	15.0
Economic stabilization activities[3]	36	2.5	0.0
Income-redistribution activities	27.7	17.1	5.3
Health & welfare	1.6[4]	14.8	4.6
Social Security, etc.[5]	25.2	0.7	—
Housing programs	0.9	1.5	0.7
Public Schools	—	28.1	2.1
Resource-allocation activities	20.7	55.0	7.1
Highways	0.1	14.0	4.1
Natural resources	7.8	2.3	0.2
Higher education	—	8.8	1.8
Postal service	6.2	—	—
Police, correction & fire	0.4	5.6	—
Transportation (except highways)	2.4	2.4	0.1
Water supply & water treatment	—[6]	4.3	0.1
All other	3.8	17.5	0.8

Note: Because of rounding, detail may not add to totals.

[1] Direct expenditure only; grants to state-local governments spent by these units are shown in the last column.

[2] Excludes defense, international relations, space programs, veterans' services, interest on the federal debt (mainly war-related), and employee retirement benefits.

[3] Includes farm price support and unemployment insurance activities.

[4] Excludes federal health research expenditure, assigned to "resource allocation."

[5] Includes, in addition to old-age, survivors, disability, and health insurance, state workmen's compensation and temporary disability programs.

[6] Federal water programs included under "natural resources."

Source: Adapted from U.S. Census Bureau, *Governmental Finances in 1966–67* (1968), taken from Dick Netzer, "Financing Urban Government," *Economics and Urban Problems: Diagnoses and Prescriptions,* New York: Basic Books, Inc., 1970, p. 170.

ernments are unable to provide the urban services and urban way of life that Americans desire; and, so far at least, the federal government has not aided them effectively. A suggested substitute for the property tax is revenue sharing — the federal government would share some of its income tax revenue with cities, the share being based on need, or on population, or on another formula. Some economists also suggest user fees, tolls on freeways, for example.

The complexities of the existing fiscal imbalance run deep. One complexity is found in neighborhood effects, or "spill-overs"; in the fact that a city may negatively effect a neighboring city and yet cannot be held responsible, in any way, for the "damages."

Fragmentation of local governments has made region-wide solutions difficult. It has made region-wide tax policies impossible. Regional government, or at least regional planning, is called for by such questions as pollution, transportation, and education (what with American mobility, the benefits of schooling are, in eighty per cent, it is estimated, of the cases, received outside of the school district that provided the education).

Microeconomic theory is useful in analyzing tax problems, since the effects of a given tax on demand and supply may be substantial. Estimates of expected tax revenue can be calculated from market conditions for the products being taxed. The shifting of taxes to suppliers or buyers can be analyzed with microeconomic concepts — as can other effects on output and price.

Macroeconomic theory is used to study the impact of income taxes, both personal and corporate. A large and important body of knowledge exists to measure and evaluate equity, ability to pay, and other normative aspects of tax decisions.

Simulation models have been successful in describing and analyzing various types of tax proposals. Planners have felt free to suggest many types of taxes, some of which have been enacted by legislatures.

For the most part, tax proposals for urban governments are subjected to benefit-cost analyses, since many different types of factors must be considered, and the overall effects of a proposed tax may be substantially different from its initial impact. Furthermore, some of the social and equity considerations require judgment and balance — in political and other terms.

23 Reforming the Real Estate Tax to Encourage Housing Maintenance and Rehabilitation

JAMES HEILBRUN*
Fordham University

An attempt to apply some of the land value principles laid down by Henry George, more than one hundred years ago, to today's United States — to the motivations of landlords who let their properties run down and to the incentives for maintenance.

INTRODUCTION

Since the early 1950's urban-housing policy in the United States has increasingly emphasized the conservation and rehabilitation of existing buildings. Bulldozer methods have been widely criticized as unnecessarily destructive of both physical and social structures. Consequently, those interested in raising housing standards have tried to develop less drastic and more selective methods. Although new construction is still considered indispensable, a good deal of attention is now paid to the problem of maintaining quality in the standing stock. The following two questions will therefore be examined in this chapter: Does the traditional American real estate tax have unfavorable effects on the quality of existing housing? Would alternative ways of taxing real estate be preferable?

Since the urban housing problem is largely within the rental sector, analysis is limited to the effects of taxes on rental housing. Moreover, the present yield of the real estate tax is taken as a datum. I do not propose to investigate the question of whether the federal-state-local tax system as a whole is or is not neutral in its approach to real estate or rental housing and other economic activities. That is, of course, an important and interesting subject.[1] Here, however, I wish to investigate the narrower question of whether the real estate tax at its present level of yield could be reformed to the advantage of housing quality. By holding yield constant, I am able to focus on the relative merits of the several varieties of the real estate tax itself without entering into the larger question of comparing real estate levies in general to other kinds of taxes.

Because local real estate taxes absorb something on the order of 16 to 20 per cent of gross housing rent, it seems likely that they have significant effects on the

---

From James Heilbrun, "Reforming the Real Estate Tax to Encourage Housing Maintenance and Rehabilitation," Arthur B. Becker, editor, *Land and Building Trades* (Madison: The University of Wisconsin Press; © 1969 by the Regents of the University of Wisconsin), pp. 63–79. Reprinted with permission.

condition of existing rental structures, but the matter has received no systematic treatment in related literature. Occasionally, one finds a statement to the effect that this or that variety of real estate tax would be more favorable to the maintenance of housing quality than is the traditional American levy on assessed value. Unless such statements are based on a systematic analysis of the way in which the rental-housing firm and industry operate, however, they remain unconvincing. The housing market, including the rental-housing sector, has been analyzed fruitfully in works by Chester Rapkin, Louis Winnick, and David M. Blank, by William G. Grigsby, and by others.[2] The house-operating firm, however, has received scant attention. Thus, my first task must be to outline a theory of the house-operating firm and of the rental-housing industry to provide a foundation for tax analysis.

A THEORY OF THE RENTAL-HOUSING FIRM

The quality of service offered is one of the variables that the owner of a rental structure can manipulate in attempting to maximize his return. This quality depends upon three elements:

1. The original cost of building the structure and subsequent investment in remodeling, if any. These expenditures establish the layout and spaciousness of the apartment units and determine the kind and extent of equipment they contain.
2. The level of quality at which structure and equipment are maintained.
3. The level of operating outlays that the owner applies to the given structure and that determines the quality and extent of operating services he can offer.

Two other factors that have important effects on housing quality when broadly defined are:

1. The social characteristics of tenants. The quality of service afforded in a given apartment is affected by the character of the other tenants in the building.
2. Influence of the neighborhood. The quality of service afforded in a given building is affected by the quality of the neighborhood as an environment.

While no attempt has been made to incorporate either of these factors systematically, I believe that their omission does not affect the qualitative conclusions of the study.

The owner of a rental-housing property can vary the quality of service he offers by varying his outlays on structure, maintenance, or operation. At the same time, expenditures by consumers in the form of rent paid provide a market evaluation of the services provided. In general, the higher the quality of housing service offered the higher the rent consumers will pay. Depending upon the problem at hand, the output of service in a given building can therefore be measured either by the annual cost of factor inputs or the annual gross rent receipts. Of course, rent and cost are acceptable units of account for intertemporal comparisons only if we abstract from cyclical and secular changes in prices.

The rental-housing industry in a large city can be described as a case of monopolistic competition among a large group of sellers. The product is differentiated by quality, location, layout, rooms per unit, and the like. In general, the number of sellers is large enough and the largest firm is small enough in relation to the size of the whole market so that the effects of one firm's decisions on the others can be safely ignored, and it can be assumed that each building owner behaves as an atomistic competitor. The supply of space offered by the industry takes the form of a distribution of space by rent level per room, with the higher-quality units commanding the higher rents. Within this rent-quality distribution and constrained only by housing codes, the building owner can "move" his building either up or down, depending upon possibilities for profit indicated by the market. He accomplishes such a move by remodeling, by varying his outlays for maintenance or operation, or by some combination of these three.[3]

In fact, these three matters are interdependent and decisions concerning them must be made simultaneously. For analytical purposes, however, I will examine them separately. Consider first the problem of choosing the optimum level of operating outlay. Assuming that the owner has already made any desirable changes by remodeling and has found the optimum maintenance policy, what level of operating outlays will be most profitable? Operating outlays cover such items of expense as fuel, janitorial and other labor services, painting (insofar as it is the owner's responsibility), repairs to structure and equipment, and administrative expenses. Within a considerable range these expenses are variable. Although housing, health, and sanitary codes establish certain minimum standards, the landlord may try to provide more (or, often, less) than the required level of service. For example, cleanliness in public areas and the speed with which minor repairs are attended to both depend upon the level of janitorial expense the owner is willing to undertake. Certain operating expenses are built into the structure, so to speak, but there remains a significant margin for variation. We all know what is meant by a well-run or badly-run building.

In fact, what I am suggesting is that in the short run a building can be regarded as a piece of fixed equipment to which the owner applies inputs in the form of operating outlays in order to obtain the output of housing services for which the tenant pays rent. The supply of such inputs is highly elastic since the owner will provide services as long as tenants are willing to pay at least their cost.

Moreover, I believe it is a reasonable hypothesis that for each type of property there is a more or less known best order in which services should be provided, proceeding from the most to the least profitable. (Such an hypothesis is supported by inference in numerous statements in property-management literature.[4]) For example, if a service costs $200 a month to provide and will enable the owner to enjoy a $300-a-month increase in gross rent, he will provide the service. He will undertake all such services until he reaches one that does not at least pay for itself. To choose a far-fetched example, it does not pay to provide a doorman in a building catering to low-income groups, even though that service would increase the security of tenants; the poor are unwilling to pay the cost of the additional security. Owners are well aware of which services pay and which do not. They push service output to the point at which marginal revenue equals marginal cost.

Next consider how the owner can vary his outlays for maintaining the quality of structure and equipment. I refer here not to ordinary repairs, which are an operating outlay, but to replacement of worn-out structure and equipment. The dividing line between repairs and replacement is not logically clear in an entity as complex as an apartment building, but let us assume that a conventional dividing line can be drawn.

Replacement must also be distinguished from remodeling. In discussing replacement, layout and equipment are held constant. Suppose that the owner is committed to his present layout and to the retention of all existing types of equipment. The question reduces to one of how often an old item, such as a plumbing fixture, should be replaced by a new one.

Since much equipment and many parts of a structure deteriorate gradually over time, the more frequently they are replaced, at least up to a certain point, the better the average level of service rendered in the building will be and the higher the rent the tenants will be willing to pay. Instead of speaking of individual parts separately, we could, indeed, generalize by saying that the shorter the average period of replacement in a given building, the higher the quality of housing service rendered and the higher the attainable level of gross rent.

The owner regards each expenditure for replacement of structure or equipment as an act of investment that must compete with other possible uses of capital. He will undertake replacement whenever he expects the rate of return on such an outlay to exceed the opportunity cost of the necessary funds. The expected rate of return will, of course, be dependent upon the expected increment to future gross rent attributable to the act of replacement. This increment will be the difference between the series of annual gross rents the building would yield if replacement were undertaken and the series of smaller annual gross rents it would yield without replacement.[5]

A given piece of equipment will be kept in use not until it is thoroughly "worn-out" and ceases to yield *any* service, but only until the annual value of the service it renders has fallen far enough so that replacing it will produce a rise in gross rent sufficient to make the necessary investment in replacement profitable. Those who wish to obtain high-quality housing service must be willing to pay a high-enough absolute rent premium for new as compared to old equipment so as to make frequent replacement investment profitable to the owner. Tenants who do not seek high quality will not be willing to pay as large a premium for "newness." Owners of buildings catering to such tenants will find that replacement becomes profitable only after a longer period has elapsed. Thus, the average period of replacement in such buildings will be longer than in buildings serving the high-rent, high-quality segment of the market.

Of course, replacement policy and operating policy are interdependent; any change in the average period of replacement is likely to be accompanied by a change in the level of operating outlays as the owner "moves" his building into a new rent-quality class.

Finally, consider the possibility of moving a building by remodeling. Remodeling takes place when interior layouts are changed or additional equipment is installed. Like replacement, it involves an investment decision of the conventional variety. Remodeling requires the commitment of additional capital. The return on past investment in the building is not relevant. What matters is the expected return on the added funds. The owner will remodel if he expects the return on the additional funds he invests to exceed the opportunity cost of his capital. It is hardly necessary to add that remodeling is likely to result in a change in operating and replacement policy as well.

The argument so far can be summed up with the help of a simple diagram (Figure 1). Annual gross rent is measured on the vertical axis, total annual cost on the horizontal. The curve, which I will refer to as a revenue-cost curve, shows the annual gross rents obtainable by varying the level of operating outlays (OC) given a constant level of fixed costs (FC). For simplicity it is assumed that rent falls to zero when operating outlays fall to zero. As the building owner moves from lower

Figure 1

Equilibrium of the House-Operating Firm

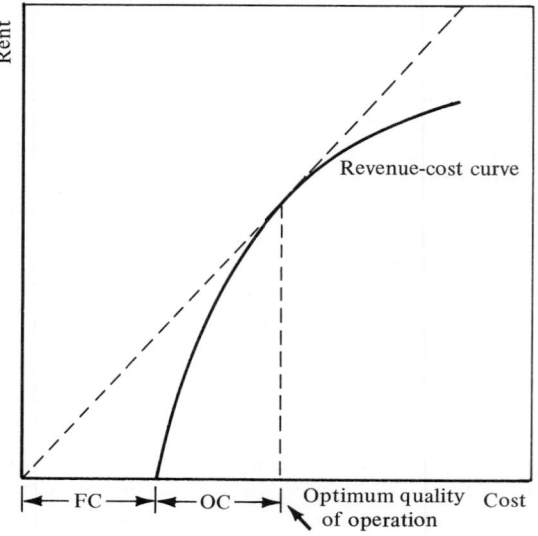

to higher levels of operating outlay, he moves from more to less revenue-productive input dollars. He earns maximum net income where the slope of the revenue-cost curve is equal to 1. At that point the marginal dollar of operating-cost outlay just brings in one dollar of additional rent. On the cost axis the associated level of cost indicates what might be called the optimum quality of operation.

It is assumed that all properties are owned debt-free and, for the present, that no taxes are levied. Annual fixed costs (*FC*) therefore consist of planned net income plus the annual charge for replacement needed to maintain a given average period of replacement of structure and equipment. Since net income is included as a cost, total annual cost will just equal total rent when normal returns are earned. In that case a firm in equilibrium and earning normal returns will operate at the point where the revenue-cost curve is just tangent to a 45° line from the origin.

If the diagram is altered slightly to show rent per room and cost per room instead of total rent and cost, the housing market can be depicted schematically by a set of revenue-cost curves (Figure 2) in which the higher fixed costs necessary to build and maintain (in the replacement sense) more spacious or elaborate apartments are generally also associated with the higher operating costs that the tenants of the more luxurious buildings are willing to pay for. Since site rent is a part of planned net income, locational advantages of particular buildings would also be reflected in higher fixed costs and would bring in higher rents.

EFFECTS OF REAL ESTATE TAXES ON OPERATING DECISIONS

We are now ready to analyze the effects of real estate taxes on the quality of urban rental housing. Assuming that we are dealing with a single housing market that falls entirely within one taxing jurisdiction and, moreover, that this housing market and

Figure 2

Diagram of a Rental-Housing Market (Schematic)

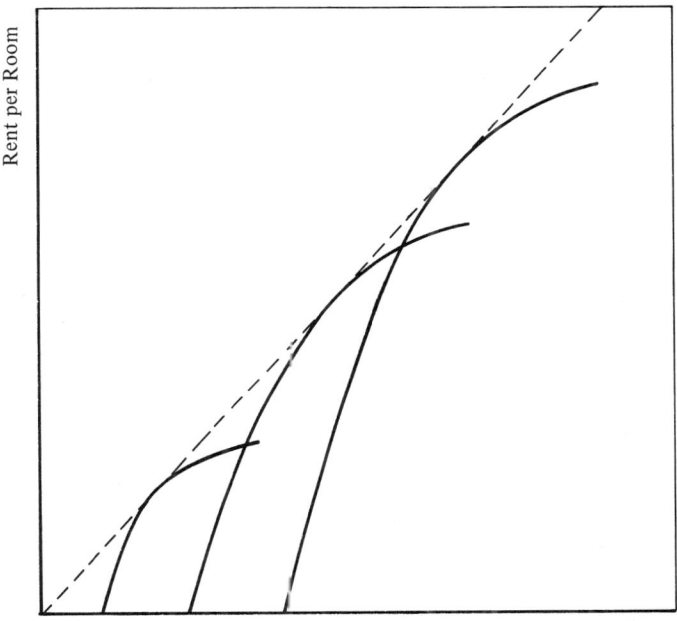

taxing jurisdiction are isolated from all others, then inter-area competition can be ignored. I have chosen to use the method of differential incidence in comparing the effects of various kinds of real estate taxes. Thus, I can treat governmental expenditures as fixed and concentrate on analyzing the changes that take place as one real estate tax system replaces another of equal yield.

The following taxes will be compared: (1) an *ad valorem* tax on assessed site value; (2) an *ad valorem* tax on the assessed value of site and improvements combined (the traditional American levy); (3) a proportional tax on the actual (not the assessed) gross rent of site and improvements combined; (4) a tax on the net income of site and improvements combined; and (5) any of the above combined with a tax abatement to encourage maintenance and rehabilitation. With the exception of the net income tax, these alternatives (and a few more) have been or are now employed in many parts of the world and hence must be regarded as feasible systems.[6]

Let me begin by examining the impact of these taxes on operating decisions. Assuming that a site value tax is already in effect, then the impact of other levies can be compared with the effects of the site value tax. The latter provides a convenient starting point because it is neutral to both operating and investment decisions and cannot be shifted forward to tenants.

It is not necessary to repeat here the familiar explanation of why the site value tax cannot be shifted from owner to tenant.[7] As for its neutrality, the tax is, in effect, a lump-sum payment that the owner must make regardless of the existence, absence, or condition of any buildings on the site. Since the tax is fixed without regard to improvements, it cannot have any effect on the owner's operating decisions. If the situation when the site value tax is in force is compared to a no-tax situation, the only possible difference arises as a consequence of changes on the expenditure side; the tax itself does not cause the optimum operating point for any building to shift.

Suppose now that the voters in the taxing jurisdiction decide to replace the site value levy with a tax on the combined assessed value of site and improvements, at the same level of yield. Will this new tax affect the quality of operation of existing buildings in the short run? Apparently, it will not, if the following argument is valid.

Let us assume that properties are uniformly assessed at full market value or at some given proportion of full market value. Market value, in turn, tends to equal the present value of expected future net returns. It has been shown that the annual net return from a given building is maximized when the building is operated at the optimum level of quality. Above or below that level of quality, present income is reduced. It does not follow, however, that if the owner were to operate away from the optimum quality level, the market value of the property would be lowered. Market value is based upon the market's estimate of the potential earning power of a property and will not be influenced by the failure of a particular owner to realize the property's full potential. Thus, if assessments are based on market value, they will not vary with operating decisions. In the short run, the quality of operation of existing buildings will not be altered if the community changes from a site value tax to the traditional American levy on combined assessed value.

To look at the matter another way, we can say that the amenities provided by operating outlays do not have any capital value. They do not represent stored-up wealth, since their expected life is, by definition, short. Hence, they do not create liability for a tax on assessed capital value. According to the assistant director of assessment in the tax department of the city of New York, his department takes no account of the operating condition of a building in assessing its value.[8] I did not undertake any empirical investigation of this point, but I think it well deserves such study.

Suppose that instead of replacing the site value tax with the traditional American property tax, the community had voted to adopt a tax on the actual gross rent of site and improvements combined. Here is a tax that, unlike the first two, would *not* be neutral to operating decisions in the short run. The effect of changing over to a tax on gross rent would be to discourage operating outlays. Owners would now find maximum profits at a lower level of quality of operation than before. I argued, in discussing operating expenditures in the absence of taxation, that owners push them to the point at which the marginal dollar of outlay just brings in a marginal dollar of rent. That same point would provide a profit optimum in the short run under the first two taxes I analyzed. When gross rent is subject to tax at rate t, however, owners will proceed only to the point at which a marginal dollar of outlay brings in $1/(1-t)$ dollars of rent. That point is encountered at a lower level of operating expense since owners proceed in order from more to less revenue productive operating outlays. Thus, compared with the site value tax as a neutral standard, a gross rent tax would cause a general contraction in operating outlays and therefore would reduce the general quality of rental-housing services. Since a tax of 15 to 20 per cent on gross rent would probably be needed to match the yield of the present American property tax, the effect at the quality margin would not be trivial.

Next consider a tax on the net income of site and improvements combined. Like a site value tax, this variant will be neutral to operating decisions. The argument is a familar one in the theory of the firm; taxing net income at so much per cent per annum does not induce the owner to operate differently than he would in the absence of taxes. Hence, in the short run, shifting from a site value tax to a net income tax would not alter operating outlays in rental housing.

The last variant I wish to take up is a tax abatement. This device may be very useful in stimulating the improvement of housing quality through its effect on investment decisions, but it is hardly relevant as a means of encouraging operating outlays. An abatement is most likely to take the form of an agreement not to raise the tax base of a property during some limited period if the owner undertakes specified improvements in quality. Such a scheme is meaningless in connection with a site value levy. Under the combined assessed value tax and the net income tax, the owner is already operating at the level of quality that maximizes tax liability. Thus, an agreement not to increase liability further if the owner expands operating outlays cannot induce him to do so while those taxes are in force. Only in connection with a gross rent tax would an abatement plan alter operating decisions: its effect would be to remove the tax on rent at the operating margin, thus inducing the owner to expand operating outlays to the same level he would have chosen in the absence of taxes. The unfavorable impact of the gross rent tax on operating quality would be removed.

EFFECTS OF REAL ESTATE TAXES ON INVESTMENT DECISIONS

Thus far I have analyzed only the operating effects of real estate taxes, and these only as they would appear in the short run. In the longer run taxes will also affect investment decisions; since it is through such effects that tax shifting can occur, I must now discuss tax shifting as well.

Herbert A. Simon has shown that the division of the burden of a tax on urban real property between land and improvements cannot be determined *a priori;* the proportion of the tax borne by the site owner may be less than, equal to, or more than the proportion of site rent to total rent, depending upon the assumptions of the analysis.[9] For the present purpose it will suffice to say that at any rate a significant part of the burden falls on the rent of improvements. In other words, when the community votes to shift from a site value tax, which is neutral to investment decisions, to a tax on the combined value of site and improvements, the tax on improvements is at best only partly offset by a fall in the rent of land gross of tax, consequent upon taxing improvements. A new burden thus falls upon all projects for investing in structure. For purposes of argument I assume a tax on real property only. Thus, such personal property as producer's durable goods and inventories remains untaxed when the community replaces the site value levy with a tax on the combined value of site and improvements.[10]

I assume that before the imposition of the tax on improvements capital earned the same marginal return in all its uses, due allowance being made for differences in risk. The new tax on improvements therefore pushes the return on investment in housing and other structures below the margin of profitability. Investment in housing ceases until housing rent can rise sufficiently to yield an after-tax marginal return equal to that obtainable on untaxed uses of capital. I have ignored the possibility that a tax on building capital may slightly reduce the equilibrium rate of return to capital in general, the expected normal return on housing investment and, to that extent, the increase in rents necessary to induce new housing construction.[11]

It is worth emphasizing that real estate is far more capital intensive than most economic activities. In 1957 the ratio of capital (as measured by value of all tangible assets) to output (as measured by national income originating in each sector) was 1.9:1 for all nonfarm businesses, excluding residential real estate. For all nonfarm housing the ratio in the same year was 18.9:1; almost exactly ten times higher.[12] Thus, a uniform tax newly imposed on capital value would have much stronger effects on housing than on nonfarm activities as a whole. This will be true, *a fortiori*, under the assumption that the new tax applies only to real property. Even after allowing for the fact mentioned above, that a fall in land rent gross of tax and a fall in the equilibrium rate of return to capital net of tax might absorb some of the burden of the new levy on improvements, it is evident that the percentage rise in housing rent necessary to shift the remaining burden of the tax forward to consumers would be far larger than the percentage rise in price necessary to achieve the same shift for the aggregate of other activities.

The required increase in housing rent could occur only through shrinking supply (that is, diminution of the standing stock), rising demand, or both. In a declining community the necessary conditions might be permanently absent. In the usual case, however, we would expect demand to increase sufficiently over time so that the remaining tax burden could be passed on from owners of improvements to their tenants.

A rise in demand may, in fact, take place for several different reasons with somewhat different consequences for the quality of housing. For example, the rise may occur as a result of increasing income per capita with no change in population or, by contrast, as a result of increasing population with no change in per capita income. The different consequences to be expected in the two cases can, however, be reached only at the end of a chain of deductive arguments too long to be attempted here.[13] I will therefore confine myself to more general points.

First, let us look at the effects on the average period of replacement of structure that would follow a changeover from the site value tax to one of the other types.[14] Suppose that before the tax change takes place a given owner was in equilibrium, maintaining the average period of structural replacement that was optimal for his segment of the market. If the community then adopts a tax on the combined assessed value of land and improvements, what will be the effect on the owner's replacement policy? The argument concerning the effect of the traditional American tax is as follows: the structural condition of a building is properly of concern to the tax assessor since replaceable structure and equipment certainly have capital value and this value is greater, the longer their remaining useful life. The older the equipment in a building, the less the annual tax. It follows that each investment in structural replacement adds an increment to the taxable value of the building. Projects for replacement that were on the margin of profitability before the tax change thus fall below the margin after the tax on building value is adopted.

It will be recalled that in the absence of taxes, a given piece of equipment will be kept in use until the annual rental value of the services it renders has fallen far enough so that replacing it will produce a rise in gross rent sufficient to make investment in replacement profitable. Given the general level of housing rent, when a building tax correlated with capital value is imposed, a piece of equipment will have to remain in use longer (that is, depreciate farther) before the necessary margin between its annual rental value and the rental value of its replacement is sufficient to make replacement attractive. Thus, imposing a tax on building value would immediately lengthen the average period of replacement in rental structures.

In the course of time, however, tax shifting will occur. As a result of rising demand, shrinking supply, or a combination of the two, housing rent will rise and this will tend to increase the absolute differentials between the rental values of old and new equipment upon which replacement depends. The higher level of rent, however, in effect puts a higher price on the amenity of "newness" provided by replacement. This amenity is one of the constituents of housing quality. Since the demand for quality is probably quite price elastic (more elastic, indeed, than the demand for housing space), the rise in rent necessary to cover tax payments will, so to speak, reduce the quantity of "newness" demanded.[15] Thus, even after tax shifting has worked itself out, the average period of replacement will be longer and housing quality lower than before the changeover to a tax on the combined assessed value of land and improvements.

If the community decided to adopt either a tax on gross rent or a tax on net income instead of the tax on combined assessed value, the results would be much the same as those just recited. Upon impact, both of those taxes would cause an immediate lengthening of the average period of replacement. As in the previous case, tax shifting through a rise in rent would fail to restore the pre-tax situation, since higher rents would, in effect, raise the price of replacement amenities and therefore reduce the amount demanded.

Before concluding the analysis of the effects of tax changes on rate of replacement and on remodeling, I must return to the discussion of the "moving" of buildings. In a world in which buildings last for decades or centuries, while tastes, technology, population characteristics, and the level and distribution of income change continuously, the housing stock is always in the process of adapting to new patterns of demand. Adaptation usually involves moving certain buildings either up or down in the rent-quality distribution, and the move is accomplished by remodeling, by changing the rate of replacement and the level of operating outlays, or by both.

In the preceding section, I assumed that the house-operating firm was in equilibrium at a profit optimum when a change in the tax system occurred and I examined the effects various tax changes would have on that equilibrium position. Now the case is reversed; the tax system is held constant, but a new pattern of demand emerges, that is to say, demand curves shift. The former level of operating expenses and replacement outlays, perhaps even the former design or layout of the building itself, is no longer optimal for the firm. How do various taxes affect the process of adapting to the shift in demand? Since adaptation through change in quality is essential to a well-functioning market, it is important to analyze such tax effects.

When adaptation consists in moving a building *up* in the rent-quality distribution (for example, in response to an improvement in the general character of the neighborhood), it almost always requires a significant commitment of additional capital. The owner is likely to have to overcome past deficiencies in maintenance by making a substantial immediate investment in replacement. He will often have to invest in remodeling as well. But even when adaptation consists in moving a building *down*, it frequently requires capital investment. If, for example, the neighborhood population is gradually changing from middle- to lower-income class, owners may wish to break up large apartments into smaller units better suited to local demand. To do so will require investment in remodeling.

The site value tax in no way impedes either remodeling or outlays for catching up on replacement. However, a tax on combined assessed values, on gross rent, or on net income imposes a burden on projects for investing in structure. The owner will elect to move his building by remodeling and by making the investments necessary to shorten the average period of replacement as soon as he finds that the expected return on the necessary investment exceeds the opportunity cost of capital. Under a site value tax the expected marginal return is tax free, but under the other systems the return creates either taxable value, taxable rent, or taxable income. The owner will therefore proceed only when the expected additional return *after* tax exceeds the opportunity cost of capital. The absolute amount of the prospective rise in rent necessary to induce him to invest will be larger by the amount of the expected rise in tax liability. The response of the market to changes in the pattern of demand is thus systematically distorted and the housing stock adapts less efficiently than it might to consumer preferences.

At this point a tax abatement could conceivably come to the rescue. It is assumed that the abatement takes the form of an agreement not to raise the tax base during a limited period if certain improvements are undertaken through remodeling or replacement. Such an arrangement would reduce (although, since the abatement is temporary, not entirely remove) the disincentive to investment that occurs under the three taxes discussed above. The more widely it is used, however, the more likely it is to have adverse effects on revenue, reducing tax receipts below what they would otherwise have been. One of the terms of the present discussion is that tax revenues (rather than rates) are to be held constant. In that case, an abatement on some properties might require the community to raise the tax rate itself, with consequent harmful effects in other directions (for example, on new construction).

Louis Winnick has made the interesting suggestion that an abatement for rehabilitation of existing buildings could be limited geographically to slum areas. Such geographic discrimination, he believes, would concentrate rehabilitation in areas where it is most needed but least likely otherwise to occur. Thus, it would reduce or perhaps eliminate adverse effects on revenue.[16] His argument is that with a tax abatement (and perhaps mortgage assistance) it would be possible to take, for example, a $40-a-month slum apartment and rehabilitate it to rent for $50 or $60 a month instead of the $80 a month that would be required under ordinary cost conditions. The low-income slum resident would willingly pay $50 or $60 for the improved housing. He could never have afforded to pay $80, however, so such abatement-induced rehabilitation does not reduce the demand for ordinary commercially rehabilitated housing and consequently does not reduce property tax revenues below what they would otherwise have been.

This proposal certainly merits consideration. It is one way of grappling with the problem of revenue maintenance under an abatement program. I doubt, however, that it would protect the revenue as effectively as Winnick suggests. Can one, for example, exclude from the rehabilitated building the not-quite-so-low-income families who would otherwise willingly have paid $80 a month for housing of like quality?

I have not dealt explicitly with the effects of taxes on new construction but it is, of course, obvious that those taxes that discourage investment in remodeling will in the same fashion discourage investment in new housing. Likewise, an abatement policy can be extended to new construction to offset in part such tax disincentives; over a certain period, taxes on any new development could be limited to those previously paid on the parcel or even forgiven entirely. Once again, however, a likely result is that tax rates would have to be higher then they would otherwise have been.

CONCLUSIONS AND RECOMMENDATIONS

The choice among alternative methods of real estate taxation certainly cannot be made solely on the basis of their effects on the quality of existing housing or even on the basis of those effects plus their impact on new construction. Many other criteria must be applied. Those I have examined elsewhere are the following: other resource allocating effects, applicability to owner-occupied as compared with rental housing, administrative feasibility, adequacy and stability of yield, and equity.[17]

Among the taxes considered here only the site value levy and the tax abatement are more favorable to housing maintenance and rehabilitation than is the tax on combined assessed value. While the site value tax emerges as the only variant with no harmful effects of any sort on housing quality, I believe that it must be rejected as an outright substitute for the traditional American tax on two related grounds: adequacy of yield and equity. Land rent is difficult to measure, but if my estimates are correct, revenue from the real estate tax has reached such enormous proportions that it may now almost equal or even exceed the rent of land in some localities. If we were to load the whole burden onto the site value base we might, therefore, expropriate, or very nearly so, the entire rent of land. That is why the proposal to change over to a site value base at the present level of yield raises the equity problem in such an extreme and, to me, disturbing way.[18]

The equity problem would be somewhat ameliorated if removing the tax on buildings were to cause an increase in the rent of land gross of tax. As I have indicated, the theoretical grounds for expecting such an effect are not entirely clear. I am not convinced, moreover, that even with the most favorable assumptions a 15 per cent reduction in shelter cost could be expected to stimulate an increase in construction and hence in land rent substantial enough to make a significant difference, given the magnitude of the problem. In short, I am unwilling to recommend taking the plunge, or more accurately, forcing landowners to take it. As I will shortly explain, however, I would not object to lowering them into the water part way.

While a tax-abatement plan would not stimulate improvement in housing quality as much as would shifting to the site value base, it nevertheless remains an attractive possibility. True, it might cause some administrative difficulty and also some loss of revenue. Its principal drawback, I think, is again failure to meet the criterion of equity; an abatement discriminates unfairly between qualifying and nonqualifying property owners. I would agree, however, that none of these objections comes near being decisive.

In conclusion, I would recommend adopting one of the three following reforms:

1. Using the Pittsburgh plan of moving gradually toward a building tax rate set at only half the land rate. Such a plan reduces the disincentive effects of a tax on improvements, while still protecting the revenue, and it reduces the pain to be

inflicted on landowners to the point where, if they cannot bear it, at least we economists can.

2. Retaining the present tax on assessed value of land and improvements but combining it with a tax abatement to encourage housing rehabilitation and perhaps new construction.

3. A combination of the first two reforms, involving the following elements: (a) setting a ceiling on building tax rates at their present level; (b) leaving the rate of tax on land value free to rise as necessary in the future; and (c) using tax abatement to encourage rehabilitation and perhaps new construction.

REFERENCES

* For a fuller discussion of many of these issues see my longer study, *Real Estate Taxes and Urban Housing* (New York: Columbia University Press, 1966). I wish to thank the participants in the TRED conference and especially Professor Carl S. Shoup for his comments on an earlier draft of this chapter which led me to clarify or revise several points.
1. It has most recently been analyzed by Dick Netzer in *Economics of the Property Tax* (Washington, D.C.: The Brookings Institution, 1966), pp. 26–31, 67–74.
2. See Chester Rapkin, Louis Winnick, and David M. Blank, *Housing Market Analysis* (Washington, D.C.: Housing and Home Finance Agency, 1953); and William G. Grigsby, *Housing Markets and Public Policy* (Philadelphia, Pa.: University of Pennsylvania Press, 1963). Lionel Needleman's *The Economics of Housing* (London: Staples Press, 1965), came to the author's attention after this study was completed. Important unpublished works are Sherman J. Maisel, "An Approach to the Problems of Analysing Housing Demand" (Ph.D. diss., Harvard University, 1948); and Wallace F. Smith, "An Outline Theory of the Housing Market, with Special Reference to Low-Income Housing and Urban Renewal" (Ph.D. diss., University of Washington, 1958).
3. The possibility of "moving" buildings was apparently first pointed out by Herbert W. Robinson in *The Economics of Building* (London: P. S. King, 1939), p. 83.
4. Consider, for example, the following explanation of how to prepare a "plan for operation and service" of a rental property: "The successful operation of an income property depends a lot on the quality of service rendered *in* the building. . . . When the manager prepares his program for the year, he must decide exactly how the building is going to be operated and how far he can go beyond bare necessity in offering those special services which may increase tenant satisfaction and thus have tangible influence on the maintenance of gross income. . . . He considers each possibility in relation to the effect it may have on securing tenants and keeping them happy . . . he tries to come out with the best possible combinations." — H. G. Atkinson and L. E. Frailey, *Fundamentals of Real Estate Practice* (Englewood Cliffs, N.J.: Prentice-Hall, 1946), pp. 192–193.
5. The analysis of replacement decisions in this paragraph follows closely the argument of Smith, "Outline Theory," Chapter 6, and differs considerably from the approach used in my earlier study, *Real Estate Taxes and Urban Housing* (New York: Columbia University Press, 1966), pp. 32–35, and in the first draft of this chapter. I am indebted to participants in the TRED conference discussion for persuading me to revise my analysis of this matter and of the effects of taxes on replacement decisions that follows from it in the second half of the chapter.
6. See, in this volume, Chapter 11 by Daniel M. Holland and Chapter 8 by A. M. Woodruff and L. L. Ecker-Racz; as well as Heilbrun, *Real Estate Taxes,* Chapter 9; and Netzer, *Economics of the Property Tax,* Chapter 8.
7. The argument is summarized in Netzer, *Economics of the Property Tax,* pp. 33–34.

8. Interview with the late Alfred Jacobsen, 8 June 1962.
9. Herbert A. Simon, "The Incidence of a Tax on Urban Real Property," *Quarterly Journal of Economics,* 57, No. 3 (May 1943): 398–420; reprinted in *Readings in the Economics of Taxation,* eds. Richard A. Musgrave and Carl S. Shoup (Homewood, Ill.: Richard D. Irwin, 1959), pp. 416–435.
10. In the United States tangible personal property is often, but not always, included in the tax base. The overall effective rate of taxation is well below that on real estate, however, since much tangible personal property is legally exempt, much otherwise escapes taxation, and rates or assessments are often low on the remainder. Netzer estimates that tangible personalty accounted for 17.7% of nationwide property tax revenues in 1957. He estimates the 1956–1957 effective rates of taxation as follows: on manufacturing personalty, 0.7%; on manufacturing realty, 2.1%; on the two combined, 1.0%; on all nonfarm business (excluding all residential real estate), 1.1%; on nonfarm housing, 1.3%.

   Intangible personalty is now so widely exempt from property taxation that it produced, according to Netzer's estimate, only 2.0% of property tax revenues in 1957. See Netzer, *Economics of the Property Tax,* pp. 24–29, 138–153.
11. On this point see *ibid.,* pp. 36–37; and Simon, "Incidence of a Tax," pp. 416–422.
12. Netzer, *Economics of the Property Tax,* Tables 2–4, 2–7. If the value and rent of land were excluded from both ratios, the difference between them would probably be somewhat less, but still very substantial.
13. On this point see Heilbrun, *Real Estate Taxes,* pp. 90–104.
14. See note 5, above.
15. For a fuller analysis of the demand for space and the demand for quality, see Heilbrun, *Real Estate Taxes,* pp. 37–45.
16. Dr. Winnick advanced this suggestion at the TRED conference on 13 June 1966 during the discussion of the preliminary draft of this chapter.
17. See Heilbrun, *Real Estate Taxes,* Chapter 10.
18. For a fuller discussion of these issues, see *ibid.,* pp. 150–154, 162–167; and Netzer, *Economics of the Property Tax,* pp. 208–212.

24 Alternatives to the Property Tax

DICK NETZER
New York University

A few alternatives: taxes on consumption or income and a general value added tax.

When the property tax is compared on economic grounds to other revenue sources for local governments, the issue is really a twofold one depending on the following questions: First, is a tax on housing, equivalent to a very high excise on housing expenditures on the average, better or worse than the alternatives as a means of local finance? Second, is a fairly substantial *ad valorem* property tax on business

From "Alternatives to the Property Tax," *Economics of the Property Tax,* by Dick Netzer, Washington, D.C.: The Brookings Institution, 1966, pp. 166–170. © 1966 by THE BROOKINGS INSTITUTION. Reprinted with permission.

property — substantial on the average but widely varying geographically and by industry and firm — the best way to tax business on the local level, if indeed business *per se* should be locally taxed?

In hypothesizing conceivable alternatives to the property tax, it is useful to commence by assuming complete revenue replacement for this removes from the area of argument a wide range of lesser taxes, in particular the selective sales taxes, which are utterly incapable of producing adequate revenues on their own. For example, in 1963, personal consumption expenditures for alcoholic beverages and tobacco products amounted to $19.2 billion, excluding excises; excises used by all levels of government equalled about 40 per cent of this total.[1] Local property tax collections in the calendar year 1963 amounted to about $20 billion; complete replacement by tobacco and liquor taxes would require sales tax rates in excess of 100 per cent.

Table 1 suggests the level of nationwide average rates which would have been required for complete replacement of the local property tax in 1963. A gross receipts tax, uniformly despised (with good reason) by public finance analysts, would have required a 2 per cent rate. A value added tax or a personal income tax without exemptions or deductions would have involved average rates in the 5 per cent range. A net income tax with federal exemptions and deductions or a personal consumption tax of the conventional nature (excluding most outlays for services) would have required rates in the neighborhood of 10 per cent. Any narrower base — such as business profits — would produce much higher rates.

INCREASED TAXATION OF PERSONAL CONSUMPTION

A case can be made for partial replacement of the property tax on housing by increased, across-the-board taxation of personal consumption. In 1963, property taxes on housing probably amounted to nearly $9 billion, equal to an excise on housing expenditures of 17–18 per cent. . . . General retail sales tax revenues were in the neighborhood of $6 billion, implying an overall average rate of tax, including jurisdictions not using the tax, of less than 3 per cent against consumption expenditures.[2] A reduction of the average housing property tax rate by about two-thirds, together with a near-doubling of average sales tax rates to replace the lost revenue, would yield a more nearly uniform consumption tax, with average rates in the 5.5–6.0 per cent range.

Such a uniform tax would answer some of the main objections to the present housing tax: its lack of horizontal equity among individuals and its deterrent effects on housing construction. It is, perhaps, the best conceptual solution, on the assumption that consumption will continue to be a major basis for state-local taxation in any event. This basis can be challenged, of course: any general consumption tax is likely to be more regressive at the extreme ends of the income distribution than a proportional income tax yielding the same revenue.

This conceptual solution does raise a side issue: if a reduced property tax on housing is to be retained as the housing counterpart of a general tax on nonhousing consumption expenditures, should not the base be housing expenditures rather than property values? One argument against this is the problem of what to include. If all actual expenditures connected with housing are taxed, then differences in size of mortgages and in debt service payments on mortgages, which are determined by both the initial financial position of the purchaser and the recency of purchase, will cause differences in taxes on otherwise identical housing. The resolution of this

Table 1

Estimated Nationwide Average Tax Rates Required for Alternative Replacements for Local Property Revenue, 1963[a]

TAX FORM	ESTIMATED 1963 TAX BASE (BILLIONS OF DOLLARS)	RATE REQUIRED TO YIELD $20 BILLION (PERCENTAGE)
Gross receipts[b]	$981	2.0
Value added in private business[c]	373	5.4
Business profits[d]	99	20.2
Corporate profits	49	41.0
Payrolls	312	6.4
Individual income:[e]		
Federal adjusted gross income	367	5.5
Federal taxable income	204	9.8
Personal consumption expenditures:		
Money outlays for goods[f]	216	9.3
Money outlays for goods, excluding food and ethical drugs	152	13.2
Money outlays for goods plus selected consumer services[g]	247	8.1
Liquor and tobacco	19	104.2

Sources: U.S. Department of Commerce, Office of Business Economics, *Survey of Current Business*, July 1964; U.S. Treasury Department, *Statistics of Income, Individual Income Tax Returns, 1962 (Preliminary)*, Publication No. 198 (1964).

[a] Calendar 1963 local property tax revenues estimated at $20 billion.

[b] Total retail and wholesale sales plus corporate sales in other industries.

[c] National income originating in business less net rental of owner-occupied dwellings and net imputed interest paid.

[d] Corporate profits before tax plus proprietors' income.

[e] Based on 1962 relationship of federal tax items to personal income.

[f] Expenditures for goods excluding in kind consumption and expenditures abroad.

[g] Services include utilities, admissions and amusements, and personal, clothing, appliance and auto care and repair.

difficulty is to tax assessed net or gross rentals. As argued in the next chapter, if the former is taxed, the distribution of liabilities is no different from that under a tax on values, which in concept equal capitalized net rents. If gross rents are taxed, there is a real deterrent to maintenance of rental properties. And, in practice, since most American housing is owner-occupied, assessment of rents would be no easier than assessment of values.

"SOCIAL OVERHEAD" CHARGES

Because of both theoretical and practical difficulties of measurement, the business component of the property tax is essentially levied on the basis of a set of proxies for the market value of the properties involved; some of the proxies are relatively close parallels, but many are not. By and large (and this is discussed further in the next chapter), this type of tax on business has no more merit than other general taxes on business as a user charge for public services consumed by business. Similarly, all general taxes on business seem equally bad considered as a form of "social diseconomy" charge — that is, as compensation for some of the external diseconomies arising from business operations, such as air pollution, congestion, and unpleasant esthetic effects. The relative volume of output, receipts, profits, and property value are all poorly correlated with consumption of public services or production of diseconomies.

Aside from pure opportunism — taxing business solely because it is a convenient source of revenue — the principal remaining argument for a general local tax on business is that business operations should contribute to "social overheads." The costs of maintaining a functioning government and a going community, without which business could not operate, are in part a justifiable component of the costs of production, to be paid as taxes by business, and to be reflected in the prices at which output is sold so that tax payments are recouped from consumers. But the notion of taxation as a contribution to social overheads is by no means a clear-cut concept. The package of local public services is a diverse one, with both collective and individual benefits and major geographic spillovers. It may be that opportunism is the only defensible argument for local business taxation. But allocational efficiency appears to demand that social overhead charges, if any, be distributed among businesses not in proportion to investment in plant, equipment, and inventories, but in proportion to the scale of business activities in the community. Indeed, if business is to be taxed to support local government in general, the most reasonable basis seems to be the value of output — that is, value added.[3] As Table 1 indicates, replacement of the $10 billion or so in taxes on farm and business property would have required a value added tax rate of close to 3 per cent in 1963.

These strictures on the relative economic demerits of the business property tax — and, indeed, of the housing property tax — do not apply to the land component of the tax. Taxation of the bare site value of land will not deter investment in physical capital and will not change the composition of inputs, since the capitalization of site value taxes into lower land prices will maintain the cost of land as an input at its tax-free level. But the land component aside, general taxes on consumption or income and a general value added tax seem clearly preferable alternatives on economic grounds to both the housing and business property taxes.

REFERENCES

1. U.S. Department of Commerce, Office of Business Economics, *Survey of Current Business,* July 1964, Tables 14, 19, and 20.
2. The characteristic tax base includes some intermediate business purchases.
3. This argument is fully and explicitly developed by Harvey E. Brazer in "The Value of Industrial Property As a Subject of Taxation," *Canadian Public Administration,* Vol. 55 (June 1961), pp. 137–47.

25 Beyond Grants-in-Aid

WALTER W. HELLER
University of Minnesota

"Beyond grants-in-aid" lie new methods of providing states and localities with federal revenues — per capita revenue sharing, for one.

A consideration of ways and means of enlarging Federal support for states and their subdivisions should begin with a recognition of the powerful assist that they are already getting from Federal aid, tax cuts, and policies for sustained prosperity.

The rise in Federal aid to state and local governments (including loans and shared revenues as well as grants) has been little short of spectacular. From about $4 billion in fiscal 1957, such aids have grown to a programmed $14½ billion in fiscal 1967. And they now represent one tenth of total Federal cash payments to the public, double their proportion a decade ago.

Less direct is the state-local bounty derived from huge tax cuts in a slack economy. An estimated $3 billion extra a year is flowing into state-local coffers from the 1964 income tax cut alone, a 7 per cent increase for both state and local tax revenues. Most of this comes from economic expansion generated by the tax reduction. But some comes from the direct additions to the tax base of the nineteen income tax states that allow Federal income taxes as a deduction. The broad excise tax cuts of 1965 provided further stimulus and presumably opened some opportunities for states to rush in where the Federal angel no longer treads. Yet the list of attractive opportunities growing out of the excise tax reductions proved to be surprisingly short.

The ever-firmer commitment of the Federal government to maintain a high-employment, high-growth economy under the Employment Act of 1946 provides a firmer base for the states' and localities' own fiscal efforts. They can afford to be less fearful of repeated recessions, and they can count on higher average revenue yields at any given level of tax rates. Also both the management of Federal economic policy, which requires timely declaration of fiscal dividends, and the results of successful policy, which keep federal coffers full, provide a favorable setting for more generous support to the states. This is reflected partly in the great growth of federal aid, and partly in the new emphasis on "creative federalism" — for example, on the sharing of money and responsibility with community groups in the poverty program, with various state and local units in the fields of air and water purification, mass transportation, and urban development, and with municipal authorities under the proposed Demonstration Cities program.[1]

Reprinted by permission of the publisher from Walter W. Heller, NEW DIMENSIONS OF POLITICAL ECONOMY, Cambridge, Mass.: Harvard University Press, Copyright, 1966, by the President and Fellows of Harvard College.

As we parcel out future fiscal dividends, grants-in-aid will be near the head of the queue. Conditional grants for specific functions play an indispensable role in our federalism. They unite federal financing with state-local performance in a fiscal marriage of convenience, necessity, and opportunity:

convenience, because they enable the federal government to single out and support those state and local services in which there is an identified national interest. I have in mind particularly those services, like education and health, whose benefits in a country with a mobile people spill over into communities and states other than those in which they are performed. Functional aids enable the federal government to put a financial floor under the level of specific services that is consistent with our national goals and priorities.

necessity, because without his financial support the states and municipalities would be unable to meet the demands on them for essential services. Failure to meet these demands would eventually mean yielding the functions to the Federal government and thus weakening the fabric of federalism.

opportunity, because putting the grants in conditional form enables the federal government to apply national minimum standards, ensure financial participation at the state and local levels through matching requirements, and take both fiscal need and fiscal capacity into account.

But, on several counts, virtue gives some ground to vice. The aids that so admirably serve the national purpose may put state-local finance at cross purposes. In drawing on a limited supply of resources to finance and staff particular functions, the matching grant tends to siphon them away from the nonaided programs. And the poorer the state, the greater the tax effort that must be made to achieve any given amount of matching, and hence the less that is left over for the nonaided functions. To some extent, then, the state-local government trades fiscal freedom for fiscal strength.

Federal grants to serve highly specialized objectives have proliferated in recent years.[2] And once established, they do not yield gracefully to change or abolition. Unless this trend is reversed, federal aids may weave a web of particularism, complexity, and federal direction which will significantly inhibit a state's freedom of movement. The picture of Gulliver and the Lilliputians comes to mind.

We must move toward broader categories that will give states and localities more freedom of choice, more scope for expressing their varying needs and preferences, within the framework of national purpose.

Perhaps we should replace our myriad categories of educational aids with broad classes such as elementary, secondary, and higher education. Or perhaps the Elementary-Secondary Education Act of 1965, which goes against the tide of particularism, points the way. Funds under this act are distributed in proportion to the number of school children in low-income families. Within the general requirement that monies are to be applied to the needs of educationally deprived children, considerable latitude is allowed local and state boards of education to formulate specific plans.

Federal aids have risen from about 3 per cent of state-local revenues in the 1920's, to 10 per cent in the late 1940's, and 15 per cent in 1965–66. This trend will and should continue. We have reached the point, though, where some restructuring of our system of federal aids — some movement toward less conditional and less specific grants — is needed to maximize their contribution to the national interest not only in strong services but in a strong federalism.

But the conditional grant for specific purposes, for all its good works and even in its optimal form, falls short of the full fiscal needs of our federalism. Part of this is simply a recognition that even the rapid expansion of aids now in prospect will not enable state and local governments to make ends meet on acceptable terms. Part of it is that they need help in financing their nonaided functions — and it is only right that the federal government temper the wind to the lambs it has shorn. And part of it is that the conditional grants are not well-suited to serve the intangible objectives of greater self-reliance and over-all vitality in state and local government. What we seek, then, are major new "methods of channeling federal revenues to states and localities which will reinforce their independence while enlarging their capacity to serve their citizens."[3]

Such new methods must run the gauntlet of the several demanding criteria that emerge from our examination of the fiscal problems of federalism. Ideally, any new plan or approach should supply federal funds to the states in ways that will (a) not only relieve immediate pressures on state-local treasuries, but hitch their fiscal wagon to the star of economic growth; (b) improve the distribution of federal-state-local fiscal burdens; (c) reduce economic inequalities and fiscal disparities among the states; (d) stimulate state and local tax efforts; and (e) build up the vitality, efficiency, and fiscal independence of state and local governments.

The device that can serve all of these ends at once is yet to be found. But I believe that per capita revenue sharing, or some allied form of unfettered general assistance, will come closer to doing so than any alternative proposed thus far.[4]

REFERENCES

1. An interesting examination of the nature of creative federalism, as viewed from the White House, was presented by Joseph A. Califano, Jr., Special Assistant to the President, in an address before the National Lawyers Club, Washington, D.C., May 19, 1966.
2. The Legislative Reference Service of the Library of Congress has prepared for the Senate Committee on Government Operations a *Catalog of Federal Aids to State and Local Governments* (Washington, D.C.: G.P.O., April 15, 1964, together with supplements of May 17, 1965, and April 6, 1966). This very useful catalog takes over 450 pages to list, index, and summarize the present aid programs.
3. Presidential Economic Issues Statement no. 6, "Strengthening State and Local Government," October 28, 1964 (White House press release).
4. See Harold M. Groves, *Financing Government,* 6 ed. (New York: Holt, Rinehart & Winston, 1964), Chapter 20; and Pechman, *Federal Tax Policy,* pp. 225–231 and 306–307 (the latter pages, for further references on this subject).

26 Tax Credits

HAROLD SOMERS
University of California, Los Angeles

If federal tax laws were rewritten to provide, for every dollar paid to the state, generous tax credit against federal income tax liability, then states could raise revenue without squeezing their own taxpayers. Further, if the principle were extended to cities, then central cities could capture much of the revenue which their wealthier businesses and individuals now pay to the U.S. Department of the Treasury.

A thoroughgoing tax credit scheme provides a superior alternative to a revenue-sharing plan. All state and local taxes would be credited against federal income tax liability up to a certain percentage of state and local taxes — or other limitation. The credit could be given immediately as in the case of unemployment insurance taxes and may be called an instant tax credit. This would avoid liquidity problems for the taxpayer. And there could be inducements to achieve conformity and interstate uniformity in matters of detail. The states would not only spend the money themselves, they would raise it themselves. This puts the tax credit plan doubly on the side of the angels.

Tax credits avoid some of the defects of revenue-sharing plans. Any grants tied to a fixed percentage of the federal income tax revenues would be procyclical and would get more money to the states in prosperity than in depression. A trust fund or a variable percentage, if used, would introduce the element of discretionary authority and its political and economic complications. At best, revenue sharing makes no contribution to the much-needed improvement of state tax structure and the elimination of multiplicity of tax forms and tax provisions, unless conditions are attached to the revenue-sharing plan in which case we no longer can call the grants "unconditional" grants.

One is reminded of the episode in the musical "Call Me Madam" in which a leading political figure in the mythical Duchy of Lichtenburg refuses to accept a large American loan because it would scuttle the basic economic reforms he had been advocating for years.

In addition to encouraging the reform of state and local tax structures and elimination of the multiplicity of tax forms and tax provisions and the multiple taxation of interstate corporations, a comprehensive tax credit scheme has three important merits:

(1) It gives help to taxpayers in the same income or property classes by the same amount whether they happen to be located in a rich state or a poor state.

From "Revenue Sharing and Its Alternatives: What Future for Fiscal Federalism?," Hearings Before the Subcommittee on Fiscal Policy of the Joint Economic Committee, Congress of the United States, 90th Congress, First Session, 1967, pp. 171–172.

Under most revenue-sharing plans the poorer states are helped more than the richer states per capita but what benefit accrues to particular taxpayers in those states is unpredictable.

(2) It helps the taxpayers of the core cities directly and does not depend on the generosity of the state or the operation of a pass-through provision of the so-called unconditional revenue-sharing grant. Any help to the taxpayer of the core city strengthens the ability of the core city to raise taxes for its own needs.

(3) It can have built-in countercyclical effect by enabling state and local governments to increase tax rates in depression to maintain public services rather than contributing to and aggravating an economic decline.

Tax credits constitute a form of general purpose, unrestricted assistance to state and local taxpayers which leaves them entirely free to make the decisions on how to use the resources that are thereby made available to them. The state and local taxpayers are allowed to offset part or all of their payments of specified state taxes in computing their federal income tax liability. This is equivalent to receiving a full rebate from the federal government of all or part of the state and local tax paid. When a state or locality imposes or increases its taxes the taxpayer will get part or all of the money back when he makes out his federal income tax form. The state and locality will still be making the decisions on their own tax system and on the spending of the money; reimbursement is a matter between the taxpayer and the federal government.

Tax credits are not new. Proposals to credit some or all state-local taxes have been made by many authors in this country for a period of more than 40 years. No one in his forties or fifties can accept credit for credits unless he was a child genius. The Advisory Commission on Intergovernmental Relations and the Committee for Economic Development recently suggested partial tax credit for state income taxes paid. I believe that it would be preferable to make all state and local taxes, and not only income taxes, eligible up to a certain percentage or at least to have a "bloc tax credit" consisting of property, sales, and income taxes. This leaves the state and local governments more degrees of freedom in selecting the taxes which they will impose.

Existing examples of state-federal credits are the federal estate tax credit and the credits against payroll taxes under the unemployment compensation system. The federal estate tax credit unfortunately has not actually accomplished uniformity of death taxation and it is an open question how much it has contributed to that end. Certainly death taxes in the various states present a mosaic of types — inheritance or estate of both; exemptions — that is, insurance exemption — and rates. Despite the credit and the resulting costless nature of this portion of the tax to the states, one state (Nevada) levies no death tax at all. Prospective decedents — our gloomy way of referring to all living persons — are undoubtedly grateful for the credit in all the other states.

Tax credits should not be confused with tax deductions. State and local taxes are generally deductible in computing federal income tax liability. The deductibility feature tends to reduce the burden of state and local taxes to some extent. For instance, if the relevant federal tax rate is 50 per cent, a state tax of $100 costs the taxpayer only $50 — in his capacity as a state taxpayer, that is. This looks fine but it has a serious defect. If there is a federal tax cut, the actual burden of state and local taxes appears to increase. For instance, if the federal rate is reduced from 50 to 25 per cent, a state tax of $100 rises in net burden from $50 to $75.

The taxpayer gains in making out his federal return, on balance, but the burden of state taxation appears heavier on him.

Tax credits do not have this defect. A $10 tax credit is $10 in the taxpayer's pocket even if federal rates change.

27 General and Specific Financing of Urban Services

WILLIAM W. VICKREY
Columbia University

User charges could help us to improve a number of public services and to avoid waste (among other uneconomic practices). Their value is special for fire protection, water supply, transportation facilities — even for police and health services.

The purpose of this paper is to re-examine the degree to which municipal services are financed from (1) general purpose taxes, levied without close attention to the way in which the taxpayers benefit from public services or affect the costs of rendering them, and (2) specific taxes, fees, and prices that attempt to reflect these costs and effects more closely. To some extent the concern with bringing payments more closely into line with costs and benefits is related to concepts of equity, in that it is conceived to be in some sense proper that those who enjoy benefits or give rise to costs should, in the absence of countervailing considerations, pay accordingly. But more weight, on the whole, is given in the current investigation to the possibility that such correlation of charges with costs and benefits can be made to increase the efficiency with which services are utilized, prevent waste, and in general improve the patterns along which our mushrooming metropolitan areas will grow. Indeed, it is this latter consideration that leads to a dissatisfaction with a mere statistical or average balance or proportionality between benefits and contributions and an insistence on a greater precision of detail: situations can easily arise in which groups of more or less similarly situated individuals share a cost equally and hence no individual is in fact treated unfairly, yet if the institutions are such that no one person can reduce his share in the cost by suitably economizing or restraining himself, the amount of the service demanded and supplied may be grossly excessive.

GENERAL CRITERIA

In determining whether an attempt should be made to pay for a municipal service by means of a specific charge, a number of general principles or criteria can be

---

From "General and Specific Financing of Urban Services," by William W. Vickrey, in *Public Expenditure Decisions in the Urban Community,"* Howard G. Schaller, editor, Washington, D.C.: Resources for the Future, Inc., 1962, pp. 62–90. Reprinted with permission.

referred to; their specific impact varies, of course, from case to case. One of these concerns the distributional impact of the charge relative to that of the general tax that it might displace. In many cases this differential will be small enough or uncertain enough in its direction to be considered a wholly secondary matter, but in particular cases it is important and even paramount. In New York, for example, a straight increase in transit fares can be considered almost tantamount to a poll tax in its incidence, and certainly far more regressive in its distributional impact than even the sales tax. The distributional impact of an attempt to finance educational, hospital, or welfare services entirely by direct charges would obviously be so unacceptable as to preclude such a solution, at least in its simple and direct form.

Another general principle that can be appealed to is the extent to which the proposed charge can be related to benefits derived from the service in a way which will appeal to concepts of equity. This immediately raises the question of how to measure the benefit: should it be in terms of the cost of providing the service to the individual concerned or in proportion to the amount that the individual would pay rather than go without the service altogether? To what extent, for example, should water charges be based on the income of the user, or be differentiated according to the cost of his obtaining water from another source? It seems fairly clear that answers given to such questions will vary widely from case to case and that the variation will have to be explained on grounds other than a general adherence either to cost or to utility as a basis.

Indeed, one factor that will often enter into the general attitude taken is the nexus, as perceived by the public, between the payment made and the benefit received. In many cases this perceived nexus will be significantly influenced by historical development. A new service accompanied by a new charge is likely to generate a vivid conception of a *quid pro quo;* a new charge made for a pre-existing service is more likely to create a feeling of inequity, even if the charge is a necessary means of preserving the value of the service, as in the case of the ferry that is worthless as long as it is free (because then queues accumulate until it is just as quick or convenient to detour via a bridge or tunnel), or where transit services are subsidized in part from funds obtained from highway use charges. Another element in the perception of this nexus is the manner of payment: a toll is immediately visible as an out-of-pocket cost financing a distinctive service; a gasoline tax is slightly less so; payment for a sewer connection may evoke different attitudes, even though computed on the same base, according to whether it is merely included in a global tax bill to a municipality performing all of the various functions itself, or paid as a separately itemized item on a consolidated tax bill, or paid separately as an entirely distinct transaction. All of these may have a significant effect on the way in which the relation between benefit and burden is perceived by the general public and in the degree of acceptance of this relationship.

More attention is to be paid here, however, to the matter of allocational efficiency. This in effect means extending the concept of marginal cost pricing as far as possible into the realm of municipal services with the intent of attaching, to each choice by individuals that affects municipal operations or that has an impact on others in the community, a differential charge that will properly represent these impacts to the individual. Ideally, this charge would serve to co-ordinate decentralized decision making on the part of individuals into a harmonious whole. In many areas, however, it will be an adjunct, though an important one, to more centralized planning activities as represented by building codes and zoning ordinances.

Moreover, even in the absence of pressures arising from considerations of progressivity and of equity perceptions, it will in practice be impossible to approach even very closely to this theoretical ideal. The relative social costs occasioned by alternative choices contemplated by individuals cannot be measured, in many cases, with anything like complete accuracy, and in other cases the costs of carrying out the measurements would be such as to outweigh the benefits. Even where the costs can be ascertained with adequate accuracy, the costs of assessing the corresponding charges may be great, and in some cases the terms of the assessment might tend to become so complicated as to be beyond the comprehension of the individual making the decision, and thus be ineffective in securing the improvement in the allocation of resources that was the original *raison d'être* of the more elaborate assessment. And finally, allowance must be made for the fact that in nearly all cases, even with the fullest possible utilization of specific charges, municipalities are almost always in such pressing need of funds that they must have recourse to general taxes that themselves have adverse effects on allocation. Consequently, by virtue of the general principle of "second best," if any specific charges are to be made, they should in nearly all cases be designed in part to contribute to the public treasury over and above the amount that would flow in on the basis of charges strictly reflecting marginal costs.

SPECIFIC CASES

General principles are seldom as enlightening in the abstract as in their application to specific cases, and accordingly some specific examples are discussed in the remainder of the paper which will serve to illustrate their application and explain their meaning. In considering specific cases, we will include on the one hand some items that may not ordinarily be thought of as municipal services, but which would lend themselves to financing by methods ordinarily associated with municipal finance; and on the other hand some municipal services, including some of the more important ones, will not be considered because of the inherent difficulty of applying to them the methods being considered here.

Fire Protection

Fire protection accounts for some 7.6 per cent of all general expenditures by cities. It serves here as a striking example of the difference between benefit and cost as a basis for charging.

Actually, fire protection is considered most appropriately paid for on the basis of property assessment, and in terms of benefit this is a fairly good basis. Benefit can be roughly measured in terms of the reduction in insurance rates on protected as against unprotected property, and in terms of the enhancement of land values in view of the provision of the protection to any structures built on the land. The value of land plus improvements would accordingly seem to be a good measure of benefit. Even here, of course, there are cases where increased property value fails to indicate increased benefit: replacing an old, obsolescent building with a modern fireproof one may lessen the amount of benefit obtained from fire protection even though the value of the property be increased.

Viewed from the cost side, however, the picture is entirely different. Providing a given grade of fire protection to an area is almost entirely a matter of providing an engine company within a suitable distance of the property, or more operationally, within a suitable number of minutes of travel time. The National Board of Fire Underwriters, in setting standards for fire protection, requires as a rough rule of thumb that in residential areas a company be stationed within about 1.5 miles for a property to be considered adequately protected; for industrial and commercial property, apartments and the like, the distance is shortened to .75 miles, while for areas containing only widely scattered residences a distance up to 3 miles is tolerated. There are in addition minor differences in the cost per engine company: in business and industrial areas a complement of seven men on duty is considered normal, whereas in residential areas five men on duty may be considered sufficient; in addition the property occupied by the fire house may be more valuable in the former case. Roughly speaking, therefore, the ratio of the cost of protecting an acre of residential area and that of protecting an acre of business area may be about one to five (leaving the fringe areas out of consideration, for the moment). This is a much smaller range than the corresponding range in assessed values, in most cases.

From the point of view of resource allocation, however, it would not be sufficient to remain content with property values as the basis for paying for fire protection even if it could be shown that these costs in fact varied in proportion to assessed value. An increase in the value of the improvements in a given area, through new construction or otherwise, does not in any significant way increase the cost of furnishing a *given grade* of protection to the property already there, even though it may make it worthwhile to provide a higher and more costly grade of protection. Even though in principle the construction of new buildings in a given area may increase the frequency of fires within the area and thus might increase the probability that the equipment might be out on another call when fire breaks out in a given property, this is normally a very minor factor, made quite negligible in most cases where alternate protection is normally available from adjacent fire companies. The basic act that is causally related to the need for added fire protection is the occupancy of land in the protected area. It is the exclusive occupancy and not the nature of the occupancy that counts: if an acre of land is used for tennis courts or a clay products depot, involving of itself almost no fire hazard, the displacement of the occupancies that might have used this land to outlying areas where new fire protection will have to be provided is a cost that should properly be assessed against such uses. Similarly it makes no difference to the cost to be assessed against a given acreage whether it is developed with residences on half-acre lots or row houses cheek-by-jowl, even though this might make a difference to the way an insurance company might rate the hazard.

Accordingly, the appropriate way to charge for fire protection would be on the basis of area. Possibly some gradation in the charge might be made in terms of distance from the fire house, but in most cases this would be a negligible factor. An exception might be made where the protected area dependent on a given fire house includes both residential and business property: areas zoned for business and located within the .75 mile distance might be assessed at a higher rate based on the higher degree of protection offered and the need of business for this higher grade of protection if it is forced to locate elsewhere by inferior occupancy of the business-zoned area. In this case it would be the nature of the zoning rather than the nature of the occupancy that would be the appropriate basis for the distinction in the charge. Moreover there is in a sense a joint product problem here: a given fire house required to provide residential-grade protection for the 1.5 mile radius necessarily provides incidentally for business-grade protection within its .75 mile radius. On the one hand, if the inner zone thus generated is greater than the demand for business sites, the business-grade protection is a by-product to be provided at no marginal cost, the residential occupancy bearing the full burden; on the other hand if the business demand increases so as to require the provision of an additional fire house, the additional residential protection, if enclosing some unoccupied but developable land, is likewise a by-product, and the full cost of such a fire house should be borne by the business protection area.

Translating the charges thus indicated into an actual tax is of course another matter. In the long run it would probably not make too much difference if the assessment were made on the basis of land value rather than land area, as any difference between the two forms of charge could readily be capitalized into the land value. In the short run transitional effects would arise, but consideration of these effects will have to be relegated to another analysis. In any event it is clear that on a cost basis, the basis for assessment is clearly land value, exclusive of improvements, in spite of the fact that at first glance the benefit basis would seem to indicate that it is improvements that should be assessed.

Another factor associated with fire could be the basis for the assessment of charges — the external economies associated with what are technically termed "exposure fires," i.e., fires not starting on the premises under the same ownership. Individuals who take precautions against fire are not only reducing their own risk, but that of their neighbors. To the extent that they are reducing their own risk in recognizable ways, they may qualify for lower insurance premiums, but since neighboring properties are insured by independent companies, and indemnities are paid regardless of the source of the fire, these rating allowances of necessity include no allowance for reductions in the likelihood of contagion or exposure losses. It would accordingly be of some merit for property tax assessments to make some small concession to structures that are fireproof or are sprinklered or are otherwise protected, over and above what building codes may make mandatory. The tax concession could even be more widely applied than building codes, since the latter are often full of grandfather exceptions; in some cases the tax concession might even motivate an improvement where otherwise the owner would be willing to hide behind an excepting clause.

Too much should not be made of this, however: over the period 1953–59 the property loss claims from exposure fires amounted to $221 million, which is 7.2 per cent of losses from known causes, which in turn was 45 per cent of total losses. Since exposure fires probably constituted a relatively low percentage of the "causes unknown" category, such losses probably amounted to not more than 4 per cent of the total. Though the principle may be applicable, the practical consequences are *de minimis*.

Water Supply

In water supply we are faced with a wide range of situations as to source of the bulk supply, but the over-all characteristics of distribution tend to be somewhat more uniform, and we will discuss the latter first.

In some fortunate areas, reasonably pure water may be available from a nearby source in ample quantities, so that the main problem is one of distributing this supply to users. Moreover the economies of scale in water main size are so substantial that it is only a minor oversimplification to say that the cost of the mains is proportional to their length and relatively independent of the required volume of flow. Another factor tending to warrant such a simplification is that for fire protection purposes a certain minimum size main is required to provide the flows needed for fire-fighting purposes.

The problem is how to relate the total length of main required to the nature of the occupancy of the area. It is tempting to say again that area is the critical factor, but this is overruled by the observation that if we take two communities that are laid out in a similar pattern, but on different scales so that streets and mains are twice as far apart in the one community as the other, while lots are four times as large, the second community will only require twice the length of mains. The simplest rule would be to use the front foot as the unit; this however produces awkward results when applied to corner lots, but even so is perhaps the best simple rule available. One can of course expect any minor variations in the system of charges to become capitalized in the price of the lots, in this case, so that the corner problem is perhaps not a crucial one. The same is true of variations in the relative amount of frontage associated with various lots due to odd shapes, curves in the street, and the like. It would be tempting to try some more general linear measure of lot size, such as the square root of the area, or the maximum diameter, but these would produce results that make the aggregate charge for a group of lots vary according to the way the total area is subdivided in ways that bear no very close relation with the length of mains required.

In smaller communities endowed with an ample source of supply this may be all that marginal cost pricing requires: there would remain, in addition to the cost of the mains, the cost of the collection and purification system and the transmission aqueduct from the source to the edge of the community. In many cases the incremental cost of added capacity may be so low as not to warrant the cost of installing and reading water meters. These intra-marginal costs not covered by explicit charges for mains can then be covered out of general revenues, or from any other source on the basis of "least harm." One source would be surcharges on the cost of the mains; not only would this probably not be too much of a distorting influence, but it would have considerable public appeal on equity grounds. Actually, data for 1959 indicate that over-all expenditures for water supply amount to $1,423 million as against revenues of $1,201 million, indicating some support from general revenues, though since expenditures are largely on a cash rather than an accrual basis, with considerable confusion between current and capital outlays and probably a considerable understatement of real interest and amortization charges, this conclusion should be made with caution.

In many cases, however, especially in the more densely populated areas and arid regions, the incremental cost of the gross supply will be a significant factor. The problem is complicated by the large size of the lumps in which increments to supply are often available, the great durability of the facilities, and by the significant seasonal and random fluctuations in the supply furnished by given facilities. Under such circumstances charges according to the amount of water used are obviously in order, but have in the past been justified far more on grounds of equity than on grounds of controlling the use. Indeed, the idea of using water charges to ration use seems quite at variance with typical attitudes of water supply engineers, who seem to view their function as one of providing an ample supply almost regardless of the cost of meeting whatever standard they decide to set, and limiting the charges to the user to whatever minimal rates prove necessary to finance the scheme over all, regardless of what the incremental cost of the particular supply involved happens to be.

Reluctance to use water charges as a means of rationing use is illustrated in the fact that rates generally remain much the same from one season to another and from one year to another. To some extent this is the result of sheer administrative inertia, but to a considerable extent it represents the view that to raise rates at a time of shortage represents exploitative profiteering that is considered undesirable and even immoral, regardless of whether the beneficiary is a private individual or a public body. Nevertheless, to an economist, at least, the possible improvement in the allocation of resources through such variation in rates should be fairly obvious, the main question being how difficult such variation would be and how important the benefits that would result.

Variations in supply may arise either as a regular seasonal phenomenon, or irregularly as a result of variations in rainfall or large accretions of capacity. In all three cases variation in rates would improve resource allocation, but the difficulty of applying the changes varies considerably. One difficulty common to all three situations is that meters are usually read quarterly, and often on a rotating schedule, so that it would be difficult to bring the impact of the rate change to bear on all consumers simultaneously. In a system having large reserves, where a situation of shortage or abundance can be expected to persist over several quarters, or in the case of the addition of large increments of supply, it may be sufficient to continue a quarterly pattern, simply prorating the consumption indicated for a given quarter into the portions of the quarter falling into the low and the high rate periods. This works fairly well with utility bills at present, where rate changes occur, but in such cases the rate changes are relatively minor and the principal issue is one of equity; it would be relatively less satisfactory where rate changes are of a magnitude intended to be sufficient to affect consumption. Then the discriminations would be somewhat more severe and the dilution of the incentive to economize during the latter scarcity part of a quarter, by reason of the fact that such consumption would be prorated back to the earlier or abundance part, (and vice versa in case of rate reductions) would be of significant concern. Ideally, extra meter readings should be arranged as nearly as possible to the time of the rate change, so as to minimize this proration effect; possibly this might be done economically by combining them with electricity and gas meter readings. Self-reporting by the consumer, such as is often practiced either for interim readings or where the regular reader was not able to gain access to the premises, would seem somewhat less feasible here than where no rate change is taking place: with constant rates there is ordinarily no significant incentive for the consumer to falsify or fudge his report of the meter reading, and even where there is, the consumer would often have to be fairly sophisticated and prescient about his future consumption to take advantage of the opportunity; where a substantial rate change is involved, both the magnitude of the incentive and the clarity to the consumer of the direction in which it is to his advantage to misreport would operate to make misreporting more of a problem.

One objection to fluctuating rates is that they make it more difficult for the consumer to budget, particularly with rates that fluctuate with unpredictable variations in rainfall. The problem would be less significant with predictable seasonal fluctuations in rates. Unlike a private utility, a municipality is in a position to offset changes in water charges with changes in the general property tax rate, so that what the average consumer would gain on a given occasion in lower water rates he would lose in higher property taxes, and vice versa; the incentive for conservation of water in times of shortage would remain. In effect, a substitution effect is generated while the income effect is minimized.

With water more than with most other utility services, the tenant who turns the tap is often insulated from the impact of water rates by their inclusion in his overall rent, and for this reason rate variations may be less effective here than with other services. Such use is however relatively inelastic to price in any case, and control at such points is hardly worthwhile. There remains, in any case, the incentive for the landlord to pay special attention to leaks and other outright wastage and for economizing in large-scale industrial use, lawn watering, and the like.

One need not necessarily maintain that rate changes can entirely take the place of water conservation campaigns in times of threatened shortage, but high water charges should provide a significant reinforcement for such campaigns, if they become necessary. Certainly such charges provide a more efficient means of rationing than such methods as the prohibition of certain uses at certain times, or in extreme cases the shutting off of the supply in various areas at various times, with the attendant danger of contamination and increased fire hazard.

Variable rates should permit considerable economies to be made in scheduling expansion of supply. Given a means of efficiently controlling the demand in cases of drought of rare intensity, it will be less necessary to expand supply quite so far to take care of such contingencies. Similarly, it will be less necessary to plan new additions to supply quite so far in advance, since a faster than anticipated growth in demand or shortage due to subnormal rainfall can be adapted to more effectively. On the other hand, new additions to supply can be used more fully and more promptly upon their completion if charges are reduced or eliminated as long as the supply is ample.

However, a policy of raising charges prior to the completion of a new project and lowering them when it is brought into production means a drastic change in traditional modes of financing public works. To the extent that funds are accumulated out of the earlier high rationing charges, the project will be more nearly on a "pay-as-you-go" basis; on the other hand, there will be no funds flowing from water charges to pay off the balance of the cost until such time as the new addition is being fully utilized and rationing charges are again needed. Whether or not this pattern can be followed in its pure form will of course depend on the over-all fiscal and financial pattern of the municipality, but substantial changes in financial procedures are indicated in any case, even if the limiting situation is not a feasible one.

There is one further difficulty with drastic variation in rates over fairly long periods: consumers may be induced to install water-using equipment, such as nonrecirculating cooling equipment, on the basis of current low rates only to find that when rates are later raised their investment turns out to have been unprofitable. In principle, of course, consumers should be put adequately on notice of the likelihood of water rates being increased in the future. Fortunately, most decisions of this sort that involve substantial fixed capital and that would be significantly affected by water rates are of a commercial or industrial nature. In such instances the decision-maker can be presumed to be sufficiently sophisticated to take account of such a prospect.

Transportation Facilities

The over-all picture of the finances of urban transportation conceals a great deal of inefficiency and distortion within an aggregate picture that seems spuriously close to being in balance. Aside from a few outstanding instances of substantial subsidy, such as the New York subways and rail commuter service, it appears superficially that the transit rider is about paying the costs of the service he uses. Likewise, for motor traffic as a whole, revenues from user charges seem to be roughly in balance with outlays on facilities: in 1957 total tax revenue from all motor vehicle related sources, including licenses, fuel taxes, manufacturer's excises, tolls, and parking meter revenues amounted to $8,162 million; expenditures directly on highways amounted to $7,931 million, not counting that part of local police expenditures of $1,290 million that could be regarded as spent for traffic control (roughly one-tenth, judging from the number of police assigned to traffic duty in New York City), or the portion of the $562 million of "other sanitation" expenditures that could be regarded as spent for snow removal and other traffic-related purposes.[1] On this basis one would be inclined to doubt whether there is any large scale misallocation of traffic between various modes, or substantial under-or-overutilization of facilities.

When looked at in more detail, however, the picture is quite different, especially when full economic costs not represented adequately in the financial accounts are added in. If we attempt to separate out the urban component of the motor vehicle revenues and expenditures, we find that in 1960 the forty-three largest cities spent $600 million on highways, exclusive of police and sanitation expenditures for traffic related purposes. Of this only $289 million was financed from vehicle user charges in terms of any explicit flow of funds: $155 million from state highway grants and $134 million from city licenses, parking fees, and user charges, leaving $311 million, or 52 per cent of the total outlay to be defrayed out of general revenues.[2] In 1957, all cities spent $2,941 million on streets and highways, of which only $1,471 million, or just 50 per cent, was derived specifically from use-related charges.

To get closer to the allocation of resources, however, we cannot stop here for the relevant matter is not through what channels the funds flow, but whether, on balance, the charges the motorist pays, to whatever governmental agency, correspond to the costs they occasion, in whatever form and by whatever agency these costs are borne. (Indeed, one could argue that the general purpose grants from state to local governments include some highway funds.) Figures of this sort are harder to come by. However, in a recent study of the Philadelphia metropolitan area, it was found that in 1957 total motor vehicle tax charges allocable to use of motor vehicles in the city of Philadelphia amounted to $30 million to all levels of government, but that motor vehicle expenditure by all levels of government for facilities within the city amounted to $46 million. Thirty-five million dollars of this was spent by the city itself, of which only $6.5 million was financed by grants from federal and state highway funds, and by user charges (chiefly parking meters), leaving $28.5 million to be financed from general revenue sources.[3] While this is only one instance, there is no obvious reason to suppose that the total cost of facilities being provided in Philadelphia is significantly higher relative to use than in other metropolitan areas, nor that the level of charges being paid by motorists is significantly lower. On this basis motorists in large cities appear to be paying only about two-thirds of the current expenditures made for the facilities they use.

To obtain the true economic cost of urban traffic facilities, however, it is necessary to go even further than this and substitute, in place of current capital outlays, an appropriate rental charge representing interest and depreciation or amortization on the value of the facilities used. The current capital outlays to be substituted for, as representing provision for future use rather than for current use, amounted to $351 million out of a total of $600 million for the forty-three largest cities; for all cities in 1957 the figure is $754 million out of $1,753 million. But what to put in place of these figures is something of a problem. Farrell and Paterick, of the Bureau of Public Roads, put the value of the depreciated investment in urban street and highway improvements at $10.2 billion as of January 1, 1953; $11 billion would seem a reasonably rough figure for 1957.[4] A figure of $8.25 billion for the value of land in city streets was produced by the Federal Trade Commission for 1922;[5] a more recent estimate appears not to be available but by considering trends in property values, a 1957 value on this basis of $21 billion seems roughly reasonable. At 4 per cent interest on the total value of $32 billion, plus 2 per cent amortization on the depreciated improvements, this gives $1,500 million to be substituted for the $754 million of current capital outlays in figuring true economic cost. The full annual economic cost of city street use thus comes to $2,319 million, as compared with actual outlays of $1,573 million, exclusive in both cases of police and sanitation. Even at this, the computation includes no equivalent for property taxes or corporation income taxes that would be covered by rental payments for the use of privately constructed property requiring comparable amounts of land and construction. If property taxes were figured at 1 per cent on the full value (in 1956, assessments of $280 billion were estimated to represent 30 per cent of full value, or about $930 billion; property tax collections were $11.7 billion)[6] $326 million would be added to the bill; in addition if as little as 20 per cent of the investment were financed by equities, with a net return to equity holders of only 4 per cent, the corresponding corporation income tax of 52 per cent would add $277 million to the cost. With these elements added in, urban vehicular traffic is found to be paying $1,050 million in charges as compared to roughly $2,916 million that users of comparable resources in the private sector of the economy have to pay.

Obviously, if there is a way in which the cities can collect an additional $1,866 million from urban vehicular traffic so as to bring the charges more nearly in line with the costs, it would not only help to improve the resources allocation pattern but would ease the financial pressure on municipal governments very substantially. (Total city revenues from all sources were $13,748 million in 1959.) Unfortunately, there has hitherto been no easy way to approximately triple the charges payable by the urban motorist without excessive interference with the smooth flow of that part of the total traffic that has a legitimate and urgent need for the use of the city streets. It appears, however, that with the aid of modern electronic equipment it is now feasible to equip each car using the urban streets with a cheap and rugged response block by virtue of which a record can be made each time such a car crosses a zone boundary, without interfering with the flow of traffic, and these records can be processed on electronic computers to produce a bill which can be made to vary appropriately with the costs occasioned by the indicated movements of the car. It remains to be seen, however, whether what is economically sensible can be made politically palatable.

Some demurrer to the assignment of all city street costs to vehicular traffic is often entered on the ground that in addition to carrying through traffic, such streets also serve as "access" to the adjacent property, and that the cost of such an access function is properly chargeable against the property owners rather than against the users as such. To be sure, if conditions are such that the roadway is no more elaborate than that which would be required to provide a mere access, and if traffic conditions are such that there is, in fact, no interference with other users of the roadway during such "access," then the marginal cost of such use is effectively zero in the short run, and charging the entire cost of the access street against the property owner would be conducive to unrestrained use of the uncongested facility, so that efficiency would be served. The bulk of the cost, however, particularly in view of such factors as the use-related character of much of the outlay for renewal of pavement and the high proportion of the property values accounted for by the downtown areas, is more nearly chargeable against users than abutting property owners. Even when a vehicle is performing an access function, its impact on traffic and on costs may be substantial; the amount of these costs is a function of the movement of the vehicles performing the access function and is not related in any direct way to the value of the property accessed. While some allowance might legitimately be made for the access function of low-traffic residential streets, this allowance would be small. Moreover, even on equity grounds, one could well raise a question as to whether the charge for the provision of common access facilities would not be more fairly allocated according to amount of use, rather than according to the value of the property accessed.

For example, even where a cul-de-sac is used almost solely for access purposes, with no traffic movement other than that destined to one of the abutting property owners, if conditions of use are such that there is interference between users, some means of bringing the cost of this interference home to them directly is needed. This can be done conveniently if the costs associated with providing the area and the pavement are assessed against users in proportion to use. It is both inequitable and inefficient to charge these costs to the abutting property owners under these circumstances, making the abutting occupant whose business requires relatively little use of the access facility pay just as much as his neighbor whose operations seriously interfere with the ease of access of the adjacent occupants. Some of the most serious congestion in New York is the result of the way in which "access" is had to firms in the garment district.

The Special Problem of the Rush Hour

The disparities in treatment between various forms of transportation are even further aggravated by the nature of rush-hour conditions. Nearly all forms of rush-hour transportation are grossly underpriced. In 1951, at a time when the fare of 10 cents on the New York subways was just about covering operating expenses, it was estimated that the marginal cost of a moderately long rush-hour ride was somewhere between 20 and 40 cents, possibly even higher in some cases. The differential between rush hour and non-rush hour or between rush-hour costs and average over-all costs varies widely as among alternative forms of service, so that even if various forms of transportation were on an equal footing over the entire week, either each paying its way or being subsidized by about the same proportion, this still would not bring about an economical allocation of traffic among the various modes during the peak hours. For one thing, transit systems can handle overloads in general much more readily than highways by putting more persons into the same vehicle, and while this causes some deterioration in the service, sometimes to a truly inhuman degree, there is no complete breakdown. On the highways, on the other hand, there is no mechanism whereby increased traffic flow results in more persons riding per car, and there is a rather strong tendency for the system to jam up once a critical flow has been reached. Another and more important factor is the distribution of traffic through the day. At one extreme, commuter railroads handle half of their total traffic during the fifteen peak hours per week; for subway traffic the figure is about one-third, while for expressway traffic on routes to and from the central city the proportion is about 18 per cent. This means that when costs are averaged over the entire traffic flow, the rush-hour traveler, who should bear the bulk if not the entire amount of the cost of providing the capital facilities, is able to shift over four-fifths of this burden to non-rush riders if he is an auto rider, but only two-thirds if he is a subway rider and only half if he is a rail commuter. Differentiation of the charge between peak and off-peak use is thus not only a matter of encouraging peak use and discouraging off-peak use, but it is also a matter of inducing the selection of a suitable mode of transportation given the time and volume of travel.

Accordingly, there can be no efficient solution to the urban traffic problem that does not include provision for charges on automobile use that are differentiated according to time of day. The most straightforward way of doing this is of course the direct recording of the passage of vehicles. It might also be possible to accomplish something indirectly through cordon tolls at the edge of the congested area, in combination with specific parking controls. This, however, is likely to balkanize the area, providing an artificial separation of economic activity on the one side of the cordon from that on the other. Tolls at an adequate level limited to main thoroughfares might reduce this balkanization somewhat, but at the cost of producing severe "shun-pike" congestion on the parallel minor streets. Special license fees imposed on city street users, in the form of a flat monthly or annual charge, hardly meet the problem: it is difficult if not impossible, without rather elaborate checking mechanisms, to distinguish between occasional use by suburban and out-of-town vehicles, which could appropriately be exempted entirely, and regular commuting for which the maximum charge would be appropriate. The usual basis for special local license fees is the location where the vehicle is customarily garaged, which is almost entirely inappropriate. For example, a vehicle which is kept in an off-street parking facility privately paid for, and is used only for weekend excursions may be responsible for relatively little congestion, even making full allowance for the weekend parkway congestion.

Parking

Whether in connection with a cordon toll or in connection with a comprehensive electronic toll system, it will be desirable to have a closer check on the time at which cars enter and leave the traffic stream from parking space. Attended parking lots may presumably be required to provide this information in suitable form, possibly not without some resistance; on-street parking may at first appear to present a more formidable problem. The proposal formerly advanced by the writer for parking meters to be operated on a post-payment basis in which the rate of charge would be varied according to the number of parking spaces occupied and such that the deposit of coins would be required to recover the parker's key seems inadequate for this purpose.[7]

A proposal for curb parking control more in keeping with the above requirement is one in which a record is made of the time of parking and unparking as follows: for each local vehicle there is issued a parking card; on parking his car the operator inserts his card in the parking meter, presses a lever on the meter down against a spring, and withdraws a key belonging to the meter. This operation locks the lever down and the card inside the meter, where it can be inspected through a window; simultaneously a record is made of the time and the serial number of the card by imprinting an embossed serial number from the card and a time indication from a clock inside the meter through a carbon onto a paper strip. Subsequently, on the return of the operator, he reinserts the meter key, which releases the lever, causing a second imprinting of time to be made and the card returned to the operator. The resulting paper tapes are periodically collected, the imprinted data read photoelectrically and converted to magnetic tape, then processed on a computer, either separately or in conjunction with records made automatically as cars cross zone boundaries.

By feeding the parking data for an area into the computer first, the occupancy rates for each group of parking meters at various times could be ascertained, and on the basis of these occupancy rates appropriate charges could be assessed for each parking of a car; the data can then be sorted by car number and matched with data for the zone boundary crossings to produce appropriate charges for the trip from the zone boundary to the parking spot, or from one parking spot to another. All the charges for any given car can then be combined, modified where indicated by a factor relating to the nature of the car, combined with any outstanding charges and a bill sent to the owner, together with a card valid for the succeeding period for those not in arrears. Payment would be enforced in considerable measure by withholding of cards from delinquent owners: it could be made unlawful to operate a locally registered car in the area without a current parking card displayed appropriately in a holder on the windshield or elsewhere.

If corresponding records can be made for cars entering and leaving private parking lots and garages, and, perhaps more difficult, for cars parking in non-metered outlying areas, it might be possible to achieve a fairly efficient system of charges by combining these records with a record made of cars entering and leaving the metropolitan area at some cordon line, without having to equip cars with any sophisticated electronic or other apparatus. Cars coming off the street into a private facility would be able to register "off" by inserting the card in a receptacle similar to a parking meter, from which it could be retrieved only by again registering "on." This would enable all cars making trips fairly directly from one registration spot to another to be accounted for fairly accurately. There remains the problem of taxicabs, delivery trucks, and similar vehicles making devious and irregular trips. This could be taken care of, though somewhat awkwardly, by simply assuming that in the absence of evidence to the contrary, such vehicles registered as "on" the streets would be assumed to be circulating in the most congested areas subject to the highest rate of charge per minute, and providing opportunities in the outlying areas for such vehicles to register so as to qualify for an appropriately lower rate, e.g., by registering in an unused parking meter, or at extra registers provided for the purpose at convenient locations; it would only be necessary to register once for each more or less direct trip or trip segment beginning or ending in an outlying location.

There seems to be no easy way to deal with non-metered parking within the cordon, however, so that the necessity for having all parking within the cordon metered is likely to require that the cordon line be put rather closer in than is altogether desirable, both from the point of view of a reasonably complete coverage of significant congestion and from the point of view of locating the cordon itself at a point where the required operations would not themselves be a congestion factor. On the other hand, with a little ingenuity, it should be possible to avoid the necessity for "toll-plaza" operations if space is at all scarce. Outbound, it is to the operator's advantage to register, so that a number of registration stations can be set up in tandem, with the driver being left free to register at any one of the stations. Inbound, while failure to register can be adequately penalized in those cases where the vehicle is going to "roost" somewhere within the cordon, there would be the possibility of evasion by those driving on through or making stops "on the run." But even here, since the operation is simply one of inserting the card in a slot, with no occasion for receipts or change requiring a human agent, it would be relatively easy to arrange for registers to be used in tandem, with signals to coordinate the sequence of use and indicate failure to register.

There remains the out-of-town vehicle. Where such vehicles are frequent visitors, it seems clear that they should be required to obtain cards on the same basis as local cars. For the occasional visitor or transient, this involves a relatively large administrative cost; moreover there is relatively little price elasticity to this particular category of use, and a considerable sentiment, arising both from commercial motives and traditions of "hospitality" in favor of generous treatment. Accordingly it seems entirely proper to arrange for such visitors to be given the "freedom of the city" insofar as street usage is concerned, to a suitably limited extent. This can be implemented by providing stations at a suitable distance outside the cordon where incoming visitors and occasional cars can obtain guest cards, valid for from two to ten days, showing conspicuously the license number of the car for which it was issued. A record is made of this license number when the card is issued, and this record is eventually checked to see that no more than the allowed number of guest cards are issued for any one car. It would probably be worthwhile to man the busier stations during hours of heavy traffic, particularly as they could be made to serve as general information booths as well; for light traffic routes and slack periods, the issuance of these cards could be automatic: for example, the applicant could be asked to write the license plate number through a plastic window and a single-use carbon on to the guest card, the carbon retaining the record; as the guest card is withdrawn, a transparent contact-adhesive film is pressed over the license number imprint to prevent further alteration. The guest card may also contain an embossed serial number, similar to those on regular cards, for further identification. Even though a guest card was issued as valid for, say, ten consecutive days, the subsequent processing of the records would show for how many days it was actually used, and it would be possible to specify that an occasional visitor was entitled, say, either to ten consecutive free days a year, or perhaps to six free days scattered through the year. It may be necessary to require the deposit of a dime for each card in order to prevent frivolous withdrawal of cards.

As compared with the cash post-payment type of parking meter, the present charge account type has one major disadvantage in that the time lag in the feedback of information to the vehicle operator as to how great the charge was for parking at a particular time and place is comparatively long, so that his response to a given level of charge may be considerably delayed. Major changes in patterns of vehicle use will probably take considerable time, however, in any case, so that this may not be as serious as it might seem at first glance. As compared with cash post-payment, the problem of the operator returning to the parked car with insufficient change to pay the accumulated charge would be avoided. The meter mechanism should on the whole be less costly, particularly as there would be no direct interconnection among meters: assessment of the level of demand in the area would be by the computer program, not by interconnecting the meters; this would be not only a considerable saving in installation costs, but would make it possible to appraise the aggregate demand with much greater flexibility and over a much wider area, so that the charges would not have to vary by such severe increments and a more stable equilibrium would be obtained. It would probably be necessary to make the release of the meter key conditional upon some pattern of holes or notches in the parking cards, otherwise there might be trouble from mischievous improper removal of meter keys; since there would be no gain to be obtained from such action, the keying need not be highly sophisticated and the meter mechanism can be kept reasonably simple.

Peak-off-peak Transit Pricing

The problem of suitable pricing of transit service to take account of the variations in cost between peak and off-peak service is relatively simple, at least for subway and commuter lines, and need not concern us here. Suitable automatic schemes for collection of sophisticated fare structures have been available, at least on paper, for some time. Recent developments in the direction of the use of subscriber cards and monthly billing (instead of cash payment, with or without refunds, as under former proposals) have been proposed for the San Francisco Bay Area Transit System, and seem well adapted to cases where the unit of sale is fairly large, as in systems that cater predominantly to medium-haul suburban traffic, as would be the case, for example, with railroad commuter service as distinct from local subway service. Also, the clientele is of a character that would give rise to less difficulty in collecting on the basis of monthly bills. The principal unsolved problem is for local bus service, where lack of space and low levels of utilization militate against the use of complicated fare collection machinery, while any complication in the fare structure tends to overload the driver and slow service. The recent abolition of bus transfers in New York is a case in point, for while it does involve discriminations of a somewhat arbitrary sort between persons whose trips happen to be catered to by single long bus routes as compared to those having relatively shorter trips requiring the use of two different routes, it does significantly ease the burden on the operator.

An interesting suggestion has been put forth in connection with subscriber fare systems for suburban service: it would be at least conceivable that the agency furnishing the service should be set up as a membership organization along co-operative lines, and if so, one might argue that the subscribers should be entitled to deduct that part of their payments representing interest on capital and taxes, somewhat as the owners of co-operative apartments do. The deduction would have at least this much rationale: commuting to relatively low rent suburban housing is a more or less direct substitute for the payment of higher rentals in close-in housing. Indeed, one could present the further case that with the commuter service the efficiency of allocation of resources is being fostered rather than otherwise by the discrimination, in that the service is one offered under conditions of decreasing costs; this much cannot be said of the deductions for interest and taxes on dwellings. But this is admittedly stretching matters pretty far.

Financing the Intra-marginal Residue in Urban Transportation

While the most urgent need is to increase charges on rush-hour service of various kinds, especially motor vehicle usage, there will remain, ultimately, a fairly substantial portion of the cost of urban transportation that cannot be fully allocated on marginal cost principles. On equity grounds many would argue for allocating this residue as a charge added to marginal cost and paid by the users, and the second best principle would support this treatment at least to some extent. Thoroughness, however, requires that some attempt be made to trace out the way in which the assessment of transportation costs affects urban land use.

In this area more than most, extreme models produce paradoxical results. Land values are widely held to be created, or at least enhanced by transportation developments, particularly those that produce changes of mode or nodes in the transportation network. Indeed at times it almost seems as if it is imperfections in transportation that create land values. Where transportation has uniform costs, models seem to indicate that the better transportation is, the lower land values will be, as for example with the assertion often made that if transportation could be made instantaneous and costless, site value would disappear. Even with less extreme models, if demand for urban land as a whole is considered to be completely inelastic, and if rents are made to vary so that for all developed urban land the sum of rents and the transportation costs of the activities carried out on the land to and from the center of the model are constant, then land rents are proportional to total transportation costs, and cutting transportation costs in half will preserve the same geographical pattern of activity with rents likewise cut in half.

A considerably different model emerges if we admit some elasticity into the demand function for access to the urban center, the amount of access being measured by the area of land occupied and the price of access being the sum of land rent plus the cost of a uniform amount of transportation per unit of land from the site to the center. If for simplicity we assume that all land uses have the same transport-to-the-center requirement, and that the demand function is unity, then the total price paid in terms of rent plus transportation cost is constant, and of this total price one-third is rent and two-thirds is transportation cost. The total cost can be thought of as a cylinder of height $h = tr$, where r is the radius of the developed area, and t the transportation cost per unit distance; at the edge of the cylinder transport cost is tr and rent is zero; at the center transport cost is zero and rent is tr; total rent can be represented by the cone fitting into the cylinder, which will have one-third of its volume. As the transport cost t increases, r shrinks (as the cube root of the transport cost rate), rents at the center rise, but the developed area shrinks, so that outside the developed area rents fall to zero. With a more elastic demand curve for access to the center, total rents would increase as transportation costs fall, but rents at the center would still fall, the increase being accounted for by enlargement of the developed area.

In order to produce a model in which improvement in transportation raises rents at the center, it would be necessary to produce a demand curve for access to the center which is in a sense perverse, i.e., in which the larger the aggregate, the more a given buyer is willing to pay for access to the center, and in which this effect is so strong as to outweigh the diminishing marginal utility of access to a center of a given size to successively less eager buyers. In other words if the Nth renter is willing to pay R for access to a center of size N, then even though the $N + 1$st renter would be willing to pay only $R - \delta$ for access to a center of size N, the Nth

renter is willing to pay $R + \delta + \epsilon$ for access to a center of size $N + 1$, and the $N + 1$st renter is thus willing to pay $R + \epsilon$ for access to a center of size $N + 1$. Such an upward sloping demand curve would indeed imply that a decrease in transportation costs would increase the marginal value of access to the center, and hence increase rents throughout the developed area. Thus it is possible for an improvement in uniform transportation to increase property values at the center; but whether the economies of scale in urban aggregations of the present size of most of our large cities are still significant enough to bring about this result would seem to be unlikely on an impressionistic basis.

On balance it seems likely that improvements in uniform transportation, as exemplified by travel in private automobiles over a standardized network of city streets, would benefit owners of outlying property more than owners of centrally located property, and that if intra-marginal highway costs are to be charged against property values at all, they should be charged primarily against peripheral property values rather than against central property values. Indeed some of the deterioration observed in downtown areas over a period coinciding with the growth of the automobile relative to transit's decline is rather suggestive of the agreement of reality with some of the above models; this result may not be an adventitious one resulting from strangulation by inadequate development of facilities, but may be an inherent property of a non-focusing transportation system.

Models Reflecting Node Effects

Models which will reflect the focusing effect of a transportation system with pronounced nodes are rather hard to come by, and it seems reasonable to suspect that a number of other facts, such as the variation in the relative demand of activities for space and for transportation, the possibility of linkages that do not pass through the center, the possibility of creating space through building upward, and the effect of the aggregate magnitude of activity on the demand for space would all interact with the existence of transportation nodes in affecting the pattern. To illustrate the lines on which analysis might proceed, I venture to suggest the following outline for a model, though without necessarily implying that the model can be worked through satisfactorily short of using successive approximations on a computer.

1. All transportation takes place along the lines of a rectangular grid, which however is dense enough to allow one to neglect the spacing between transportation lines. Initially the cost of transportation is uniform per unit of distance, with the result that the developed area takes the form of a tilted square, the diagonals of which are two of the transportation routes at right angles to each other. In subsequent stages improvements are made in transportation facilities along these two main axes, so that the marginal cost of travel along them is reduced as compared to travel off these axes. The result is to spread the developed area out in a four-pointed star.

2. A unit of activity is defined as an activity originating and terminating one unit of traffic. For simplicity the amounts of traffic originated and terminated are assumed to be equal. Activities vary according to some simple distribution as to the amount of space they require per unit of activity.

3. The frequency with which a unit of transportation is carried on between any

two units of activity is inversely proportional to some power of the cost of the transportation (the so-called "gravity" model).
4. Space can be provided at a given location by constructing buildings of varying height and lot coverage, at (linearly) increasing marginal cost of additional space as the ratio of space to ground area increases.

Specifying the conditions of equilibrium is a fairly straightforward matter, buildings being constructed to a height at which space rent equals marginal cost, the difference between marginal and average cost appearing as ground rent, which, on this basis, is proportional to the square of the building height. Activities presumably locate in such a way as to minimize the sum of rent and transportation cost; there is, to be sure, some question at this point whether the transportation cost considered to be paid by an activity should be the one-way transportation cost or the two-way transportation cost: in principle it would be the two-way cost, but one might want to consider contexts in which it is more likely that an activity bears only the costs of outgoing transportation and incoming transportation is fully prepaid by the shipper, or vice versa. Presumably, also, each activity would want to minimize not the cost of reaching a given set of correspondents by transportation, but the cost of transportation as adjusted for such shifts of correspondents as would be induced by the application of the gravity rule.

I have not had time to develop this program fully so I merely offer it as a suggestion to anyone who may be possessed of the computer programming facilities and mathematical skills required. Without going into the matter further, a guess at the results is risky, yet one might hazard the guess that significant differences would emerge between the patterns that result when transportation costs are uniform as compared to what they are when transportation along certain channels is specially favored. If this expectation is substantiated this would be a further reason for using property tax revenues to subsidize node-creating transit rather than unfocused motor vehicle transportation.

Rationale for Subsidy of One Mode by Another

If for one reason or another outside financing cannot be obtained to meet the intra-marginal residues of transportation as a whole, there still may be sound justification for financing the intra-marginal residues of mass transit by the levying of charges on urban motor traffic, even if these charges cannot be made to vary closely with the diurnal and other variations in congestion. In one sense, such a use of motor vehicle user revenues for the finance of transit would be merely the equalization of the subsidy that now is given to the urban motorist, partly in the financing of actual outlays on streets out of property taxes, and partly in the failure to account at all for the rental value of the space the motorist occupies.

In some cases a politically more acceptable rationale can be derived from adventitious historical circumstances, as when it is proposed to turn some of the San Francisco Bay Bridge toll revenues over to the Bay Area Transit Authority, on the ground that originally the bridge did carry rail transit cars of the Key System, and the tracks were later removed to make way for additional roadways. The plea is made that this diversion of tolls is in lieu of the recapture of the bridge space for rail transit use. Actually, while use of the bridge would be considerably cheaper in capital cost than the present plan to construct a new tunnel for the transit system under the bay, use of the bridge would be rather less satisfactory because of the awkward approaches that would be required and the severe speed restrictions that seem inevitably to apply to rail equipment operating over suspension bridges.

A more basic argument for subsidy of this sort can be derived from the following example, however, which illustrates how far off the "every tub on its own bottom" philosophy can get when misapplied to what seem superficially to be aggregates of similar tubs (even without an introduction of decreasing costs!). Suppose a facility of type M attracts rush-hour and nonrush-hour passengers in the ratio of 1 to 4, and costs $1.00 for each rush-hour passenger provided for and $.20 for each nonrush-hour passenger. On the other hand a facility of type T costs only $.75 for each rush-hour passenger and $.15 for each nonrush-hour passenger, or uniformly 25 per cent less; however, it attracts only one nonrush-hour passenger for each rush-hour passenger. If no differentiation between rush-hour rates and nonrush-hour rates is possible, facility M can break even with a charge of [$1.00 + 4($.20)]/5 = $1.80/5 = $.36; for facility T the break-even fare is [75¢ + 15¢]/2 = 90¢/2 = 45¢. Thus with each facility required to be self-liquidating, the passenger is offered a 9-cent fare differential in favor of facility M, alike in the rush-hour and in the nonrush-hour, whereas the consequence of his choosing facility M rather than T is to increase the costs, by 25 cents in the rush-hour and 5 cents in the nonrush-hour.

Of course, if it were true that if five rush-hour and five nonrush-hour passengers were to shift from T to M, they would automatically convert themselves in some way into two rush-hour and eight nonrush-hour travellers, then the 9-cent reduction in fare that they would obtain would be justified. But there is no reason to expect any effect in this direction, and an effect of even a fraction of this magnitude would be a highly unlikely occurrence. Actually, if peak-off-peak differentiation in charges is impossible for one reason or another, the next best thing would be to reverse the relationship between the charges, and raise the charges on M to 45 cents and lower the charges on T to 35 cents, resulting in a subsidy of about 25 per cent to T from excess revenues of M. If for the M facility we read streets and highways and for T we read suburban rail service, the correspondence with the typical facts is reasonably close. Thus if charges for peak use are ruled out, there is an even stronger case than would exist otherwise for subsidizing mass transportation at the expense of vehicular traffic.

Police and Custodial Service

Police expenditures amount to slightly over 10 per cent of city expenditures, ranking below education and sanitation, but are perhaps less amenable than most other services to financing by means of specific charges. There is, nevertheless, something to be gained by an examination of the ways in which the revenue structure can be brought more closely in line with the costs of performing this service.

Unfortunately, not very much is as yet known concerning the specific factors that influence or should influence the level of police service provided. In New York City, under a "Post Hazard Plan" promulgated in 1955 and subsequently revised, an index of the relative volume of police problems in the various areas is used as an aid in allocating personnel. The index uses the following items with corresponding weights: crimes of personal violence, .25; other crimes and offences, .20; juvenile delinquency, .15; accidents and aid cases, .10; population, .10; area, .05; business establishments, .05; school and recreation areas and crossings, .05;

and radio alarms transmitted, .05. Obviously, at most .20 of the total weight is assigned to factors that could be made the basis for some form of tax, and even here the basis is impressionistic rather than based on any rigorous study.

There would seem to be a relatively close relationship between the characteristics of buildings in an area and the magnitude of the policing problem. But even if this can be substantiated, it is not clear how this relationship could be converted into a tax base and whether it would be desirable to do so if it could be done. Buildings converted to single room occupancy may appear to increase the policing problem, but it is at least possible that a tax on such occupancy would only result in the tax being passed on very largely to tenants. Indeed, to the extent that police problems are most intense in low income neighborhoods, it may be almost inevitable that any attempt to levy a tax in proportion to some factor that seems to be causally related to policing costs will result in a severely regressive levy. This can be illustrated, for example, if it is proposed to allow some sort of tax credit for the provision of doormen, full-time janitors, and the like, whose presence would tend to reduce the policing problem.

There is, indeed, a whole array of situations where the line between private and public policing is unclear. At one time it was the practice in New York for city police to be detailed as guards to accompany payrolls and other similar transfers. This had serious ill-effects: gratuities were often offered in connection with this service, to the detriment of morale; the gratuities failed in most cases to cover the full cost, so that in effect an incentive for converting to a payment-by-check basis that should have been brought to bear was held off. A further effect was the diversion of unduly large numbers of police to this duty at peak periods near weekends. In some instances police are hired to perform such duties during their off-work hours; this also may lead to abuses. Similar difficulties occur in conjunction with sporting events and other occasions where large numbers of persons are assembled. The range over which this problem of drawing the line between that for which the public police department will be responsible and that which is a private responsibility is a wide one. At one extreme, the Morningside Heights Association has recently arranged for a corps of private police to patrol the area as a supplement to the city police. At the other there is said to be at least one case where the municipal police deliver the morning newspapers as a part of their early morning patrol. While this could obviously cause difficulty if carried too far, there are obvious complementaries between patrolling an area and performing other functions that may be worth taking advantage of, and of course if police are involved in such activities, the possibilities for obtaining revenues by appropriate charges should not be overlooked. But on the whole there is at this stage little that can be said definitely about appropriate modifications of revenue structures on the basis of their impact on police expenditures.

Recreational Facilities

Expenditures on recreational facilities account for about 5 per cent of general expenditures, or about one-third as much as highways (in terms of cash outlay). In terms of the nature of the benefit, one could argue that here is an even stronger case for the levying of specific charges. However, it is rather more difficult to isolate a marginal cost that makes very much sense because in many cases the anemity provided by a park is enjoyed by occupants of abutting property, even if they impinge in no way upon the enjoyment of others. Some uses are joint rather than exclusive, in that one goes to an event in part in order to be a part of the multitude. Even where the use is definitely exclusive, as in playing golf or tennis in periods of heavy demand, and accordingly efficient allocation would definitely call for the levying of a specific charge sufficient to equate demand and supply, there is a case to be made on distributional grounds for rationing by queue rather than by price. Many groups have more time than money, and it can be argued that it is desirable to preserve a reasonably wide variety of areas in which those who possess little coin of the realm can cash in that coin of which they have relative abundance.

Thus, while a professor of economics, accustomed to value time highly and to think of queuing as an essentially wasteful process may at first take a dim view of a system where people line up for hours to get on a public golf course, this may not accurately reflect the feelings of those who do the lining up. Existence of a queue, to be sure, is *prima facie* evidence of inefficiency, in that if somehow reservations could be handed out to approximately the same group of persons who eventually play, the waiting, at least, could be eliminated. The cost involved in handling the reservations, however, may be greater than that of the waiting (this is essentially the analog of the former situation with respect to vehicular traffic, where it was maintained that the cost of toll collection would be greater than the cost of the congestion it was to eliminate). Permitting non-transferable reservations to be made on a first-come, first-served basis involves an alternate waste of induced excessive pre-commitment to a specific plan of behavior some time in advance, on pain of forfeiting the privilege represented by the reservation. Again at first glance one might suppose that this waste could be eliminated by making the reservations transferable, to the mutual benefits of transferor and transferee, but this would only make the reservations either an attractive area for speculators to operate in, or require the application of some prior criteria for the issuing of the reservations.

Where the capacity of the facility is fairly rigid, as with tennis courts, and the demand somewhat unpredictable, because of the influence of the weather, if for no other reason, it will in any case be almost impossible to clear the market with any degree of precision through pricing alone, and in such cases a combination of pricing and queuing is likely to occur. In the absence of distributional considerations, a proper balance is to be sought between the wastes of queuing and the wastes of underutilization of the facilities: the higher the price the less the queuing but the greater the underutilization in periods of unusually low demand. On the other hand the lower the price, the lower the revenues over the range of prices that is relevant here, while the greater, presumably, is the favorable effect on the distribution of income.

The outcome of the balance of these considerations is not a cut-and-dried matter, in any particular case. In considering the weight to be given to the losses of queuing, however, it is appropriate to consider the degree of compulsion involved in the queuing: if the associated service is one easily dispensed with or for which there are reasonably close substitutes available, as for example where private facilities are available at moderate fees, then the queuing losses can be assigned a relatively low value in the appraisal of alternatives, whereas if the queuing is more nearly associated with a necessity, with only relatively remote substitutes available, the costs of the queuing are likely to weigh more heavily in the decision.

The same principles apply to the case where there is a temptation to continue the same fee that is inadequate to eliminate queues in peak periods over into periods of slack demand where the facilities are lightly used. In these cases the argument seems to be that the demand is highly inelastic over the range of prices in question anyhow, and that the redistributive effect of reducing the fees is less likely to be favorable, partly because of the absence of the selective effect of the queue, and partly on the ground that possession of leisure during the off-peak period is evidence of economic prosperity. There is also the problem of whether in view of the relatively low level of demand the facility should be closed down entirely during off-peak periods, or whether, contrariwise, only the fee collecting element should be closed down. This is not an important problem, but it is one that often seems to have been resolved more in terms of adminstrative convenience than in terms of any serious economic appraisal of the situation.

Education

Education is by far the largest single item in local government budgets, and there is no dearth of material on its financing. This is not the place to attempt a review of the volumes that have been written, but rather to sketch out new avenues of approach that might follow from an examination of the economics of the problem.

If provision of a uniform minimum standard of educational opportunity for all were more nearly a fact, rather than the rather remote aspiration that it actually is, the problem might be considered relatively simple. In fact, communities differ widely in their ability as well as in their willingness to provide a high grade of education. While intrastate differences in ability are met to a moderate degree by state aid formulae, the degree to which interstate differences in ability are met by federal aid is as yet minimal. The desire to provide adequate or even superior educational facilities thus often is severely constrained by the lack of adequate public revenue resources.

The problem is aggravated to a certain degree by the imbalance of internal migration. Regions that are net exporters of educated personnel fail to realize the tax base that would ordinarily result from the activities of the persons they educate, a process that has certain vicious circle elements in it as areas with high educational aspirations relative to their tax base fail thereby to attract the base necessary to support the aspirations without recourse to burdensome rates. It is easy to exaggerate the importance of this, but it seems clear that some means of breaking through this situation is needed. The essence of the problem is that the opportunity for a profitable investment in education is being missed because the parents of the children involved may be unable to finance the education, either individually or collectively, while the community finds it very difficult to finance an investment from which the returns will accrue elsewhere. The problem is how to arrange for the repayment to the investing community of some of the returns generated by that investment in education.

The somewhat exotic proposal that these considerations seem to point to is as follows. Each federal income taxpayer should be required to report on his income tax form the state (or school district) in which he received his public education, if any. A portion of his tax would then be turned over to the state (or school district) so indicated. The intended effect would be primarily one of making "educational export" regions more willing to upgrade their educational standards in view of an expectation that even though the region might not benefit directly from the better education of those who leave, the region would nevertheless get a return in this form.

Such a principle is of course capable of great modification in detail. It could, for example, be applied only prospectively, to taxpayers in the future that are now getting educated; presumably the incentive to educational export regions to upgrade their education would remain as strong, even though they might have to borrow to do it on the strength of the expectation of these revenues. They merely would not obtain an unexpected windfall from the incomes of their previous students. However, this would be subject to the perennial problem of the inability of any government to commit itself effectively to a program that would have to extend for so many years into the future if it were to be effective at all, and in the absence of some mechanism of effective commitment, the incentive effect on current expenditures on schools might not be realized. Also, it would be possible to limit the distributions in some way to those educational systems that represent a high degree of effort in relation to the revenue resources available. Another possibility would be to vary the amount of the income tax payable by the individual according to the degree to which his income might be considered to be the result of superior or inferior educational facilities, the variation in tax above the minimum level being the amount available for redistribution back to the educational agencies.

The difficulties of putting any such plan into practice are obvious and probably insurmountable, and accordingly it must be considered as being presented as an aid and stimulus to discussion rather than as a serious proposal. Possibly a more likely, but less effective, variant would be to propose that some of the federal grants in aid to the states might be calculated on the basis of their being, in effect, *ex post* compensation to the exporting states for the loss of human capital they experienced as a result of net emigration in the past, insofar as this capital export could be considered to reflect the value of the education given. Another way of doing it would be to make current and future migration patterns the basis for grants, without attempting to relate the grants to the income actually yielded by the investment in education.

Health and Hospital Services

The main element that is peculiar to health and hospital services is the close interrelationship between municipally financed services and services covered by insurance, and the presence of a "moral hazard" element, by which is meant the tendency to make unjustified use of the facilities because they are either free or covered by insurance. In a sense the "moral hazard" here is only an acute form of the general tendency to overuse a facility that is underpriced; if a difference exists it is mainly that here the justification for use is supposed to reside more in objective medical facts and less in individual preferences, and the moral hazard arises because the objective medical facts are never quite as objective as the concept of a welfare standard or an insurance indemnity would like them to be. The moral hazard arises from many motives, from the doctor's desire to have the patient where it is easy to visit him, or the use of the hospital as a refuge, or to the desire to take advantage of section 105(d) of the federal income tax, which allows a deduction for sick pay for the first seven days of illness only if the employee is hospitalized during that time. The problems are so diverse that about all that could be done here is to simply list the area as one in which there is the possibility of some financing by fees.

Public Utility Services

Although such public utility services as electricity supply, telephone service, gas distribution, mail service, parcel delivery, and even newspaper delivery are not ordinarily included among the services considered as part of the standard pattern of governmental activity at the local level, the lines between these services and those such as water supply, garbage collection, and sewage disposal, that more typically are so considered, are to a degree arbitrary. Of these, the one that is most frequently added to the list of municipal activities, electricity supply, is perhaps the one for which the special powers of the municipality are least needed.

Dissatisfaction with the results of public utility regulation of private utilities, plus the attractions of the availability of relatively low-cost capital and certain other tax advantages relative to federal and state taxes are among the major factors which have led to the entry of municipalities into the business of supplying electricity, but these factors are common to the other utilities as well. In some cases the establishment of a municipal electricity service is the result of such special stimuli as the TVA and other public power agencies. But to a large extent the fact that these forces were effective with respect to electricity but not to other utility services can be laid to the fact that of all of the predominantly privately supplied ones, electricity is the one that is most nearly an absolute necessity for the typical urban resident. Actually, it is precisely this characteristic that would make it possible for a privately operated utility to come reasonably close to an optimum allocation of resources through the adoption of a schedule of charges that will closely reflect marginal cost and yet at the same time extract a sufficient additional revenue from the intramarginal consumption to earn a normal return on its investment. There are several ways of doing this, but the most appropriate would be to charge rates for kilowatt-hours at the appropriate marginal cost, and assess in addition a front-foot charge to cover the basic cost of the distribution system. The front-foot charge could be expressed, if need be, in the form of a higher rate per kilowatt-hour for the first x kilowatt-hours per month per front foot; since practically all consumers would be using more than this initial block, the result would be essentially marginal cost pricing. This device is available to the electric power company primarily because the use of electricity is so nearly universal that no customers to speak of would find it advantageous to refuse service because of this initial rate.

With nearly all of the other services, however, an attempt to charge for the service according to front feet, to cover the basic costs of traversing the streets so as to cover the area effectively, would result in many potential customers refusing the service in order to escape the cost, and it does not seem likely that a privately operated service would be empowered to assess charges on property owners who do not take the service. It is here that there is a definite opportunity for improvement in the efficiency of allocation of resources through the collection by the municipality of a special frontage tax to defray the basic traversal costs of these various services, and then make available to the residents these various services at rates that would be fairly close to the incremental cost of rendering the service. It would not be absolutely necessary for the municipality to render the service on its own account: this could be done by contract, though of course in this case care would have to be taken lest abuses occur, and if anything of this sort were to be done at all, many would be inclined to favor some method that would not result in the subdivision of responsibility and the introduction of opposing monopolistic interests. Including mail delivery in this list is perhaps a bit quixotic in view of the firm preemption of this field by the federal government, yet it is technologically no more unreasonable to contemplate the local handling of mail that is transmitted nationwide by a national service than it is to contemplate local distribution of electric power generated and transmitted over a wide area by a federal agency.

SUMMARY

Enough has been said to indicate that even though the decision to provide a given facility or service may well require a weighing of costs and benefits, benefit may not provide a suitable basis for the assessment of charges to defray the costs. The decisions made by governments in deciding whether to offer a service and of what extent and character, and those made by individuals in availing themselves of whatever service is provided are of a different scope and often of a different dimension, so that the comparisons that are pertinent for the one decision are not always relevant for the other. Generally speaking, the considerations adduced in considering appropriate charges lean rather more towards the taxation of land rather than improvements, not necessarily in terms of its market value, but rather in terms of such parameters as area and frontage. Even where benefits seem to be most closely measurable in terms of improvements, the causal nexus is found to be more nearly independent of actual improvements and to relate more to the fundamental site-determined characteristics. Finally, a comprehensive approach to the pricing of municipal services may lay the groundwork for a new and more fruitful approach to over-all urban planning in terms of economic costs as well as of architectural design.

REFERENCES

1. U.S. Bureau of the Census, *Census of Governments, 1957* (federal excise taxes added).
2. U.S. Bureau of the Census, *Compendium of City Government Finances in 1960.*
3. Philadelphia Bureau of Municipal Research, *Improved Transportation for Southeastern Pennsylvania* (May, 1960), pp. 294, 314.
4. Proceedings of the 32nd Annual Meeting of the Highway Research Board, January 1953.
5. National Bureau of Economic Research, *Studies in Income and Wealth,* Vol. 12, p. 547.
6. U.S. Bureau of the Census, *Statistical Abstract of the United States, 1961,* pp. 403, 418, 419.
7. William W. Vickrey, "The Economizing of Curb Parking Space," *Traffic Engineering,* November, 1954, pp. 62–65.

PART FOUR

THE REGIONAL CONTEXT

HIGH-INCOME SUBURBS share only minimally, if at all, in the problems of the central cities. Suburban cities in Maryland and Virginia have no legal responsibility for the rising crime rate in Washington, D.C. Suburban cities south of San Francisco do not try to meet the ghetto education problems of their large neighbor to the north. Poverty, discouragement, and discrimination in the slums of Chicago are of little direct concern to the citizens of Wheaton, Illinois. Only air pollution is a leveler: it clouds the atmosphere of the city slum, the high-income suburb, and of the farms beyond.

To date, significant steps to control urban problems on a regional scale have been made in just two fields — in transportation and in pollution. But the recognition is growing that an approach to few urban problems can be made unless city and suburb are bound together through joint action. To that recognition, the Watts Riots of 1965 gave a push.

Region-wide policies are very difficult to implement because of the lack of regional government in the United States. At the regional level, a serious power vacuum exists. Voluntary regional associations have been organized in a number of metropolitan areas — in New York, Chicago, San Francisco, Los Angeles, Minneapolis-St. Paul, to name several. But such associations have been weakened by the long tradition of local home-rule and the political "necessities" of re-election.

Some urban issues are too large for solution even at a regional level — issues which tend to destabilize urban and regional economies. These include fluctuations in war expenditures (especially today in and around Los Angeles, Dallas, and Boston); stagnation due to changes in technology or to overspecialization in the production of one or two basic products; and depletion of mineral resources. Methods of helping to stabilize such economies include replacement of military with civilian contracts, poverty programs, aids to education. And, some economists would add, the federal government's assumption of its legal responsibility to maintain full employment across the nation, as written in the Employment Act of 1946.

Economic theory boasts two widely quoted approaches to the stabilization and stimulation of regional economic growth. One uses the theory of John Maynard Keynes to link economic growth to export development; the other analyzes the natural resources and productive factors which could form the basis for new economic expansion. Most cities try both export promotion and diversification to secure for their people jobs and income.

The institutional changes needed to facilitate the application of urban and regional economics can be proposed at all levels, of course, from the nationwide level to the smallest neighborhood level. The task is to match effective institutions to the size and nature of the important problems; and then to create additional institutions.

28 Reshaping Government in Metropolitan Areas

COMMITTEE FOR ECONOMIC DEVELOPMENT

The CED makes several recommendations for metropolitan America, which is "in trouble." One recommendation: a governmental system of two levels — with some functions assigned in entirety to area-wide government; others, to local government; most assigned in part to each level.

INTRODUCTION AND SUMMARY OF RECOMMENDATIONS

Metropolitan areas embrace most of our greatest resources. They are centers of commerce and industry, fashion, culture, and thought. Many metropolitan areas are wealthier and more populous than most nations.

Yet metropolitan America is in trouble. In cities and suburbs alike, citizens are beset by complexities that disturb their everyday lives. They are threatened by crime in the streets, by impure air and water, by breakdowns in public transportation. They are burdened by high taxes and inflationary prices. The deprived minorities in the slums and ghettos suffer more than other citizens of metropolis, for they are more likely to be jobless or sick, badly educated or poorly housed. What is worse, they are handicapped by racial discrimination in their efforts to improve their own condition.

Vigorous leadership is essential if the plight of metropolitan Americans of all races — in cities and suburbs — is to improve. The national and state governments must develop relevant substantive programs designed to deal with a host of diverse and elusive metropolitan problems. At the same time, metropolitan areas must develop a system of government that is capable — administratively, fiscally, and politically — of translating substantive programs into action. Such a system must be geared to respond not only to problems of metropolitan-wide concern, but to those of local communities within metropolitan areas.

We do not intend in this statement to recommend substantive policies and programs to meet the many problems of metropolitan America. Proposals for dealing with some of these difficulties may be found in earlier CED statements; proposals for dealing with others will appear in statements now under way by the Research and Policy Committee. Our purpose here is to provide guidelines for redesigning the present structure and organization of government in metropolitan areas. With-

---

From "Reshaping Government in Metropolitan Areas," A Statement by the Research and Policy Committee, Committee for Economic Development, New York: Committee for Economic Development, February 1970, pp. 9–22. Reprinted with permission.

out a more rational, more flexible system than now exists — one that recognizes local as well as area-wide needs — new policies and programs are likely to fail.

The structure of government in metropolitan areas has a profound impact on the daily lives of metropolitan citizens. But, as this Committee has long recognized, the present arrangement of overlapping local units is not serving the people well.[1] Citizens in metropolitan areas are confronted by a confusing maze of many — possibly a dozen — jurisdictions, each with its own bureaucratic labyrinth. This baffling array of local units has made it difficult for citizens — the disadvantaged particularly — to gain access to public services and to acquire a voice in decision-making.

Clearly, a fragmented system of government works better for some than for others. In gaining access to the system, citizens with greater political influence and sophistication may succeed in bypassing bureaucratic governmental procedures. Moreover, the system generally works better for suburbanites than it does for residents of the central cities. The haphazard arrangement of local governments in metropolitan areas has created great inequalities between resources and needs. In the suburbs, the combination of superior fiscal strength and fewer problems usually yields a higher quality of public service; in the central cities the situation is reversed. But it is not entirely by chance that such disparities have developed. One of the principal failings of a fragmented system of government is its inability to take an overview in matters of planning, transportation, and population dispersal. Zoning and other land-use control powers wielded by small suburban communities tend to exclude from the suburbs black citizens and other low-income minority groups.

Fragmented local governments reflect great variations in character and viewpoint. The fact that fragmentation persists indicates a determination among local communities to control their own affairs and preserve their own identities. While this attitude makes for greater local pride, it also results in failure of local communities to unite on matters of area-wide concern, such as environmental pollution and transportation congestion, which seriously undermine the quality of metropolitan life. The question to which this statement is addressed may be stated quite simply:

Can existing forms of government in metropolitan areas be modified to permit solution of area-wide problems and at the same time permit local communities to manage their own affairs and maintain their own identities?

Metropolitan Trends

Mounting population pressures which accelerated after World War II have sent Americans beyond their central cities in a quest for space. At the same time, there have been pressures in the opposite direction: the technological revolution in agriculture has forced residents of rural areas to abandon the farms and move in great numbers to the cities. This dual movement has intensified the problems of metropolitan areas.

The cities have suffered the most. The departure of business firms and a large proportion of the more affluent, white residents to the suburbs has severely weakened the cities' tax base. This, in turn, has made it more difficult for cities to deal with problems of race and poverty brought on by a heavy influx of poor, nonwhite residents. But the suburbs have suffered, too. The worsening condition of the cities has only speeded the outward movement, and the result has been many problems of the cities have spread beyond their borders. Suburbanites found that governmental patterns designed for rural areas were not suited to their needs. To cope with new problems, new governments were created, but they were not created with a rational view to the future. Rather, they seemed to spring up — in endless proliferation. These new governments, tacked on to one another around the central city, have formed the crazy-quilt that is metropolitan America today.

The U.S. Bureau of the Budget defines a metropolitan area as "an integrated economic and social unit with a recognized large population nucleus." These units are called "standard metropolitan statistical areas" (SMSA's) defined by the Budget Bureau as normally consisting of one or more entire counties, primarily nonagricultural and closely related to and including a central city, or cities, of 50,000 or more. Nearly two-thirds of the U.S. population is concentrated today in 233 metropolitan areas compared with only 55 per cent in 1940. Until the mid-1960's a majority of the residents of metropolitan areas lived in central cities; now the preponderance has shifted to the suburbs. (See Figure 1.)

Growth is still generally toward metropolitan areas. Between 1960 and 1966 their population increased 11 per cent compared to 6 per cent for nonmetropolitan

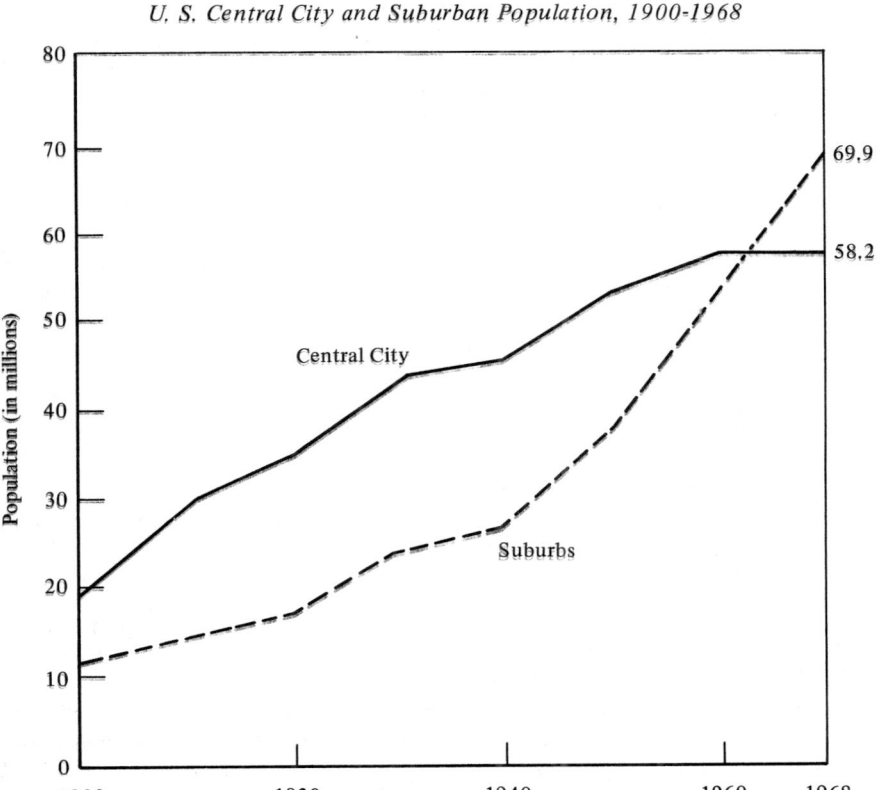

Figure 1

U. S. Central City and Suburban Population, 1900-1968

areas. By 1985 it is projected that more than 70 per cent of the population will live in metropolitan areas. The metropolitan areas of the Northeast represent the largest concentration of metropolitan population in the United States; they account for 79 per cent of the region's total population. The metropolitan areas of the West account for 72 per cent of the region's total population and are the fastest growing. Metropolitan population concentration in the North Central region is 60 per cent; in the South, 48 per cent.

There are metropolitan areas in 47 of the 50 states. Alaska, Vermont, and Wyoming have no population now defined as metropolitan. Eight states have at least 80 per cent of their population in metropolitan areas. These are led by Massachusetts with 97 per cent and California with 90 per cent. However, 28 states have less than 50 per cent of their population in metropolitan areas. (See Figures 2 and 3.)

At last count, there were 455 metropolitan counties. Nearly half of the nation's metropolitan areas consist of a single county. Fifteen metropolitan areas consist of five counties or more.

In 1967 the nation's metropolitan areas were served by 20,703 local governments, or about one-fourth of all the local governments in the United States. The average is 91 local governments per metropolitan area — 46 per metropolitan county. But these averages cover great extremes. The Chicago metropolitan area, for example, has 1,113 local governments (186 per county); the Philadelphia area has 871 (109 per county); the Pittsburgh area has 704 (176 per county); and the New York area has 551 (110 per county). At the other extreme there are 20 metropolitan areas with less than 10 local governments each.

In both population and physical size most local governments in metropolitan areas are extremely small. For example, two-thirds of the municipalities (usually cities, boroughs, villages, or towns) have a population of less than 5,000, and about half cover less than a single square mile of land area. Fewer than 200 municipalities cover as much as 25 square miles.

Most metropolitan residents are served by at least four separate local governments — a county, a municipality or a township, a school district, and one or more special districts whose functions range from garbage collection to mosquito control. Some, of course, are served by many more. The residents of Blue Island, Illinois, must contend with 13 separate, independent local governments.

Steps Toward Reform

In *Modernizing Local Government*, this Committee underscored the need for local government reform as follows:

> The bewildering multiplicity of small, piecemeal, duplicative, overlapping local jurisdictions cannot cope with the staggering difficulties encountered in managing modern urban affairs. The fiscal effects of duplicative suburban separatism create great difficulty in provision of costly central city services benefiting the whole urbanized area. If local governments are to function effectively in metropolitan areas, they must have sufficient size and authority to plan, administer, and provide significant financial support for solutions to area-wide problems.[2]

To this end we recommend thorough consolidation of the number of conflicting jurisdictions and competing tax units. We also propose that county governments — because they are less limited in area, population, and fiscal resources — be utilized where possible as the primary basis for consolidation.

Reshaping Government in Metropolitan Areas · 265

Figure 2
Standard Metropolitan Statistical Areas Defined by U. S. Bureau of the Budget to May 1, 1969

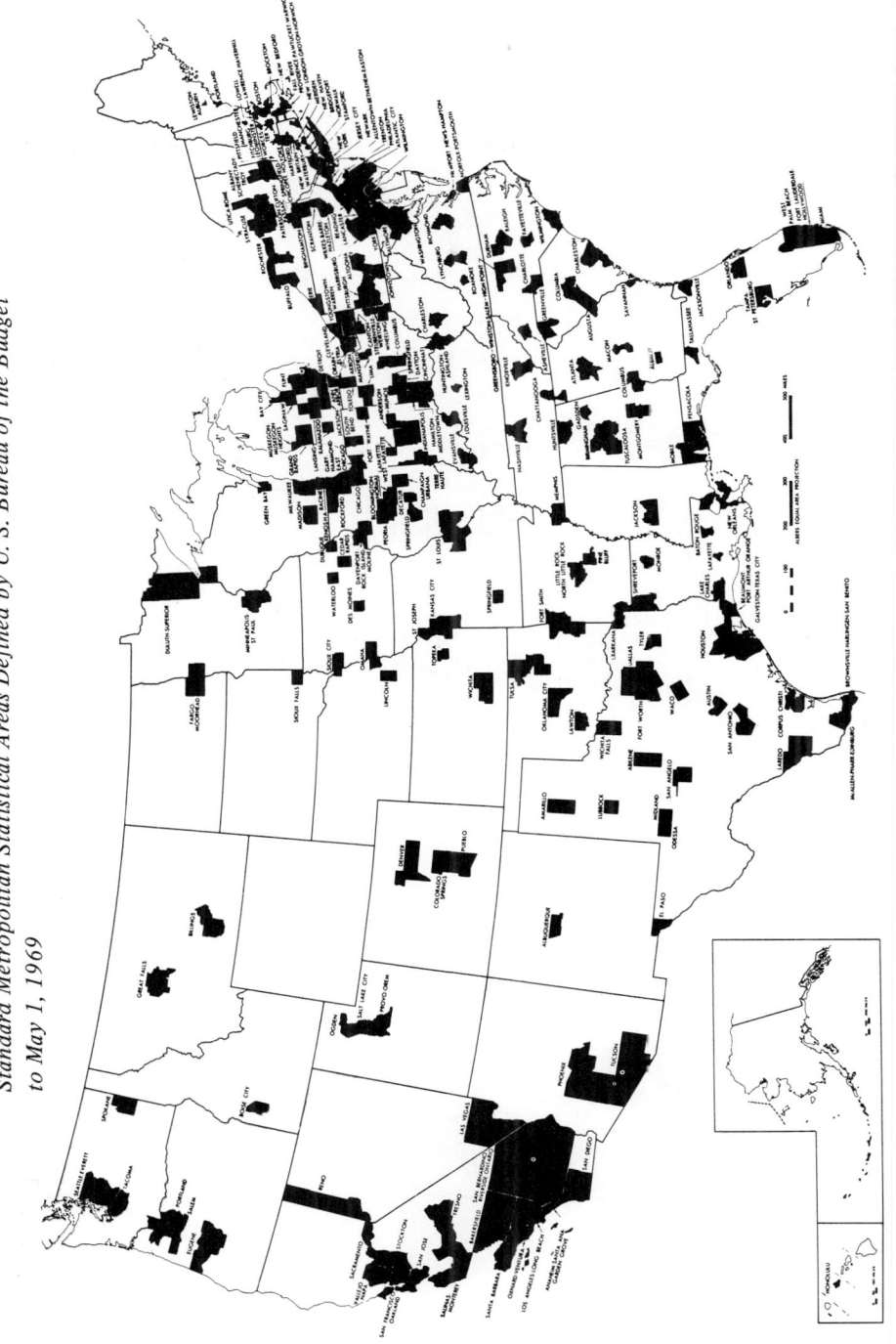

Figure 3

Proportions of State Population in Metropolitan Counties: July 1, 1966

Source: U. S. Bureau of the Census.

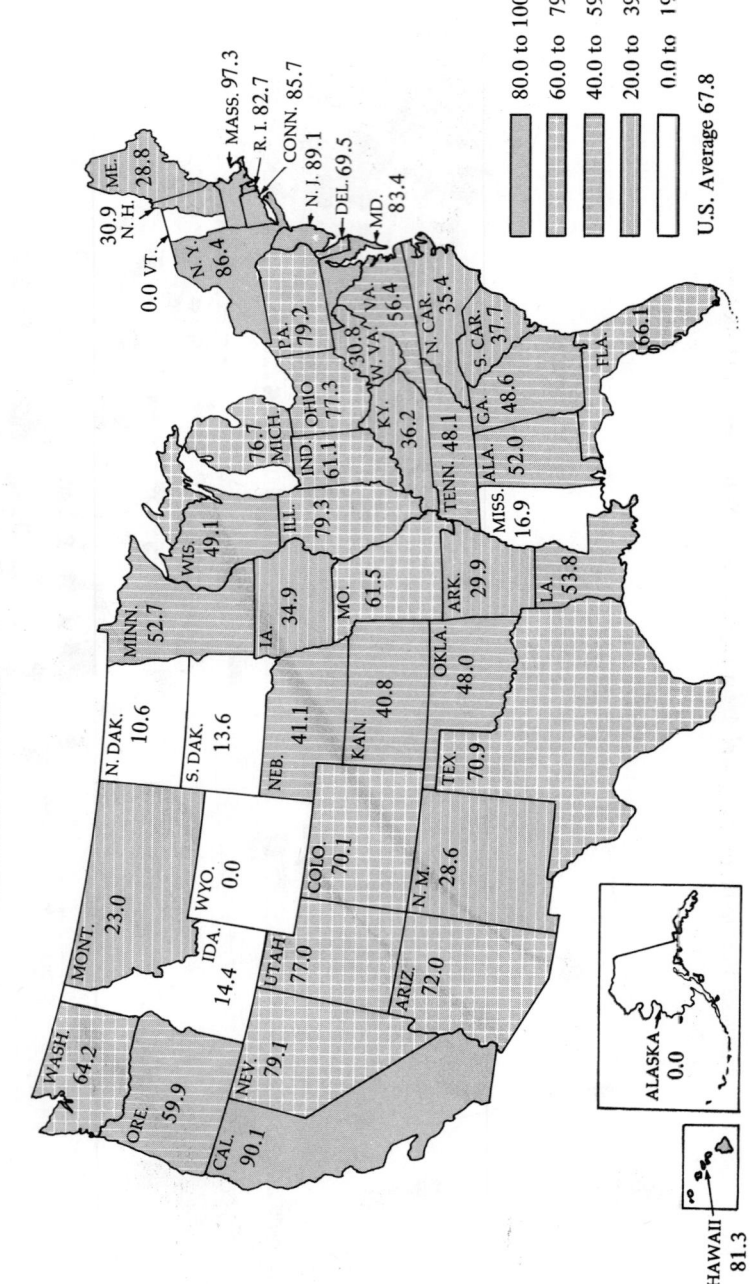

Aware of the need for change, enlightened business and civic leaders in metropolitan areas have spearheaded campaigns to replace small-scale, overlapping local governments with consolidated, federated, or other forms of metropolitan government. These campaigns have stressed the fact that the economic and social interdependence of metropolitan areas has created problems which can only be solved on an area-wide basis.

Centralization vs. Decentralization

Steps in the direction of area-wide government are not surprising when considered in their historical context. For nearly two centuries, American government has become increasingly centralized. Cities have expanded their boundaries by annexation. States have assumed new functions or have taken more responsibility for old ones. The national government has broadened its role in domestic affairs. Traditionally, much support for centralization has been based on the assumption that it leads to better, more responsive government and more humane social policies.

It may seem paradoxical, therefore, that today's growing support for decentralization should rest upon the same assumption. Much of the popular discussion of decentralization centers on current demands of black citizens for control over those institutions which most affect their lives, and for a stronger voice in the political process. The dialogue over black community control has focused public attention on many legitimate grievances of black citizens. The issue of decentralization, however, is not limited to the black community. White citizens, too, are impelled toward decentralized government (witness the suburban village) by some of the same factors that are motivating blacks: a desire for greater separatism and a stronger sense of local pride and community identity. Indeed, decentralization goes beyond questions of black and white. Its advocates see it as a means of humanizing government, giving the voter greater access to public services, more control over the bureaucracy which manages his affairs, and a more important role in decisions in which he has a stake.

The case for decentralization, however, cannot ignore the economic, technological, and social arguments which favor a centralized system. Small-unit governments are poorly equipped to take advantage of economies of scale and technological innovations; hence, they often find it more difficult to respond to the growing and desparate needs of their citizens. Proponents of centralization argue that the interests of the disadvantaged are best served by a larger rather than smaller unit of government. They point to the economic weakness of the ghetto, the historic conservatism of America's small communities, and the growing dependence on the federal government for social progress.

It is clear from the foregoing that what is needed is a system of government that adequately recognizes *both* forces, centralization and decentralization. Such a system must permit a genuine sharing of power over functions between a larger unit and a smaller unit. It must recognize a larger unit to permit economies of scale, area-wide planning, and equities in finance. It must recognize a smaller unit to permit the exercise of local power over matters which affect the lives of local citizens.

* * *

Some basic arrangements for sharing responsibility and power for individual functions between area-wide governments and community districts may be found in Chapter 4 of *Reshaping Government in Metropolitan Areas,* Committee for Economic Development, February, 1970. For each there is an area-wide component and a local component. However, no hard lines have been drawn between functions or between levels of government. The emphasis is on the *sharing of power* and not on the assignment of entire functions to either level.

SUMMARY OF RECOMMENDATIONS

All metropolitan areas are affected to a greater or lesser extent by the conflicting forces of centralization and decentralization. The interdependence of activities within metropolitan areas requires area-wide institutions for some functions or parts of functions of government. Just as clear is the need for units of government small enough to enable the recipients of government services to have some voice and control over their quality and quantity.

However, no two metropolitan areas are alike. Each has its own history and life style, and its own economic base. Both demographically and geographically, each differs from the other. For this reason, our proposals will not apply alike to all metropolitan areas. Each must examine its own capacity to govern and determine what particular organization suits it best.

It has been argued that the present governmental system already possesses the necessary combination of smallness and bigness. Small government already exists, at least in suburbia, and when area-wide action is needed, special districts may be created for the purpose. Further, the present system could govern effectively, it is often claimed, if only it had enough money.

None of these justifications for the present system is satisfactory. Uncoordinated area-wide special districts, fragmented by function, are no better than governments fragmented geographically. They do not permit a genuine regional approach to problems that are genuinely regional; nor do they create a system of decision-making and power-sharing capable of dealing with political conflicts. The state and federal aid solution within the present system has already been tried and so far has been found wanting.[3] Aid is badly allocated. Often it is wasted or assigned without proper priorities.

A Two-level Governmental System

In principle a governmental system for America's metropolitan areas must recognize the need for both a community level and a metropolitan level of government. There are many different governmental arrangements which will meet this need. As long as legitimate demands for centralization and decentralization are met, the specific arrangements may vary to fit the economic, cultural, and political characteristics of each area. Some may require greater emphasis on consolidation of local units; others may require greater emphasis on creating units which will enhance community participation.

Therefore, in the following proposals to achieve the dual advantages of a combined community-metropolitan governmental system, we would expect variations in application. In some areas a comprehensive solution may be feasible at an early date. In other areas achievement of an effective two-level system may require several steps over a period of time.

To gain the advantages of both centralization and decentralization, we recommend as an ultimate solution a governmental system of two levels. Some functions should be assigned in their entirety to the area-wide government, others to the local level, but most will be assigned in part to each level. More important than the division of functions is the *sharing of power*. Local communities will be assigned some power over functions placed at the area-wide level of government. Further, state and federal governments must be involved in most functions. This two-level system will not provide neatness and symmetry, but effectiveness, responsiveness, and adequate resources.

In those situations where the metropolitan area is contained within one county, a reconstituted county government should be used as the basic framework for a new area-wide government. This may, but need not, include consolidation of a large dominant central city with the county government in which it is located. If there are two or more sizable cities in the county, consolidation may not be appropriate. Counties in some states already have very wide powers. An indispensable requirement is the restructuring of such counties with a suitable legislative organ, a strong chief executive, and modern management.

In cases where the metropolitan area spreads over several counties or towns, a new jurisdiction should be created which embraces all of its territory. Although a federation of existing counties and towns might be considerably easier to implement, it is clear that rapid metropolitan growth makes a stronger jurisdiction considerably more appropriate, especially for purposes of long-range planning.

In addition to an area-wide level, modern metropolitan government should contain a community-level government system comprised of "community districts." These units might consist of existing local governments with functions readjusted to the two-level system, together with new districts in areas where no local unit exists. The new community districts should not be imposed from without, but created through local initiative by the simplest possible methods. A state boundary commission or similar body might be established to begin the process of delineating new districts. Citizen groups which seek community-district status might first make their appeal to this body if it is established.

In some cities there are areas which already possess strong community identity and these could become the new community districts. But in many cities, particularly the big cities, the sense of community is diminishing. Isolation and alienation, on the other hand, are increasing. Once the smaller political units are created — units with genuine power — a stronger sense of community is bound to emerge. In the suburbs, existing municipalities are likely to be retained as the community districts. Except in the most recently settled suburbs, these municipalities tend not only to represent "natural areas," but also to have well-developed community identities. Thus, local communities in both cities and suburbs can be guaranteed full participation within the metropolitan system.

Determining Size

A major difficulty in establishing community districts will be determining their size. Although much of the literature on government organization places heavy emphasis on appropriate size of minor jurisdictions, the fact is there is little hard economic evidence of what the optimum size should be. Therefore, how a community perceives its identity becomes important as well as the number of people it contains.

States should establish suggested, but not mandatory, criteria to guide the actual determination of community boundaries. The states should, in addition, set down requirements which will guarantee the representativeness of the government estab-

lished. Although the community districts should be allowed to determine their form of government — council, strong executive, commission, or some other form — the basic requirement of one-man, one-vote should be met.

State governments should assist the organization of community districts by enacting enabling legislation to permit the creation of a two-level form of metropolitan government and by establishing a procedure through which community districts may be created. Great flexibility as to size and governmental organization should be permitted.

The states should also prescribe guidelines for determining size and representation of the area-wide government. The practice exists in some metropolitan areas of representing community units — towns and villages — on an area-wide governing council. However, this form of representation rarely produces an area-wide point of view but rather a bargaining process through which the various smaller units try to protect their parochial interests. Therefore, we suggest that delegates to the area-wide government represent legislative districts on a one-man, one-vote basis instead of representing the community districts as such.

It is important to underline the full significance of the changes advocated here.

City boundaries would become less important than they now are. There would be a boundary surrounding each metropolitan area as well as boundaries surrounding community districts within each metropolitan area.

Financing the System: State and Federal Help

Reorganization of government in metropolitan areas will make it possible to increase over-all fiscal resources. America's wealth is concentrated largely in its metropolitan areas and metropolitan-wide government is advocated, in part, so this resource base may be preserved and improved. The existing system of overlapping local governments results in a poor match between needs and resources and perpetuates waste, inefficiency, and confusion.

Although the establishment of metropolitan-wide government will make possible a greater local fiscal contribution, it will by no means eliminate the need for substantial state and federal aid.

There is urgent need for a greater and more equitable state aid contribution and more attention by the states to the adequacy of their local governmental systems. The states have responsibilities for their local governmental systems. They should adapt their aid systems to the facts of metropolitanism and adjust the boundaries of local governments to fit current realities.

The states have the power to assume functions that are now performed locally, but few have assumed them. In some states, highways and welfare have become a major state responsibility, and a few municipal higher educational institutions have been taken over by the states. But there has been no major reshuffling of responsibilities to ease local fiscal burdens.

The response of the federal government to local fiscal problems has been more positive. The federal aid system, for example, through such programs as urban renewal, aid to education, and the anti-poverty program, is adjusting its assistance programs to the problems of the cities. It is possible that by giving more attention to the flow of aid the federal government will be able to help fill the gap left by the state aid program.

Both state and federal aid systems should be restructured in order to put resources where they are most needed. Equally important, state and federal aid should be used to stimulate government reorganization. The use of aid for this purpose has a precedent in its use in promoting school consolidation by the states. *Therefore, we recommend that state and federal aid should be used as an incentive to promote the kind of restructured government outlined in this statement.*

REFERENCES

1. See *Modernizing Local Government,* a Statement on National Policy by the Research and Policy Committee, Committee for Economic Development, New York, July 1966.
2. *Ibid.,* p. 44.
3. See *A Fiscal Program for a Balanced Federalism,* a Statement on National Policy by the Research Committee, Committee for Economic Development, New York, June 1967.

29 Metropolitan Growth and Regional Policy

JAMES L. GREEN
University of Georgia

Diversification is essential for a metropolitan region's growth and expansion. Excessive dependence on one export product not only makes an economy vulnerable to outside market conditions, but also inhibits secondary industries which serve to build up and to bind together a region. Diversity creates new ideas; new ideas create the incentive and energy for growth and expansion.

All metropolitan complexes harbor an agglomeration of people living in close proximity, a myriad of economic institutions, and interlocking political jurisdictions. In a general way this mix of people, firms, and government agencies create a similarity of problems, of needs, and of composition. However, the economic "basics" upon which the metro-complex developed engender shades of differences which aggravate growth problems, stimulate differences in approaches to growth and development, and determine the nature and direction of growth. These "basics" do not, in themselves, necessarily assure growth by their mere presence, singly or collectively, but they must be present if growth is to ensue.

Natural Resources

In the area of natural resources Pittsburgh and Birmingham represent metro-complexes oriented toward such resources as iron ore, coking coal, and limestone.

From "Metropolitan Growth and Regional Policy," *Metropolitan Economic Republics,* by James L. Green, Athens: University of Georgia Press, 1965, pp. 11–73. Reprinted with permission.

Growth based on the basic of natural resources has also made Birmingham one of the industrial agglomerations of the South.

Markets

If natural resources can be considered as one side of the metro-growth coin, then, market orientation must be the other as regards the location of economic activity. Atlanta represents a metro-complex deriving its place in the sun from market orientation. Located at the "end of the track" by the early engineers and surveyors seeking a way around the rugged Appalachian mountain range, Atlanta became a transportation crossroads for railroads going east and west and north and south. Today it is also a crossroads for arterial highways, communications, and airline traffic. At the heart of a major region of the national economy, Atlanta is today a major processing and distribution center, a financial center, a medical center, and a center of education for the heart of America's southland.

Human Resources

The ultimate source of economic success of any firm, metropolitan complex, or nation is correlated with the quality of its working population. Economic prosperity depends basically on the amount of work that is done and the efficiency with which it is done. It was not by accident that Detroit became the automobile capital of the world. At the time of the founding of the automobile industry Detroit was already industrialized and a center of gasoline and steam engine production. Mechanics with labor skills already developed were available to ply their trade in this advancing industry. The same orientation explains the location of much of the electronics industry in the northeastern United States in the past decade. The President's Council of Economic Advisors suggested that continued high levels of economic activity depend upon maintaining a high level of investment, a high level of basic and applied research, and a high level of education. The same, quite obviously, pertains with equal potency to the metropolitan complex as well as to the nation.

Energy and Power

Energy means power. Modern technology cannot function without adequate power. Early industrial development relied upon direct power from the waterfall. Today's transformation of water power into electric power adds mobility to power and has initiated substantial industrial development in Eastern Washington (Coulee Dam) and the Tennessee Valley (T.V.A.). And, of course, the internal combustion engine and steam generated electric power have abetted growth in those metropolitan complexes not so naturally endowed. Power, unquestionably, is a key and necessary resource for regional and metropolitan growth. Sound judgment in planning and implementing power requirements in a growing metropolis is even more important than proximity to natural power sites within the structure of modern power production and distribution technology.

The above "basics" are important considerations in site location for the individual firm as well as for entire industries. In every instance, private executive management balances relative advantages and disadvantages in the "mix" offered them in determining site location. Some type firms and industries are resource oriented; others are overwhelmingly market oriented; others compromise between the two (note the concentration of textiles in the industrial piedmont compromising effectively between cotton resource orientation and market orientation towards the industrialized and populated northeastern United States). What is required for sound growth is a diversified, balanced mix in each community sufficient to sustain continuing growth. It is in this respect that careful planning is necessary.

The concept of the old company town built upon a single product, operation, or process is well known. The sawmill town, the mining town, the textile town are examples of homogeneity. In a similar sense, Detroit may be considered an "automobile town," Texas City, Texas, a chemical town, Longview, Washington, a lumber and paper town. The economic trends in the City coincide with the economic trends in its specialized and particular supporting industry. This is not necessarily a handicap and may reflect broad specialization as per unique comparative advantages of the "basics" present in the complex. Nonetheless, economic dependency aggravates instability and sensitiveness to the fortunes or misfortunes experienced by firms and their products in markets far afield from the metrocomplex (note the problems of Duluth, Minnesota, as the Mesabi deteriorates). The economic health of the metro-region varies directly with variations in and vagaries of the national market, the particular industry, or the basic natural resource.

The forward looking metropolitan complex striving for balanced, self-sustaining growth seeks diversification. Thus the "mix" of basics generated should be planned and directed so as to meet the needs of primary industries, related servicing type industries, and supporting commercial and professional activities.

In this concept of the basic mix, we can classify patterns of economic activities supporting regional metropolitan complexes into three categories.

1. Primary Processes:
    a. Production: mining, agriculture, manufacture.
    b. Distribution: warehousing, transportation, marketing, communications.
2. General Business Service Processes:
    a. Financial institutions to service business and consumers.
    b. Insurance institutions to service business and consumers.
    c. Educational institutions to service business needs and to develop employee skills and aptitudes (both public and private).
    d. Managerial, legal, technical, engineering, and scientific advisory services.
3. Public Service Processes:
    a. Public and quasi-public capital support bases to service private enterprise needs as to site accessibility, transportation, power, communication, sewage and waste disposal, water and gas supplies, and the myriad other services required to meet the needs of primary and secondary business activities.
    b. Health and welfare.
    c. Protection of life and property.
    d. Recreation facilities.
    e. Education facilities (at all levels).
    f. Cultural facilities and outlets.

DIVERSIFICATION — THE CENTRAL CONCEPT

Diversification of the metro-economic pattern proceeds from those supporting and supplementary activities demanded by the primary industry and emanating from it in the regional complex. Basic iron and steel industries are oriented toward natural resources and support numerous foundary and fabricating type activities. The automobile industry is predominantly "skill and market" oriented as it fabricates, assembles, and distributes its product in national and international markets. The industry directly and indirectly accounts for one out of ten employed workers in the entire nation in terms of thousands of suppliers, dealers, and supplementary industries such as petroleum. Other urban agglomerations such as Minneapolis with its large concentration of milling companies process the food products of primary agriculture. Every basic industry establishes an institutional pattern reflecting its particular needs. Those metropolitan complexes which build upon several basic industries develop the more diversified economic base, provide a more stable, self-sustaining economic environment, and offer a broader economic base for secondary, service industry development.

Secondary service industries such as banking and finance, professional and technical services, and wholesale, transportation, and commercial activities build on the broader primary base. The stability of the base is enhanced by diversification which is the key to opening up the possibilities of economic growth. Diversification is a means of overcoming the inertia of the "one industry town" which frequently poses restraints upon self-sustaining, dynamic growth. Diversification also fosters further knowledge, augmented labor skills, and improvements in the inter-workings of industries.

Historically, urban development occurred as a result of the existing "mix of the basics." The mines were nearby, the natural harbor made transhipment a going business, the site was "on the railroad" or became a railroad center, or perhaps climatic conditions supported a given type agricultural pursuit and the embryo urban agglomeration with its mills, processes, brokers, etc. developed as an agricultural market outlet. Thus "natural" economic concentricity greatly influenced urban development and patterns.

Today, with modern technology, metropolitan diversified development is less restricted. The "mix of the basics" can be altered so as to change the comparative advantages. Atlanta was too late to catch the embryo automobile industry. It has, however, caught the overflow and expansion of the developing auto industry. Both Ford and General Motors have established large assembly plants in the area. Georgia is also diversifying its agriculture. Atlanta's urban neighbor, Gainesville, has become the "Chicken Broiler" capital of the world and the corn crop has replaced King Cotton as the leading farm income producer. In 1962 Georgia led the nation in the production of paperboard and was second only to Washington State in the production of wood pulp. That the Atlanta metro-complex has gained from this regional diversification is quite clear. This core metropolitan complex is growing in economic stature and strength as the regional hub or center.

Growth within the Atlanta metro-complex reflects its orientation toward diversification. Developments in the complex show forces pulling toward Birmingham to the southwest, Marietta, Rome, and Chattanooga to the north, Gainesville and Athens, and Augusta to the northeast, and Griffin, Columbus, and Macon to the south and southeast. These pulling forces stem from city sizes, their proximity to Atlanta, and their economic orientation in turn.

To the west, Atlantan tendrils reflect the economic "mix" and orientation of Birmingham. Thus, site location which facilitates accessibility to the source of varied iron and steel material needed for the processing of numerous consumer and business goods attract processing firms to western locations. Dense metropolitan traffic required of cross-town trucking is thus avoided. To the northeast we find storage, warehousing, wholesaling, and other distribution facilities seemingly pulled in this direction by the diverse industrial piedmont and the northeastern markets which lie beyond. Throughout the metropolis we find distinct residential areas and those market oriented professional and business services designed to serve the populace. The pattern is not fixed or rigid, but we could expect the kitchen utensil manufacturer or the office equipment processor to locate toward the west whereas the wholesaler and warehousing operation is more likely to be found on the other side of town.

The various Economic Republics comprising the Atlanta complex need to recognize the economic pulls influencing their growth and development. In time, a typical strip city will materialize between Atlanta and Birmingham. We will also see potential growth patterns toward the northeast with Atlanta, Athens, Gainesville, Anderson, Greenville, Charlotte and another toward Atlanta, Chamblee, Buford, and Gainesville, and yet another tendril encompassing Atlanta, Griffin, Barnesville, and Macon. This tendency toward intercity growth is strengthened by adequate planning, anticipation of new and growing markets, and provision of services which are adequate for the type economic mix that can be anticipated. Thus the "social or public" decision-maker can expect to find that his capital investment expenditures and planning have a growing importance to the development of his political jurisdiction. His decisions can so alter the basic "mix" as to promote a natural and sound economic growth or, if he laggardly allows growth "like topsy," he will be forever fighting fires stemming from coincident problems of growth which had not been anticipated because the nature of growth was not previously determined.

We thus return to the basic proposition that the flow of public investment funds must precede the flow of private investment funds. This premise now needs further amplification. A city must prepare for that type growth which existing economic pulls indicate are forthcoming. Modern technology allows some modification of the "basic mix," but public managers should plan their capital and operating base on "what comes naturally economically." This is done most effectively only if the public manager knows and understands the economic pushes and pulls impinging upon his developing community.

Through economic diversification the metropolitan complex gains in its industrial base, its human resource skills, and its market drawing power. In and through diversification lie the most feasible and greatest possible opportunities for balanced and stable economic growth and development. This is not to be taken as a pat solution for metropolitan or regional progress. However, as a guide, the pattern established by economic diversification provides the premise for sound and stable growth.

A growing enigma of affluent America today is the increasing hard core unemployment which is overwhelmingly centered in metropolitan super-urbanized areas. We have millions who are uneducated, unskilled, and unable to sell their labor services so as to survive in a highly monetized urban environment. In these people we have the resources that make a vibrant economy — resources yet uncultivated, undeveloped, and unable to participate in the stream of economic flows. As Representative Charles Weltner of Atlanta stated on the floor of the Congress, "The median income of the Negro in Georgia is $927 per year, while that of the white Georgian is $2,470. Unemployment among Negroes in the Georgia work force stands at 6 per cent, compared to 3.7 per cent for whites. . . . Here, among the poverty-stricken of the South, white and Negro, is an abundance of human resources, — undeveloped and unproductive. . . . Obviously, those families living on $20 a week cannot pay for the goods and services enjoyed by the average wage-earner. But what if they could? . . . Consumer needs in the South sustain over 7½ million non-agricultural jobs, notwithstanding the startling percentage of poor and poverty-stricken. If we could develop these resources, our people's newly derived purchasing power would easily call for more than one half million new jobs. . . . We in the South can follow the old ways or we can take a new departure. We can see every southerner — white or Negro — as a worthwhile citizen who can contribute something of value to the growth and well-being of our section."[1]

Neither the public nor the private economic decision-maker can deny the realities of the need for jobs — all types, variety, and nature of jobs — if we are to eliminate festering economic sores and social tensions in our metropolitan areas. In light of the labor skills at our disposal, we must cultivate both capital intensive and labor intensive job opportunities. Diversification is a primary means of broadening the labor market and of providing demands for all human resources — unskilled, skilled, and professional. Moreover, in 1963, 185,000 Georgians drew welfare or public assistance of some sort. If each of these persons were earning the median income of white Georgians, $2,470 per year, the State's economy would have been increased by almost half a billion dollars. If each of the 65,000 unemployed Georgians earned that median income, Georgia's total income would increase $160 million. If the 360,000 Negroes in Georgia who have jobs earned the median income of the white employed, Georgia's income would increase another half a billion dollars.

White Little Rock and New Orleans have gained national publicity by holding tenaciously to the old ways, both metropolitan complexes have paid in lost industry and deceleration of growth. Atlanta, on the other hand, has largely emerged unscathed from similar crises. In Atlanta's case, due to the new departure which the majority of its people and businesses have taken, economic growth appears to be accelerating.

FULL EMPLOYMENT AND REGIONAL POLICY

Neil Jacoby states one facet of the problem of full employment: "The Great Depression of the thirties left an indelible impression upon the minds of Americans who lived through these difficult years. The fact that millions of men and women were deprived of work opportunities for long periods, while their skills and their sense of personal dignity eroded in idleness, made full employment more important than any other goal."[2]

Implications in this statement led directly to passage of the Employment Act of 1946. Through this Act, maximum employment became a primary goal of national economic policy. The position taken here is that the goal of high employment levels is even more important at the local level where the human frustrations and economic stagnation coincident with forced unemployment are more directly encountered. Further, the local or regional problem of maintaining high employment levels is accentuated by the mobility of manpower. Movement into or out of any particular region accentuates employment problems irrespective of any national average. Five per cent unemployment across-the-board is usually taken as a danger signal at the national level. This figure is, however, an average. Regional unemployment figures may be far above or below the national average. Local officials must act on local conditions — not national averages.

Full Employment Considered

Within a changing economic structure, governmental policies and actions have contributed to the enlargement of demand for goods and services produced by the private sector. Governments at all levels, acting through the market, have contributed to improved technology and capital accumulation in the private sector. In terms of increasing productive capacity, the private sector has responded effectively. However, the relative level of employment has been in a downward trend for the past decade. This is not to say that the concept of full employment means zero unemployment. The exact meaning of full employment is left undetermined. Nonetheless, we all have a feel for what acceptable levels of unemployment are at any given place or time. As a generality, any figure above five per cent unemployment is unacceptable. Further, we need always to reconcile full employment standards with an elevation in the standard of living, with economic progress, and with individual freedom and human dignity. This means, not just jobs, but significant, productive, and satisfying employment. In terms of metropolitan regional economic health and social well-being, full employment is not only desirable, but is essential and necessary.

The Price of Full Employment

A position frequently encountered is that full employment, in a free, market-oriented economy, implies a costly inflation. This is a generality which must be supported with specifics. Are we referring to traditional inflation, i.e., an increase of money and credit at a rate so much above the rate of increase in the production of goods and services that real incomes actually decline? Or are we referring to such facets as cost-push inflationary pressures, demand-pull market price pressures, administered pricing powers, the proliferation of personnel in service type industries including government which tends to increase the overhead cost of operating the economy, or perhaps to deficit financing practices by both private firms and governments? What we mean when we use the term is of paramount importance in its policy implications. It is unquestionable that we have experienced some inflationary pressures in the last two decades. The pressures have, however, not come from any single source. More than this, the causes of inflationary pressures have been subject to considerable controversy in the past decade. We can observe that, at times, general price rises occur when aggregate demand rises without a corresponding increase in the supply of goods and services. Moreover, in some instances, rising prices have been apparent in industries with idle production capacity and excessively large inventories. Obviously, no clear-cut relationship between rising demand and "shortages" can be found to support a conclusion of demand-pull or cost-push inflationary pressures. While we can concur that true inflation caused by an accelerated expansion of the money supply beyond the needs of the economy is an unconscionable and unnecessary cost of growth, the other types or facets of general price level rises are relative costs and need to be analyzed in relation to the causes and alternative objectives being strived for.

At the same time there is considerable question as to whether or not these potential costs of full employment, and growth necessary to sustain full employment, have the same connotations at the regional level that they have at the national level. In the first place, these "costs" are endemic of a closed economy which is the case for the United States as a whole. On the other hand, the region is an open economy and the mobility of men, goods, and funds, including credit, is sufficiently free and responsive to incentives that price levels and resource availability tend to stay in line within the national market notwithstanding some stubborn and persistent regional differentials which have been subjected to much research and analysis.

Perhaps the foremost price we pay for urbanization is a loss of individual freedom. A part of this loss stems from our need to conform to the patterns of urban living. Our right to act freely and independently is limited by the rights of others. Another reason for less freedom and more limited action is that in an urbanized setting nearly all "things and activities" are monetized. Thus, we are increasingly dependent upon our ability to sell our labor services to provide income to make us free to participate in the economic market as consumers. These are two important facets limiting urban freedom as contrasted with rural life.

In the final analysis, local municipal governments can, more than any other level of government, impinge upon individual freedom. The City has powers to limit assembly and trespassing, and may pass judgment on the exercise of free speech. Agents of the City may possess powers to enter into, inspect, and pass judgment on a man's home, his place of business, and even pass upon the propriety of child care within the family unit. The City may decree behavior patterns governing the freedom to use publicly provided services. No other level of government does as much policing, makes more arrests, imposes more fines or in innumerable other ways lessens the exercise of individual freedom.

Despite these strictures imposed upon the individual, compact urbanized living offers the benefits of collective social consumption patterns. In the City, people collectively through local government and quasi-government public utilities, particularly, provide themselves with water systems, sewage systems, educational facilities, public health facilities, police and fire protection, streets and various modes of transportation, communication facilities, and the like. In this way, joint or collective social consumption requires that certain rules and regulations be administered uniformly. Persons must comply. On the one hand, this is a limitation of freedom. On the other hand, people are relieved of many basic drudgeries which, without collective consumption, would necessarily have to be individually borne. The important aspect for urbanized living does not seem to be the loss of freedom as much as the fact that the concept and pattern of the exercise of freedom change. If one can judge from the continuing migration of people from farms to the city, it would seem apparent that the amenities and opportunities found in urban living far outweigh the loss of individual freedom encountered.

Regional Policy Considerations

The concept of intensive monetization coincident with urban living gives more emphasis to the goal of high employment levels and to inflationary pressures. Both public and private officials at the local level need to modify and differentiate their decision-making processes as regards regional versus national problems. The problem of full employment as viewed from Washington, D.C. is not at all the same as viewed by local officials. The slope of the required rate of employment absorption line for the region is subject to marked aberrations from national averages due particularly to changes in the rates of in-migration or out-migration. Thus, the regional economic equilibrium may fluctuate widely with no problem being perceived in national average figures. As an example, the supply of housing, education, and other facilities may be subjected to swings of "shortages or surpluses" at the local level due to migration, which do not create a ripple at the national level.

Further than this, the federal legislators are concerned primarily with policy matters of broad economic environmental conditioning. That is, legislation at the national level is aimed primarily at providing incentives to the private sector through improving the general rules of the economic business game. Federal action and expenditures act primarily through the market rather than upon it. Decision-making processes in changing the "rules of the economic game" seldom encompass the same type maximization objective inherent in local public official decision-making.

This holds in so far as we can consider the existence of an interdependent relationship between the local public and private sectors. In the first place, local public and private officials need to "maximize" as a means of meeting the anticipated needs for specific goods and services. We must provide a given growth rate in jobs, in houses, in market facilities, in the myriad of public services anticipated for a growing population. This anticipation, itself, however, feeds an external conflict of interests which must be resolved by local officials. For a metropolitan regional area to remain dynamic, public investment funds must necessarily precede the flow of private investment funds. The sources of these funds must be those citizens and businesses who are presently members of the community. Thus, present citizens must assume the burden of expanding and anticipating the capital base to provide for future citizens who are expected to enter the labor force as private investment flows follow public investment flows and provide growing employment opportunities and growing markets. Local public officials are, in a real sense, expanding risk capital funds, for there is always the assumption that private growth in the community will follow. Growth may not follow the expenditures made and the financial burden placed upon present citizens may have been unwarranted. However, the desired growth in the private sector may well materialize. Large scale deficit financing undertaken by local governments to provide the necessary expanded capital social overhead base is one means by which local officials are able to pass the burden of capital expansion forward so that future citizens can participate in and share the public financial costs of expansion.

Metropolitan economic prosperity is an essential requisite of our national and regional life. By the turn of the century it is anticipated that some seventy per cent of a projected three hundred and fifteen million U.S. citizens will live in some fifty primary metropolitan complexes. Physically, these metropolitan units cross state lines in many instances. Economically, these super-urbanized complexes extend their influences regionally and nationally. State boundaries, like those of localized governmental units within the metropolitan complex, are economically erased, except in so far as they impede, limit, or reallocate the utilization and economizing of resources and the various economic flows of men, incomes, goods, credit, and communications. Present trends toward super-urbanization constitute a profound redesigning of political and economic power centers. Metropolitan complexes are not explicitly modeled after state structures nor county structures nor even single city structures. Yet metropolises are fast becoming a fourth major level of government. The regional Economic Republic concept is taking form and an increasing amount of attention is being given this phenomenon. Whether we direct our attention to the physical planning aspects of rapid transit, industrial parks, highway networks, public utility expansion, or to the social problems of urban renewal, juvenile delinquency, education, or perhaps technological destruction of jobs and the obsolescences of human skills, or the like, we can readily observe that the basic integrating thread of all alternative actions seems always to be *economic feasibility*.

In turn, economic feasibility is an inherent inter-dependent variable of maximum employment and income flows. This is easily recognized in the market-oriented private sector. In the public sector the objectives of maximum levels of employment and income contain answers to fiscal problems, to social problems, and to the problems of freedom in an environment in which specialization and interdependency rule and all the good things in life are monetized.

REFERENCES

1. Charles L. Weltner, "The War Against Poverty," *Congressional Record,* January 28, 1964.
2. Neil H. Jacoby, *Can Prosperity Be Sustained?,* p. 17.

30 Exports and Regional Economic Growth

CHARLES M. TIEBOUT
Northwestern University

The theory of the regional economic base — which holds that the economic activities of a region are divided between industries producing for export and industries producing for the local market; and then uses the ratio between the two, measured in income or employment, as a multiplier — may be an oversimplification, especially for larger, more complex areas.

I

The theory of the regional economic base has been bobbing around in the literature, implicitly and explicitly, for some time.[1] Its latest appearance comes as an explanatory factor in regional economic growth. In his recent article Douglass C.

From "Exports and Regional Economic Growth," by Charles M. Tiebout, *Journal of Political Economy,* April 1956, pp. 160–164. Copyright © 1956, The University of Chicago. Reprinted with permission.

North has suggested that the theory of regional development which sees the region as passing through various stages — primary, secondary, and tertiary — is not adequate.[2] As a substitute, North maintains that a region's growth "is closely tied to the success of its exports and may take place either as a result of the improved position of existing exports relative to competing areas or as a result of the development of new exports."[3] He further points out that it is necessary to look into location theory to explain changes in the export base. The point involved is that the concept of the export base in regional analysis is called on as the major autonomous variable determining the level of regional income.

The concept of the economic base has been developed largely in the works of city planners and other researchers interested in urban problems.[4] As such — and this is neither slur nor praise — no attempt has been made to relate this concept to the general theory of income determination as used in national income analysis.[5] This failure and the continual identification of the exports of a region with the autonomous variable determining income have led to some erroneous conclusions about regional income and regional development. The purpose of this note is, first, to show how the export-base concept fits within the more general theory of income determination and, second, using this setting as a frame of reference, to point out some implications for the theory of regional growth.

II

It is useful to begin by presenting a simplified version of the concept of the export base. The economic activities of a region are divided into those which produce for the export market and those which produce for the local market. In defining exports allowance is made for such items as the earnings of commuters, capital flows, government transfers, and linked industries. Given these basic or export activities, the level of non-basic or residentiary activities follows. The ratio between export activities and residentiary activities, measured in income or employment, is then used as a multiplier. For example, a one-to-one ratio would mean that an increase in exports will cause an equal increase in residentiary activities. Whether or not this function is constant at all levels of income is not stated. There is no *a priori* reason to believe it is. From here, of course, it is a simple step to the statement that the income of the region is tied to the level of exports. For a small region this may be substantially correct, but for larger regions it is an oversimplification. A general theory of income determination at the national level rests on a knowledge of the level and stability of both the dependent and the autonomous variables. These are the necessary ingredients of an economic model that forecasts income.[6]

There is no reason to assume that exports are the sole or even the most important autonomous variable determining regional income. Such other items as business investment, government expenditures, and the volume of residential construction may be just as autonomous with respect to regional income as are exports.[7] Under the assumption, which may have some validity, that the autonomous variables are the dynamic factors in determining the short-run level of regional income, these items may even be the chief source of instability. Only empirical studies will enable us to say something about their quantitative importance.

A further consideration will help to point up the error of identifying exports as the sole source of regional income change. In an exchange economy one person considered in a spatial context may be entirely dependent on his ability to export his services. Probably this is true of a neighborhood area, except for the corner grocer. For the community as a whole, the income originating in non-exports increases. In the United States economy, exports account for only a small part of national income. Obviously, for the world as a whole, there are no exports.

Thus the quantitative importance of exports as an explanatory factor in regional income determination depends, in part, on the size of the region under study. It is true that for a region considered at two different time periods, a change in the volume of exports may indicate a change in the level of income, but this is not enough. A region may grow with exports at a constant level, if internal autonomous activities are on the upswing. The larger the region, the more the dynamic forces causing income change will be found inside its borders.

The problem that arises because export volume is a function of regional size might be solved if it were possible to find some method of determining the boundaries of a region which not only made sense but allowed for interregional comparisons. North has suggested that the boundaries of a region should be determined by "its development around a common export base."[8] This basis of classification is useful, but it is by no means the only possibility.

Most researchers in the field of regional economics have come to the conclusion that there is no "ideal" region. Probably the closest approximation to the concept of an ideal region would arise in a Lösch production-oriented spatial system.[9] In this system an over-all area is mapped out according to sites of production determined by market networks. Other conditions which are also given for equilibrium need not concern us here. In the central city all goods are produced, with fewer produced in the other spatially arranged cities. If an over-all area, in this sort of orientation, could be divided into two or more identical parts, either one might be considered an "ideal" region[10] Any statement concerning the nature of one region would be applicable to any other. Unfortunately, in the nature of market networks even in the conceptual construct, such regions do not exist. Given this Lösch mapping, it follows that regional boundaries are not clear-cut and any statement concerning the importance of exports must keep this in mind.

In view of our inability to construct an "ideal" region, the selection of regional boundaries rests on other criteria. Usually, the regional boundaries are suggested by the variables one chooses to study. Non-economic considerations, such as the availability of data and the location of political divisions, may, of course, be the basis for the demarcation of a region. The important point is *not* which boundaries are chosen but the effects of this choice on the variables under study. If the researcher is aware at least of the direction of changes in the variables as a function of regional boundaries, the question of boundaries is of less importance. For example, increased regional size, with more internal trade, implies that the quantitative importance of exports decreases.

Perhaps the most surprising feature of the concept of the export base of a region is that no one, to my knowledge, has attempted to integrate this concept into the traditional foreign-trade multiplier analysis. The works of Metzler, Machlup, and Stolper are conspicuous by their omission from the discussions.[11] Usually the economic base of a region of any size from an urban area up to several states is merely assumed to be exports. Implicitly, no foreign-trade multiplier feed-back is assumed. This is probably valid for smaller areas, but for larger areas the feedback can be an important factor. An example may illustrate this point.

Consider the exports of New England. Like those of any other region, its exports compete with products from elsewhere. Thus one expects and finds that export receipts fall off as a function of distance.[12] Few of the region's exports enjoy a world-wide market. The New York area would be expected to absorb a much higher percentage of New England's exports than would a market of equal size in the Far West. Conversely, the New England area would tend to absorb a greater percentage of New York's exports than would a more remote market.

Contrast this situation with that of a mill town. Here the exports may be considered as going off into some distant space. The income of the mill town will be affected by the income of its market, but the income of the market will not be affected by the income of the mill town. This merely places the mill town in the same position as the competitive wheat farmer who is too small to affect the market but is affected by it. In this case there is no foreign-trade multiplier feedback. This is not true in the regional case, and one is left in the uncomfortable position of having exports in part a function of domestic income. Thus in the short run it appears that the determination of regional income depends only in part on the region's exports. The larger the region under consideration, the smaller the role of exports. Other variables in the structural equations must be considered if income stability is to be more fully understood.

III

The concept of the export base, or even the fuller concept of regional income determination which includes other autonomous variables, is a short-run concept. As such it may be fairly accurate. Our knowledge of consumer behavior and the relative ease of entry into residentiary activities, such as baking and retailing, indicate that this may be a fairly safe assumption, at least for small regions. To extend this relationship to the question of regional development, however, can be dangerous.

Before we consider the question of the export base in regional development, one issue should be cleared up. It involves a difference between regional growth and economic development in general. Suppose that we assume that general economic development means raising the per capita income of some area, say North America. Further, let us define regional growth as the rate of change of per capita income in some segment of this totality, say Canada. It is pertinent to ask whether these should be considered as presenting the same sort of problem. If we imagine that the continent had developed without Western influence, but assuming capitalism, some process of primary, secondary, and tertiary evolution might be expected to have taken place just as it did, in general, in the development of Europe. True, some areas might have specialized in agricultural activities; but if the concept of regional balance means anything, specialized areas of manufactures would be expected. If some island economy, unknown to the rest of the world, were studied as a case of economic development, the stage concept might be quite valid.

This sort of analysis should not be called on, however, to deal with questions of regional economic growth, which presents a different sort of problem. If a new peninsula were formed off the New Jersey coast, it would provide an ideal setting for studying regional economic growth. In this case there is no reason to expect the peninsula area to pass from the primary-subsistence to the secondary-tertiary stage as real incomes increase. If, as North points out, the region can develop an export base, it may develop in a variety of forms. It could become a center for truck gardens (primary); a site for manufacturing (secondary); or a vacation area (tertiary). Note that this does not imply that it will develop even if it *seems* to have an export base, for reasons to be discussed later. The important point about the New Jersey example is that we are dealing with a region in the neighborhood of more advanced areas. The degree of specialization and of exporting will depend on the market. The higher the incomes in the neighboring areas, given the propensity to import, the higher the volume of their imports, that is, the exports of the peninsula. The volume of exports and, in turn, internal growth will depend not only on the factor endowment but also on the income of the surrounding area. It is useful to keep this distinction in mind when contrasting regional economic growth with economic development in general.[13]

The idea that essentially the export base is the necessary and sufficient condition for regional economic growth may be, by definition, a true statement. Given the transport network, the size and location of markets, and factor endowments, it appears that a region will develop if it can compete with other regions in the export market. This implies an ability to produce at lower cost. With factor mobility, growth will take place only if the return to the factors is equal to, or greater than, the return to the same factors in other regions. If this is what is meant by the ability to develop an export base, it is correct by definition, but it does not uncover enough to predict growth. Ability to find an export base depends not only on the value of the units of output but on the cost of the inputs. These costs cannot be assumed to be equal for all regions. Yet, if residentiary activities are assumed to be endogenous and are not considered as a factor in regional growth, the analysis will implicitly assume that all unit factor costs are equal among regions. Put another way, it is possible to define the necessary condition for regional economic growth as the creation of an export base. But location theory, which is called on to explain its creation, will work only if factor costs are known. The determination of factor costs depends in part on the nature of the region's residentiary activities.

An example may serve to illustrate this point. Going back to our hypothetical New Jersey peninsula, assume that a coal deposit is found some two hundred miles out on the peninsula. Will it be mined to compete in the New York market with Pennsylvania coal? Make one further assumption about the region. Assume that the rest of the area is all sand and marshland. If workers are to mine this newly found deposit, they must eat, and hence there must be imports. If the cost of these imports is high enough, no coal will be mined, and no export base will develop.

Contrast this with a situation in which the peninsula is rolling, fertile countryside. Truck gardening and dairy farming can develop. Some imports will still flow in, but some local needs — vegetables and milk — will be supplied locally, that is, supplied by residentiary activities. Under these conditions coal may be mined because of the lower cost of production, in this example lower dollar wages.[14]

Again, formally speaking, it is the ability to develop an export base which determines regional growth. Yet in terms of causation, the nature of the residentiary industries will be a key factor in any possible development. Without the ability to develop residentiary activities, the cost of development of export activities will be prohibitive.

The objection may be raised that this is a special case. No claim is made for general validity. However, if one seeks to explain the failure of certain parts of Alaska or Canada to develop, this consideration may uncover a more complete picture. Further, it is well known that cities usually develop in locations that are surrounded by good lands and not in the middle of less fertile areas.

However, the idea of the export base is more useful when applied to certain areas, such as satellite cities in the suburban fringe. Here low transport costs and proximity to markets insure that, even if residentiary activities do not develop fully, their outputs can be imported from near-by areas. The larger the region under consideration, the less safe the assumption.

A final point is in order concerning regional growth and the ratio of export to residentiary activity. Given its population, boundaries, transport network and costs, markets, and factor endowment, a region must divide its energies between residentiary and export activities. If too little is devoted to one or the other, the economy will not be maximizing per capita income. Supposedly there is some optimum division. If export activities are relatively too large, it will pay to move resources into residentiary industries (witness the enviable position of the storekeeper during the gold rush), and the region's income will increase. Here we find an example in which regional growth is possible with a reduction of exports.

IV

This note has tried to show that the concept of the export base is merely one aspect of a general theory of short-run regional income determination. In the case of large regions, other variables may play as important a role as exports. Furthermore, the concept of the export base may be useful in describing regional income growth, but this need not be considered the same problem as general economic development. As an explanatory factor in regional growth, the idea of the export base should not subsume the key role of residentiary activities in determining factor costs of possible regional exports. Finally, since a region must optimize the use of factors as between exports and residentiary outputs, a decline in export activity may even be accompanied by rising regional income.

REFERENCES

1. See Richard B. Andrews, "The Mechanics of the Urban Base," *Land Economics,* Vol. XXIX (1953), No. 3 (continuing series). For a more explicit statement see George Hildebrand and Arthur Mace, Jr., "The Employment Multiplier in an Expanding Industrial Market: Los Angeles County, 1940–47," *Review of Economics and Statistics,* XXXII, No. 3 (August, 1950), 241–49.
2. "Location Theory and Regional Economic Growth," *Journal of Political Economy,* LXIII (June, 1955), 243–58.
3. *Ibid.,* p. 251.
4. See Richard Andrews, "The Mechanics of the Urban Economic Base: Historical Development of the Base Concept," *Land Economics,* XXIX (August, 1953), 161–67; and Homer Hoyt, "Homer Hoyt on the Concept of the Economic Base," *Land Economics,* XXX (May, 1954), 182–86.
5. It is interesting to note that the work of Hildebrand and Mace (*op. cit.*), which deals with an employment multiplier, is rarely mentioned in discussions of the economic base. North's article is a notable exception.
6. See Lawrence Klein, *Econometrics* (Chicago: Row, Peterson & Co., 1953).

7. North's consideration of the possible outlets of a region's indigenous savings suggests these considerations (*op. cit.*, p. 255).
8. *Ibid.*, p. 257.
9. August Lösch, *The Economics of Location* (New Haven: Yale University Press, 1954).
10. In terms of set theory, this implies that the over-all area can be partitioned into disjoint subsets which map one-to-one into each other.
11. Lloyd A. Metzler, "Underemployment Equilibrium in International Trade," *Econometrica*, X (April, 1942), 97–112; Fritz Machlup, *International Trade and the National Income Multiplier* (Philadelphia: Blakiston Co., 1943); Wolfgang Stolper, "The Volume of Foreign Trade and the Level of Income," *Quarterly Journal of Economics*, LXI (February, 1947), 285–310.
12. See Walter Isard and Merton Peck, "Location Theory and International and Interregional Trade Theory," *Quarterly Journal of Economics*, LXVII (February, 1954), 97–114.
13. The development of the Pacific Northwest and the Canadian development cited by North (*op. cit.*, p. 246–47) may be analogous to the New Jersey example. Both occurred after the process of industrialization was under way. In contrast to this case, the position of the earliest colonies typifies the case of general economic development. Of course, this is a matter of degree and should not be taken as a statement that exports were unimportant to the early colonies.
14. In both cases the real wages of the coal miners would be the same, but in the former case, because of the high cost of living, dollar wages would be higher. In location theory it is the dollar cost which determines location and development.

31 A Reply — to Professor Tiebout

DOUGLASS C. NORTH*
University of Washington

To long-run economic growth, regional economic base theory applies. For, the ability of a region to sell to other regions determines its ability to attract the capital and skilled labor essential to its growth.

Professor Tiebout's comment is a welcome addition to the literature on regional economic growth. The role of the export base in regional development requires further analysis, and Tiebout has raised some important questions that merit discussion.

The bulk of his criticism of the role of the export base in regional growth hinges on one critical point at issue between us. His is a *short-run* analysis, in which the export base is conceived to be only one of a number of important factors in income determination. I have no quarrel with this position, but it has little relevance for

From "A Reply," by Douglass C. North, *Journal of Political Economy,* April 1956, pp. 243–258. Copyright © 1956, The University of Chicago. Reprinted with permission.

my article, which was explicitly concerned with *long-run* economic growth. Short-period income determination and long-run economic growth are not the same thing. In the former case the analysis is concerned with changes in the level of employment and the variables that will affect the rate of utilization of productive factors. In this case increased business investment will result in expanded employment and income in periods of less than full employment. Such analysis, however, has little relevance for long-run economic growth, where the objective is to determine the factors that will affect the decade-to-decade changes in the real aggregate and per capita income of an area under conditions of full employment. In the latter case secular expansion comes about because of increased output per unit of resources or an increase in the supply of productive factors, or both. Historically, this increase in labor and capital has come about as a result of long-run expansion of the demand for productive factors within the area. Not only has there been mobility of productive factors within the American economy, but also during a substantial period of our growth there has been international mobility of capital and labor for the entire Atlantic economy. Therefore, while the study of short-run income determination has been concerned with the rate of utilization of productive factors, the study of long-run growth has dealt with the determinants of changing efficiency and the immigration of labor and capital into an area. The variables used in income analysis are of limited use in the study of long-run growth. Indeed, the aggregates used tend to obscure rather than to illumine the factors generating secular expansion. An examination of Tiebouts major points will further clarify this distinction and highlight some important problems for further research.

I

Tiebout and I are in agreement that there is no "ideal" region. Since he concedes that the question of boundaries is of less importance if the researcher is aware of the significance of increased regional size, there is no apparent difference in our position. Yet one point requires emphasis. The usefulness of a region as an economic unit of analysis rests upon its specialization. It is this geographic division of labor, with different areas having special factor endowments and transfer costs, which makes the concept of the region valuable in economic analysis. The region's significance lies in its being a specialized part of the whole. If the size of the region is to be limited by its individual economic characteristics, then the concept of a geographically contiguous area held together by its development around a common export base is a useful (though certainly not the only) basis of classification. It has the added advantage that, in terms of the long-run growth of different areas in America, the export base has been influential in shaping a good deal of the history of the region.[1] Such a classification necessarily limits the size of the region and minimizes the problems raised by Tiebout.

II

Given the region as defined, the role of the export base in regional growth may now be more precisely delineated. Tiebout and I are in agreement that it is not the sole source of regional growth,[2] but we are in disagreement when he states that it may not even be the most important factor in regional expansion. An examination of the differential rates of growth of regions throughout America's development inevitably focuses on the ability of areas to attract productive factors. Initially it was the rich land and resources capable of producing extractive goods in demand in existing markets which were the primary attractions. At a later date, with changing factor combinations and technological developments, it was frequently the opportunities in manufacturing for the United States market which led to immigration of labor and capital into a region. The important point is that the pull of economic opportunity as a result of a comparative advantage in producing goods and services in demand in existing markets was the principal factor in the differential rates of growth of regions.

Since residentiary industry depends on income within the region, the expansion of such activity must have been induced by the increased income of the region's inhabitants. Therefore, increased investment in residentiary activity is primarily induced investment as a result of expanded income received from outside the region, and, correspondingly, expanded employment in locally oriented industry, trade, and services primarily reflects long-run changes in income received from the export base.[3] The qualifications to this argument require examination in order that the significance of the export base in regional growth may be properly evaluated.

1. Disproportionate federal government expenditures in a region (as compared with tax withdrawals) can serve and have served as a cause of regional expansion. Not only may the character and amount of federal expenditure in a region be expansive, but also investment in social overhead facilities in a new area may alter its competitive position with other regions.

2. Migration for non-economic reasons may lead to expansion of residentiary activity without any expansion of the export base. In a high-income society such as ours the lure of pleasant living conditions — "amenities," to use Professor Ullman's term[4] — has been a force attracting immigrants (with capital) into California and other areas and leading to an expansion of residentiary activities.

3. The relationship between residentiary activity and imports changes in the course of regional development. With the opening up of a new area, almost everything must initially be imported. Gradually, residentiary activity increases until locational factors effect a balance between imports and locally oriented economic activity at a given level of technology and transfer costs. Since techniques and transportation have undergone radical changes over time, this relationship has been subject to important changes. Moreover, as a region's population and income grow, its regional market will become large enough to make it feasible to produce some goods and services locally which had previously been imported.[5]

Clearly, therefore, residentiary activity does not play a purely passive role in regional growth. Tiebout's point about factor costs is a good one. Both the nature of the supply curve of labor and the level of transfer costs are important determinants of the ability of a region to produce export commodities. Typically, new regions have been opened up and developed because they had such a tremendous advantage in natural-resource endowments that they could produce and market their export commodities at a cost competitive with other areas despite this disadvantage in labor and transfer costs (and in the case of the earlier development of American regions, when institutions for financial mediation were immature and capital was less mobile, higher capital costs as well). The subsequent inflow of capital and labor and the development of social overhead facilities typically reduced these cost disadvantages and made it possible to produce other export commodities whose comparative resource advantages were somewhat less pronounced. However, when the growth of residentiary industry is "stunted" and transfer costs remain high, then the export base will not expand in this manner. Alaska is an excellent case in point.

This examination of the major alternative sources of regional growth clearly indicates their secondary importance as compared with the export base in long-run regional growth. The first two qualifications are exceptional in character, while the third, though more important, is clearly not a primary determinant of growth but rather a factor that will exert some influence upon a region's rate of growth.[6] Any analysis of the secular growth of a region must be primarily focused on the success of its export base, and Tiebout's contribution here has been to point out some of the factors that must be considered.[7] However, his discussion of short-run factors in income determination, significant though these may be in determining the level of employment (or effecting a shift in resources in the case of full employment), is irrelevant to the analysis of long-run regional economic growth.

III

Tiebout's distinction between regional growth and economic development in general is surely a spurious one. It is hard to conceive of the economic growth of one region which would not favorably affect the per capita income of the nation as a whole (even though it might have adverse effects upon another region). In fact, America's entire development has illustrated this relationship. Growth has been generated in particular geographic areas which, as a result of favorable factor endowments and transfer costs, could produce goods in demand in existing markets. Whether it was the opening up and development of a new region in the West capable of producing wheat for the world market or the development of an industrial region in the eastern and central states producing manufactured goods for the domestic market, the result in each case was to attract labor and capital (from Europe as well as internally) not only into the expanding export industry but also into a wide variety of residentiary activities to meet the expanding needs of the region's population. The process of urbanization, which was an integral part of the growth of manufacturing regions, was as expansive in its effects as was the opening up of new regions, their development, and their assimilation into the economy. In both cases the expansion of the region required a vast increase in imports from outside the area. The result was to induce investment throughout the rest of the economy. The multiplier-acceleration process that resulted was an essential part of America's economic growth.[8]

Tiebout's footnote about the difference between the later development of Canada and the Pacific Northwest, when there were well-developed markets, and the case of general economic development which typified the American colonies is, to the best of my knowledge, likewise incorrect. America was settled partly for the explicit purpose of producing goods in demand in the expanding European market. The prosperity of the colonies did not rest upon subsistence farms but resulted from the rich land and resources of the New World, which could produce tobacco, rice, indigo, ships, fish, cereals, and other products that were in growing demand in England, Europe, and the West Indies. The whole development of the New

World has been within the context of the rapidly expanding Western world, and the prosperity of the colonists reflected the growth of income throughout the North Atlantic economy, which resulted in an expanding demand for their services (particularly important in the case of New England) and commodities.

REFERENCES

* I am indebted to my colleagues Philip Cartwright and Donald Gordon for suggestions which have clarified some of the points at issue in this discussion.
1. A brief account of the role of the export base in shaping the character of a region's economy is given in my article, "Location Theory and Regional Economic Growth," *Journal of Political Economy,* LXIII (June, 1955), pp. 249–51.
2. See the qualifications in my article, *ibid.,* p. 250, n. 34.
3. The employment multiplier has been conceived by Hildebrand and Mace ("The Employment Multiplier in an Expanding Industrial Market: Los Angeles County, 1940–47," *Review of Economics and Statistics,* Vol. XXXII, No. 3 [August, 1950]) to be primarily of use in short-run analysis. However, the study by the Federal Reserve Bank of Kansas City of "The Employment Multiplier in Wichita" (*Monthly Review, Tenth Federal Reserve District,* Vol. XXXVII, No. 9 [September 30, 1952]) strongly suggests that residentiary employment does not adjust to short-run changes in employment in export industries but does reflect long-run movements in export employment.
4. Edward Ullman, "A New Force in Regional Growth," *Proceedings of the Western Area Development Conference, November 17, 1954* (Palo Alto, Calif.: Stanford Research Institute, 1955).
5. The changing character of residentiary activity with regional growth requires further research both in expanding regional markets and in the historical development of regions where changing technology and transfer costs have changed the character of residentiary goods and services.
6. Tiebout's final point deals with the possibility of regional growth with a decline in exports. This is conceivable but flies in the face of the experience of growing nations, where international trade has typically increased with rising incomes rather than the reverse.
7. In this regard the changing terms of trade of a region have been important. Regions whose export base consists primarily of agricultural commodities have been particularly affected.
8. James S. Dusenberry has an excellent account of this entire process in his article, "Some Aspects of the Theory of Economic Development," *Explorations in Entreprenurial History,* Vol. III, No. 2 (December, 1950).

32 The Economic Impact — Industrial and Regional — of an Arms Cut

WASSILY LEONTIEF
Harvard University

ALISON MORGAN
Harvard University

KAREN POLENSKE
Harvard University

DAVID SIMPSON
Harvard University

EDWARD TOWER
Harvard University

The input-output method of measuring economic impact was developed in the 1930's by Professor Leontief, from the ideas of a French economist. The method is an extension of conventional supply and demand analysis, with a table or "matrix" arrangement for lining up all supply elements and comparing them with all demand elements for a particular region or sector within an economy. Like most other economic tools, input-output analysis, to be useful in urban problems, must be followed by policy recommendations. Here, Professor Leontief's study suggests: the federal government offer civilian contracts to regions from which military contracts are withdrawn.

I. THE PROBLEM AND ITS ANALYTICAL FORMULATION

1. The object of the computations described in this paper was to determine what effect a hypothetical reduction in military accompanied by a compensating increase in non-military demand would have on the industrial composition and regional distribution of employment in the continental United States. By compensation is meant the maintenance of the total level of employment in the economy.

In a paper published four years ago,[1] input-output analysis was used to estimate the effect of such a change in the structure of final demand on the industrial distribution of the labor force for the country as a whole. The present study carries

---

From "The Economic Impact — Industrial and Regional — of an Arms Cut," by Wassily Leontief, Alison Morgan, Karen Polenske, David Simpson, and Edward Tower, *The Review of Economics and Statistics*, Volume 47, August 1965, pp. 217–228. Reprinted with permission.

that inquiry one step further. The impact of the hypothetical shift from military to civilian demand is projected here not only in inter-industrial, but also in inter-regional terms. Specifically, the territory of the continental United States has been subdivided into 19 distinct regions, and the shift in the industrial composition of output and employment was assessed for each one of them.

Had we attempted to study each region separately and then simply to add the results to arrive at corresponding aggregates for the country as a whole, the total national output figures and the corresponding total input figures for each distinct category of goods and services could not have been expected to match. In other words, the results of such isolated regional studies would not comprise a consistent picture of the national economy as a whole. The simple scheme of multi-regional analysis on which the present computations are based provides for simultaneous balancing of all input-output flows from the point of view of each individual region, as well as for the U.S. economy as a whole.

For some goods — let them be called Local — a balance between production and consumption tends to be established separately within each region; for other goods — let them be identified as National — such a balance typically is achieved only for the country as a whole. Within each region the output of a National good might exceed or fall short of its total input, the deficit or surplus being evened out by exports to or imports from other regions. Retail Trade and Auto Repair services are characteristically Local industries while Coal Mining and Aircraft Manufacturing are typically National. The difference between the two obviously should be explained in terms of the relative mobility or transportability of their output.

To separate National industries from the Local, all sectors were arranged in order of the increasing magnitude of inter-regional, as compared with the intra-regional, trade of their respective products. Then, an admittedly somewhat arbitrary cut was made across that array, setting apart the Local industries, serving mainly users located within the region in which production occurs, from the National industries, supplying the entire national or even international market, whose products typically are being shipped for this reason in comparatively large amounts across regional lines.[2]

2. The multi-regional input-output computation itself can be visualized best as being performed in three distinct, successive rounds. The first consists of a conventional input-output calculation designed to determine the direct and indirect effects of the given shift from military to non-military final demands on the total output of all — that of Local as well as of National — goods for the country as a whole. The regional distribution of these total figures is determined in the second and the third rounds. All basic information on the input structure of each Local or National industry used again and again throughout these computations stems from the same large input-output table of the American economy. This common source of structural data ensures the internal consistency of all the final results.

For National industries the regional apportionment of the increase or the reduction in the total U.S. output is based in each instance on a simple, but in the first approximation, well-justified assumption of a uniform percentage change. For example, if the first stage computation indicates that as a result of curtailed military purchases and a simultaneous expansion of deliveries serving various types of final civilian demand, the total U.S. output of Electronic Equipment will fall by 5 per cent, then in the second stage that aggregate cut is allocated among the different regions on the assumption of an equal 5 per cent cut applied across-the-board.

That presupposes, of course, knowledge of the actual output and employment levels maintained by the National industries in each region before the shift occurs.

The third and last step determines the geographic distribution of changes in the level of activities of Local industries producing goods for which the balance between supply and demand tends to be maintained within each region with relatively limited recourse to inter-regional trade. The input requirements that must be covered in each region by the output of its Local industries comprise: deliveries to final military and civilian users located in the same region, input requirements of the National industries operating in it, and the input requirements of the Local industries themselves.

Thus, the calculation of regional outputs of Local industries requires not only a knowledge of final demand for the U.S. as a whole, but also a breakdown of military and non-military final demand by regions. While changes in the level of final deliveries of Steel, Chemicals and other National goods need to be specified only for the country as a whole, the given shifts in military procurement and civilian purchases of Electric Power, Gas and Water, Office Supplies and other Local goods have to be specified separately for each region before the analysis of their regional impact can begin. The amounts of Local goods absorbed in each particular region by National industries operating in it can be ascertained easily by applying appropriate sets of technical input coefficients to the regional output figures derived for all National industries in the previous, second round of computations.

The regional output levels of Local industries, finally, can be derived through separate input-output computations in which the deliveries of Local goods to final users located in each region and to National industries operating within it play the role of a given bill of goods.

3. In this last stage of the multi-regional analysis, Households is treated as one of the Local industries — the largest one in fact. The output of that industry consists of labor services of various types. In contrast to previous computations of this kind, *for reasons of practical convenience the quantities of labor services are measured in this study not in man years but rather in terms of the total wage and salary payments received for them.*

The input of the Household sector are consumer goods purchased by it. Its input structure, like the input structure of any other industry, can be described accordingly by an array of consumption coefficients, each of which represents the amount of one particular type of good absorbed by the Household sector per unit of its own output, i.e., per dollar of salaries and wages received by it.

That means, of course, that in the third stage of the multi-regional input-output computations, the given regional bill of goods is redefined so as to include all military and nonmilitary governmental purchases and private investment expenditure, but not the private consumption expenditures. Since Households is treated at this stage of the computations as one of the Local industries, all goods absorbed by it appear not as final deliveries, but rather as components of that part of all output of each sector that serves indirect demand.

The internal consistency of the entire procedure is demonstrated by the fact that, if separated from deliveries to other Local and all the National industries and summed for the country as a whole, these regional inputs into Households will match exactly the private consumption column of the final bill of goods introduced into the computation in its very first stage.

4. That bill of goods itself, of course, must reflect the anticipated effect of a hypothetical reduction of military and a corresponding increase in civilian expenditures. For purposes of the present analysis, such a shift has been assumed to have occurred in the year 1958, which at the present time is the latest year for which a detailed input-output table of the U.S. economy has been compiled. The final bill of goods is represented by three components: Military Purchases, Private Household Consumption, and Non-Household Civilian final demand.[3] The latter demand "contains" non-military deliveries to the federal, state, and local governments, private and public gross investment, and net exports.

The hypothetical cut in military expenditure is visualized to take the form of a 20 per cent across-the-board reduction in each kind of military purchase. With the total 1958 defense expenditure included in the military vector amounting to 31.3 billion dollars, that means reducing it by $6.3 billion to $25.0 billion.[3] The compensating rise in non-military demand was assumed, on the other hand, to be represented by a proportional across-the-board increase in all kinds of non-military final deliveries. Its total magnitude is chosen deliberately with the view of maintaining the total level of employment, or rather the combined wage and salary bill of all industries, at its original — that is, the actually observed — 1958 level.

Had the military shopping list contained the same goods and in the same proportions as the civilian, each million dollars' worth of additional non-military demand could re-employ the same number of hands and heads — commanding the same amount of wages and salaries — as would have been released by each million dollars' worth of military budget cut. However, the military product mix is very different from the civilian. A comparison of the results of two auxiliary input-output computations has shown that in 1958 the total wages and salaries paid for all the labor engaged directly and indirectly in production of one million dollars' worth of goods and services combined in the proportion demanded by the military are some 21 per cent larger than wages and salaries paid for labor inputs required for production of one million dollars' worth of outputs delivered in amounts reflecting the average product mix of all non-military final users.

Thus, it would take $7.6 billion of additional civilian demand to compensate the cancellation of $6.3 billion worth of military spending. Non-military final demand, as defined for this study, amounted in 1958 to $418.0 billion.[3] Stated in percentage terms, the shift in the economic impact as described below combines a 20 per cent cut in military purchases with a 1.8 per cent increase in the amount of goods and services absorbed by each of the two categories of final civilian users.

With the total labor input and wage bill remaining constant, a 1.8 per cent increase in the amount of all goods and services allocated to private consumption can be described as a proportional increase in all consumption coefficients. Accordingly, the column of technical coefficients used in the last stage of the multiregional input-output computations to describe the input requirements of Households was obtained by raising by 1.8 per cent the consumption coefficients derived from the 1958 U.S. input-output table . . . .

II. SUMMARY OF THE PRINCIPLE FINDINGS

1. When the numerical conclusions presented are based on a straightforward application of a systematically developed theoretical theme, the results need little

additional explanation. In the present instance most of the explaining was done when the procedure was described by which the primary factual information fed into an analytical machine is transformed into final figures describing the results of the entire computation. They appear in the form of tables which describe in great detail changes in the inter-industrial and the inter-regional distribution of output and employment that would be brought about by a hypothetical 20 per cent reduction in the military bill of goods, combined with a compensating proportional increase in the non-military components of the final bill of goods. This non-military demand comprises consumption by private households, total investments, which includes new construction, and non-military governmental expenditures . . . .

The number of industries in terms of which the productive apparatus of the American economy is described is 58, and the number of regions into which the territory of the continental United States was sub-divided for purposes of this description is 19; thus, the total number of output and employment figures resulting from this multi-regional input-output computation could exceed one thousand . . . .

Since the hypothetical shift in the composition of final demand was balanced so as to leave the overall level of employment for the country as a whole the same as it was before, its economic impact takes the form of shifts in the labor force among different industries and among different regions.

The magnitudes of changes in output and employment that we are about to examine are — when expressed in relative terms — at most on the order of a few percentage points up or a few percentage points down; in most instances, they are even smaller. Considering, however, that an employment rate of 5.5 per cent commonly is interpreted as a sign of serious malfunctioning of our economic system and that an eventual reduction of that figure to 4 per cent has been recognized as one of the major goals of national economic policies, even a half-of-one per cent change in employment level in one region or another must be taken to represent a noteworthy shift. The percentages to be examined may not meet that degree of accuracy, but they should indicate the direction of change in regional employment levels.

2. Table 1 describes the impact of a postulated de-militarization of the final demand in terms of individual industries. The percentage figures here show that of the 56 sectors listed,[4] only 10 will experience a reduction in total output and employment; Aircraft, Ordnance and, significantly, Research and Development will take large cuts of over 13 per cent, while Electronic Equipment, Non-Ferrous Metals and Instruments will drop between 1.59 and 5.40 per cent. Among the four other industries registering losses rather than gains is Iron and Steel, which with its token 0.04 per cent cut barely maintains the traditional standing as an armament industry. Positive changes are, on the other hand, distributed more evenly and among a much larger number of industries.

Food Products, other soft consumer goods, and services gain most, basic industries such as Chemicals, Petroleum Products and Paper least; Printing and Publishing, Motor Vehicles and other branches of processing show intermediate gains a few points above and below 1 per cent. The skewness of the entire distribution, specifically the bunched negative and widespread positive shifts reflect, of course, the contrast between the specialized nature of military demand and the broad product mix of the civilian.

Table 1

Percentage Changes[1] in Output and Employment[2] by Industries, After a Compensated[3] 20% Cut in Armament Expenditures

SECTOR NUMBER[4]	INDUSTRY	PERCENTAGE CHANGE (%)	SECTOR NUMBER[5]	INDUSTRY	PERCENTAGE CHANGE (%)
36N	Aircraft	−16.05	27N	Stone and Clay	1.10
40N	Ordnance	−15.42	1L	Printing, Publishing	1.12
41N	Research and Development	−13.26	10L	Business Services	1.14
34N	Electronics Equipment	− 5.40	8N	Fabrics, Yarn	1.19
29N	Non-Ferrous Metals	− 2.21	15N	Office Furniture	1.19
38N	Instruments	− 1.59	20N	Drugs	1.21
32N	Electrical Apparatus	− 0.92	35N	Motor Vehicles	1.21
37N	Other Transportation Equipment	− 0.23	39N	Miscellaneous Manufacturing	1.23
28N	Iron and Steel	− 0.04	2L	Electricity, Gas, Water	1.24
31N	Non-Electrical Machinery	− 0.03	12N	Lumber, Wood Products	1.26
18N	Chemicals	0.15	5L	Communications	1.26
13L	Maintenance Construction	0.20	14N	Household Furniture	1.27
24N	Rubber, Plastics	0.30	12L	Medical, Educational Services	1.31
33N	Appliances, Lighting	0.34	3L	Forestry, Fisheries	1.33
22N	Oil Fields	0.38	4L	Trade	1.40
23N	Petroleum Products	0.45	6L	Finance, Insurance	1.48
3L	Transportation	0.48	9L	Auto Repair Services	1.48
21N	Paint	0.48	8L	Personal Services	1.56

SECTOR NUMBER[4]	INDUSTRY	PERCENTAGE CHANGE (%)	SECTOR NUMBER[5]	INDUSTRY	PERCENTAGE CHANGE (%)
30N	Fabricated Metals	0.54	25N	Leather	1.57
11N	Miscellaneous Fabricated Textiles	0.54	7L	Real Estate, Rentals	1.57
19N	Plastics, Snythetics	0.59	2N	Other Agriculture	1.65
26N	Glass	0.81	11L	Amusements	1.66
16N	Paper	0.83	10N	Apparel	1.66
17N	Paperboard Containers	0.93	6N	Food and Kindred Products	1.66
9N	Miscellaneous Textiles, Rugs	0.97	1N	Livestock	1.67
14L	Government Enterprises	0.98	7N	Tobacco	1.76
5N	Coal Mining	0.98	17L	Households[5]	1.81
13N	Wood Containers	1.05	4N	Agricultural Services	2.14

[1] Each figure represents the change in output and employment in each industry as a percentage of total output and employment in that industry before the arms cut.

[2] Employment and its regional distribution is measured in each industry by labor earnings.

[3] Compensation is assumed to consist of a uniform proportional increase in all components of non-military final demand sufficiently large to maintain the aggregate employment in all sectors (consequently in all regions) taken together unchanged.

[4] Note that the two local sectors which are dummy industries have been omitted from this ranking. N refers to National industry number, L to Local industry number.

[5] Note that this percentage reflects the 1.81 per cent increase in all consumption coefficients. It represents the change in employment of employees in households such as domestic help or baby sitters.

3. The regional projection of the economic impact of disarmament is summarized in Table 2. As can be seen from the percentage entries, in 10 of the 19 regions employment can be expected to contract while in the other 9 it will expand. The largest loss, —1.85 per cent, will be experienced in California; the biggest gain, +1.54 per cent, in the mid-western region comprising Minnesota and the two Dakotas.

Neither the shift from one industry to another, nor the move from one region to another, considered separately, measures the total magnitude of readjustments that will be required of the members of each regional labor force. Such a measure must take both into account, simultaneously. What is needed is a figure which shows what proportion of all men and women initially employed in all the different industries operating in a given region will lose their jobs and will have to look for

Table 2

Percentage Change in Output and Employment by Region After a Compensated 20% Cut in Armament Expenditures

REGION NUMBER	REGION	TOTAL NET CHANGE (%) (1)	TOTAL GROSS INCREASE (%) (2)	TOTAL GROSS DECREASE (%) (3)
19	California	—1.85	0.54	2.39
16	Colorado, New Mexico	—1.40	0.67	2.07
17	Arizona, Nevada, Utah	—1.35	0.69	2.04
9	Maryland, Virginia, Delaware, W. Virginia, D.C.	—1.36	0.66	2.02
14	Texas	—1.00	0.73	1.73
18	Oregon, Washington	—0.81	0.91	1.72
12	Mississippi, Alabama	—0.73	0.89	1.62
8	Georgia, North and South Carolina	—0.57	1.02	1.59
10	Florida	—0.43	1.12	1.55
1	New England	—0.06	1.05	1.11
13	Arkansas, Louisiana, Oklahoma	0.21	1.26	1.05
7	Kansas, Iowa, Nebraska, Missouri	0.44	1.46	1.02
11	Kentucky, Tennessee	0.37	1.31	0.94
2	New York	0.66	1.44	0.78
3	New Jersey, Pennsylvania	0.53	1.26	0.73
15	Idaho, Montana, Wyoming	1.28	1.83	0.55
4	Michigan, Ohio	0.89	1.43	0.54
5	Indiana, Illinois, Wisconsin	0.93	1.46	0.53
6	Minnesota, North and South Dakota	1.54	1.96	0.42
	Total United States	..	1.16	1.16

new jobs in a different industry in the same region or in another region; in the latter case, the jobs they find in another region might or might not be in the same industry in which they worked before.

The figures entered in column 3 of Table 2, accordingly, show what proportion of all the wage and salary earners will receive discharge notices and will have to look for new jobs. To emphasize the importance of these figures, the sequence in which the 19 regions are listed on the table reflects the order of decreasing magnitude of these "gross displacement" rates.

California, again, is at the head of the procession with the highest rate of 2.39 per cent, and Minnesota with North and South Dakota ranks lowest with only 0.42 per cent. A comparison of entries in column 1 with those of column 3 reveal that one region can experience a larger expansion in the total level of employment than another, but at the same time be subject to a greater stress as measured by the gross displacement figure. According to the computations, the New York State region, for example, would expand its total employed labor force by 0.66 per cent while the corresponding figure for the Kentucky-Tennessee region is 0.37 per cent. At the same time 0.78 per cent of the original job holders in New York would have to change their jobs as against 0.94 per cent in Kentucky-Tennessee.

Employment agencies might be interested in the total number of new jobs created in a particular region, i.e., in the sum total of the increases in employment figures of those industries expected to expand in each region. Expressed as percentages of total labor force initially employed in the region, these "gross job gains" figures are entered in column 2. Strictly speaking, they do not present us with any new information since by definition they can be obtained simply by adding pair-wise the corresponding entries in column 1 and column 3.

The regional impacts of disarmament as summarized in Table 2 are described graphically on Chart 1. Each set of bars depicts the impact of the same hypothetical shift from military to non-military demand on the employment situation in one of the 19 regions. The total length of the bar extended downward from the horizontal baseline measures the gross job loss (described in column 3 in Table 2). The total length of a bar extended upward represents the corresponding gross gain in jobs (described in column 2 of Table 2). The solidly shaded section of the longer of the two bars shows the difference between their length; in other words, it measures the change in the total level of employment in a particular region. That change is negative when the solid bar extends below the horizontal line, and it is positive when it is above.

The geographic picture confirms the well-known fact that most of the resources serving directly or indirectly Final Military Demand come from the West, South-Western and South-Eastern regions, while the Mid-West, the Great Lakes region and the North Atlantic and New England states depend to a large extent on civilian demand. A cut in military expenditures, accompanied by an expansion of the non-military bill of goods, thus will create more serious readjustment problems in the first than in the second group of regions . . . .

III. CONCLUDING OBSERVATIONS ON FURTHER RESEARCH

The same analytical scheme that permitted us to assess the economic implications of a hypothetical step toward disarmament, implemented by the same body of factual data, also can be used for evaluating the probable effect of specific measures

300 · THE REGIONAL CONTEXT

Chart 1

Percentage Change in Output and Employment Resulting from a Hypothetical 20 Per Cent Cut in Military Spending and a Compensating Rise in Civilian Final Demand

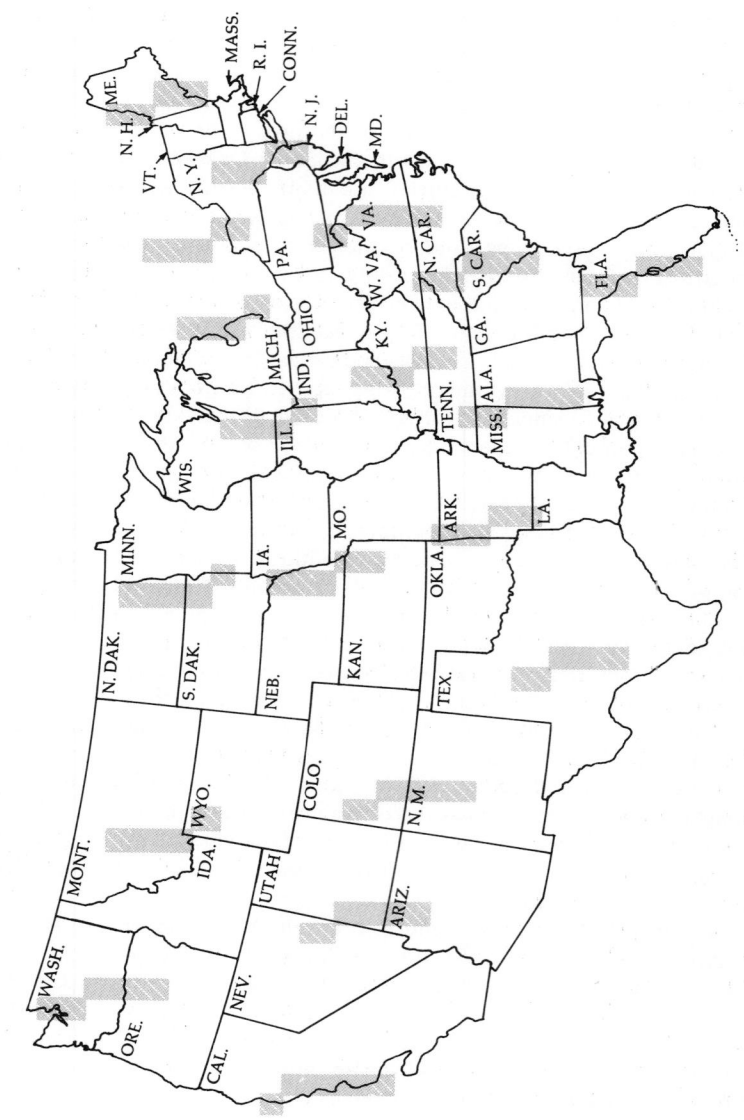

of economic policies intended to mitigate the stresses of the transitional period. Such measures are usually designed to modify directly or indirectly the level, the composition and the regional distribution of the new civilian bill of goods. To assess their effect on the inter-industrial and inter-regional distribution of outputs and employment, it will be necessary only to repeat the sequence of computations described above with these readjusted versions of the final bill of goods. Whenever information on specific military budget cuts becomes available, this information can replace the hypothetical assumption of the proportional 20 per cent cut in military spending and the compensating 2 per cent increase in civilian purchases.

The following two refinements can be introduced into the procedure described above without changing the analytical basis of the general approach. The admittedly rigid assumption that whenever the total output of a National good goes up or down, it increases or decreases in the same proportion in all regions, can be relaxed. After completion of the three-stage computation described above, the new regional distribution of consumption of each National good can be determined and then compared with the old. Some regions will turn out to be increasing their relative shares at the expense of the others. Accordingly, the geographic distribution of the output can be expected to be affected by this, at least to some extent. If the demand for steel were to contract in a Western but to expand in the Eastern regions, the share of the latter in the total output of steel might be expected to increase somewhat and the share of the Western mills to fall. To take account of this, a second round of multi-regional input-output combinations can be undertaken in which the set of the regional distribution coefficients applied to each of the National industries would be revised in the light of the numerical results of the first round.

The second refinement of the original procedure consists in breaking the regions into sub-regions.[5] The region, for example, which in the present computation includes Illinois, Indiana and Wisconsin can be subdivided into two parts, one comprising Illinois and Indiana and the other — Wisconsin. Their percentage figures describing the participation of these three states in the total production of each National good would have to be split into two separate figures. The output of the industries originally classified as Local can be treated in two different ways. The regional outputs of some Local goods might balance the demand not only for the three states together, but also separately, in each of the two sub-regions. That might be true of automobile repair services and retail trade. Other Local goods, while not moving in sufficiently large amounts across the borders of the three-state region, still might be traded freely between its two parts. For such goods the distribution of the total regional output between the two sub-regions might be described better by a set of constant sub-regional coefficients. On the lower sub-regional level, these empirically determined coefficients would play a role analogous to that assigned to regional coefficients in determining the inter-regional distribution of the total output of each National good. Without elaborating the technical details of such a complicated analytical scheme, involving not one but several layers of regional breakdowns, it suffices to observe that while the successive rounds of such computations can be introduced one by one without modifying the results of the higher rounds, the overall results always will be internally consistent at every state.

Finally, an entirely different non-linear, multi-regional input-output scheme was proposed several years ago.[6] It is being tested now in the United States, in Latin America, and also in Europe. All of these inter-regional input-output schemes require detailed regional information which is not always available.

Thus, highest priority should be assigned to improvement of the basic data. For statistics which are collected on a national level, a systematic, regional breakdown becomes more and more important. On the other hand, most data collected by local and state organizations — often in connection with various programs of regional economic development — are limited in their usefulness because of lack of comparability with other regional and national statistics. This needs to be remedied by agreement on and compliance with certain common classifications and standards.

REFERENCES

1. Wassily Leontief and Marvin Hoffenberg, "The Economic Effect of Disarmament," *Scientific American,* April 1961.
2. The concluding observations at the end of this article describe a possible refinement of this approach which introduces a graduated distinction between National, Regional and Sub-regional industries and goods.
3. Morris R. Goldman, Martin L. Marimont, and Beatrice N. Vaccara, "The Inter-Industry Structure of the United States, A Report on the 1958 Input-Output Study," *Survey of Current Business,* U.S. Department of Commerce, November 1964, Washington, D.C. A detailed description of the definitions and composition of the final demand vectors used in this study is given. The vectors only include estimates of final purchases from endogenous industries, e.g., the military vector does not include purchases from new construction since this is exogenous in this study. Thus, the sum of the elements included in the vectors does not represent all Final Demand.
4. Two Local sectors, 15L Office Supplies and 16L Business Travel and Entertainment, are not included in this tabulation.
5. See Wassily Leontief (ed.), *Ibid.,* Chapter 4.
6. Wassily Leontief and Alan Strout, "Multi-regional and Input-Output Analysis," Tibor Barna (ed.) *Structural Interdependence and Economic Development,* (Macmillan: London, 1963), Ch. 7.

SUGGESTED BIBLIOGRAPHY

PART ONE: AN URBAN OVERVIEW

Boulding, Kenneth E., *Beyond Economics: Essays on Society, Religion and Ethics,* Ann Arbor: University of Michigan Press, 1968.

Chinitz, Benjamin, *City and Suburb,* Englewood Cliffs: Prentice-Hall, Inc., 1964.

———, "Contrasts in Agglomeration: New York and Pittsburgh," *American Economic Review,* Vol. LI (May 1961), pp. 279–289, pp. 299–302.

Hirsch, Werner Z., "The Supply of Urban Public Services," *Issues in Urban Economics,* Harvey S. Perloff and Lawdon Wingo, Jr. (eds.), Baltimore: The Johns Hopkins Press, 1968, pp. 477–524.

———, *Urban Life and Form,* New York: Holt, Rinehart & Winston, Inc., 1963.

Hoover, Edgar, and Raymond Vernon, *Anatomy of a Metropolis,* Cambridge: Harvard University Press, 1959, Chapters 1–8.

Jacobs, Jane, *The Death and Life of Great American Cities,* New York: Random House, Inc., 1961.

Margolis, Julius, "The Demand for Urban Public Services," *Issues in Urban Economics,* Harvey S. Perloff and Lawdon Wingo, Jr. (eds.), Baltimore: The Johns Hopkins Press, 1968, pp. 527–564.

Rothenberg, Jerome, "Urban Renewal Programs," *Measuring Benefits of Government Investments,* Robert Dorfman (ed.), Washington, D.C.: Brookings Institution, 1965, pp. 292–367.

Vernon, Raymond, *Metropolis 1985,* Cambridge: Harvard University Press, 1960.

Wilson, James Q. (ed.), *Urban Renewal: the Record and the Controversy,* Cambridge: MIT Press, 1966.

PART TWO: URBAN ISSUES

A: Poverty, Unemployment, and the Welfare System

Batchelder, Alan B., *The Economics of Poverty,* New York: John Wiley & Sons, Inc., 1966.

Becker, Gary S., *The Economics of Discrimination,* Chicago: University of Chicago Press, 1957.

Becker, Joseph M., *Guaranteed Income for the Unemployed: the Story of SUB,* Baltimore: The Johns Hopkins Press, 1968.

Clark, Kenneth B., "The Negro and the Urban Crisis" in *Agenda for the Nation,* Washington, D.C.: The Brookings Institution, 1968.

Downs, Anthony, "Alternative Futures for the American Ghetto," *Daedalus* (Fall 1968), pp. 1331–1379.

Kain, John F., "Coping with Ghetto Unemployment," *Journal of the American Institute of Planners* (Spring 1969).

———, "The Distribution and Movement of Jobs and Industry," *The Metropolitan Enigma: Inquiries into the Nature and Dimensions of America's Urban Crisis,* James Q. Wilson (ed.), Cambridge: Harvard University Press, 1968, pp. 1–40.

Miller, Herman, *Rich Man, Poor Man,* New York: Thomas Y. Crowell Co., 1964.

Rainwater, Lee, "Crucible of Identity: The Negro Lower-Class Family," *Daedalus* (Winter 1966), pp. 172–216.

Seligman, Ben P., *Permanent Poverty,* Chicago: Quadrangle Books, 1968.

Walker, Mabel L., *Urban Blight and Slums,* Cambridge: Harvard University Press, 1938.

Weisbrod, Burton A., "Investing in Human Capital", *Journal of Human Resources,* Vol. 1 (Summer 1966), pp. 5–21.

B: Housing

Abrams, Charles, "The Housing Problem and the Negro," *Daedalus* (Winter 1966), pp. 64–76.

Downs, Anthony, "An Economic Analysis of Property, Values and Race," *Land Economics,* Vol 36 (May 1960), p. 181.

———, "Moving toward Realistic Housing Goals," in *Agenda for the Nation,* Washington, D.C.: The Brookings Institution, 1968.

Frieden, Bernard J., "Housing and National Urban Goals: Old Policies and New Realities," *The Metropolitan Enigma,* Cambridge: Harvard University Press, 1968, pp. 159–202.

Glazer, Nathan, and David McEntire, *Studies in Housing and Minority Groups,* Berkeley: University of California Press: 1960.

Grigsby, William G., *Housing Markets and Public Policy,* Philadelphia: University of Pennsylvania Press, 1963.

Heideman, M. Lawrence, Jr., "Public Implementation and Incentive Devices for Innovation and Experiment in Planned Urban Development," *Land Economics,* Vol. 45 (May 1969), pp. 261–267.

McEntire, David, *Residence and Race: Final and Comprehensive Report to the Commission on Race and Housing,* Berkeley: University of California Press, 1960.

Muth, Richard, "The Spatial Structure of the Housing Market," *Papers and Proceedings of the Regional Science Association* (1961).

Neutze, Max, *The Suburban Apartment Boom: a Case Study of a Land Use Problem,* Washington, D.C.: Resources of the Future, Inc., 1968.

Taeuber, Karl E., and Alma F. Taeuber, *Negroes in Cities: Residential Segregation and Neighborhood Change,* Chicago: Aldine Publishing Co., 1965, Chapters 1, 3, 5.

Weaver, Robert C., "The Impact of Urban Renewal," *Land Economics,* Vol. 36 (August 1960), pp. 235–251.

Wingo, Lowdon, "Some Suggestions for a Statistical System for Regional Housing Policy Decision," *Journal of the American Institute of Planners,* Vol. 32 (May 1966), pp. 143–154.

C: Transportation

Beesley, M. E., and John F. Kain, "Urban Form, Car Ownership and Public Policy: An Appraisal of Traffic in Towns," *Urban Studies,* Vol. 1, No. 2 (November 1964).

Kain, John F., and John R. Meyer, "Interrelationships Between Transportation and Poverty," *The Public Interest* (Winter 1970).

Kain, John F., "The Journey-to-Work as a Determinant of Residential Location," *Papers and Proceedings of the Regional Science Association,* Vol. IX (1962), pp. 137–161.

Owen, Wilfred, *The Metropolitan Transportation Problem,* Washington, D.C.: The Brookings Institution, 1956.

Southern California Research Council, *An Approach to an Orderly and Efficient Transportation System for the Southern California Metropolis,* Los Angeles: Occidental College, 1960.

Strotz, Robert H., "Urban Transportation Parables," in *The Public Economy of Urban Communities,* Julius Margolis (ed.), Washington, D.C.: Resources for the Future, Inc., 1965.

D: Public Health and Education

Auster, Richard, et al., "The Production of Health: An Exploratory Study," *Journal for Human Resources,* Vol. 4 (Fall 1969), pp. 411–436.

Fein, Rashi, *Economics of Mental Illness,* New York: Basic Books, Inc., 1958.

Glazer, Nathan, "Is 'Integration' Possible in the New York Schools?," *American Race Relations Today,* Earl Raab (ed.), Garden City: Anchor Books, Doubleday and Co., Inc., 1962, pp. 135–153.

Kneese, Allen V., "Rationalizing Decisions in the Quality Management of Water Supply in Urban-Industrial Areas" in *The Public Economy of Urban Communities,* Washington, D.C.: Resources for the Future, Inc , 1965.

Report of *National Advisory Commission on Health Manpower,* Washington, D.C.: U.S. Government Printing Office, 1967.

Revelle, Roger, "Pollution and Cities" in *The Metropolitan Enigma: Inquiries into the Nature and Dimensions of America's Urban Crisis,* James Q. Wilson (ed.), Cambridge: Harvard University Press, 1968.

Ribich, Thomas I., *Education and Poverty,* Washington, D.C.: The Brookings Institution, 1968.

Ridker, Ronald G., *Economic Costs of Air Pollution: Studies in Measurement,* New York: Frederick A. Praeger, 1967.

Somers, Herman Miles, and Anne Ramsay Somers, *Medicare and the Hospitals,* Washington, D.C.: The Brookings Institution, 1967.

U.S. Commission on Civil Rights, *Racial Isolation in the Public Schools,* Washington, D.C.: U.S. Government Printing Office, 1967.

E: The Economics of Crime

Harris, J. R., "On the Economics of Law and Order," *Journal of Political Economy,* Vol. 78 (Jan.-Feb. 1970).

Kerner, Governor Otto (Chairman), *Report of the National Advisory Commission on Civil Disorders,* New York: Bantam Books, Inc., 1968.

Stigler, G. J., "The Optimum Enforcement of Laws," *The Journal of Political Economy,* Vol. 78 (May-June 1970).

U.S. Riot Commission, *Report of the National Advisory Commission on Civil Disorders,* New York: E. P. Dutton & Co., Inc., 1968.

Wilson, James Q., *Varieties of Police Behavior,* Cambridge: Harvard University Press, 1968.

PART THREE: URBAN FINANCING

Baumol, William J., "Urban Services: Interactions of Public and Private Decisions" in *Public Expenditure Decisions in the Urban Community,* Howard G. Schaller (ed.), Baltimore: The John Hopkins Press, 1963.

Brazer, Harvey E., "Some Fiscal Implications of Metropolitanism," *City and Suburb: the Economics of Metropolitan Growth,* Benjamin Chinitz (ed.), Englewood Cliffs: Prentice-Hall, Inc., 1964, pp. 127–150.

Netzer, Dick, "Financing Urban Government," *The Metropolitan Enigma,* James Q. Wilson (ed.), Cambridge: Harvard University Press, 1968, pp. 71–88.

Perloff, Harvey S., and Richard P. Nathan (eds.), *Revenue Sharing and the City,* Baltimore: The Johns Hopkins Press, 1968.

Subcommittee on Fiscal Policy of the Joint Economic Committee of Congress, *Revenue Sharing and Its Alternatives: What Future for Fiscal Federalism?,* Washington, D.C.: U.S. Government Printing Office, 1967.

PART FOUR: THE REGIONAL CONTEXT

Alonso, William, *Location and Land Use,* Cambridge: Harvard University Press, 1965.

Anderson, Martin, *The Federal Bulldozer: a Critical Analysis of Urban Renewal, 1949–1962,* Cambridge: MIT Press, 1964.

Banfield, Edward C., "Why Government Cannot Solve the Urban Problem," *Daedalus* (Fall 1968), pp. 1231–1241.

Chinitz, Benjamin, "Appropriate Goals for Regional Economic Policy," *Urban Studies,* Vol. 3 (February 1966), pp. 1–7.

Hoover, Edgar M., *The Location of Economic Activity,* New York: McGraw-Hill Book Company, 1963, Chapters 1–8.

Margolis, Julius, "Municipal Fiscal Structure in a Metropolitan Region," *The Journal of Political Economy* (June 1957).

Mills, Edwin S., "An Aggregative Model of Resource Allocation in a Metropolitan Area," *American Economic Review* (May 1967), pp. 197–211.

Moses, Leon M., and Harold F. Williamson, "The Location of Economic Activity in Cities," *American Economic Review* (May 1967).

Rodwin, Lloyd, *The British New Towns: Problems and Implications,* Cambridge: Harvard University Press, 1956, pp. 3–6, pp. 165–183.

Rothenberg, Jerome, "Strategic Interaction and Resource Allocation in Metropolitan Intergovernmental Relations," *The American Economic Review* (May 1969), pp. 494–503.

Tiebout, Charles M., "Intra-Urban Location Problems: An Evaluation," *American Economic Review,* Vol LI (May 1962), pp. 271–278, pp. 299–302.

———, *The Community Economic Base Study,* Supplementary Paper No. 16, New York: Committee for Economic Development, December 1962.